The FBI and the
Catholic Church,
1935–1962

The FBI and the Catholic Church, 1935–1962

⸺⟡⸺

STEVE ROSSWURM

University of Massachusetts Press

AMHERST AND BOSTON

Copyright © 2009 by
University of Massachusetts Press
ALL RIGHTS RESERVED
Printed in the United States of America

LC 2009040219
ISBN 978-1-55849-729-0

Designed by Steve Dyer
Set in Fairfield by House of Equations, Inc.
Printed and bound by Thomson-Shore, Inc.

LIBRARY OF CONGRESS
CATALOGING-IN-PUBLICATION DATA
Rosswurm, Steven
The FBI and the Catholic Church, 1935–1962 / Steve Rosswurm.
p. cm.
Includes bibliographical references and index.
ISBN 978-1-55849-729-0 (cloth : alk. paper)
1. United States. Federal Bureau of Investigation—History.
2. Catholic Church—History.
3. United States—History—20th century.
I. Title.
HV8144.F43R67 2009
282′.7309045—dc22
2009040219

British Library Cataloguing in Publication
data are available.

CONTENTS

Acknowledgments   ix

Introduction   I

1. The Creation of a Catholic Protestant and
   Protestant Catholics   9

2. The Boss's Bishops   53

3. Assistant to the Director Edward Tamm and His
   Chicago Connections   97

4. Father John F. Cronin and the Bishops' Report on
   Communism   133

5. A Jesuit Informant: Father Edward A. Conway, S.J.,
   and the National Committee for Atomic Information   180

6. Anti-Communism in the CIO: Monsignor
   Charles Owen Rice and the FBI   226

Afterword   275

Abbreviations   279
Notes   283
Index   325

ACKNOWLEDGMENTS

I AM MOST GRATEFUL to the librarians and archivists who have provided such useful assistance over the years. The interlibrary loan librarians at Lake Forest College—Guynell Williams, Rita Koller, Ping-Chih Keil, Ruth Henderson, and Susan Cloud—have done an excellent job of tracking down and obtaining hard-to-find material. Susan's efforts over the past decade have been particularly useful, as have Rita's for various projects. Libraries are only as good as their circulation desks, and Lake Forest has been blessed with some wonderful supervisors: Karen Ludlow, Alie Stansbury, and Kristen Kinsella.

Early on, I did considerable research in two archives that convinced me that this book was possible: the Archdiocesan Archives of Chicago and the Catholic University of America Archives. Tim Slavin, then an assistant archivist at the former, answered endless questions and retrieved box after box of documents. Jac Treanor professionally oversaw the archives then and continues to do so today. Jac's encouragement and support over the years has meant a great deal. John Shepherd at Catholic University is not only an excellent archivist, but also a friend who repeatedly has done me kindnesses.

The staff at the following places ably assisted me: Archdiocesan Archives of Baltimore; University of Pittsburgh; University of Notre Dame; Chicago Historical Society; Wayne State University; Detroit Archdiocesan Archives; Franklin Delano Roosevelt Library; Georgetown University; Hartford Archdiocesan Archives; Pennsylvania State University; Harry S. Truman Library; Library of Congress; Marquette University; National Archives (Washington, D.C.); National Archives (Chicago); Seattle Archdiocesan

Archives; Toledo Archdiocesan Archives; University of Chicago; Rutgers University; University of Virginia; University of Missouri–St. Louis.

The story in chapter 5 would have been considerably different if some generous folks had not provided me access to material. William Higinbotham's son gave me copies of his father's diary. Those entries gave a day-to-day inside perspective that was irreplaceable. Jessica Wang, at UCLA, sent me her copies of the FBI's Washington Field Office files on the Federation of American Scientists. Without these, a good deal of Father Edward Conway's relationship with the FBI during several critical months would be unknown. Finally, Marge Wannarka, Archivist at Creighton University, and Father David Smith, S.J., Minister of the Jesuit Community at Creighton, tracked down and provided the space for me to examine Conway's papers.

Documents obtained through the Freedom of Information Act are the foundation of this book. For many years, Mrs. Joan Mills was who I referred to as "my person at the FBI." She and I exchanged hundreds of letters—hers always under the name of a supervisor—but I came to know her a bit better through our telephone calls. Mrs. Mills, who worked for the FBI when J. Edgar Hoover ran it, could have put many more obstacles in my way, but she didn't.

Several institutions provided significant financial aid. The National Endowment for the Humanities awarded me a Fellowship for College Teachers and Independent Scholars in 1996. During that year, I drafted the bulk of the book. Successive Deans of the Faculty at Lake Forest College—Bailey Donnally, the late Steven Galovich, and Janet McCracken—oversaw the awarding of summer research grants that proved extraordinarily useful. Deans Donnally and Galovich were especially generous and I appreciate their initial support and belief in the value of the project.

Lake Forest College students also deserve thanks. Kathleen Ferraro, Kelly Harmon, Deborah Kane, and Eleanor Shirley served as my research assistants over the years. Alison Freund and Lindsay Ross assisted me as Richter Fellows. Freund's work was particularly useful. I learned more than I could have imagined from teaching Women in Modern America and Europe and Topics in Gender and History. The students in those classes consistently stimulated and challenged my thinking.

Dawn Abt-Perkins, Andy Eisen, and Ellen Schrecker generously read a draft of the entire manuscript. Their acute comments forced me to rethink parts of my argument and correct more than a few misjudgments and mistakes. (Jim Fisher's, provided as a press reader, were just as useful.) Bill Burr and John Earl Haynes did the same for chapter 5, as did

John Donovan for chapter 4. Michael Meranze pointed out, before I saw it, one of the most significant implications of my work.

The following helped in a various ways, for which I am grateful: Steve Avella; Bill Burr; Jo-Anne Carr; Monsignor James Cronin (1919–2008); John Donovan; Monsignor George H. Dunne, S.J. (1905–1998); John Fox; Josh Freeman; John Earl Haynes; Monsignor George G. Higgins (1916–2002); Harvey Klehr; Sister Nora Klewicki, O.S.F; Pat McCarthy; Mark McColloch; Patrick McGeever; Robert P. Newman; Ken O'Reilly; Bill Pratt; Monsignor Charles Owen Rice (1908–2005); Dave Roediger; Ellen Schrecker; Ellen Skerrett; Tom Slaughter; M. Wesley Swearingen; Leslie Tentler; and, Athan G. Theoharis.

Working with the University of Massachusetts Press has been everything I expected it would be. Clark Dougan's advice has been wise, and his support essential. Amanda Heller's editing greatly improved the book.

Wonderful friends have sustained me over the years. Les Dlabay and Ivory Mason, of the Juan's Chuck Wagon Breakfast Club, remind me of what really matters and how to do it. Derek Lambert walks the walk in ways that are truly inspiring. Jill Van Newenhizen was generous with her time at points of serious need. Ignacio Alvarez, Andy Eisen, Elsi Rodriguez, and Kanwal Shakeel were my students at Lake Forest College: I now am lucky to count them as friends. All writers need good neighbors to bring them out into the world; I am grateful to mine: David Dallison and Lee Luu. Finally, Dawn is my best friend and supporter and sharpest critic.

The FBI and the
Catholic Church,
1935–1962

Introduction

THERE "IS NO GROUP," the Archdiocese of Baltimore's *Catholic Review* argued in 1942, that held J. Edgar Hoover (1895–1972), director of the Federal Bureau of Investigation, in "higher esteem" than U.S. Catholics. Six years later *Novena Notes*, the publication of the enormously popular Our Sorrowful Mother devotion, noted that Hoover was so respected by Catholics that he might as well have been a "Catholic priest or bishop." In 1952 Anne Tansey, in *Our Catholic Messenger*, wrote that it was quite understandable that many believed Hoover was a Catholic. John Patrick Gillese, in *The Magnificat*, a widely read Marian publication, explained why this was the case: "So often has J. Edgar Hoover been quoted by the Catholic Press, so often has he spoken to Catholic gatherings, so many times has he been eulogized and honored by Catholic institutions."[1]

Catholic "hero-worship" of Hoover, as Gillese put it, was not unrequited: Hoover's profound admiration and respect for Catholicism and its values laid the basis for a working alliance that stood firm for about thirty years, perhaps even a bit longer, until Catholic opposition to the war in Vietnam first fractured and then destroyed the relationship. Nothing better captures this rupture than the running battle between Fathers Philip Berrigan, S.S.J., and Daniel Berrigan, S.J., and the FBI: whether it be Catholic FBI agents—including one trained by the Jesuits—arresting them, Dan's "An Open Letter to J. Edgar Hoover," or the Boss's vendetta against them.[2]

Hoover and the Church shared a commitment to a set of values, to a certain vision of the world. To some extent the man long known simply as "the Director" has become a buffoonish figure in American history, laughed at by many, revered by few, including conservatives, who—one might think—could manage at least a tepid defense of one of their own. Most professional historians, seemingly more interested in scoring political points or fulminating against his sins, which were many, than in explaining his extraordinary popularity and influence, have not done much better. This study takes his values and commitments seriously because almost everyone in the United States did so during his lifetime. It does the same for Catholics, whose treatment at the hands of historians, while different from Hoover's, has often been equally dismissive.

At its core this is a book about men and power—or, more broadly, about gendered values and institutional authority. It is about how members of the American Catholic Church, especially its hierarchy, worked with Hoover and his FBI—many of whose agents were Catholic—ultimately to defend, among other things, patriarchal authority in society and family because they could not imagine a good social order in which power was not exercised in that way. While the leading Catholic actors, as we will see, were clerics, there is plenty of evidence that the mutual admiration shared by Hoover and the laity was as strong as that of the priesthood and the Director.[3]

For more than twenty years I have been filing the Freedom of Information and Privacy Act (FOIA) requests that have produced one of the primary evidentiary bases for this book. I began in 1984 by soliciting FBI surveillance records for the Farm Equipment Workers, a Communist-led member union of the Congress of Industrial Organizations (CIO), and still have requests pending as I write this introduction. Doing research via the FOIA is time-consuming, difficult, and enormously frustrating, but without this material, the book could not have been written. At the same time, I could not have relied on FBI files alone because most of them have been redacted (that is, censored) before FOIA release. The often fragmented information that remains, moreover, not only tends to reflect the FBI's point of view but also makes it difficult to connect the dots—to know where one piece of evidence fits in with other pieces. Fortunately many missing parts of the story have been provided by Catholic sources, including the Catholic press, which I have researched extensively.

Chapter 1 lays out the values that the Church and Hoover shared. Both saw the world through the lens of what we would now call antimodernism, perceiving virtually every manifestation of change as a sign of decline, albeit it from different vantage points. For the Director, it was the nation's Founding Fathers who had established the standard against which innovation should be measured; for the Church, it was pre-Reformation Europe. Although Hoover never adopted the Catholic view of history, toward the end of the period under study the Church increasingly embraced the heroic and mythic aspects of the American past, including the quasi-sacred view of the Founding.

Of all the changes that troubled these men, the ones that threatened them most were those that challenged their essentialist readings of gender. Any alteration in the way women acted or were expected to act called into question the verities of a world in which men defined themselves in terms of what they were not (women) and over whom (women) they reigned. (The self-activity of women, therefore, while little discussed, is this book's ever-present backdrop.) A commitment to the patriarchal family and patriarchal authority flowed directly and logically from such presuppositions. The problem, of course, was that patriarchy—and all that went with it—was at risk, besieged everywhere in the modern world. Not surprisingly, the metaphors that the Church and Hoover used to describe these dangers coded them as female, and these figures of speech did considerable cultural work: they confirmed the value of masculinity, held at bay their femininity and desire, reinforced assumptions of male authority and expertise, and provided the framework from within which others could understand the gravity of what was at stake. As a poster in the FBI's Los Angeles Field Office in the early 1970s put the question: "WHAT SHALL IT BE? LAW & ORDER or CHANGE & CHAOS"[4]

Hoover's childhood and high school years were primarily responsible for producing the kind of man he became: pugnacious, plain-speaking, driven. He knew he was right, and he knew why he was right. The values he espoused—including those related to issues of gender—were universal and absolute. Those who disagreed with him were quite simply wrong or misguided. His body, steeled in childhood as well as by his experiences in his high school cadet corps, was as disciplined, routinized, and bounded as his ideas. He was, in fact, the embodiment of the FBI and the nation. For Hoover, an attack on one was an attack on all.

The men the Church produced—the laity as well as the priests—performed precisely the masculinity that Hoover desired. Raised for the most part in respectable and patriarchal working-class, often Irish American families and in a church that espoused similar values, these Catholic men were trained in a neo-Thomism that was as schematic, dogmatic, and anti-intellectual as any traditional Marxism. The seminaries, the prep schools, and the colleges aimed at building strong bodily borders that could keep in check the flowing and surging within and without.

Many people have commented on the large number of Catholics who joined the FBI, but no one has framed the issue more acutely than Garry Wills. Catholics, he argued in *Bare Ruined Choirs*, learned from "the structure of their Church" a "deep respect for authority" and a familarity "with doctrinal ways of testing that respect." Their inclination toward intelligence agencies was as "natural as the drift of other young [Catholic] men to the discipline and authority of the priesthood." Wills's assessment leaves out the insights of feminist analysis; other than that, he says it all.[5]

The chapters that follow have two different but related focuses. First, they examine the ways in which Hoover's FBI and the Catholic Church explicitly worked together. This cooperation flowed directly from their shared values and commitments and also aimed at reinforcing them. Both sides were fighting a rear-guard antimodernist action against change coded in decidedly dangerous terms. It is therefore not surprising that there was a crisis mentality evident in virtually every social commentary either side produced during this period. Second, chapters 2 through 6 elaborate on what brought the FBI and the Church together. Values as basic as those laid out in chapter 1 are often unspoken and assumed, so their implementation often provides clarity in ways that are not otherwise possible. This will be seen in relation to issues as apparently unrelated as crime, Communism, salacious literature, and juvenile delinquency.

In chapter 2 I examine Hoover's relationships with five powerful members of the Church hierarchy and take a briefer look at several more. Hoover's interactions with these men were for the most part businesslike, a matter of pursuing common interests and goals. Only with Archbishop Michael J. Curley of Baltimore did he develop a real friendship, in part because the two men lived near each other but also in part because they had similar personalities, including unapologetically blunt speaking styles. They also shared a hatred of Communism, though on that score Hoover's affinities with Richard Cardinal Cushing of Boston, another notoriously plain speaker, were even stronger.

There was virtually nothing about twentieth-century American society that Bishop John Francis Noll of Fort Wayne, Indiana, liked or with which he was comfortable. What he did not seem to understand though was that he could not simply ban those things and make them go away. Hoover shared his disgust with the salacious literature and immoral movies that seemed to be everywhere, but unlike the bishop, he understood the limits of his ability to control them. Noll's publishing empire, especially the ubiquitous *Our Sunday Visitor*, promoted Hoover's speeches and writing more than any other Catholic publication I am aware of.

The relationships between the Director and the two remaining members of the hierarchy, Bishop Fulton J. Sheen and Francis Cardinal Spellman of New York, were each different from those between Hoover and their colleagues. In Sheen's case, the Bureau apparently provided a good deal of help when it came to his renowned convert-making, especially for his work with Louis Budenz, the former Catholic editor of the *Daily Worker*, who returned to the Church in 1945. Nothing approaching a friendship seems to have developed between Spellman and Hoover, but they certainly did a good deal of business fighting their common enemies.

Edward A. Tamm, the subject of chapter 3, provides an opportunity to examine how a Catholic functioned at the Bureau's highest levels. The third-ranking FBI official, below Hoover and Clyde Tolson, when he retired in 1948, Tamm was the most powerful Catholic in Hoover's Bureau. Prospering under Hoover's managerial regime, he moved up the ranks by consistently demonstrating that he was the Director's kind of American man. He also forged extensive contacts with the powerful Catholic Church in Chicago that greatly benefited both institutions.

By 1945 Tamm had become very concerned about the Communist problem in the United States. Like Hoover and Tolson, he was well aware of the extent of Communist influence, especially in some CIO unions, as well as the operation of Soviet espionage rings. But he could do little about any of this because much of the Bureau's evidence of Communist activity had been obtained illegally. To get their message out, Tamm and his colleagues needed non-Bureau conduits. Along came Father John Cronin, S.S., the subject of chapter 4, to whom the FBI funneled hundreds of pages of information that later appeared in a report he wrote for the Catholic hierarchy.

Historians have long known of Cronin's work for the bishops, but its full story is recounted here for the first time. Always ambitious to do good works for God and his church, Cronin started out as an obscure seminary professor whose enormous appetite for work and willingness to take on additional responsibilities brought fresh opportunities, including his selection by the administrative board of the National Catholic Welfare Conference to write its research paper on Communism. Cronin had many sources for the assertions he eventually made in his report, but the FBI was the most important. Not only did he get help from Bureau Headquarters, but he received intelligence from field offices and individual agents as well.

The Bureau's leak of information to Cronin was the opening salvo in an anti-Communist war that it would wage for the next fifteen years. During that period Cronin became a central figure in the anti-Communist camp, serving as liaison for the FBI in the Alger Hiss case and as a speechwriter for Vice President Richard Nixon. Others, following in his footsteps, also laundered information for the FBI—intelligence that was for the most part accurate if illegally obtained—contributing to the success of the anti-Communist cause.

Of course, not all anti-Communisms were the same. For numerous reasons, the kind that Joel Kovel calls "black-hole" anti-Communism, which said more about the fears and anxieties of its adherents than the actual activities of their presumed enemies, is greatly underrepresented here.[6] Although there was a good deal of this anti-subversive sentiment among Catholics, that does not mean their concerns were completely unfounded or that Communists were without significant power and influence in the United States, as Kovel implies. American Communists were, rather, like the "disorderly women" in eighteenth-century New England evangelical communities, who "became," Susan Juster argues, not just "a metaphor for disorder in the revolutionary era," but "a living metaphor."[7]

Father Edwin Conway, S.J., was considering giving up his battle with subversives in the National Committee for Atomic Information (NCAI), an organization established in late 1945 to educate the public about the atomic bomb, when Cronin introduced him to several Bureau agents. From that point on he worked closely with the FBI in his successful effort to drive the Communists and "fellow travelers" out of the committee. He picked up some important allies in his battle, and he may have revealed his Bureau connections to some of them, but most of those with whom he worked had no idea who lurked in the shadows.

Conway's work in the NCAI, the topic of chapter 5, not only shows how readily a Jesuit priest could conspire with the FBI but also demonstrates how fragile U.S.-Soviet unity during World War II had been. To most Catholics and FBI officials, of course, that friendly cooperation never really had any legitimacy, though to others, including most liberals, it had resonated greatly. As that "grand alliance" fell apart under the pressure of both international and domestic events, the ties that held together the popular front unraveled. All of this would have happened without the advent of the atomic bomb, but the U.S. monopoly on the world's first superweapon exacerbated tensions between the two powers and hastened the disintegration of their wartime partnership. Fears that the Soviets might try or were trying to steal America's atomic secrets fueled widespread suspicions of Communist infiltration and subversion throughout the United States, particularly within the national security establishment. In organization after organization battle lines were drawn, names taken, and decisions made. It was unclear in how many of these the Bureau participated, but its work with Conway in the NCAI was surely not an isolated episode.

Conway and the Bureau were not, however, inventing a danger. There were at least a few Communists and even more fellow travelers among those who quit after the NCAI executive board fired Daniel Melcher, its director. Melcher, the primary target, was well connected with men and women who were themselves closely associated with leading members of Washington, D.C., Soviet espionage rings.

Nowhere did the issue of how to handle a living metaphor work itself out more visibly than in the CIO, where the American Communist Party, the CPUSA, had much power and considerably more influence. Yet because most of both had been gained with few members revealing their Communist affiliations, these individuals were vulnerable to attacks that targeted their loyalty to a conspiratorial political party that answered to a foreign country. Monsignor Charles Owen Rice, the topic of chapter 6, not only specialized in launching such assaults but also had the will and determination to carry them through. From 1939 to 1941 he fought a sustained campaign against the Party and its allies in the huge Westinghouse local of the United Electrical, Radio and Machine Workers of America (UE) in East Pittsburgh, Pennsylvania. After the war Rice resumed the fight, playing a central role in organizing a national opposition in the UE while also taking on the Communist Party in other CIO affiliates. This second period ended when the CIO expelled the Communist-led unions.

According to James B. Carey, the leader of the anti-Communists in the UE and the president of the rival IUE (International Electrical, Radio and Machine Workers of America), the CIO's alternative union, there was a "trade union approach" to handling Communists in the CIO and a "government" approach. In the first case, he explained in the late 1950s, the "union puts its own house in order and engages in its own investigations, establishes its own standards for leadership and membership." In the other it "becomes a matter for the Government and some Government agency, a matter for legal authorities." The problem with the latter, in Carey's view, was that it became "an invitation to McCarthyism," tantamount to a "Communist or totalitarian approach."[8]

Carey's distinctions make sense. Process *does* matter. How the anti-Communists handled their adversaries had serious implications. The irony here, though, is that Carey himself offers one of the best examples for the "government approach." As will become clear in chapter 6, he and his staff maintained close working relationships with the FBI. So too did Monsignor Rice, although, after his connection was revealed, he did what he could to hide its reality from historians.[9] This labor priest did not stop with the FBI, however, but also got help from the House Committee on Un-American Activities and assorted others.

For Rice and many others, the Communist threat was so dangerous, so widespread, and so imminent that virtually any tactic seemed justified in the battle against it. When Rice confessed to having done things he wished he had not done in this engagement, I think he was referring to the political implications of his actions, not the morality of any given act. It was, as he told me, a "just and beautiful fight."

CHAPTER 1

The Creation of a
Catholic Protestant and
Protestant Catholics

I T MUST HAVE BEEN a pretty heady experience for the 120 Holy Cross men who heard J. Edgar Hoover's commencement address that warm June day in 1944. Few of them, after all, had spent much time outside the Catholic ghetto in which they had been born. Beyond that world of family, school, and parish, though, they knew—either firsthand or through others' stories—that there was much Protestant dislike, even hostility, toward them and their fellow Catholics. Hoover's mere acceptance of the invitation from Holy Cross did much, at least momentarily, to counteract that enmity. His talk went much further, though, for not only did he compliment the graduates by sharing a rousing jeremiad about American social morals, but also he asked them to join him and the FBI in redeeming the country.

There is little in either the current popular imagination or the historiography to suggest why this pure product of white Anglo-Saxon Protestant America would find common ground with the Jesuits, historically one of his culture's worst (religious) nightmares. In hindsight, however, the connection between Hoover and the Jesuits—indeed, between him and Catholics in general—seems eminently reasonable, even somewhat predictable. By 1944 Hoover had good reason not simply to trust the Jesuits but to reach out to them in an alliance-building move.

The good relations he had developed with several local Jesuit institutions apparently laid the basis for this trust. Georgetown University was

a close enough neighbor for Hoover to have learned that it was producing his kind of men. One of its faculty members, Father Edmund Walsh,
S.J., spoke regularly at the FBI's National Police Academy, and in 1939 it
awarded Hoover an honorary degree. Beginning in 1937 Catholic FBI employees began making annual retreats at Manresa-on-Severn in Annapolis,
Maryland, where Father Robert S. Lloyd, S.J., was the director. Lloyd and
Hoover wound up liking each other very much.[1]

The Boston Field Office also had had, since 1937, "cordial and frequent
contact" with the College of the Holy Cross, a small Jesuit school located
in Worcester, Massachusetts. The Director had written an article for its
literary magazine that year and another for the *Holy Cross Alumnus* in
1941. There had been some rather formal correspondence between its
presidents and Hoover from 1938 through 1941; in 1942 the Boston special
agent in charge (SAC) spoke at the college.[2]

It was how Catholics, including the Jesuits, and Hoover interpreted
what was happening on the home front during the Second World War
that seems to have cemented the alliance. Social change and turmoil—
whether it be women working outside the home, the coalescence of male
homosexuals and lesbians in the military, decreased supervision of teenagers, increased geographical mobility, social hygiene lessons in the
armed services, relaxed sexual mores—loomed large and were read as
threatening the patriarchal family and ordered desire, the basis for a good
society. For the Director and Catholics alike, it made no sense to win the
battle overseas only to lose it at home.[3]

As it turned out, Hoover could not get away from FBI Headquarters
(FBIHQ) to deliver the commencement address himself, but Special
Agent John J. McGuire was the perfect replacement. After attending
Fordham and Brooklyn preparatory schools, he received his B.A. from
Holy Cross and his LL.B. from Fordham Law School. McGuire began his
FBI career in 1935 and made SAC in Buffalo in 1939. Next came service in
New Haven, Cleveland, and Omaha; he returned to FBIHQ in 1942. From
1943 to 1959 he was the "Number One Man" in the Records and Com-
munication Division, where he supervised the Crime Records, Statistical,
Communications, and Mail Dispatch sections. In 1948 he was elected
second vice president of the Holy Cross Alumni Association; in 1956 "an
old friend and classmate" was the college's Jesuit president.[4]

The Director's message, delivered through McGuire, was a simple one.
There were enemies everywhere you looked. They included, of course,
Communists and Nazis, but others as well: the coddler of the killer, the
kidnapper, the "youthful desperado," the criminal (157 crimes, he noted,
were committed every hour), the cynic who thought money the highest

value, the citizen who bought black market goods, the destroyer of home life.[5]

The solution was elementary: return to the values of old—the "fundamentals," Hoover called them—while there was still time. The bedrock was religion, the home, and discipline. Religion—"a necessary factor in a healthy and well-ordered society"—was of course most important. Next came the home, for there was no "character-building agency" that could "take the place of a good home," the "basis of our social order," the "basic unit of society." Without discipline, American liberty could readily turn into the "license" that had existed in the 1930s.[6]

Hoover laid a heavy burden on the Holy Cross men who received their degrees that day. The Founding Fathers not only had won "life, liberty, and the pursuit of happiness" against "superior foes" but also had "preserved it against doubt and uncertainty." It was the graduates' responsibility to defend that heritage and keep it intact for the future. George Washington's words concluded Hoover's address: "Let us raise a standard to which the wise and honest can repair; the rest is in the hand of God."[7]

There was considerable coverage of this speech in both the Catholic and the secular press, and Hoover received letters for weeks from people requesting a full transcript of his remarks, asking permission to reprint them, or just wanting to let him know how much they admired his words. Two of these stand out because of what they tell us about the Director's evolving relationship with the Catholic community.

The first suggests that it was not just what Hoover said but how he put it that was so impressive. William Edward Broome, a Holy Cross alumnus and a Boston doctor, had heard the speech. It reminded him of a similar address, "fashioned along the line" of the Director's, delivered in 1906 by the Holy Cross president, "a very clear-thinking school man." Broome wondered where Hoover had "studied philosophy." The talk's straightforwardness had greatly impressed him and his friends: "We all wonder, and with pleasure, at your clear cut expressions constructed without fear and forcefully."[8]

The second letter, from Father J. W. Hynes, S.J., at Manresa House in Convent, Louisiana, focused on the speech's message. A Catholic, he wrote, "could not have better expressed our Catholic views and principles in face of the crisis that confronts us and the worse crisis that impends and will come with the end of the Great War." Nothing "less than a full-hearted return to these fundamentals will save U.S. and through us the world." The Jesuit then paid Hoover the ultimate compliment: "Talis cum sis, utinam noster esses." Someone at the Bureau provided the translation: "Since you are such an [sic] one, would that you were of us."[9]

In this chapter I look at the values, the language, and the sexual and gender politics that brought Hoover and Catholics together to defend what Gayle Rubin has described as a "sex/gender system." Already in decay, even though of relatively recent origin, this sex/gender system was rooted in the subordination of women, the normalization of heterosexuality, and the patriarchal family. The particular contribution of Hoover and Catholics to this complex of values was a commitment to an essentialist reading of sex and gender that not only provided the basis for a good society but also served as a diagnostic tool for discovering why things were not going the way they should. One aspect of this commitment was a rigorous homosociality, which served as a way of enforcing male domination and heterosexual norms.[10]

A couple of issues require discussion, though, before we proceed to an examination of what united Hoover and Catholics. One has to do with the reason for my focus on the Jesuits. The second has to do with the ways in which the values of the Church and the Director interacted. Let me take up the Jesuit matter first.

There are many reasons why the Jesuits play such a prominent role in the discussion that follows. First, they were the largest religious order in the United States. Second, their order was devoted mainly to education: their colleges and universities, which numbered twenty-five in 1942, were the largest Catholic ones in the country at a time when most Catholics attended only their own institutions of higher education. Third, because of their focus on the life of the mind, Jesuits produced a large body of material that discussed what they were doing in their schools and classrooms (the two, as we will see, were not necessarily the same). In their work, moreover, they self-consciously sought—and often obtained—an intellectual and organizational coherence to which other religious orders could only aspire. The Jesuit "plan of study," as Hoover noted in an article he wrote in 1947 for the Holy Cross student newspaper, was "originally designed," and still was, he would argue, "as a plan of living."[11]

What seems to have set the Jesuits apart from their fellow Catholics was not, as we will see, the focus on self-control and a disciplined body, or on patriarchy, or even coherence. Rather it was the continuing need to prove one's manhood through contest. This in turn derived, I believe, from the Jesuits' intense homosociality. Extra-parish Catholic educational institutions were organized almost entirely along single-sex lines until the 1960s. Since the Jesuits did almost no parish work, they had little or no contact with females.

Jesuits, to sum up, were Catholic only more so; or to put it a bit differently, they were more conscious of their faith than most other Catholics, even most Catholic intellectuals. Nevertheless, in what follows, the reader should be ready to mentally translate "Jesuit" into "Catholic," since there is considerable evidence from non-Jesuit Catholicism that parallels the Jesuit evidence. This chapter, for example, could have begun with the speech that Hoover gave at Notre Dame in 1937 rather than with his talk at Holy Cross in 1944.[12]

As for the way in which the values of Hoover and Catholics related to each other, the concept of "elective affinity" is a good place to begin. The term, in Michael Löwy's formulation, means "a very special kind of dialectical relationship that develops between two social or cultural configurations, one that cannot be reduced to direct causality or to 'influences' in the traditional sense." Beginning with a "certain structural analogy," the "relationship consists of a convergence, a mutual attraction, an active confluence, a combination that can go as far as a fusion."[13]

Bishop John J. Wright of Pittsburgh got at part of what this meant for the FBI and the Church when, in an address to the Eleventh Annual FBI Mass and Communion Breakfast, he "likened the FBI to the hierarchy of the church as being the two most disciplined organizations in the world." They, of course, shared many other structural and organizational characteristics: they were both rigidly hierarchical, functioned on a command/ obey basis, and included virtually no women in positions of authority or decision-making power. The values they shared were implicit in that organization: respect for authority, a corporate ethos, reverence for tradition, hostility toward innovation.[14]

The FBI and the Catholic Church could have had all this in common even if the values they shared had different origins, as long as members of each organization allowed themselves to see themselves in the other. This would have required each, of course, to put aside that which set it apart. For some in the FBI and the Catholic Church, I think, this is exactly what happened. There was, then, in Lowy's words, a "convergence" of values. For still others, there could have been something more, a "mutual attraction." Finally, for many—if not most, if the correspondence is to be taken at face value—the relationship became "an active confluence." "Fusion" was not a possibility, though, because each institution had its interests to protect.

Hoover and the Church agreed on several central twentieth-century social and cultural issues: the nature of the family, its place in society, and the distribution of power and influence within it; how authority was defined and who should wield it; the shape of freedom and its relationship to the individual. At every point gender was deeply implicated in this active confluence between the two organizations, but it was considered such a given, so natural, that neither side discussed it at any length. As we will see, though, the FBI and the Church both responded sharply when they sensed that their gender values were under attack.

Ghostwriters produced much of what Hoover published and delivered over the years—the output was so prodigious that it is hard to believe that contemporaries thought he was writing his own material—but there is no doubt that everything appearing under his name reflected his values. His readers and listeners certainly took his words at face value: Hoover's speeches and articles were one of the central reasons why the American public supported him so enthusiastically. I look at them, then, not only because I want to show that Catholics and Hoover agreed about basic values, but also to understand the vast majority of Americans who so fervently championed him.[15]

Two articles, both published in 1946, are particularly good explications of Hoover's commitment to the primacy of the family. He made his point, as he so often did, in a negative way: his explanation of the good became apparent during the course of his discussing how to correct the bad. America, the Director asserted, was "sick," suffering from the "illness" of crime. If a "cure" was to be found, the "infection" had to be identified and "destroy[ed]" at its "source": the home. In a series of prescriptions Hoover explained what parents had to do to ward it off. First, they had to pass along America's "heritage": the "promise of life, liberty, and the pursuit of happiness." Next, they had to teach (and live) a "true belief in God and the teachings of Jesus." Mothers and fathers, moreover, were reminded that "proper social behavior necessitate[d] obedience in the home," since "uncontrolled freedom" created a child whose only goal was to "satisfy his own selfish interests." Finally, parents had to provide a "strong foundation of moral fortitude," for without it children would succumb to the "corruption and decay" prevalent in a world that "worships at the shrine of materialism." That moral fortitude could come only from God, the "Supreme Arbiter of good and evil."[16]

Hoover came at the problem a bit differently in the second article but wound up in the same place. He began, as he sometimes did, with stories drawn from FBI case files to show the "pattern of future conduct for many of today's delinquents." After providing examples of "modern manifestations of perverted family life," Hoover gave his diagnosis. "Lack of parental guidance," he argued, "is at the root of the juvenile problem." The "best insurance against delinquency" was the "impregnation of discipline, love, tolerance, and obedience" in children. While sorely needed—and the

Director spent the rest of the article discussing them—other efforts to deal with the delinquency problem were merely "synthetic."[17]

The clearest expression of Catholic commitment to the family—one that matched Hoover's—is the Church hierarchy's 1949 statement "The Christian Family." Convinced that what "amount[ed] to a calculated attack upon family life" was under way, the administrative board of the National Catholic Welfare Conference (NCWC) came to its defense. The state, it argued, "measures its true strength by the stability of family life among its citizenry," for the family, it continued, "is the social cell. It is the family that produces the citizen. No nation can be greater than its families." The school, even "at its best," was "only a strong aid to produce good citizens."[18]

But it was not just any family to which Hoover and Catholics were committed. For both, the patriarchal family was *the* family. For both, it was an ongoing assumption that the only kind of family that was a family was the one headed/mastered/dominated by the father. They therefore did not always specify the particular kind of family to which they were committed. In the right circumstances, though, the details became clear.

The Director explicitly clarified his advocacy of the patriarchal family twice in 1938. In a speech he argued that the "only way" to end crime in America was "by a re-establishment of respect for the law by the *head* of our homes." That same year the editor of Notre Dame's *Religious Bulletin* reprinted an article by Hoover, "If I Had a Son," in which he laid out his ideal family more clearly than anywhere else I know of. He stressed here the importance of fathers' truthfully answering their sons' questions. If they did not, they would shatter their image as patriarch: "This matter of the whole truth is doubly important because every boy is a hero-worshipper. His inclination is to look up to his father as head of the house, a repository of all knowledge, the universal provider, the righteous judge. He cannot do so if he's continually catching his father in half-truths. A liar is a weakling and a boy admires strength. No matter how difficult it might be, I'd tell my boy the truth."[19]

The Catholic commitment to the patriarchal family was both clearer and more frequently stated. A reason for this might have been that one of the main functions of the Catholic press was to reinforce the values of the faithful. But in statements meant for the public, since there was no consensus in America about the patriarchal family, which was in fact disintegrating, it was often as circumspect as Hoover. For example, in "The Christian Family," it was never stated outright that it was the patriarchal family about which the hierarchy was speaking.

Two examples from the Catholic popular press will suffice. In 1951 Father Thomas Meehan, editor of Chicago's *New World*, nostalgically discussed his childhood, when the rosary was said as a family, leisure time was spent together, and his "father held forth on every subject." The popular weekly columnist of *Novena Notes*, Father Hugh Calkins, O.S.M., strenuously argued for a patriarchal form of the family in a radio talk that headlined "Who Wears the Pants in the Family?" He soon became connected with the *Integrity* group, which sought to restore the father as "boss."[20]

Catholic academics also weighed in on this subject. For some, such as the Notre Dame sociologist John Kane, the author of a popular Catholic text on the family, patriarchy was the only family form. In his discussion of the "extermination" of the "patriarch" in the middle-class family, he argued that its demise had produced a "rising matriarchy" and a "femino-centric society." For others, such as Father John L. Thomas, S.J., who received his Ph.D. from the University of Chicago, patriarchy needed to adapt to changing conditions. "In the Catholic family system," he argued, the "father is considered the head of the family." This was "an ideal or value premise which must be maintained." Yet its implementation would "vary according to different cultural situations."[21]

Women had a significant role to play in this patriarchal family. Father Ignatius Cox, S.J., a popular professor at Fordham in the 1930s and 1940s, concisely summarized the Catholic position. There should be "co-operation" within the marriage, but "authority should belong primarily to the father as the superior." By the "Natural Law both parents are vested with the natural authority over the children," but "in such wise the father is the superior in this society." That authority, though, "never remains so completely in the father alone that its varied functions are not distributed to both parents." The mother was "particularly committed" to her "domestic provision, admonition, and the physical and moral care of the children, especially in the state of infancy and childhood." To the father, Cox argued, "especially belongs general provision for the domestic regime."[22]

Catholic thinking here, in its most benign and abstract form, argued for complementary gender roles. Since there could be only one source of power and/or authority in a given unit, it went to the male. Leaving aside the particular Catholic gloss, the ideal family looked very much like the middle-class Protestant family of the nineteenth century. Woman, inherently possessed of greater virtue than man and unequipped for struggle outside the home, was the family's source of morality, goodness, and purity. Man, inherently competitive, aggressive, and commanding, was the head of the family and its source of firmness and solidity.

This commitment to women as moral guardians of the family and society laid a heavy responsibility upon them. This related, in turn, to Catholics', and Hoover's, definition of masculinity. When women did not act as they ought, neither the world nor men could be as they ought to be. As the Director argued: "Where the women of a community inculcate, by precept and example[,] the highest ideals of ethical living, these communities have progressed and life within their borders has brought peace and happiness. In those communities where the women have been indifferent to the high duty of inspiring their children, sweethearts, brothers, and husbands to better things, conditions have rapidly deteriorated and ultimate moral chaos has been the result."[23]

Calkins echoed this prediction of chaos. "Woman's true role," he wrote in *Novena Notes*, was to create a "real home." If a "woman scorns her greatest job, home-making, if she neglects her task in the family, nothing takes her place. The family breaks down and with it the whole society." Sometimes, though, as with nineteenth-century Protestants, it was necessary for Catholic women to "go outside their homes to save their homes." Accordingly, in November 1948 Samuel Cardinal Stritch delivered to the Archdiocesan Council of Catholic Women a "Call to Arms" to drive "printed filth" out of Chicago. His assumptions undergirding this exhortation had been revealed two years earlier when he argued that "where womanhood is noble and pure there is always hope for genuine social well-being."[24]

Catholics might have argued with the theological anthropology that underlay Hoover's thinking about gender, but they certainly would not have disagreed with his principles. As early as 1933 those were quite clear, as evidenced in a reporter's interview with the Director. After the mother's "strong moral influence," Hoover said, came "the father's loving discipline and immovable insistence upon obedience to parental command."[25]

That authority for Catholics, as for Hoover, was patriarchal, paternal, and familial can be assumed from everything that has been said so far. Sometimes, though, it was made explicit. Father John LaFarge, S.J., an influential journalist and civil rights advocate, once described the relationship between a member of the Society of Jesus and his superior as "the relationship between a son to a father." The superior's authority, he argued elsewhere, "should be paternal"; he should "exercise his authority in the manner not of an official, but as the father of a family." Good Jesuits were sons of several mothers (and fathers): "Sons of good mothers try to become sons of the Society, of the Church, and of the Mother of God herself."[26]

Hoover, as far as I know, never discussed his directorship of the FBI in this way, but he ran the Bureau as a patriarch. His contemporaries understood this. Lynda Johnson Robb, who had been about to interview him the day he died, had a conversation with her mother, Lady Bird Johnson, first lady at the time, in which they noted that there was no one to whom condolences could be sent: "All that were left were the two cairn terriers and the FBI, which after all, was his true family." Historians have understood this too. "Hoover's managerial style," writes Richard Gid Powers, "combined authoritarianism with collegiality." As a former agent put it in explaining why he did not last long at the Bureau, "I just never adopted the Director as my father, which seems to have happened in the case of many other employees."[27]

Catholics and Hoover also shared an overriding sense of the public good and a resolute disdain for individualism. Neither believed that anyone had the right to be wrong, or that liberty ought to be unlimited. Both grudgingly accepted pluralism but never welcomed it or integrated it into their basic philosophies. Liberty, for Hoover, was the freedom to do what was right. As he put it in 1943: "Tolerance is a virtue, to be sure, but the greatest crime of our age has been the toleration of wrong. In this there is no middle ground." Liberty, Hoover asserted over and over again, was not license. "License" and "licentiousness" were two of his favorite epithets. Speaking in 1942 he said, "While we fight for religious freedom, we must also fight the license sought by the atheist and those who ridicule, scoff and belittle others who seek spiritual strength." The FBI, he argued two years later, is what "stands between [subversive forces] and their desire to abrogate liberties by installing their own treacherous and ruinous philosophies of rule by license."[28]

Fordham's Cox was one of the Jesuits' most vociferous opponents of what he called "arbitrary license." As he wrote in the preface to his text on ethics, *Liberty: Its Use and Abuse*, "there is liberty true and liberty false—there is liberty well used and liberty abused. This book champions the one and provides weapons against the other." Another Jesuit targeted what he called "individual absolute license," while the Jesuit presidents of Fordham and Georgetown dismissed "academic freedom" on the same grounds Hoover did.[29]

Both Hoover and Catholics identified their vision of what was good and right with what was good and right for the whole country. They also conflated their real and metaphoric bodies with the metaphoric bodies of their country and their organizations. Or to put it a bit differently, they perceived threats to the institutional bodies they headed as endangering their own bodies and read threats to their own bodies as menacing the institutional bodies they led. But it was not just this identification of the individual's vision and body with that of the institution and nation that was significant. These were male bodies on which their thinking was founded and through which they read the dangers around them. And for numerous reasons Hoover and the FBI as well as Catholic leaders and laymen read the dangers to them, their institutions, and their country as female.

The starting point for one set of these metaphors was the distinction they made between the solid and bounded (male) and the flowing and un-bounded (female). No matter how one identifies the origin of the process—my own personal preference is to see it as an eclectically psychoanalytic one—the notions of damming and flowing, boundaries and borders, were central to their understanding of the world.[30]

George Cardinal Mundelein of Chicago explicitly used these concepts of damming and flowing in his speech to a gathering of Catholic women in 1930. The cardinal likened his audience, to a "clear bubbling mountain stream" whose "limpid and sparkling and pure" water is "pretty to look at" but, lacking a dam, "does not do much good as far as the general community is concerned." Then an "experienced engineer" comes along, builds a dam, and "stores the water of the little stream." This stream can now help the community because "it became organized and was given something to do." Once the "engineer and the scientist" put "bit and bridle and harness on it" and "[bind] it to the turbine wheel and the electric generator," the stream can provide light and power to the community. "Do you know, my dear Catholic woman," Mundelein, who once depicted himself as a "breakwater" against Communism, continued, "that is just what you can do if you have organization."[31]

Women, elemental and boundless energy and desire, needed (male) circumscription and direction in order to be effective in the wider (male) world. Without this, (female) desire, hunger, and passion could wreak havoc in the (male) world. This is how Hoover used these same images in an article published in 1950. In this piece, "Law Enforcement Views Education for Leisure," the Director noted that Americans' recreation time had "become a challenge" for law enforcement officers since never before had people had so much of it. There was a connection between the wrong use of free time—Hoover called it "perverted leisure"—and crime. Then, as was his custom, he illustrated his points with stories, here about teenagers who, being "bundles of energy," got into trouble because they "just had to do something." After recounting a favorite tale of a teenager who tried to create a train wreck because he wanted to make something big happen, Hoover argued that "this energy is bubbling in the hearts and souls of every normal youngster—it needs an outlet." Scouts and recreation programs provided "worthwhile channels in which these energies may drain." The alternative was frightening: "If [energies] are allowed to flow promiscuously, without the dikes of morality, honesty and clean living, they will run a muck, seep underground, and eventually pollute and undermine the very foundations of society."[32]

Images of surging water, or stagnant, contaminated water, or watery substances constantly endangered the boundaries of Hoover's real and metaphoric bodies. In dozens of cases Hoover used the terms "flood," "tide," and "wave" to refer to crime, juvenile delinquency, lawlessness, and Communism. "Slime" and "slimy" were employed for profits, politics, racketeering, subversion, corruption, and selfishness; "cesspool," "morass," and "swamp" were used in the same contexts.

Catholics just as frequently described danger as gushing water or as dank, contaminated fluid of some kind. "Waves," "tidal waves," and "floods" referred equally to obscene literature, Communism, and the Protestant revolt. "Swamp" described nineteenth-century society, while immorality was a "cesspool." Watching an indecent movie was to be immersed in "slime."

The answer of Hoover and Catholics to all these watery dangers was to erect some sort of barrier. "Bulwark" was an image in which Hoover found great comfort, for it signaled the solid, the impermeable, and the protective: in other words, the male. The first time he seems to have used it was in 1935, but he went on employ it many more times in speeches and articles. Sound institutions, individuals, and values were bulwarks—also "dikes" and "bastions"—against all kinds of threats. Catholics, too, used these metaphors of hardness, stability, and rigidity. Writers and speakers frequently employed "bulwark" to describe the exclusively male Holy Name Society. In 1947, for example, a Chicago pastor noted that in this time of "challenge to manhood and society," it was necessary for "real Holy Name men" to serve "as the bulwark of the laity."[33]

There was a second set of metaphors that Hoover and Catholics favored to describe those things that most endangered them and their country. Sometimes they were used in conjunction with the first set, sometimes not, but the goal was the same in either case: to present the danger as a medical one. Communism and crime were, among other things, a cancer, a malignancy, a disease, an epidemic, a growth, an illness, a malady, a pestilence, a plague, a sickness, a germ, a tumor, a contagion, and a virus. They infected and contaminated the muscles, arteries, bloodstreams, fibers, and sinews of those with whom they came in contact. The solution was an antidote, an inoculation, a quarantine.

Both Hoover and Catholics, in the hundreds of examples I have collected, engaged in a good deal of cultural and political argument medicalizing social problems. In taking the "position of a doctor vis-à-vis their patient," they produced and reproduced the notion that the health or security of "the larger population is dependent upon the specialized knowledge of an elite." They dramatically narrowed the number and kinds of explanations and solutions considered legitimate for approaching the problem being examined.[34]

The few occasions when either explicitly assumed the role of doctor are quite instructive. Hoover, as far as I know, referred to himself as a doctor just once, describing a meeting he was addressing as "a clinic in which we have gathered as physicians looking to the cure of a malignant disease, namely crime, which has fastened itself upon America, viewing its symptoms and its possible remedies and seeking to correct any defects in a selected mode of treatment, through frank and sincere cooperation and consultation." There are several examples of Catholics metaphorically stepping into a medical role. Father Edmund Walsh, S.J., a professor at Georgetown and a specialist on the Soviet Union, argued that power alone would not solve the problem there. It would rather "leave the roots of the infection uncured." Something more drastic, he argued, was needed: "The ax must be laid to the roots of the evil and the scalpel applied to the ulcered spot." Father John Cronin, S.S., the subject of chapter 4, gave a radio address in which he offered his solution for the problem of Communism in the labor movement: "Be mercifully harsh like the doctor who removes a festering limb, lest life itself be snuffed away by contagion."[35]

When the Director and his Catholics characterized the source of the danger as exterior to the body—his, theirs, the nation's, the Church's, or those of like-minded citizens—and threatening it from without, they reaffirmed the integrity of the boundaries under attack. They not only policed the borders but also laid out the appropriate values and behavior for those inside them. More generally, in their attention to "bodily boundaries," as Mary Douglas has put it, they were actually dealing with "social boundaries." Those inside the borders were "clean," those outside "dirty" or even "filthy." Clean was good, dirty bad. Because of their concern with the reproduction of the proper man, Hoover and Catholics alike often used these terms in connection with boyhood and its attendant institutions. Hoover told an interviewer that sports had been a particularly important source of "manly cleanliness" for him. The first president of the Archdiocesan Union of the Holy Name Society in Chicago, the *New World* noted, came from a "family of notable athletes" and was a "ardent promoter, as well as a devotee of clean athletics among youth in Catholic circles."[36]

None of this focus on the metaphorical way in which these men interpreted the world around them is to deny the reality of what they defined as a problem. Criminals, Communists, juvenile delinquency, and obscene literature existed. What they were doing, however, was more than simply identifying a problem that required attention. Not only were (male) boundaries being reinforced and (male) solutions being offered, but also Hoover and Catholics were projecting onto those things they opposed that which they most feared within themselves: the desiring feminine. In so doing, they denied, eliminated, and destroyed what they coded as female within and without.

As we have seen, these men who were constantly erecting, reinforcing, and preserving the boundaries between themselves and women were doing so from within an extraordinarily homosocial position, for they spent most of their lives within all-male environments. It was their fear of women, I believe, that helped produce the imagery of the bulwark/male against the flowing/female that was so vital to their worldview. Their worship of the Blessed Virgin Mary, in the case of Catholics, and the idealized mother figure, in that of Hoover, brought them together as males united in pursuit of this one perfect woman, who provided them with a yardstick for judging all real women as deficient.[37]

The social institutions that produced these men—Hoover and the Catholic leaders—were similar in ways that most scholars have not understood, for they have focused too much on the distinction between Catholic and Protestant. In this section I lay out the experiences, especially in the disciplining of the body, that seem to have formed in both Hoover and his Catholic allies—or in Catholics and Hoover, their Protestant ally—a commitment to male domination of women and the female, a patriarchal family form, homosociality, and ordered desire.

Hoover grew up and reached maturity during the tumultuous and transitional Progressive Era, but his life was marked by continuity and stability. They provided him with one of the central foundations for the control and mastery that came to typify his personal life and the FBI he created in his image. These were values, as we will see, that the Catholic experience also produced.

The FBI director lived at the same address, 413 Seward Square, in Washington, D.C., for the first half of his life. Born on January 1, 1895, he resided there until his mother died in 1938. She had grown up in Seward Square and his father nearby; a grandmother lived across the square when Hoover was young. The neighborhood was white, Protestant, and self-consciously middle class. Government employees, especially clerks, predominated, for the federal office buildings where they worked were just a few blocks away. A child of Seward Square during this period, a Hoover biographer has noted, "would have grown up knowing no one who was, in any essential respect, different from himself."[38]

Annie Hoover, Edgar's mother, is central to understanding his life and personality. He lived with her until she died, and he never married. Virtually every observer of their relationship, and of the dynamics of the Hoover family more generally, points to her overwhelming influence. The earliest discussion of Hoover's formative years emphatically makes the point that his mother dominated the family. Annie had provided the "knack for discipline" that, in combination with an "unusually intense boyish nature," produced her son's many high school accomplishments, according to a 1937 New Yorker profile. "Mrs. Hoover came from a long line of Swiss ancestors who were mercenary soldiers, and she kept alive the disciplinary tradition in her home, rewarding obedience and punishing disobedience with impartiality." Hoover's father, a "quiet and diligent minor government employee," received little attention in this profile, which added only that his "career was a short one."[39]

No one has disputed this central argument. As Hoover's niece put it: "Edgar would have never been able to get married. Nanny was the true matriarch, a woman with a very independent streak—she would have stopped anything rumored." Annie was stern and uncompromising; her surviving letters to her son were "affectionate, but did not show as much emotional vulnerability as her husband's." From his mother Hoover learned to be detached and objective, disciplined and orderly.[40]

All but one of his grade school years was spent at Brent Elementary, a block from his house. Citizenship and discipline were stressed, and dress was formal. Prayer began the school day, and Bible study was a regular feature of the curriculum. Brent demanded much of its pupils. Eighth-graders read Dickens, Shakespeare, Defoe, and Hawthorne. Algebra was required. Even so, the emphasis was on mastering received knowledge. Only whites attended Brent, since Jim Crow laws dictated separate black and white schools in the District of Columbia.[41]

Hoover's family made religion central to his life at an early age. The Lord's Day, which was spent at Sunday school and church services, concluded, Edgar remembered, with his great-great uncle leading the family in prayers and Bible reading. In one of the few adventuresome moves of his life, Hoover followed his older brother away from the family church and into another when they both transferred their membership to the Old First Presbyterian Church, "the highest level of Capitol Hill's middle-class respectability." Hoover joined his brother's Sunday school at thirteen and quickly became a leader. At fourteen he rose from secretary of his class to corresponding secretary of the whole school. He began teaching his own students at fifteen and continued to do so throughout his high school years, eventually becoming assistant superintendent of the Junior Department.[42]

The Sunday school experience apparently reinforced some of Hoover's incipient character traits and initiated new ones. Because post–Civil War reformers were convinced that "uniformity of thought and action" would "create a deeper *unity*," lessons were exactly the same in all Presbyterian Sunday schools. Uniformity also "provided a simple, efficient, sabotage-proof system that could be run by amateurs." Religious education was "organized like a legal brief to lead the class to accept the moral lesson and render a verdict for Jesus." The purpose of the uniform lesson was to promote not only godliness but also "unity and power as well as efficiency."[43]

In later life Hoover often testified to the importance of Sunday school and sometimes asserted that no one who regularly attended it would become a juvenile delinquent. He may have meant this literally, but more likely he was thinking of Sunday school as part of the larger whole of the Victorian Sabbath that in turn was embedded in a life lived righteously. "The fabric of that day had many strands: church, Sunday School, special clothes; roast beef and the Sunday newspaper for more casual families; and cold meat, hymn sings, Bible reading and peaceful walks for stricter households."[44]

In 1909 Hoover entered Central High School, three miles away, rather than attend a closer but inferior school It was in Central's competitive environment that he "hit his stride as an achiever." The best secondary institution in the city, white and middle class, Central affected his development in several ways. First, it "reinforced the sense of self" that he "had acquired in his early years on Seward Square." Second, it was where Hoover learned the tools and strategies to defend that identity and that community. He flourished at Central High. Its basic requirements were stiff for the times, yet he surpassed them, taking four years of math rather than two; four of history rather than two; physics, the toughest elective in the school; and Latin. He missed only four days of school and placed near the top of his class, which elected him valedictorian.[45]

Later on, newspaper columnists consistently referred to Hoover as having been "athletic" during the height of his popularity in high school, but they did so on the basis of flimsy evidence. He tried out for football and track, but was too small for one and too slow for the other. It was rather the cadet corps and the Debate Club in which he excelled while at Central, and it was these activities that most influenced him. Hoover joined the Debate Club his sophomore year; he judged its intramural contests and was part of an undefeated team his junior year. (Among the issues taken up were women's suffrage and the annexation of Cuba.) He was one of four senior boys chosen to debate Baltimore City College. The question involved presidential primaries; Hoover was the first speaker and also gave the final rebuttal for the victorious Central team.[46]

Debate helped shape the character of Hoover's later engagement with the world. He learned "how to lend authority to his opinions by presenting them, not as his own beliefs, but as truths apparent to any serious and honest intelligence." Furthermore, Hoover learned that in order to do this, he had to master his opponents' arguments and collect as much detail as possible. Debating produced—or perhaps reinforced—the combativeness and shrewdness that he would exhibit continually throughout his life.[47]

Hoover's thoughts about the significance of the debate experience are illuminating:

> Debate offers benefits in many forms. It teaches one to control his temper and free himself from sarcasm; it gives self-possession and mental control; it brings before the debater vividly the importance of clean play, for debate, like other interests, offers loopholes for slugging, but when the referee is a committee composed of three lawyers, slugging in the form of false arguments and statements proves of little use; and lastly, it gives to the high school debater a practical and beneficial example of life, which is nothing more or less than the matching of one man's wit against another; such is debate.
>
> These are the benefits that one derives from debate, benefits which are more than could be obtained from a study of math or of modern languages; benefits which serve to aid one in the practical struggles of life.[48]

Hoover's cadet experience may have been even more important than his participation in debate. He spent his freshman and sophomore years drilling in the ranks and served as second sergeant in Company B his junior year. During his senior year Hoover was one of three captains of Company A. One of the others, a football star and class president, became an all-American at West Point and later its head football coach. The third co-captain became a general. All three Central High companies marched in Woodrow Wilson's inaugural parade on March 4, 1913.

This experience in the cadets must be viewed within a larger American cultural context: the attention to—some might say obsession with—class and gender that gripped white middle-class Protestant men from the 1890s through the 1910s. These men found themselves besieged on one side by economic changes that called into question their independence, from another by a growing (and often foreign-born) working-class presence, and from yet another by women who refused to accept their subordinate position. Among the reactions to this situation was that of middle-class "character builders," who responded by "retiring to fixed positions and doubling efforts to keep the garrison loyal." They sought to keep "respectable boys apart and [strengthen] them for leadership in later life."[49]

Military drill teams were an early and important part of this effort to (re)invigorate middle-class masculinity by "building character" among boys. Central's drill team was founded in 1882—among the country's earliest—and was mandatory for freshmen during Hoover's years there. Its founders undoubtedly shared former president Benjamin Harrison's hope that disciplining the body would do the same for the mind: "A military drill develops the whole man, head, chest, arms, and legs, proportionately; and so promotes symmetry. . . . It teaches quickness of the eye and ear, hand and foot; qualifies men to step and act in unison; [and] teaches subordination. . . . If rightly used, it will wake [boys] up, make them more healthy, develop their pride, and promote school order." The end result of this disciplined mind and body, its advocates hoped, would be a militant Protestant. Drill, according to one advocate, "subdues and controls the contentious spirit of the boy; teaches him to obey and enables us to hold him under influences . . . that lead him to become a loyal soldier of Jesus Christ."[50]

It is virtually impossible, especially in light of Hoover's latter years, to overestimate the importance of his cadet experience. First, he learned to inculcate group cohesion, identity, and discipline. Becoming a cadet leader, said Hoover, "means work all the time. Attendance, fight and set-up are the three essentials." Second, he discovered that he excelled at this kind of leadership. Third, the cadet experience explains much about the older Hoover's leadership of the FBI. As biographer Richard Gid Powers argues, "so much of the routine that later consumed Hoover's FBI, and seemed so pointless to his critics, becomes understandable in light of the youthful Hoover's pleasure in organization for its own sake." Fourth, the cadet experience disciplined Hoover's body and routinized the regime of self-control he had learned as a child. Finally, it was an important ingredient in his social bonding with men at the very time when many of his peers were becoming heterosexually oriented.[51]

Hoover's final report on Company A indicates its importance to him: "This year has been a most enjoyable one, for there is nothing more pleasant than to be associated with a company composed of officers and men who you feel are behind you heart and soul. The saddest moment of the year . . . was when I realized I must part with a group of fellows who had become part of my life. And in conclusion, let me say that I want every man of Company A of 1912–1913 to look upon me as their friend and helper whenever we might meet after this year."[52]

The J. Edgar Hoover we see at his high school graduation was fully prepared to be the man he would become. In many ways Hoover *had* become the "loyal soldier of Christ" for which the advocates of drilling had hoped. Fond of teaching his Sunday school class in his Central High cadet uniform, Edgar was competitive and achievement-oriented. The most important lessons he had learned at Central were concerned, he wrote, with the "practical struggles of life." (He believed, in fact, that "the book learning" had been the "least of high school life.") Disciplined in mind (debate), body (drill), and spirit (Sunday school), Hoover was now well trained to take up life's battles. "A gentleman of dauntless courage," the caption under his picture in the yearbook noted, "'and stainless honor."[53]

Hoover's definition of life as "nothing more or less than the matching of one man's wit against another" was both literally and figuratively true. He seems to have had little if any interaction with female students at Central High. The cadets, of course, were all male; the Debate Club was heterosocial, but the team that took on Baltimore City College was all male. The place where Hoover and his pals regularly ate lunch was off-limits to girls. Former classmates, when asked if he had dated during high school, said yes but could not remember anyone in particular. One, though, noted that "he was in love with Company A."[54]

All this of course takes on quite a different significance from the perspective of Hoover's lifelong bachelorhood, let alone lurid insinuations that Hoover was a practicing homosexual. His high school days look quite normal, though, when viewed from a turn-of-the-century perspective. White, Protestant, middle-class men and women very often lived in homosocial worlds; they frequently spent their time with those of their own sex and saw them as their primary emotional reference group. Nonetheless, Hoover never became comfortable around women, and though it obviously is impossible to be sure, he seems never to have focused his sexual energy on them. His social relations with men, moreover, would often assume the characteristics of what Anthony Rotundo calls "boy culture," writing: "At the heart of nineteenth-century boy culture . . . lay an imperative to independent action. Each boy sought his own good in a world of shifting alliances and fierce competition."[55]

Annie Hoover, along with his male friends, sustained Edgar during the Red Scare of 1919–20, when he was working long and stressful hours as the young head of the General Intelligence Division of the Justice Department, overseeing the arrest of "alien radicals." In 1920, too, he became a Master Freemason. He switched his membership from Federal Lodge No. 1 to a Justice Department lodge when it was founded in 1926 and later to the FBI's Fidelity Lodge when it formed. For many years, it has been asserted, Masonic membership provided a key to promotion within the FBI.[56]

While attending George Washington University, where he received his law degree, Hoover joined Kappa Alpha fraternity. He became its president and house manager and Annie Hoover its "unofficial mother." (Both must have been quite popular despite the fact that Annie had a strict moral code and Hoover, according to a former member, "took a dim view of such antics as crap games, poker, and drinking bouts.") Once Hoover became the Bureau's director, he often filled its top positions with men who were members of Kappa Alpha, graduates of George Washington, or both. There also were many Kappa Alphas (just one of many fraternities represented) employed in the ranks.[57]

Hoover's father, also a Mason, died in 1921 after spending time in a sanatorium. Edgar, who had more or less supported his parents after his father's retirement, now became the "man of the house." He found in Kappa Alpha and the Masons the kind of male emotional support and comradeship on which he had come to depend and that he would foster, perhaps inadvertently, and albeit in an extraordinarily hierarchical fashion, at the Bureau. This male tribalism requires women in practical terms to do, privately and publicly, the work that men did not or would not do. It requires women in ideological and cultural terms to be what men were not. Both meant subordination.[58]

During the 1920s Hoover spent a great deal of time with his mother: they ate breakfast together every day and never missed a Christmas. When he was on a trip to a Bureau field office, he called her often and brought back a present on his return. He also spent time with his niece, whose stories about her uncle suggest that his fondness for routine was already beginning to harden into the rigidity of his later years.[59]

Annie and Edgar frequently played bridge with T. Frank Baughman and his mother, a widow, at 413 Seward Square. Baughman, who "anticipated the wholesome G-Man of the 1930s, with his short well-groomed hair, impeccable suits, and courtly manners," was a Kappa Alpha who also earned his law degree at George Washington. Hoover had hired him into the General Intelligence Division several weeks before the first raid that picked up radicals. They became best friends and were inseparable for a time. While playing cards, the two men "exchanged anti-Communist confidences."[60]

Some deep homosocial relationships could survive marriage and some could not. At about the same time Baughman got married, Clyde Tolson came along to replace him in Hoover's world. Tolson, typical of the men who ran the Bureau in the early days, was born in Iowa in 1900 and took his first Washington job as a War Department clerk. In 1920 he became the confidential secretary to the secretary of war and continued in that post for the next eight years. He went to George Washington University Law School at night and received his law degree in 1927. Shortly after being admitted to the bar in 1928 he became a special agent. Taking an immediate interest in Tolson's career, Hoover apparently decided early in their friendship that Tolson should be his second-in-command and promoted him "rapidly through a series of positions to provide him with the paper experience necessary for his dossier." By 1931 Tolson had become an assistant director and, in 1936, assistant to the director.[61]

On February 22, 1938, Annie Hoover died. She had been "bedridden" for about three years. The family, one of Hoover's nieces remembered, suspected cancer, but "it was in the days when nobody mentioned" such things. We know nothing of Hoover's reaction to her death, but it must have been devastating, for she was the "only personal anchor he had known in his life." His relatives had all moved out of town, and Hoover was now alone in Washington. He sold the Seward Square house and bought one near Tolson's. It was there that another Annie, his housekeeper, would find him dead on the morning of May 2, 1972.[62]

Tolson was Hoover's "only close relationship" after his mother died. They were, in fact, inseparable. They shared at least two meals every day, vacationed together, attended official Washington functions together (an invitation to Edgar soon included one to Clyde), and went to the track together. Tolson possessed those "attributes that Hoover most admired in men . . . athleticism, toughness, virility, loyalty, and . . . piety," and so "came as close as anyone to fulfilling Hoover's dream" of the ideal man.[63]

Were Hoover and Tolson homosexuals? Did they engage in what we would now consider homosexual acts? Many of their contemporaries thought so, and such suspicions have increased since their deaths. It is true, as Hoover's biographers have noted, that his "social interests were overwhelmingly male-oriented." It also is true that his and Tolson's "relationship was so close, so enduring, and so affectionate that it took the place of marriage for both bachelors." Still, none of this answers the question: Did they have a homosexual relationship?[64]

This is not, I think, a fruitful or even an interesting question. First, in the mid-1990s Anthony Summers marshaled all the available evidence in an effort to demonstrate that Hoover not only was a homosexual but also was being blackmailed for it. A close reading of his book at the time of its publication, however, made it clear that Summers's "evidence" was a combination of gossip, circumstance, and secondhand stories that originated with people long since dead. Hoover biographer Athan Theoharis, moreover, has taken apart Summers's argument bit by bit until nothing remains of it. Second, there is little reason to think that we will ever find evidence to provide a sure answer—one way or the other—to this question. The trail has gotten colder, not warmer: Summers's book should be seen, therefore, as an end point of this line of inquiry, not a beginning.[65]

Finally, the issue of homosexuality per se distracts us from a larger and much more significant one: the way in which Hoover's embeddedness in a male-only world—a homosocial world—solidified his commitment to gender politics that planted both him and his organization squarely against any change in the social position of women. This homosociality served several purposes. It emotionally replenished and sustained Hoover so that he could work amazingly long hours. It also provided a continual reminder to him of what he was (a man) and what he was not (a woman). For Hoover, chaos resulted when men did not act like men and women did not act like women. Participation in male-only activities continually affirmed and reaffirmed Hoover's commonality with other men and their "maleness" and his separateness from women and their "femaleness."

The Catholic seminaries of the United States produced male selves, bodies, and minds that were surprisingly congruent with Hoover's and laid the basis for the clerical alliance with him. These seminaries—all male, except for, in some cases, the nuns who did the menial work—helped these men turn their desires into the proper channels, discipline their bodies, and order their minds.[66]

The Catholic seminary trained men to become priests. Minor seminaries consisted of at least four years of high school and sometimes two years of college (though the trend was to drop the two years of college). After successfully completing this course of studies, the seminarian went on to learn not only philosophy and theology but also some subjects appropriate to college. This training in the major seminary lasted anywhere from eight to ten years. Religious orders—those priests who took vows of poverty, chastity, and obedience—required at least one further year, the novitiate, a time of intensive spiritual training. The Jesuits—as we will see, a story unto themselves—demanded even more years of education.

Seminary training, relatively haphazard and locally controlled in the nineteenth century, became increasingly uniform and controlled from Rome. This was especially true after the intellectual crises of "modernism" and "Americanism" that shook the U.S. Church around the turn of the twentieth century and led to a papal crackdown. There was little change in seminary training from about 1910 to the post–Vatican II period.

The "rule" is key to understanding the way in which the seminary worked on the self and the body. At the simplest level, it was a schedule of what the seminarian had to do during the day. At every minute there was a place where he was supposed to be and something he was supposed to be doing. Through its stipulations, moreover, the rule laid out the seminarian's spiritual obligations (for example, weekly confession and daily meditation) and his duties to his fellow seminarians (for example, the necessity of participating in community recreation). In addition, the rule dictated when the seminarian should speak (very seldom) and keep silent (almost always). Finally, the rule included, even if it did not formally mention, regulations such as whether or not seminarians could smoke, and if so, when and where.[67]

That it was God-given gave the rule its significance. As Father Thomas Dubay, S.M., noted in his 1954 study: *"The seminary rule is the expression of God's signified will for the seminarian. It points out to him at any given moment of the day exactly what God wants him to do."* Or as the rector of Immaculate Conception Theological Seminary in Darlington, New Jersey, put it, "the seminarian should be impressed with the idea that during his seminary day, the rule indicates definitely the will of Almighty God manifested through his superiors."[68]

There were two reasons why nothing less than absolute obedience to the rule was required. First, it was a way of determining who was priestly material and who was not. Second, in the process of becoming obedient the seminarian developed those character traits necessary to be a good priest. The kind of obedience demanded also was twofold. It was first to be external, but also eventually internal. Seminary disciplinarians knew that one kind of obedience was not necessarily the other, but they tended to assume, as they almost had to, that the external ultimately signified the acquisition of the internal.

Father Joseph Mohan, the spiritual director of Chicago's Quigley Preparatory Seminary from 1938 to 1955, provides in his graduate school thesis an excellent discussion of both obedience to the rule and its monitoring. Obedience, "the foundation of the priestly life," typified the Church: "If there is any organization in the world that demands obedience, it is the Catholic Church. The laity obey the priest; the priest obeys the bishop; the bishop obeys the Pope; the Pope leads all others in obeying Almighty God."[69]

Both the supernatural and the natural world demonstrated the reasons for this obedience. "In all things," Mohan asserted, "the future priest looks to Christ himself as the model he is to follow in living his life." It was obedience that characterized that. "St. Paul summed up the life of our Lord in this sentence: 'He humbled himself, becoming obedient unto death, even to the death of the Cross.'" The *Seminary Rule Book* for Quigley, which included two years of college-level instruction in addition to high school, put it this way:

> The foundation of a Christ-like character is the spirit of obedience, prompt, cheerful, exact. This was the outstanding virtue of the Boy Christ. A student for the priesthood should be more like the Boy Christ than any boy in his neighborhood. He should willingly obey the rule, not to please superiors or to avoid punishment, but because he wishes to fashion himself after Christ, and because he sees in the rule a detailed plan for imitating the obedience of Christ. Obedience to the rule will serve as a measure of your resemblance to Christ.[70]

But the secular world also demonstrated the need for the development of discipline. There is no "well-balanced leader," Mohan argued, "who has not a trained will." Obedience, "also called self-control or self-discipline," is a "basic qualification of leadership." The priest then called upon a familiar figure to back him up: "J. Edgar Hoover, the capable director of the Federal Bureau of Investigation[,] has aptly said: 'You don't acquire self-discipline, if you never learn what discipline is.'"[71]

A look at how Quigley monitored behavior is revealing. At the beginning of the quarter, each student received a personal conduct card which he had to carry at all times. When a student violated one of the seminary's eight rules—for example, through "tardiness" or "disorder in free time" or "disrespect"—he received a certain number of demerits. Each multiple of five produced a confiscation of the card and a trip to the prefect of discipline. Fifteen demerits in a quarter meant a visit to the rector and a letter home. Five more led to a "Final Conduct Warning." Another five, bringing the total to twenty-five, meant expulsion. Since many students, according to Mohan, did not take the rules seriously until they received close to twenty demerits, the *Rule Book* stipulated that "habitual violation of the rules of the seminary or a manifestation of a spirit of contempt for them renders a student liable to expulsion."[72]

There were many advantages to this system, which "in a way," Mohan acknowledged, was "an adaptation of the method used in the United States Military Academy at West Point." First, it allowed, once demerits were totaled, for the giving of a grade in conduct each quarter. Second, since "the teaching and maintenance of discipline, order, and good conduct in the Seminary" was "not confined to the Prefects of Discipline," professors had the "right and duty" to give "demerits for behavior whenever" they saw fit. Finally, students who had to leave the seminary because of demerits clearly were "not proper candidates for the priesthood." If they reached this point, it was "due either to deliberate disobedience, or to lack of will-power, or downright carelessness." Any of these signaled a "serious defect of character."[73]

West Point was not the only origin of the demerit system at Quigley— and presumably other seminaries—but it was a source of inspiration and legitimation for another Catholic authority in his discussion of the seminary: James Cardinal Gibbons (1834–1921). The "spirit of discipline"— according to him "one of the most essential elements in ecclesiastical training"—was acquired through the seminarian's daily routine. A "habitual compliance with the rules" of the seminary "quickens his attention, strengthens his will, invigorates the energies of his soul, gives him decision of character, makes him prompt in responding to the call of duty, impels him by force of habit to sacrifice personal comfort to legitimate obligations, endows him with docility and elasticity of mind, and renders him a well-equipped soldier of Christ." In addition, "the custom of rising promptly at the sounding of the bell, of repairing to the prayer-hall and to the chapel, the refectory and the class-room" will, Gibbons argued, "afterward enable him with ease to be punctual at the altar, alert in attending sick-calls and in performing the other functions of the ministry."[74]

At West Point, Gibbons noted, "the recruit" was "schooled for stern warfare by his peaceful military evolutions," just as by "making the daily rounds of the seminary exercises, the young levite" was "unconsciously preparing himself for the battle of ministerial life." Just as West Pointers played such a prominent role in the Civil War because of their professional training, so have the "great bulk of our successful apostolic leaders" been "qualified for their work by spending a series of years of rigid discipline in the school of Christ."[75]

The discipline at West Point and Annapolis was, according to the cardinal, "far more severe" than in Catholic seminaries. If the cadets were willing to "subject themselves to so rigid a discipline" in the "hopes of being enrolled among their country's defenders," surely "the young soldier of Christ should not be less generous in cheerfully submitting to the salutary yoke of the seminary, especially as he is the disciple of Him whose watchword is self-denial, and whose standard is the cross." There was nothing "degrading or slavish in obedience. It was, on the contrary, a most rational duty." It was not an "act of servility paid to man, but an act of homage paid to God."[76]

The extraordinary isolation of many seminaries made the rule's work on the seminarian self even more exacting. Most seminaries, at least when originally built, were geographically isolated. Erected in rural or semi-rural areas, with spacious and bucolic grounds surrounded by large trees and/or fences, the seminary buildings often were not even visible from the outside. This geographic isolation, however, was only the physical context for a deeper, more significant isolation.

The secular world quite literally stopped at the seminary gates. In a decree issued in 1910 Pope Pius X ruled that "we absolutely forbid" seminarians to "read newspapers and reviews, however excellent these may be, and we make it a matter of conscience for a superior who fails to take precautions to prevent such reading." Radios usually were banned as well. A "young lad," as a priest put it in 1933, was "sent to the seminary to get away from the world and its spirit. But there is everything of the world save sensible presence in the radio." It took the inauguration of the country's first Catholic president, John F. Kennedy, to generate the installation of television sets in each of the seminary buildings of the Philadelphia archdiocese. (Major seminarians had been allowed to watch the election returns the previous November.)[77]

A discussion of the supervision of movie watching in a Redemptorist minor seminary illustrates both its isolation from the world as well as its animating values. The seminary directors, who watched the movies and decided if they should be shown, operated on a specific set of principles. First, seminary training was to help the seminarian to "overcome the world, the flesh, and the devil. One of the chief means of overcoming these enemies is the avoidance of unnecessary contact with them." Second, movies "by and large," did not "center human life in God," yet they had a "unique power to influence minds and morals." Third, movies rated Class B, a Legion of Decency classification that permitted their viewing under certain circumstances, were not to be shown. Fourth, movies that included or gave "considerable emphasis to teen-age good times, dates with girls, dancing, kisses and caresses, boy and girl stories" were excluded, even if rated A. Why? "Many well acquainted with seminary life" were convinced that "seminarians are particularly susceptible and disturbed by vivid representations of the beauty of the opposite sex and the charm of their society." Not only did the seminary's "all male environment" offer no "immunization," but also seminarians lacked a "normal family as an outlet for the affections." Fifth, seminary officials had the responsibility not just to decide which movies could and could not be seen but to view them before making that decision. Films deemed unsuitable were not to be shown at all. A "censorship which involves having someone stand in front of the projector while objectionable scenes are running is as bad as no censorship at all," for the "adolescent imagination is probably stirred unduly in the natural attempt to guess just what it was that was cut."[78]

Guests posed a particular problem for seminary authorities. If the outside world was full of danger and evil, then those visiting the seminary were certainly suspect. A 1933 study suggests the ways in which minor seminaries handled the issue. Of the more than forty that responded to a questionnaire, five banned visiting altogether, and the rest drastically limited it. Four restricted it to Sunday afternoon, five to two Sundays per month, and fourteen to one day a month. Many circumscribed visitors' access to the grounds and limited visiting to parents or close relatives. Visiting days, Dubay argued, were yet another part of the seminarian's training. He "should not forget even then that he is living a supernatural life" and "should be making the visit an act of love for God." He does this by "sublimating his natural love to the supernatural level—which means that he loves those who are near to him because he loves God."[79]

Day students—those who commuted to and from their homes to minor seminaries—represented yet another significant problem. Brooklyn's Cathedral College enrolled about four hundred day students, some of whom traveled as much as forty miles daily to attend. In 1935 its prefect of discipline, Father Richard B. McHugh, published a paper in which he laid out some of the practical problems involved in "moulding" the character of seminarians he had under his care for only five hours per day. The priest counted on the help of parents and pastors to enforce seminary regulations. "For the promotion of the student's spiritual welfare, and to protect him from harmful influences," McHugh wrote, the seminary had "several fundamental rules." The use of report cards, signed by either parent, monitored the requirement of daily Mass attendance. (Daily Communion was the norm, but not obligatory.) Seminarians were not allowed "out of their home at night without the permission of the prefect of discipline, or a priest of their parish." There were, moreover, "strong recommendations with regard to attendance at moving-picture shows or theaters, and care in choice of companions, and reading material."[80]

The minute supervision of a seminarian's life carried over even into the few recreation periods that he was allowed. This recreation, of course, was to be purposeful. "Leisure time properly used," wrote Father Wilfred

Brennan, S.A., vice rector of St. John's Atonement Seminary in Garrison, New York, "is beneficial to the whole man, to his soul and body." If used "improperly," however, it could "work havoc in a man and in the case of the young seminarian be the cause of the development of many grave faults eventually leading to the loss of his vocation." Supervision of this recreation "attempt[ed] to develop good habits especially of fraternal charity and industry," while it was also meant "to uproot and abolish those evil habits which idleness breeds."[81]

The daily recreation requirement, which seems to have developed about the middle of the period I have been considering, best illustrates Brennan's point. Held in the afternoon, it usually lasted anywhere from one to two hours and was compulsory. (Labeled "community recreation" in the rule of Holy Ghost Fathers' Junior Seminary in Ann Arbor in the mid-1960s, it was derided by seminarians as "forced fun.") Since it was obligatory, "ordinary games which appeal to the average boy and in which a large group" could "participate" were "played during this period." One problem, of course, was that some students preferred not to participate. Brennan suggested that they should not be excused from the "more virile sports" until they had put in a good deal of effort at trying them. If exempted, they were "obliged to be present at least as spectators. Many times they can be of some help as timekeepers and cheer leaders."[82]

Other recreation periods—the occasional free afternoon or the much briefer period after supper—were less supervised and permitted some freedom of choice. These, however, were seldom spent alone, and never in the company of just one other seminarian because of the ban on "particular friendships." They therefore fell into the pattern of the seminary's group recreation.

Smoking was another important issue for seminary officials. While some completely banned it, others generally permitted it. Many established quite specific and detailed regulations as to when and where it could occur. Smoking was prohibited at St. John's, the Boston archdiocesan major seminary, from 1884 until 1911, when diocesan authorities allowed it "in certain conditions during each walk day." Patrick Cardinal Hayes of New York "repeatedly and vehemently" banned smoking at Dunwoodie, his major seminary. Philadelphia's seminary forbade smoking until Bishop John O'Hara became archbishop in 1952.[83]

Seminary authorities put "so much stress on the smoking rule," Dubay argued in his discussion of it, for three reasons. First, it was "especially fit for use as a criterion in judging a seminarian's seriousness of intent." If the prohibition is broken, "the faculty can be reasonably sure that the seminarian concerned places no great value" on "any seminary rule." Dubay conceded that the offender might "change his attitude after monition" but leaves little doubt that he considered the offense virtually irredeemable: "Smoking is a *fully* deliberate act, and consequently quite an apt criterion by which to judge the seminarian's attitude toward the rule in general." An infraction such as "breaking silence" could happen by "surprise or unprepared weakness," but "smoking against the rule" had to be "prepared." Second, the smoking rule was a "means of acquiring the detachment from creatures that is so essential to holiness." Even a seminarian who obeyed the rule could "still ardently desire to smoke (with his *will*)." Although smoking was not a sin, the "seminarian will immensely aid his spiritual development and progress in perfection if he breaks even this attachment to a creature." Finally, the ban "furnishes the smoking student with splendid opportunities to build up and develop his will power." Quitting smoking was "exceedingly difficult"; even cutting back took "much will power." But just as the "unpleasant task of lifting or pulling" developed arm muscles, so the will was "strengthened by the unpleasant task of saying no to the yearnings for tobacco pleasure—or any pleasure for that matter." Furthermore, conquering one's hunger for tobacco aided in one's struggle against the desire for sexual pleasure: "Because smoking and sex are in the same *general* class of sense pleasure, mortification in one's use of tobacco is an excellent means of counteracting and overcoming temptations against purity." Denial of "sense gratification" was the way to deal with "sins (or temptations) of sense."[84]

Virtually every essay written on seminary training made the same connection—at least implicitly, if not explicitly—that Dubay makes here between disciplining the body and refusing sexual and/or sensual pleasure. This was further connected to celibacy, according to Gibbons the "most glorious, most distinctive, and the most indispensable ornament of a priest." The priest's "spiritual armor" would be "incomplete if it were not crowned with the helmet of sacerdotal chastity." Everything else in his life gained "additional lustre from the aureola of a stainless life." Christ's life was the primary motivation for chastity: "The incentive," the Baltimore cardinal wrote, "to a chaste life is furnished by the example and precepts of our Lord."[85]

There were other reasons, though, for leading a celibate life. First, in reasoning derived from one strand of Church thinking about the relationship between mind and body, Gibbons argued that the suppression of the latter left the former unencumbered in its pursuit of God: "Purity of heart illumines the mind in contemplation of God and in the investigation of heavenly truths; while sensuality obscures the intellect, 'for the animal man perceiveth not those things that are of the Spirit of God.'" Second, more practically, chastity enhanced the priest's mission in the world. Since he led a celibate life, the cleric was "regarded by the community as a superior being." Why? The "greatest evidence of moral strength," Gibbons asserted, was "self-control and the highest manifestation of self-control is in the victory over the carnal appetite." The laity, then, would come to him as "their spiritual physician, to obtain an antidote against the sins of the flesh from which he is happily exempt!" The lack of "family cares," more-over, meant that the priest could "devote himself with entire freedom to the service of his Master and of the people committed to his charge."[86]

Then followed a discussion of the ways in which the priest was to main-tain his chastity. It began with prayer, then the "mortification of the flesh," for as Gibbons puts it, chastity is "a fragrant flower that blooms among the thorns of self-denial." Gluttony and intemperance were to be avoided, as were occasions of sensual sin: "Keep custody over your senses, which are the avenues leading to the citadel of the soul. If the avenues are left unguarded, the enemy can easily enter and take possession of the spiritual fortress." Finally, his reader was cautioned to be "vigilant and circumspect on all occasions. Be ever animated by a salutary fear of the Lord. There should be no truce to this vigilance and fear."[87]

The priest's "ministerial life" would bring him "daily face to face" with evil, yet he would be protected. In a sentence laced with somatic refer-ences, Cardinal Gibbons explained how "God, who calls you to be the soul's physician, to cleanse the leprosy of sin, to be a light to them that are in darkness, to purify the poisonous atmosphere, will make you proof against its infection." Indeed, "happy" was the priest whose "flesh" was "subject to the law of reason and of the Spirit of God." The priest's "tri-umph in conquering self" was "[m]ore glorious" than if he had won a military victory.[88]

Gibbons assumed here—the title of his chapter is "sacerdotal chastity"—that the seminary already had done its job in creating a chaste and chas-tised body, that is, an ordered body. Order was what resulted when the rule was followed and the body disciplined. Order was what resulted when desire—used here to include not only the sex drive but also nonsexual passion, need, energy, and longing—was properly educated and trained. Disorder was the outcome when desire was ill disciplined and not directed or contained appropriately.

Seminary officials seldom discussed the mechanisms through which a celibate body and mind were produced. Rather they seem to have assumed that outer discipline would sooner or later yield inner discipline. "Peda-gogically viewed," a seminary rector wrote, "discipline is orderly train-ing." The purpose of "external discipline" was the "orderly direction of the outward acts of seminarians, so that internal habits or virtues, which will be the foundation of Christlike sacerdotal character, may be brought into being." Internal discipline was the "regulation of the movements (*affectus*) of heart and mind." External discipline was the "means by which internal discipline is acquired."[89]

In 1949 there appeared an article that addressed the issue of training for the priesthood and sexual desire as straightforwardly as any I have seen. Written by Father Frank Gartland, C.S.C., the spiritual director of Holy Cross Seminary in Notre Dame, it spoke, though written about minor seminaries and sex education, in sophisticated ways to the much larger issues of desire and the Church.

The place to begin, Gartland argued, was with the presumption that sex was "good, and even holy; that God planned and made it just as He planned and made every other faculty of the body, every power of the soul." As for the best place to show the seminarian the "positive side, indeed to give him the 'whole story,' the book of Genesis" could not "be beaten." Adam came first and then Eve, but along came much more: "the two sexes male and female," "their complementary character, the aggressiveness of one, the passivity of the other," and "how God himself witnesses their marriage, authorizes their intimacy." Furthermore, Gartland argued, as the "principal purposes of marriage" were the "procreation of children and the mutual support and encouragement of husband and wife," only "by the virtuous exercise of the sex life in human marriage" could "heaven be peopled with saints for all eternity." The "pleasures of sex" were, however, only for those who took on the "responsibilities of marriage." God "reserved" them for "the married alone as a reward for fathers and mothers who fulfil [*sic*] the arduous duties of parenthood."[90]

The seminarian—remember, Gartland was explaining to fellow clerics how to approach sex education in a minor seminary—should be told that the prohibition on sexual pleasure applied to anyone who was unmarried: "Therefore, no unmarried person may, alone or with another, indulge in any thought, word, or action which stimulates this marital pleasure." This would be "convincing and inspiring to the minor seminarian," who would be "willing to fight as a hardy soldier for what is right."[91]

Adam and Eve's disobedience to God's command—original sin— provided the explanation for what Gartland knew would be the seminarian's question in response to what he had just been told: "But why do I have these violent thoughts and desires, this fascination for pleasure, these physical stirrings by day and 'wet dreams' by night?" He then would realize that there "was nothing abnormal, queer about him if he experiences bad thoughts and desires," because everyone has them as a result of original sin: "There is a fierce civil war going on within every one of us, the flesh struggling against the spirit, the spirit willing (to do God's will) but the flesh weak."[92]

Priests had to "be brave men," and the "earlier" seminarians realized this, the "better for them and the priesthood." What the minor seminarian had to do "from the start of his training" was to "generously and consistently sublimate sex and all human love, however good; he must supernaturalize all his attractions, all his struggles." How was he to do this? Gartland's list began with "the necessity of modesty," "high motivation," and "training the will through self-denial." Finally, the soul needed to be "strengthen[ed] through prayer and the sacraments," and "devotion to the Blessed Virgin Mary especially," for she, "alone of all men, was conceived immaculate, free from the first moment of her existence, and always free, from the domination of evil."[93]

Here are, I think, the two ways that the seminaries handled desire, including sexual desire. The first was to reeducate it. As Father Felix M. Kirsch, O.M.Cap., who taught at Catholic University, approvingly quoted a monsignor: "We do not rise to our full spiritual stature by eradicating passions. The ideal man is not a passionless man. He is rather one whose passions are turned into the right channel. The ideally pure man is not the sexless man; he is the man who loves violently what he ought, as he ought." G. K. Chesterton, Kirsch thought, spoke the same truth in fewer words: "Chastity does not mean abstention from sexual wrong; it means something flaming, like Joan of Arc."[94]

Desire was reeducated in several different ways. First, it was turned toward the Blessed Virgin Mary. Thus Mary, the most complete woman of all, and the woman against whom no other woman could compete, became an object of the deepest (and safest) desire. This redirection took place within a system of gender and familial relations that already provided women with primacy over spiritual matters. To this was added the emotionally weighted biological, psychological, and spiritual connection that already existed between the seminarian and his mother. All of this provided the experiential basis on which desire could be reoriented. There was good reason why dozens of devotions to Mary sprouted up from 1900 to 1960.

This reeducation of desire turned in another direction as well: toward the Church itself. Always coded as female, the Church was simultaneously spouse and mother to the priest. At his ordination he married the Church, yet he called her his Holy Mother. At one level, then, the seminarian was preparing to marry his mother. Operating from within a theological and familial system that was explicitly as well as implicitly patriarchal, the seminarian or priest passionately loved Mary and Holy Mother Church as he would an equal, yet simultaneously saw them requiring protection and defense as he would an inferior. Those who threatened either one, then, were threatening his sense of himself as man, patriarch, and priest.

While much of the seminarian's desire was being redirected, the resulting ordered body and mind drove some of it, perhaps the most dangerous part, underground. Here it was kept at bay—in its proper place—behind borders and boundaries that required continuous surveillance. That place was ultimately not safe, however, for every sort of change deeply endangered the self that repression had helped to create. Because issues of gender were central to the creation of this self, virtually every menace, real or imagined, was read in terms of gender relations. Changes in gender relations, moreover, were especially threatening. Furthermore, the metaphors and figures of speech used to understand these dangers were primarily somatic ones, and in this way they raised the stakes even as they helped the user understand what they referred to.

Order, then, was everything to the seminarian and the priest. In a study of Dunwoodie, the New York archdiocesan seminary, Father Philip J. Murnion repeatedly found this. Whether it was in the many interviews he conducted with priests who had attended the seminary or in their spiritual reading, regularity, discipline, and routine were recurring themes. So did Raymond Hedin in his interviews with his former classmates at St. Francis Seminary in Milwaukee: "In discussing the seminary, nearly all my classmates talk first about the rule." If Herbert Marcuse was onto something with the concept of "surplus-repression"—the "restrictions necessitated by social domination" beyond those required for civilization—then the repression required in the seminary was far in excess of this surplus.[95]

The result was a "brotherhood of priests" connected, in the words of a Hartford labor priest, by "an intimacy" that was "more reckless" and "more profound" than any other in the world. The "strange sympathy" of one priest for another was "too tender to be called friendship" and "too sturdy to be called love." United, then, in a homosocial bond that rivaled Hoover's and Tolson's, and committed to a masculinity that had as its foundation the subordination of women, priests were logical allies as the FBI went about its business.[96]

During the first fifteen years or so of his directorship, Hoover preferred to hire white Protestants from small towns, especially in the West and the South, as special agents. In 1940, however, he began specifically recruiting in New York City, where Catholics constituted a large portion of the pool. Hoover and his executive committee, having learned that Catholic agents were ideologically sound, increasingly hired them when the FBI greatly expanded during World War II. At the same time, Jesuit educators were producing large numbers of undergraduates who went on to earn law degrees, thus fulfilling one of the Director's requirements for serving as a special agent. As Father Robert I. Gannon, S.J., the president of Fordham, wrote to Hoover in 1945, "I like to think the FBI and Fordham have the same ideas."[97]

Good public relations were the foundation for the Bureau's recruiting at Jesuit schools. This had begun with the war against crime in the early 1930s, as the Justice Department's Division of Investigation was being transformed into the Federal Bureau of Investigation, resulting in G-Man mania. FBI movies, radio shows, documentaries, comic books, pulp fiction, and Junior G-Man clubs were everywhere as the FBI accumulated the cultural capital on which it would draw for decades. If the young men at Boston College were typical, students at Jesuit institutions as early as 1938 had, in the words of the Boston special agent in charge (SAC), a surprising "familiarity" with "the accomplishments of the Bureau."[98]

Providing speakers and movies for classes and student organizations was an important aspect of the FBI's recruiting efforts. Whenever possible the Bureau furnished both. At Canisius College, for example, the Buffalo field office supplied a copy of its documentary *You Can't Get Away with It* for a criminology students' study group; later that same year the SAC spoke on "Law Enforcement—the Protection of Americanism"—to an audience of about 350 at the Communion breakfast of the Canisius Alumni Sodality. The FBI regularly provided a speaker for Boston College chemistry majors, some of whom were working in the FBI's lab as early as 1938. In 1961 the FBI speaker had been a chemistry graduate student there twenty years earlier. He was deemed eminently qualified to "sell" the FBI in "giving a clear picture of its service to the country, its technical skills, its zeal and its integrity."[99]

Only the barest outlines of the actual recruiting process are illuminated in the FBI files on Jesuit colleges and universities. In 1940, for example, the St. Louis SAC arranged for a special agent to speak to all third-year law students as well as seniors in the College of Commerce and Finance at St. Louis University. In the former case, the agent spoke to about 200 students and met privately with those interested; in the latter, he talked to about 150 and then held individual conferences. The SAC spoke to between 80 and 100 law students at Boston College in February 1940. After a talk of about forty-five minutes and "many questions," he privately interviewed "several," some of whom intended to apply. None were "exceptionally outstanding," but everyone had exhibited "keen interest."[100]

The results of this recruiting are considerably clearer than the process: not only did many graduates of Jesuit schools join the FBI, but also these institutions took immense pride in their Bureau alumni. While the Bureau claimed publicly that it did not keep statistics on how many agents came from any particular school, it clearly did so. In the right situation, the FBI not only willingly produced those numbers but cooperated with the school as well in its publicity efforts. A look at just one school provides further insight into the connection between the Church and the Bureau.

Among Jesuit schools, Fordham University probably ranked first in the number of alumni who were FBI agents. In 1952 the editor of its student newspaper, *The Ram*, wrote the Bureau, saying that he wanted to do a story on Fordham's FBI alumni. In response it produced a blind letterhead memorandum—a document not identifying its origin—titled "Re: Fordham Men and the FBI." Several weeks later this memorandum, its source acknowledged but underplayed, appeared more or less verbatim as a three-part series in *The Ram*. More than 180 men with a degree from Fordham, slightly up from the 176 figure of the year before, were special agents. The memorandum, which argued that the Bureau's values and Fordham's were essentially the same, presented specific examples of Fordham alumni who had excelled at the FBI, for example, Paul J. Shine, class of 1936, the current Cleveland SAC, who graduated from the college and the law school. Two members of Fordham's undefeated 1937 football team, including one of the legendary "Seven Blocks of Granite," were special agents.[101]

The term "granite" came up again in 1957, when Fordham asked Hoover to write an article for its alumni magazine. That Fordham had so many alumni—173—in the FBI, Hoover noted, was "indicative of the type of training which has molded their character." Eight FBIHQ supervisors were from Fordham, as were four assistant special agents in charge (ASACs). "I like to find men of granite," the Director wrote, "men of physical, mental, moral and spiritual strength."[102]

In 1960 the Bureau, in response to another request from *The Ram* for an article, produced a detailed piece for publication. Of the 5,900 special agents in the FBI, 170 were Fordham alumni. An assistant director, a special agent in charge, three ASACs, and twelve supervising special agents at FBIQ were among them. In its discussion of the alumni who were special agents, the Bureau emphasized athletes: more than a few had played football, others baseball, and another had starred on the swimming team.

Ultimately, however, the article came back once again more generally to the way in which Fordham had prepared its men to be agents: "All, however, work tirelessly and ceaselessly in the true spirit of Fordham and exemplify in Government service the traditions and standards which were imparted to them during their college days."[103]

Similar requests from other Jesuit schools produced similar results. In 1940, we learn, Georgetown had fifty-four graduates in the FBI. Holy Cross had forty in 1944 and St. Louis seventeen in 1947. In 1961 Canisius, one of the smallest Jesuit schools, had twenty-eight alumni working for the FBI. One of its basketball teams from the late 1940s produced four special agents.[104]

Other, non-Jesuit Catholic schools, of course, turned out many special agents. (Notre Dame ranked number one.) These educational institutions, though, apparently had less intellectual coherence and somatic integrity than the schools the Jesuits created out of their experiences as seminarians and priests. It was Jesuit thinking in particular that produced the "Christian manhood" Hoover so desired.[105]

Jesuit training, which aimed at creating a "militia of Christ" or a "Jesuit corps" to "undertake campaigns on many fronts," began with a two-year novitiate. Three things are striking about this experience. First, it was an all-male world where Jesuit brothers (men) did the physical labor that was often done in other seminaries by sisters (women). In an editorial titled "These Are Men!" a Jesuit publication, perhaps a bit anxious that these brothers' role in the seminary might gender them as female, asserted that they were doing a "man-sized job" of being a "whole man who uses mind and muscles and heart." Second, it was a world where authority and social relations were patriarchal. It was not just LaFarge, as we have seen, who described it that way. Patriarchy, as David G. Schultenover, S.J., brilliantly argues, was embedded deep within the Jesuit mentality. In early 1942, for example, the U.S. Jesuit provincial, in pledging his order's support for the war effort, noted that "we who are the sons of a Soldier Saint will not be found wanting." Third, aspiring Jesuits began the process of creating a self that imitated the example of Ignatius: "A good soldier, Ignatius conquered first the closest part of the kingdom, himself." In the seminary a young man began learning, in the words of one Jesuit, "guts," and in another's, "to say *no* to himself." At novitiate's end came vows and admittance into the Society of Jesus. Next came two years of Latin, Greek, and English classics. After three years of philosophy Jesuits then served their regency, a three-year teaching stint in a Jesuit high school. Here teachers were not only "drilling boys in the languages or the sciences" but also, in the words of a Jesuit Seminary Aid Association magazine, "trying harder still to mold their characters to [the Jesuits'] own high ideals of Christian manhood."[106]

This brand of manhood, according to Lance Morrow, recalling his education at Gonzaga High in Washington, D.C., encapsulated a "spiritual core that was as hard as a stone, an intellectual will that seemed to me grim and impressive: a hard bright black rock with blue flame flickering around it." The Jesuits exuded "an aggressive sort of humility" and a "black and alert kind of anger." Patrick Buchanan, also writing about his years at Gonzaga, remembers those serving their regency as "serious, self-confident men who tolerated neither nonsense nor disobedience." There "was not much playfulness about them." The "Pope's Marines," as he calls them, were there to "teach the truth about God and man."[107]

The four years of theology that followed the regency shared much, for our purposes, with the three of philosophy that preceded it. Here Jesuits learned what they would teach "to defend the faith" and to render their "students immune from those infections of skepticism and materialism that are in the air we breathe." Here they learned Aquinas, "the only buoy which can keep men afloat in the midst of the whirlpool of doubt and confusion called modern thought."[108]

An "agonistic" pervaded not only the teaching of philosophy and theology but also its content. This agonistic, argues Walter Ong, S.J., "resulted from a disposition to organize the subject matter itself as a field of combat, to purvey, not just to test, knowledge in a combative style." Pervasive intellectual battle, then, characterized the seven years of philosophy and theology. These classes, moreover, were taught in Latin, the homosocial language of men, with its echoes, for Ong, of Renaissance puberty rites.[109]

A continuing need to prove one's masculinity through contest, originating deep in the unconscious, seems to have typified Jesuit manhood. An anecdote about Fordham's Father Ignatius Cox gets at this from one perspective. On Sunday afternoons he would go downtown to debate a *New York World Telegram* columnist at a Protestant church, then on Mondays he "regal[ed] his classes with how he had demolished agnosticism with logic." Another story, this one about Cox and William Casey, the future CIA director, also captures this Jesuit characteristic. Casey "forever remembered" how Cox concluded a lecture on courage: "God give us men who will not shrink from the battle. . . . God give us men who will not flee the fray. . . . God give us *men*!"[110]

Jesuit higher education produced the same sort of men that the seminaries did. First, they were men who were very comfortable in—indeed probably preferred—an all-male environment. It was not until after 1960 that the liberal arts divisions of Jesuit colleges and universities began to enroll women. Father Vincent T. O'Keefe, S.J., president of Fordham University from 1963 to 1965, had wanted to enroll women in the College, but there was too much opposition from "many people, especially the Jesuits." Instead O'Keefe founded the all-female Thomas More College, which did not merge with Fordham College until 1974.[111]

The sense on Jesuit campuses was that the type of learning conducted there was not simply for men but primarily male in nature. At Fordham, for example, Anne Anastasi became the fourth female professor on the Rose Hill campus when she arrived in 1947. She found a situation that perfectly illustrates Mary Douglas's argument about how notions of pollution effectively patrol borders: "I was told that a female assistant or secretary could not even enter a classroom to put a notice on the blackboard if the regular instructor was absent."[112]

Second, Jesuit education produced men who not only understood authority and hierarchy, but also whose personalities were congruent with them. No matter the level, it was never just the imparting of "facts"; rather it was about the "formation and training" of a "truly Christian character." Because proper respect and reverence for authority were a necessary condition for "Christian manhood" and "manly piety," they were woven into the daily experience of Jesuit education.[113]

Discipline and self-control, the third characteristic of the men produced by Jesuit education, were closely aligned with authority. Jesuit educators provided the appropriate context, both inside and outside the classroom, within which the student could develop these traits on his own. This was of course a central focus in the Jesuit high schools, but it was no less essential at the college and university levels.

Authority and discipline began with the course of study. The "system of education," the "one in use in all" Jesuit colleges, was guided by the "famous *Ratio Studiorum*," which constitutes an "essential requisite" for success in education: "natural, thorough, and effective methods of teaching, employed uniformly by all the teachers." Wanting no part of a "system of ever-changing theory and doubtful experiment," Jesuit institutions never wholly surrendered, at least during the period under study, to "electivism." Students for the most part "took a prescribed set of courses chosen by "*men whose profession is education*," not by "*inexperienced youth just entering on the process of education*."[114]

Jesuit institutions, a 1927 catalogue conceded, provided "closer supervision" of student life than "is usual at the present day in most of the large colleges." At Fordham in the 1920s and 1930s, students living on campus had required nightly study in their rooms; lights-out came at 11:00.

Into the 1950s a Jesuit prefect lived in each building in Martyrs Court. Students were to be in by 11:00 each weekday night and had to check in with the prefect. Joseph Califano, President Jimmy Carter's secretary of Health, Education, and Welfare, remembers that during his Holy Cross days in the late 1940s and early 1950s, two bed checks were performed nightly, and a Jesuit priest lived on "every floor of every dormitory."[115]

The emphasis throughout these regulations was on the necessity of a "paternal" authority to create a disciplined and orderly environment for community life. This can be seen in class attendance policies. At Fordham and Holy Cross, no one was allowed to enter the classroom late. Creighton University punished every unexcused absence from class with two hours of physical exercise or campus work. At Holy Cross no exceptions were permitted to the rule that vacations could not be extended, because doing so would be "unfair to other students and injurious to discipline." The most elaborate explanation for attendance policies, and the one most revealing of the Jesuit value system, was Georgetown's. Missing a class denoted not just "a loss of mental training" but also a "serious menace to the regularity of College discipline." The "absence of one [student] suggests, perhaps encourages, the absence of another," and "so gradually a noticeable absenteeism arises which enervates regular attendance and discourages the teacher."[116]

Students at Jesuit schools, whether secondary schools or institutions of higher education, thus grew accustomed to highly disciplined and hierarchical all-male environments and organizations in which patriarchal authority was deeply embedded. That is not the end of the story, however, for two other attributes—of which we have already caught glimpses—characterized Jesuit education and intensified the gender consciousness of its products: a military rhetoric of battle and struggle, and a continuing immersion in competition as a mode of learning.

"Military metaphors, as applied to spiritual warfare," LaFarge argued, "are as old as the Church." But like other metaphors, they are sometimes called upon and sometimes not, and are at times fitting and at other times inappropriate. Jesuits often found such imagery congruent with their situation; one is struck with the emphasis on battle and military vocabulary in their writings about the world and themselves during this period.[117]

Examples from one important Jesuit document will have to suffice. On September 20, 1954, Father Martin Carrabine, S.J., gave the sermon to Chicago-area Jesuits gathered at the National Shrine of Our Sorrowful Lady to honor Mary, the "Queen of the Society of Jesus." Here are just some of the military and agonistic terms and metaphors from Carrabine's sermon: "militant loyalty," "struggle," "fighting man," "commander of Christ," "fighting force," "fought to turn the tide," "turned back a tide," "became a fighting issue," "militantly," "glorious army of militants." The best illustration of the way in which military thinking permeated Carrabine's consciousness is his description of the Jesuits' discovery of the need to include laymen in their campaigns: "The first ten members of the original Company were quite inadequate to the demands made on them. Heartbreaking it was to recapture a vantage point, then to be summoned away to another crisis. What to do? How to hold each hard-won position? A partial answer lay in discovering dedicated laymen, turning them into men of decision by that best of disciplines—the Spiritual Exercises, developing them into a force which would hold till reinforcements might come."[118]

"Emulation" was an essential part of the *Ratio Studiorum* and therefore a fundamental component of Jesuit education. A 1950s teaching manual acknowledged the increasingly negative evaluation of competition as a teaching device but characterized this as "nonsense." The "spirit of rivalry," says *Teaching in Jesuit High Schools*, is in "the fibre of the American boy. All his life he will be facing competition, which seems to grow fiercer as the years go on. To form the habit of flinching and shying away from competition will do the youth more harm than learning the attitude of welcoming it and facing it."[119] Competition apparently was integral to daily classroom work in Jesuit high schools, as teachers worked ingeniously to combine athletic contests and the liberal arts. Father John Nash, S.J., who taught first-year Latin at the University of Detroit high school for thirty-eight years, used Army-Navy baseball games, for example, to teach his subject. There were, moreover, yearly Latin contests between Jesuit high schools in the Midwest.[120]

It is not known exactly how many students in Jesuit institutions of higher education, in Ong's words, "learned subjects largely by fighting over them," but we do know that contest and competition continued there. The "friction of mind with mind in the classroom, the work of emulation and work in concert" were some of the benefits of class attendance at Georgetown. Twice a year students and faculty assembled to hear marks and standings "publicly proclaimed."[121]

An anecdote recalled by a Fordham graduate of 1932 wonderfully illustrates the connection between learning as contest and the Jesuit disposition for thinking in the vocabulary of warfare. Father Joseph Assmuth's general biology exams in the 1920s were called "*Blitzes*—unannounced flashes of lightning that would last five minutes—no more." He entered the classroom, announced "Blitz," and placed a time clock, set for five minutes, on the lecture table. When the bell rang at the end of the five minutes, writing stopped and papers were passed in, and "Woe to the student who tried to dot an i or cross a t!" At the next class period Assmuth "read out the names of those who had 'fallen in battle,' the failures, those who had done very well, and finally the one to whom the laurel wreath was given, the one who got the top grade."[122]

From one perspective, then, combat and struggle typified these male communities gathered together on Jesuit college campuses. In contrast to this individuation, however, these men often were brought together in unity. One such occasion was during the mandatory spiritual exercises. On some campuses attendance at Mass was required daily, on others four times per week, and at yet another only on Friday. At Fordham prayers were said before class, crucifixes hung in classrooms, and numerous sodalities formed in which students performed spiritual activities under the patronage of various saints. Georgetown's sodalities were active enough that by 1957 they were publishing a newsletter that was distributed weekly in the dorms.[123]

Devotion to the Virgin Mary was particularly intense on Jesuit campuses. Most of the sodalities were under either the patronage or the invocation of Mary; others had the Mother of God as their object of devotion. May, the month for Marian devotions, saw considerable activity. Students attended daily Mass, said the Rosary, and gathered around the most centrally located statue of Mary for devotions. Several Fordham alumni had warm memories of what one called the "outstanding event" of the day: one senior each day would give a short talk on some aspect of Mary to students gathered in front of the statue of the Virgin in Edwards Parade. William Casey's topic was "Mary, Mother Most Pure."[124]

The increase in Marian devotions that developed nationwide during the Cold War also occurred on Jesuit campuses. At Loyola in Chicago in 1947, students initiated an annual participation in the Rosary Crusade; more than six hundred gathered on October 7, the Feast of the Most Holy Rosary. In addition to gathering for prayer and hymns each day at noon, Loyola students also involved themselves, in 1949, in another event that became annual, a Marian hour at Chicago's Catholic colleges. By 1950 enthusiasm for daily Marian devotions in October ran so high that they continued into November. The Marian Year of 1954 saw an even further increase in devotions. The increased Marian piety at Georgetown also was intertwined with anti-Communism. In 1950, for example, the graduating class gift was a statue of Our Lady of Fatima.[125]

That these all-male gatherings were intensely praying to Mary—one of the few females present in their lives, even if only symbolically, is significant. Mary as intercessory—in Elizabeth Johnson's words, "heavenly interaction modeled on a patriarchal household"—reinforced the patriarchal notion of God as the Father who is most approachable by his sons through their Mother. In so doing, this image of Mary fortified some of the participants' most basic suppositions about gender and the gendered nature of authority. As Fordham's Gannon once put it, "God [the Father] is the source of all legitimate authority." At a time when the patriarchal form of the U.S. family was disintegrating and patriarchal authority was being increasingly questioned, these young men were affirming and reaffirming both in their prayer life.[126]

These also were profoundly homosocial gatherings of men united in competition to love (and for the love of) the Blessed Virgin Mary. She was of course the perfect woman—as was their mother, the only other woman in their lives. No woman could compare with either Mary or their mother. Yet these were the standards by which real women were consistently judged. Is it any surprise that they came up lacking, that they were continually found to be undermining the way the world ought to be?

In 1959 Father James Martin, S.J., reported to Hoover on the seventy-two FBI men who had just completed a retreat at Manresa-on-Severn. It was "not easy," he noted, "for every man to come to Loyola and follow the regulations and the discipline entailed in going through a retreat." The Director's men, though, "got through every part of the services" as if they "were in a manner born to this life." So "permit me," Martin continued, "to thank you most sincerely for the interest you have always manifested in the spiritual life and conditions of your boys. You are truly a credit to the moral life of this country."[127]

There is nothing surprising in what the priest wrote. Hoover wanted the men the Jesuits produced, because they (and those who trained them) exhibited those things he "admired most in men"—"athleticism, toughness, virility, loyalty, and . . . piety." Character, a word often used by both Hoover and the Jesuits, was what these graduates had: "Character, thus initiated and habituated, is not a stucco front but polished granite, unmoved for the most part by the storms of greed, passion, or expediency."[128]

This chapter has focused on the values and personality traits that led Hoover and Catholics to find so much common ground and so many arenas for cooperation in the period before Vatican II. By 1959 FBI men had been making retreats to Manresa for twenty years. During the first fifteen or so its director was Father Robert Lloyd, S.J., who moved there from Georgetown Prep in Garrett Park, Maryland. Lloyd and Hoover had met during the Lindbergh kidnapping case and developed a particularly close friendship. The Jesuit consoled the Director when his mother died in 1938. "In the past year," Hoover testified, "I have had my trials and sorrows, deep sorrow, and I can say from my heart tonight that if it had not been for the steadfast friendship of Father Lloyd and the consolation he gave me I do not know how I would have stood them." Values, too, helped Hoover and Lloyd grow close. In *The Manresan*, in editorial after editorial, the Jesuit attacked virtually everything that Hoover opposed and supported virtually everything Hoover espoused. He did all this in the gendered but plain language of the spiritual athlete and warrior that he had learned at home and in his Jesuit training.[129]

Hoover and the FBI expressed their affection for Lloyd, who gave the invocation at the National Police Academy's graduation exercises thirty-nine consecutive times, in three unprecedented ways. One incident, which occurred after his death, involved the collection of money for a plaque commemorating Lloyd. Presented to the director of Manresa, where it was to be hung, it portrayed the Holy Family.

The other two incidents are even more significant. On the twenty-fifth anniversary of his ordination as a priest, a special agent called Lloyd to Washington on a matter of urgency. After lunch five agents took him to the Director's office, where Hoover presented him with a chalice engraved: "1925–1950. Rev. Robert S. Lloyd S.J., in Grateful remembrance of 25 Years as Priest. Your FBI friends." Lloyd also received Hoover's personal message of congratulation, along with more than $700 that Bureau employees from around the country had contributed beyond the sum necessary to pay for the chalice. Upon his return to Manresa, the Jesuit found that the FBI had installed a metal filing cabinet with a built-in safe to hold the chalice.[130]

Lloyd framed his comment on the FBI's gift within the context of the worldwide struggle against Communism:

> Think of Cardinal Mindszenty! Think of Cardinal Stepinac! Think of the persecuted priests and nuns and the Christian laity behind the Iron Curtain of terror and godlessness!
>
> Then, think of the Chalice of Salvation presented to your most humble and unworthy servant from the hands of Director Hoover— the head of the greatest law enforcement agency in the world!

The chalice is a direct rebuke to Communism. It shall be lifted as long as I live daily at the altar, for Director Hoover and all the wonderful men and women of the FBI. God bless them all! America is safe in their hands.[131]

But the FBI was not done. Later than same year Hoover presented Lloyd with the FBI Service Award key at the National Police Academy's commencement exercises. In so doing the Director referred to him as "our chaplain of the FBI."[132]

CHAPTER 2

—❧—

The Boss's Bishops

JOHN CARDINAL O'HARA, C.S.C. (1888–1960), spent most of his childhood in Peru, Indiana, a small farming town in the Fort Wayne diocese. After his father was appointed American consul to Uruguay in 1905, O'Hara lived with his family in South America for three years. Entering Notre Dame in 1909, he received his B.A. there and then joined the Congregation of the Holy Cross. Ordained in 1916, he went on to become Notre Dame's prefect of religion, dean of the College of Commerce, then vice president of the university and president from 1934 to 1939. During World War II O'Hara became a military delegate, assisting Archbishop Francis Spellman, the military vicar of the U.S. Armed Forces. Appointed bishop of Buffalo in 1945, he served there until becoming the archbishop of Philadelphia in 1951. He was made a cardinal in 1958.

As prefect of religion at Notre Dame for more than a decade, O'Hara was responsible for shaping the spiritual lives of the men under his care. Working within an environment quite different from that of secular educational institutions—students, for example, had to attend morning and evening prayer and Mass on Saturday as well as Sunday—O'Hara motivated them to great heights of spirituality. Through the force of his own personality, the power of his office, and the influence of the *Religious Bulletin*, which he originated in 1921, O'Hara was instrumental in the dramatic increase in attendance at daily Communion at Notre Dame. He was the first, moreover, to draw the explicit connection between piety and success on the football field that has become such an integral part of campus life. It was his Notre Dame that a football player and future athletic director remembered as a "man's school."[1]

In 1937 J. Edgar Hoover, director of the FBI, spoke to Notre Dame students and received enthusiastic applause. One observer noted his "quiet mask-like face, piercing eyes, black, cropped hair, and short compact body." After first addressing America's crime problem, Hoover moved on to the matter of subversion through a discussion of Notre Dame's campaign against Communism which O'Hara had initiated, and which was to begin shortly. He noted how "easy" it was for "agitators, spouting magical formulas, to seize the imagination of youth" and "lead it into false paths, making of young men and women missionaries to impossible gods." Not so, though, at Notre Dame: it "has devoted excellent efforts toward the practical eradication of such fantasies. I am sure that its work in the future will be along the same course of common sense." As for the future plans of these young people themselves, there "can be no higher ideal for the student of Notre Dame or any other university in America than that he should consecrate his life to the virtue of justice."[2]

O'Hara liked Hoover's speech so much that he had ten thousand copies of it printed, so it is no surprise that the *Religious Bulletin* reprinted a year later an article by Hoover titled "If I Had a Son." In it, as we saw in chapter 1, he described how a father must function in the family if his son was to "grow up to be a fine, honest man, a good citizen in every sense of the word." O'Hara "carried the matter a step further" in his sermon for the "Mission to the Freshmen." "I told them," he wrote Hoover, "that you had beat me to the sermon on the fourth Commandment. I then went on to draw a lesson on the whole principle of authority, and the importance of discipline as against individualism if we are to protect our country from dictatorship, whether of communistic or fascistic origin." Hoover's response indicated his complete agreement with O'Hara: "As you indicated, the inculcation into youthful minds of ideals and principles which are fundamentally false and which if carried to their logical conclusions would lead to the eradication of all authority, whether it be religious or civil, is fast becoming one of the greatest dangers facing the youth of our country today."[3]

"Salacious magazines" were one of the influences endangering young people that O'Hara and Hoover detested. In late 1937, having misplaced the speech that Hoover had delivered the previous year to the Holy Name Society Convention, in which he had "spoke[n] of salacious magazines as a source of temptation to crime," O'Hara wrote to the Director requesting a copy. The need was urgent. "We hear rumors," said O'Hara, "that Communists are fostering indecent literature for the purpose of corrupting the youth, in order to make them easier victims of Communism." In 1943 he went to the FBI with a complaint about obscene literature at an Oregon

army base. "In view of Bishop O'Hara's position and his great friendliness to the Bureau," the New York SAC recommended that the matter
be looked into. In 1959 Hoover praised an article of O'Hara's titled "Label
It Poison and Lock It Up," in which the cardinal had lauded Hoover as a
"common sense leader" who was trying to "wipe out" juvenile delinquency
and stop its "greatest breeding ground—pornographic literature, motion
pictures and the like."[4]

O'Hara and Hoover both responded dramatically and directly to the
danger, which they saw all around them. Hoover acted illegally and extralegally again and again to undermine the Communist Party and those
who worked with it in order, he said, to protect Americans. Convinced,
moreover, that only the FBI stood between the United States and chaos,
and that only he knew what was best for the FBI, Hoover shaped the
Bureau in his own image, often running it tyrannically and capriciously.

O'Hara combined, in virtually the same measure as Hoover, self-
righteousness and authoritarianism. Perhaps the best example is his
destruction of library books. Shortly after becoming president of Notre
Dame, O'Hara asked the university librarian for a master key to the building. "In his free time," his biographer tells us, "and especially in the hour
after lunch he visited sections of the library to search out books that he
thought did not belong on the shelves." He "particularly eliminated many
books on sociology, anthropology, and criminology," but also some American and English literature. He carefully saved the title pages of those
books he destroyed so that the library could pull the cards from the catalogue. One packet contained nearly twenty-five title pages.[5]

The good relations between O'Hara and the FBI continued after he left
Notre Dame. He surely had something to do with the decision to award
Hoover an honorary degree in 1942. Having a fondness for Hoover's "verbal punches," the military delegate must also have liked the Director's
wartime commencement address, in which he praised the institution's
patriotism—"Red-blooded Americanism, typified by the valorous men of
Notre Dame, will not permit our Nation to bow in defeat"—and railed
against license, materialism, softness, and foreign "isms." He also noted
the "scores of graduates" of Notre Dame who "are today enlisted in the
ranks of the Federal Bureau of Investigation, carrying on its motto,
'Fidelity—Bravery—Integrity.' "[6]

O'Hara's Catholicism was an especially masculinist and conservative
one that ultimately rested upon the principles of patriarchy. His social
values mirrored his Catholicism in that they, too, rested on a foundation of male domination. Despite his Protestantism, Hoover found little
if anything with which to disagree in O'Hara's values. They both fought

as vigorously as possible against everything that called into question their vision of the world.

O'Hara and Hoover's comradeship was the rule, not the exception, when it comes to characterizing the relationship between the FBI and the Catholic hierarchy from the mid-1930s to the early 1960s. Thousands of pages of FBI files indicate, though, that it was not just values that brought together the FBI and U.S. bishops, archbishops, and cardinals; it was also self-interest. The stories I tell in this chapter of two cardinals and two bishops exemplify this complex connection.

J. Edgar Hoover, who had not planned on speaking, acceded to Archbishop Michael J. Curley's "personal request" to say a few extemporaneous words to the nearly eight hundred Catholic men who had gathered to celebrate the establishment of the Laymen's Retreat League in Baltimore and the silver jubilee of Curley's episcopacy, which had begun in 1921 when he became bishop of St. Augustine, Florida. Curley (1879–1947), who had been born and ordained in Ireland, then immigrated to the United States, had served as a pastor in Florida for ten years prior to his promotion.[7]

Hoover first complimented the audience, declaring: "I am a Protestant. As a Protestant, I say sincerely and from experience that the Catholic Church is the greatest protective influence in our nation today." Turning his attention to Curley, he praised him highly: "Your archbishop is a great Churchman and he is a great patriot. He speaks the truth and none can deny what he says. He is fearless. He speaks out what he thinks, in short, simple, clearcut words, no $2.50 words for him."[8]

Curley, after a rousing ovation, followed Hoover with a vigorous jeremiad. American could not long survive "the moral rottenness" brought on by secularism. The danger, according to Curley, was internal, not external: "This nation of ours will never be overcome by any outside material power. The greatest dangers to our country come from internal subversive forces which are spoiling the hearts and souls of men, particularly of young men."[9]

The next morning Hoover wrote a letter to Curley in which he expressed warm and deep feelings of friendship. I know of few other occasions when the Director genuinely displayed such sentiments and none when he expressed them to a Catholic. "One should always value friendships," he wrote, "but when I say to you that to have your friendship and confidence means more to me than that of any other man I know in this country, I make that statement from my heart." In more pro forma language Hoover praised Curley's "fearless manner" in championing "those forces and causes which stand for decency and for Americanism," but his closing was unprecedented: "Sincerely your friend."[10]

What produced this friendship? Part of it, surely, was owed to the fact that they lived so near each other. Until 1947 the nation's capital was part of the Baltimore archdiocese, so Curley got to Washington quite frequently. There is evidence, moreover, that Hoover often went to Baltimore for both work and relaxation.

But there was more. Agreement about what constituted masculinity was central, as we have seen, to the ways in which the Director and Catholics connected across religious differences. In the case of Hoover and Curley, plainspokenness seems to have been a particularly important ingredient of their shared sense of "masculine authenticity." Curley's follow-up reference to Hoover's use of the phrase "$2.50 words" led the *Catholic Review*, the Baltimore archdiocesan paper, to caption a picture of Hoover and the bishop conversing at the banquet with "Neither Uses $2.50 Words." Later that year Curley thanked Hoover for sending him the reprint of a speech, which he had appreciated much: "[You] call a spade a spade." Curley and Hoover also had similar personalities. Monsignor John Tracy Ellis, who had much experience with Curley during his teaching career at Catholic University in Washington, wrote that he had a "quick temper" and "deep-seated likes and dislikes." Both men, moreover, had well-earned reputations for making arbitrary decisions. FBI agents, unprotected by civil service regulations, often felt the Director's unpredictable wrath. Curley's efforts in 1937 to move Father Raymond McGowan out of the Social Action Department of the National Catholic Welfare Conference into one of his parishes was just as autocratic.[11]

Just as Hoover and Curley shared the same habits of authority and the same sense of manhood, they also had the same political and moral values. By the time of the silver jubilee banquet in January 1939 they had been communicating with each other for some time. For example, in 1936 Hoover had sent Curley a copy of his speech to a Holy Name Society convention. Promising to read "every word of it," Curley offered Hoover the "warmest congratulations" on the FBI's "fine work" on behalf of the "nation's welfare." Then in 1940 Curley complained to Hoover about the tourist camps on the Baltimore-Washington Pike; the conditions in them "indicated possible violations of the White Slave Traffic Act."[12]

Curley's anti-Communism also matched Hoover's. The headlines of several newspaper articles reporting his speeches prior to Pearl Harbor illustrate this similarity: "Awakening to the Foe—Communism," "Reds Blasted as U.S. Peril by Archbishop," "Communism Held Self-Condemning,"

"Archbishop Hits Pretense of the 'Reds,'" "Communism, Birth Control Scored," "Archbishop Hits Coddling of Reds," "Curley Flays U.S. 'Flop' to Stalin." Support for the demagogic Father Charles Coughlin flourished in Baltimore, moreover, as it did in many other dioceses whose bishops did not firmly oppose him.

The *Catholic Review* reflected Hoover's and Curley's similar reactions to the social upheaval produced by World War II. In November 1942 the paper excerpted one of Hoover's speeches in an editorial and discussed the talk—"The Need to Return to God"—in a lengthy article. The following year it editorialized against a U.S. Public Health Department publication that argued for the separation of sex and morality in relation to "any self-induced, sensual pleasure." In a wide-ranging critique of this position, it invoked Hoover in asserting that children need to be raised in a religious home, not as "beasts." In 1944 and again in 1946 the paper republished portions of Hoover's speeches.[13]

Perhaps the best example of the dovetailing of views between Hoover and the Catholic Church is a 1943 editorial in the *Catholic Review* against the sexual license unleashed by the war. In an effort to "head off the hellbent drive for Paganism which is capturing the United States," the editorial cited several news stories it apologized for having to quote: a statement from the NCWC's Family Life Bureau about *Fortune* magazine's recent survey on "the value or uselessness of virginity," an appeal to women made by Planned Parenthood urging them to write to *Reader's Digest* and thank it for a recent article praising birth control, and one of Hoover's recent speeches about immorality. The paper also inveighed against the easing of divorce laws in many states as well as a recent *Washington Post* editorial which argued that a good way to prevent abortion was to teach people about birth control. Hoover, who, the newspaper continued, "knows probably more about immoral conditions in this country than any man," had shockingly reported that there had been "an 89 per cent increase among women in the committing of crimes against moral decencies." He had also pointed out that there "are children who despise their parents" and "countless" homes in the United States "which are dens of wickedness."[14]

The editorial concluded by echoing the same point that Hoover had made in the speech to which it referred: "What is the use of fighting for Democracy which must be based on the stability of the homes of the country when we are seeking to destroy those very homes?" As Hoover had put it: "Our war is a holy crusade. It is to protect the dearest of all our institutions—the home and the hearthside, under the double blessing of liberty and freedom."[15]

The close connection between the *Catholic Review* and the FBI persisted long after Curley's death in 1947. The paper continued to publish Hoover's speeches and gloss them. It also weighed in with support during the "smear" campaign of 1958, which I discuss later in this chapter. What stands out ultimately, though, is the significance of the personal relationship between Curley and Hoover. It would stand the Church in good stead, as we will see in chapter 4, when Father John F. Cronin needed help for his report on Communism to the bishops of the Church. One final anecdote suggests how important such a connection could be to both church and state.

In August 1940 a special agent from the Oklahoma City Field Office made a serious mistake. On the basis of a complaint received over the telephone, the agent, with his SAC's tacit permission, had searched the basement of a Catholic church, St. Joseph's at Fourth and Harvey, looking for boxes of weapons. Instead he found altar furnishings.

Upon hearing of the search, Francis C. Kelley, the bishop of Oklahoma City, wrote a scathing letter of complaint to Hoover. He had sent a representative to the field office, but the agent in charge would give him no information about the person who had made the telephone call. Since Catholic churches were always open during the day, Kelley pointed out, if any weapons had been discovered, anyone could have planted them. Yet it was the pastor who would have been labeled a "fifth columnist." Kelley had not yet publicized the incident, but sooner or later it would have to come out. He did not see how he could "avoid warning my fellow bishops of the United States that such an outrage has been committed once and may be committed again." He was writing to Hoover first because he wanted to include the Director's explanation with his statement. (There had been, Kelley hastened to assure Hoover, no discourtesy on the part of the agent or the SAC.)[16]

Hoover ordered an immediate investigation, only to discover that the error was more serious even than Kelley thought. The original complainant "at one time was confined in an insane asylum." The SAC had therefore not only "exhibited an obvious lack of judgment in the handling of this situation" but also ignored Bureau instructions about "psychopathic complaints."[17]

FBI Headquarters immediately began trying to figure out how to stop Kelley from informing his fellow bishops. Their first step indicated how little some FBI executives understood about the authority structure of the Catholic Church. Having learned that there was no archbishop in Oklahoma City with jurisdiction over Kelley, FBIHQ determined that the ranking archbishop in the area was in San Antonio. San Antonio's assistant special agent in charge then tried to contact the archbishop, only to discover not only that he was in the hospital but also, more important, that no bishop outranked another.[18]

Quinn Tamm then entered the picture. The younger brother of Edward Tamm, a fervent Catholic, third-ranking official at the FBI, and the subject of chapter 3, Quinn was well on his way to his own successful career with the Bureau. He contacted an "acquaintance" at Catholic University, who confirmed that "Archbishops and Senior officials of the Catholic Church exercise no control over Bishops except in purely Church matters." They "would not interfere otherwise, particularly to the extent of suggesting that someone refrain from writing a letter."[19]

Tamm then suggested that E. A. Soucy, the Baltimore SAC, contact Curley. Curley's characterization of Kelley made it even more essential that he be persuaded to put the incident behind him: he was "a great journalist, and a brilliant man who is capable of writing an excellent letter and filling it with dynamite." Curley did, however, propose a way for Soucy to handle the problem. According to an internal FBI memo on the matter, "a ranking official of the Bureau personally representing Mr. Hoover [should] go to Bishop Kelley and advise him that there had been a mistake in judgment; the Agent was going to be disciplined, and Father Kelley, he felt sure, would not want the man disciplined or removed, and that he would ask that no action be taken." Curley went even further in his efforts to be helpful. If Kelley "wanted to know anything about the Director," he should write him. There was, finally, a bishops' meeting scheduled at Catholic University in November. "If the matter has not been adjusted by them," Curley "thinks he can straighten things out with Bishop Kelley."[20]

Soucy was delegated to go to Oklahoma City to talk with Kelley. The bishop was initially "somewhat antagonistic," but they discussed the problem "practically all morning and grew personally friendly with each other." While Soucy at first feared "that the situation might have been bad," Kelley eventually made it clear that he was "satisfied with the explanation," and by the end of the morning the two men were getting along so well that the bishop invited Soucy to supper. Unless he phoned again later that evening, Soucy reported, the Bureau could assume that everything was all right. The FBIHQ supervisor who took Soucy's call praised his "splendid handling of this matter."[21]

Soucy filled in some additional details upon his return to the East Coast. Before going to Kelley's residence, he had talked with the two agents involved and also the Oklahoma SAC, who was "embarrassed, worried, and deeply chagrined." Kelley asked to meet him, and Soucy arranged it. The bishop, who was "friendly," asked the SAC how he felt. He responded, "I am plenty worried right now," to which Kelley replied: "There is no need for your worrying. I am sure everything will work out all right. . . . I want you to feel free to call on me at any time and I want to get to know you better." During Soucy's dinner with Kelley and several priests, the incident did not come up.[22]

Curley's friendship with Hoover and his enormous respect for the FBI were the keys to solving this crisis. Once the FBI began to think nationally rather than locally and Quinn Tamm brought Curley into the picture, the problem, given a certain deftness on Soucy's part, was essentially solved. As Soucy reported to Curley once he returned to Baltimore, "Everything went off splendidly and everything is forgotten." Curley had told Kelley that if he should ever think of writing about the incident, he should "take his typewriter out and place it under the wheels of a heavy truck."[23]

The association between J. Edgar Hoover and another influential Catholic prelate, Richard Cardinal Cushing, began with Hoover's attendance at a banquet held in 1952 to honor the cardinal. Although their relationship began later than those developed between the Director and the other bishops just discussed, it quickly turned into a close and warm one that both deeply treasured. This friendship was embedded in a series of close connections between Bureau personnel in Boston and priests of the archdiocese. As Cushing told the special agent in charge in 1953, "You know in these parts if I quote J. Edgar Hoover, it's just like quoting the Pope."[24]

Deciding to accept a speaking engagement and/or attend an honorary banquet was a well-considered act on Hoover's part. Not only was he very busy, but also he must have received a dozen requests a week to give a speech. The paperwork delineating the decision to come to the 1952 banquet has not been released, but his reasons probably ran along the same lines as those involved in the Director's determination to speak at the 1956 convention of the National Council of Catholic Women (NCCW) in Chicago.

The Crime Records Section, actually the FBI's public relations arm, headed by Louis B. Nichols, did the necessary background research. A lengthy memo provided Nichols and Hoover with the information they wanted under the following headings: "Background on the NCCW," "Information in 'Bufiles' on the NCCW," "Speech declines by the Director at NCCW functions—3," "Speeches by Bureau Personnel Before NCCW Units—3," and "Speech declines by Director in Chicago, 1954 to Present—78." The first addendum indicates that Hoover had turned down twelve invitations from the Executive Club of Chicago since 1939, while a second summarized several telephone calls from longtime Bureau friends urging Hoover to accept the NCCW's invitation.[25]

Though considerably less voluminous than that for the NCCW, the paperwork surrounding Hoover's decision to attend Cushing's banquet is revealing. First, the invitation came not from Cushing or one of his aides but rather from the banquet chairman, Father Christopher P. Griffin, the pastor of St. Catherine of Siena in Norwood, Massachusetts. Griffin, who was "noted for his wonderful organizational ability and particularly, for a series of public forum lectures," had invited Hoover to speak several times before, in 1943, 1945, 1946, and 1947.[26]

Second, Nichols's contact for the event was not the Boston SAC but rather Special Agent Larry Quinn, who was "active in Catholic circles in Boston." Quinn, who told Nichols that the banquet would be "attended by many prominent Catholic laymen," passed along the information that Special Agent Thomas McLaughlin, a "close personal friend of Griffin's, told him that Cushing's first words on hearing that Hoover had decided to attend the banquet were, "My God, that is wonderful." Griffin also told McLaughlin that the banquet "had started out as a Testimonial for the Archbishop but it was looking like it will end up as a Testimonial for the Director."[27]

This elaborate dinner brought together dozens of Catholic leaders, both clerics and laymen. There were forty people at the head table, which was arranged in three tiers. The toastmaster was Monsignor Jeremiah Minihan. On one side of Minihan sat Hoover, on the other Cushing. Other guests at the head table included two bishops; the governor of Massachusetts; the mayor of Boston; the ambassadors from Spain and Ireland; J. Howard McGrath, the former attorney general; Congressmen John W. McCormack and John F. Kennedy; Senator Leverett Saltonstall; James Farley, the former postmaster general and onetime chairman of the National Democratic Committee; the Supreme Knight of the Knights of Columbus; the president of the National Council of Catholic Men; and labor leader Daniel Tobin.

FBI employees provided Hoover with two memoranda on the bishop sitting to his right, the "brilliant" John J. Wright of Worcester. The first, which came from Nichols's office, had turned up limited Bureau information. The second, from the Boston SAC, informed Hoover that Wright, who had been secretary to both Cushing and his predecessor, was one of the youngest bishops in the country. Important for Hoover's purpose was the notation that Wright's "future activities in the Catholic Church will undoubtedly lead him to high responsibility."[28]

Among the many testimonials to Cushing heard by the 1,300 men assembled that evening was J. Edgar Hoover's. Praising Cushing's life as witness "to a dedicated heart and a magnificent soul," Hoover referred to the archbishop as a "prince among princes," who "sees in every human being, young or old, in tattered rags or in imperial purple, a part of God's great creation." What most impressed Hoover was Cushing's struggle against Communism:

> Archbishop Cushing stands as a crusader in arms, with militant and defiant courage, against the godless forces of everyday life. He has always fought, with tenacity and vigor, the evils of Communism. His towering figure has become a rallying point, encouraging his fellow citizens to battle against this heinous foe. To Archbishop Cushing, as to all right-thinking men, Communism is the mortal enemy of freedom. It would make the state, rather than the individual supreme. The fountain springs of religion, love, charity and faith in an eternal God, would be quenched. Society would become a bleak, barren and inhuman institution.

Cushing, Hoover concluded, was "not only an outstanding prince of his church, but a champion of everything good and decent."[29]

Hoover, despite a very short stay in Boston, granted the *Pilot*, the archdiocesan newspaper, an exclusive interview, in which he discussed the twin problems of Communism and crime that endangered America. Both, he said, originated in America's "spiritual starvation." Both had the same simple solution: "The problem of crime and Communism is not a complex one. The factors of life have been predicated by the Bible, and the interest of all faiths is the focal point for building decency in our national life." What the country needed, Hoover concluded, according to the *Boston Globe*'s coverage of the interview, was "inspired and virile leaders—men like your Archbishop Cushing."[30]

Hoover presumably attended this 1952 testimonial dinner to strengthen existing friendships and make new ones. Some of this activity went on at the dinner, while some occurred more indirectly through the exclusive *Pilot* interview and the resulting daily newspapers' coverage of it. The real evidence of the visit's success, however, lay in the future.

The Cushing dinner initiated a close and mutually beneficial relationship between the head of the FBI and Monsignor Jeremiah Minihan. Their friendship never approached the depth of that between the Director and Cushing, but it was of importance for both men and the institutions they loved so dearly and served so loyally.

One of the unwritten job assignments of special agents in charge was to make sure that Hoover followed up speaking engagements and appearances with the requisite "glad to meet you" letter laying the basis for future interaction. Minihan was among those recommended to receive such a letter after the Boston visit. Hoover complied, praising his performance of the toastmaster's job—done in a "clever manner"—and thanking him for his "kind references to the FBI and my administration of it."[31]

Minihan's handwritten answer to Hoover's somewhat pro forma letter both clinched the connection between the two men and reveals something of what they shared. In the course of discussing their alma maters, they had fallen into a discussion of Georgetown's football team and one player in particular. "I was most happy that you remembered Gene Golson," said Minihan. "While we were competitors for the same job on Lou Little's Georgetown team of 1924, we had deep respect and affection for each other and I was sincerely saddened by the news of his untimely death." (Minihan later received an honorary degree from Georgetown, where his name graces a football award.) Minihan even ventured a joke: "Many of my friends have kidded me about sitting beside such a prominent figure at the dinner and I have told them that I was a 'G' man, having made my letter about the same time that you started awarding them to the finest American defenders we have."[32]

The Director surely sensed in Minihan a life lived the right way. It was not just that he had played football (Minihan had been an undersized center at 150 pounds). More than that, he had become William Cardinal O'Connell's secretary in 1933 when he was only thirty and then served as Cushing's chancellor. According to his onetime secretary, he "was a manly guy, but a priest through and through." Minihan also understood hierarchy, command, and authority. He was "always a *Churchman*, not just a churchman. There is a big difference you know. He had the same mind as the Church in all things—not a day later, or a day sooner, but when the Church says so!"[33]

Minihan remained a loyal friend of the Bureau until his death. In 1954, the year he became an auxiliary bishop, the Boston SAC recommended that Minihan be made a "SAC Contact." He was "an outstanding Catholic clergyman" whose "contacts and associates extend to every field of endeavor and interest." He has "been most cordial in providing any assistance which the Bureau has requested of him as the result of his position, and holds an exceedingly high regard for the Bureau's work." The following year Minihan was one of the "key people" in Boston" whom a new SAC made a point of meeting, then provided the Director with a report of the contact.[34]

What little specific information the files offer on how Minihan helped the Bureau is revealing. In 1953 he accompanied a new SAC on what apparently was the man's first encounter with Cushing. The archbishop arranged by phone during their "nice visit" for the SAC's children to be enrolled in their parish school. Minihan and McLaughlin then took the SAC to the school to meet the principal. The new SAC, in Minihan's estimation, "was a worthy representative of his great chief." Several months later Minihan arranged a meeting with Cushing for Cartha DeLoach, who worked out of FBI Headquarters in Washington, and he apparently introduced yet another new SAC, H. G. Foster, a Notre Dame alumnus, to Cushing the following year. In 1956 Minihan reported to Hoover on the "very pleasant evening" he had spent with Foster: "I am always thrilled by the loyalty, and affection of all your men toward their chief. I share that admiration and esteem."[35]

Minihan, one of whose brothers was married to the sister of a Boston special agent, outlived Hoover, dying on a trip to Ireland in 1973. Clarence Kelly, then the Director, sent condolences to a family member.

Plain speaking, which, as we have seen, was central to the affinity between Hoover and Curley, undoubtedly was significant in that between the Director and Cushing as well. A man forthright in his public statements, the cardinal did not use flowery prose and diplomatic language. Cushing sugarcoated nothing. As one of his biographers described him at the height of his influence, he was "the earthy, open man-of-action; the blunt, salty, sometimes unpredictable public commentator on church and state."[36]

It was not, though, just how Cushing said things but what he said that drew Hoover to him, for there apparently was nothing of substance about which he and the Director disagreed. Throughout the 1950s Cushing waged an unceasing war against the wickedness he saw all around him. While some episcopal leaders began to make peace with the contemporary world and others discovered greater enemies to combat, Cushing continued to joust—in word and print—with the evils of modernity. By the late 1950s other bishops had decided that Communism in the United States was too insignificant a factor to warrant their attention; but not Cushing, who continued to denounce it well into the 1960s.

Secularism, for Cushing and Hoover, was the key to understanding all of America's problems. Whether it was the breakdown of the family or creeping materialism or growing juvenile delinquency or subversion, the exclusion of God from daily life had produced it. While both men willingly sought the amelioration of these problems, neither passed up the

opportunity to remind his audience of the real culprit. That the alliance
between Hoover's FBI and Cushing's Catholic Church was predicated on
an obdurate opposition to modernity is evident in the speech that Cushing
gave when he presented the Lantern Award to Hoover in 1957.

The annual Patriots Dinner of the Massachusetts Knights of Columbus
was a long-standing tradition, but 1957 was the first year the Lantern
Award was bestowed. It was to be given annually to a "man who exemplifies the patriotic and religious devotion of the founding fathers of the
country." There were many "differences of a superficial and secondary
kind" between the worlds of Paul Revere and Hoover, Cushing admitted,
but "the essential work of Paul Revere is still done by Mr. Hoover and the
spirit of Paul Revere and the Minute Men is the spirit of the FBI." The fate
of the nation depended on the "readiness with which the FBI's modern
cry of alarm to every American village and farm—a cry of defiance to evil
and not of fear—is heard and loyally seconded by present day Americans."
Like Hoover, Cushing said, the men of the Revolution "feared God and
therefore had no need to fear any man. Their theology was not mine, but
my God was theirs."

Those who criticized the FBI were not only unpatriotic but also anti-
Catholic: "The fault finding and sniping against the FBI come almost
exclusively from people who are at once open to suspicion in the matter of
their loyalty to the United States and openly hostile to our religions traditions, notably, be it said with great pride, hostile to the Catholic Church
in particular." Cushing found it "unintelligible to the point of being preposterous, but even somehow perverse," that someone would be upset that
more than one thousand agents and employees of the FBI received Holy
Communion together and then had a Communion breakfast.[37]

Hoover noted, in accepting the award, that he had long admired Cushing "as a man of God, as a patriot and as an outstanding leader." Moreover, in "his stalwart, rugged form, he is democracy personified." After a
discussion of the "twin evils of communism and crime," Hoover recommended that they be "counteract[ed]" by "a return to the influence of
religion in American homes."[38]

Cushing and Hoover often lent each other a hand in the 1950s. One
of the ways in which the FBI helped Cushing was to provide him with
off-the-record information for his speeches and the column he regularly
wrote for the *Pilot*. The first instance came in 1953, when Cushing asked
the Boston SAC for information for a speech to be titled "Juvenile Delinquency and Parental Delinquency." Since "the chief gives such wonderful
talks on this subject," he wrote, referring to Hoover, that "anything in the
way of helpful data will be appreciated." The SAC met with Cushing on

the very day he received the letter and gave him a recent article by Hoover on juvenile delinquency. After looking through it, Cushing told the SAC that it "answered his every purpose."[39]

The information that the FBI provided Cushing most often dealt with Communism. In 1958 SAC Leo L. Laughlin, who had received his B.A and L.L.B. from Catholic University then joined the Bureau in 1935, accompanied by Agent McLaughlin, visited Cushing, who told them that he thought the ongoing criticism of Hoover would continue since the Communists knew that the Director "represent[ed] the last bulwark against their nefarious activities." The defense of Hoover and the Bureau, Cushing argued, therefore "must be a continuing thing." Since he did not have the time or resources to do the research for his own speeches, he told them that he "would appreciate it if he could be furnished with specific factual data on a periodic basis which he might incorporate into his public remarks where the occasion was propitious."[40]

In 1959 Cushing wrote to ask Hoover if he knew of any current book that provided information on Communism in catechetical form. After consulting William C. Sullivan, his Catholic in-house specialist on Communism, Hoover told Cushing that none existed. Cushing then wrote one, which the FBI's Central Research Section reviewed for errors. Worried that several significant mistakes he found could "destroy the anti-communist message of the pamphlet," Sullivan recommended that Cushing be informed of them. The Bureau's intervention allowed the archbishop to correct the errors before their critics could capitalize on them.[41]

Another significant way the Bureau helped Cushing was with his travels. His trip to Europe in 1958 is a good example of this kind of aid. After going to Ireland to receive an honorary degree from the National University of Ireland, Cushing then planned to travel throughout Europe and wind up in Rome. Hoover provided Cushing with the names of the Bureau's representatives in London, Paris, and Rome and assured him that they would do whatever they could for him. He let the special agents know that he wanted "*every possible* courtesy" given to Cushing. In turn, Cushing thanked Hoover and promised him, "Wherever I go I will remember you at the altar."[42]

For his part Cushing helped Hoover and the FBI in many ways, but two were especially important: the promotion of Hoover's book *Masters of Deceit* and the opposition he mounted to the 1958–59 "smear" campaign against the FBI. In each case Cushing firmly aligned himself and the Catholic Church with Hoover and the Bureau.

To begin with *Masters of Deceit*, in late February 1958 Cushing received an advance copy specially inscribed: "To his Excellency, the Most

Rev. Richard J. Cushing, Archbishop of Boston, whose magnificent fight against atheistic communism inspired the writing of this book. Sincerely, your friend, J. Edgar Hoover." Convinced that "we now have the classic text book pertaining to Communism in our country," Cushing immediately contacted the publisher about sending one thousand copies to the "leading clerical, religious, and lay teachers of the Archdiocese of Boston." The publisher in turn asked Cushing to provide a blurb for the book. He gladly complied, writing:

> This is the book which I and countless others have been expecting. It presents a thorough and accurate account of the communistic conspiracy as it has operated in the United States by one who knows it from day by day experience. I pray that it will overtake the fraudulent, rolling propaganda machine of the Communists and that it will be read with such indignation that it will arouse the great body of average men and women of this country and elsewhere from their apathy and indifference towards the most destructive "ism" that ever attempted to dethrone the Almighty, rob man and conquer the entire world![43]

The archbishop ceaselessly promoted *Masters of Deceit*. He not only discussed it during a sermon at a noontime Mass at General Electric's Lynn, Massachusetts, works but also offered to send it at a reduced price to any GE worker who wrote him. "I'll send a copy to any Communist free," he added. During a speech at the "first annual ladies night" of the Massachusetts Chiefs of Police Association meeting, he praised Hoover's book and again offered to send copies out at a reduced price. Cushing also made an advertisement for the book that was shown on Boston television stations.[44]

By March, Cushing wrote Hoover to say that after several weeks of promoting *Masters of Deceit*, his stock of two thousand copies would soon be gone. (The publisher was giving him a good discount, and someone who had heard Cushing talk about the book promised to contribute $2,500 to help get it out to the public.) "Honestly, I never enjoyed anything more than the thrill I have had in the last couple of weeks advocating this book on television, the radio, and speaking to the multitudes," he told Hoover. "They are thrilled, but it is your name that captivates them." Cushing concluded with thanks "for the opportunity of being on 'your team.'"[45]

The second form of help that Cushing provided the FBI was his effective and vocal opposition in 1958 and 1959 to what Hoover referred to as a "smear" campaign. Stung by an issue-long critique of the FBI in *The Nation* in October 1958 and other signs that American enthusiasm for militant anti-Communism was waning, Hoover and his men sprang into action. As in previous "smears" in 1940 and 1950, they provided their firmest supporters with the information and arguments necessary to organize petition and letter-writing campaigns in favor of the FBI and against its critics. Cushing defended the FBI many times during the anti-smear campaign, but several times, even more significantly, he helped produce the concerted action that overwhelmed Hoover's opponents.

On November 16, 1958, he gave a lengthy speech to a Communion breakfast of employees of the Commonwealth of Massachusetts. Giving much detail, Cushing put the "smear" into the wider perspective of periodic efforts by Communists and their allies to undermine the FBI, the "one chief obstacle" between subversives and their "conquest" of the United States. He took particular aim at *The Nation*, whose article he vilified as a "hodge-podge of ignorance, half-truths, and misrepresentation." He then tied together this smear campaign with the persecution of the Catholic Church in Eastern Europe. The Massachusetts governor then asked the audience to stand to endorse a telegram of support for the FBI. With unanimous backing, the message went off to Hoover.[46]

Cushing's speech, which was reprinted in the *New York Journal-American*, combined with a three-part series on the gains made by U.S. Communists published in 1958 in the *Brooklyn Tablet* (again reprinted in the *Journal-American*), produced other actions similar to those taken in Massachusetts. The Rhode Island American Legion publicly thanked Cushing for his defense of the Bureau and castigated Hoover's critics. The New York Knights of Columbus took several actions: besides adopting a series of resolutions supporting Cushing and defending the FBI, its general assembly for Queens and Nassau counties sent copies not only to the two New York senators and the four congressmen from Queens but also to every Knights of Columbus council on Long Island, urging them to take action. Cushing clearly worked in concert with the FBI in this counter-offensive. There is no direct evidence that the Bureau wrote Cushing's Communion breakfast speech, but Laughlin, in sending along the text to Hoover, noted that the "remarks of the Archbishop are in keeping with his previous request for information pertaining to the recent attacks made upon you and the Bureau." FBI Headquarters, told ahead of time that the Massachusetts Communion breakfast meeting was going to send a message of support, had a telegram of thanks already prepared and ready to send out the day before the meeting.[47]

It is not surprising that Cushing worked so hard to defend the FBI. Though a relative latecomer to the near worship of J. Edgar Hoover and the FBI, Cushing was no less sincere in his commitment. He believed, as Laughlin paraphrased in a report to Washington, that "the entire structure of American society depended upon the success of the FBI in its battle against Communism."[48]

In November 1960 Special Agent John Quinlan decided to spend his ten days of vacation time in Boston, where he had been born. Apparently a deeply religious person, he had a brother who was a Jesuit missionary and two sisters who were members of the Community of Sisters of Charity. Quinlan's phone call to Cushing produced the following response: "I never heard of him but I was thrilled that as an FBI agent he felt free to contact me." Since the agent had no place to go on Thanksgiving Day, Cushing invited him to join "a program that I think took more out of him than any FBI project." Quinlan, Cushing, and two priests attended several parties for large poor Catholic families and also visited disabled children. Hoover thanked Cushing for the letter about his special agent and praised the cardinal: "Of course, your devotion to your vocation is always a source of inspiration to me."[49]

John Francis Noll (1875–1956), bishop of Fort Wayne, Indiana, surely was the most conservative cleric and most militant defender of Catholicism with whom Hoover and his FBI worked. Through cooperation with Noll's *Our Sunday Visitor*, which had more than a million subscribers nationwide, Hoover reached a multitude of Catholics who also were deeply disenchanted with the direction of American society. Perhaps no one in the hierarchy was more capable of speaking for them than Noll. As one Catholic newspaper noted, he "wag[ed] a relentless war against secularism and filth in periodicals and movies."[50]

Noll was born and lived his whole life in northeastern Indiana. In fact he was baptized, confirmed, ordained, and consecrated as bishop in the same parish, the Cathedral of the Immaculate Conception in Fort Wayne. As a result of his experiences with anti-Catholic prejudice during his years as a pastor in rural Indiana, where Catholics were a minority, Noll became convinced that he had a special responsibility to explain the faith and oppose anti-Catholic bigotry.

One of Noll's primary means of doing this was through the publication of *Our Sunday Visitor*, which initially contained no local news. The paper never lost its original focus, but the ambitious Noll, its editor, was soon putting out local editions for dioceses in addition to the national one. By 1943 six different editions of *Our Sunday Visitor* were appearing, and by the mid-1950s more than a dozen were coming out. Noll also had several other publications. In 1908 he founded the *Parish Monthly*, which became the *Family Monthly* in 1938 and the *Family Digest* in 1945. In 1925 he began publishing *The Acolyte*, a magazine for priests; in 1945 its name was changed to *The Priest*.

Noll, then, was a force with whom other Catholic bishops had to reckon. During the 1930s and into the mid-1940s he served the NCWC in many different positions, among them as an elected member of its administrative board from 1931 to 1937 and again from 1941 to 1946. He also was a member of the Bishops' Committee on Motion Pictures, which founded the Legion of Decency, and chairman of the Bishops' Committee on Obscene Literature. Other bishops might not approve of how Noll went about implementing his moral and political positions, but he had far too many resources at his disposal, and his views were too close to those of the Catholic mainstream, for him to be entirely dismissed.

A man who saw himself surrounded by enemies of the Church, decline and decadence, and ensnaring evil, Bishop Noll spoke for other Catholics who felt just as embattled. There was little in contemporary America with which Noll and his publications did not stand in sharp disagreement: birth control, an absolutist definition of free speech, sex education, secularized public education, expanded opportunities for women, diminished parental authority, "easy" divorces. He was, of course, an early opponent of Communism and may well have temporarily lost his administrative board position because of his outspokenness on Communist infiltration of labor unions. Noll, who had fought anti-Catholic bigots who were members of the Socialist Party of America in the 1910s, closely associated anti-Catholicism with Communism in the 1930s and 1940s.

What seems to have angered Noll the most, though, was the obscene literature that he saw everywhere. It was his effort to drive "dirty" magazines out of Fort Wayne that highlights his relations with the FBI and J. Edgar Hoover. Noll died in 1956, but the connection between *Our Sunday Visitor* and the FBI survived him. That relationship, too, was based on a profound distaste for modernity. We will look first at Noll and then at his newspaper.

In August 1937 a South Bend druggist came to Bishop Noll asking for advice. He objected to some of the magazines he was given to sell in his store, but his distributor told him that he had an "all or none" policy: the druggist had to take every periodical the distributor gave him or he would get none. A "devout Catholic," the store owner "was having considerable conscience-trouble about the moral value of some of the magazines he was being asked to peddle. He wanted Bishop Noll's advice."[51]

Out of Noll's admonition to make a "good fight" came not just a campaign against "smut" in the Fort Wayne diocese but eventually the formation of the National Organization for Decent Literature (NODL), headed by Noll, in January 1938. With *The Acolyte* serving as the campaign's official publication, the NODL, an NCWC organization, began reviewing magazines and listing those that violated its code. Publications were "objectionable" which "glorify crime and [the] criminal," were mostly "sexy," habitually carried articles on "illicit love," and contained "disreputable advertising" or "illustrations and pictures bordering on the indecent."[52]

On numerous occasions Noll sought to involve Hoover and the FBI in the NODL campaign. On one level, Noll wanted the FBI's investigative help in an effort to legally suppress "indecent" publications. On another, though, what the bishop really desired was the moral prestige that the Director's name would lend his efforts. Noll generally was unsuccessful in persuading the FBI to participate in NODL activities. Hoover opposed "salacious" literature as vehemently as Noll but could not involve the FBI if there was no legal basis for its participation.

Noll's first attempt to recruit the Bureau, which occurred in December 1937, even before the formation of the NODL, set the tone for the rest of his efforts. He had targeted fifty magazines that were sold primarily to "youths" or in drugstores near "public schools," had large print runs, and whose "every advertisement" spoke "to the lowest in human beings." Noll, who was convinced that the "growth of sex criminality is largely due to the sex mindedness produced by reading such literature," asked Hoover for a letter that would give his "view point, which should carry weight." He also suggested that several of the magazines "would merit investigation by" the Bureau, since postal laws were being violated.[53]

Hoover gladly provided Noll with a letter in which he voiced his opposition to smut. Proclaiming, "I heartily disapprove of obscene and lewd literature being circulated among the youth of this country," the Director informed Noll that the interstate transportation of such literature violated federal law and therefore fell within the FBI's jurisdiction. Since Noll believed that postal laws were being violated, Hoover urged him to write to the postmaster general. The Indianapolis SAC would soon be contacting him.[54]

The case then proceeded at two levels. One was legal and involved the Indianapolis SAC and his special agents, the U.S. attorney, and Noll. The SAC visited Noll, who gave him the names of eighteen magazines he thought "obscene in contents and advertising." After the agent had purchased copies, the U.S. attorney contacted the bishop, telling him that several of them were indeed "obscene within the law." Noll then asked about those that advertised contraceptives; he was told that the ads were not obscene. In the end, the U.S. attorney, did not think it was possible to move legally against any of the magazines. In early February 1938 Hoover informed Noll that since the government had declined to bring legal action against the magazines, the FBI was withdrawing from the matter.[55]

At the second level at which the case continued, though, Noll's campaign was more successful. The FBI's involvement produced "quite some publicity" in Fort Wayne, where a *Journal Gazette* headline, for example, read, "G-Men Tracing Magazine Sale." Noll also used Hoover's letter to good advantage. A copy of it, along with an even more noncommittal letter from the postmaster general's office, appeared in *Our Sunday Visitor* under the headline "National Support for Decent Literature Drive." The February issue of *The Acolyte*, under the banner "The Fight against Filth," also reprinted Hoover's letter.[56]

The grassroots organizing that accompanied this publicity campaign apparently worked. Magazine distributors in the Fort Wayne area agreed to discontinue those periodicals that the League for Clean Reading condemned, and "bookleggers," truckers who transported smut, left Indiana. The periodicals that Noll and those Catholics who supported him had driven out of the state were, ironically, not all that objectionable in comparison to those being sold elsewhere. As Edward Tamm informed Hoover: "For your further information the magazines of which Bishop Noll is complaining are not the true obscenity which we have come in contact with in other cases involving the interstate transportation of obscene literature, but are the magazines which are generally sold on [news] stands in the U.S."[57]

Hoover continued to take Noll's complaints about obscenity seriously, but the Indianapolis Field Office repeatedly found that the material did not fall within its jurisdiction. In early 1942 Noll complained about "small lewd picture books" that were being distributed at South Side and Central Catholic high schools in Fort Wayne. The U.S. attorneys in Newark, New Jersey, where the "strip-tease novelty booklet" was made, and in Fort Wayne, both judged that it was not obscene under the law. The Indianapolis SAC tried to explain the legal issues involved, but Noll did not understand—or said he did not—why the FBI could not simply prohibit certain things from being distributed.[58]

Two more complaints produced the same result. Later in 1942 Noll went to Hoover about an issue of *Burlesk* magazine. First the U.S. attorney in Fort Wayne declined to prosecute, then the one in New York City did the same. Noll, who was "disappointed" when the Indianapolis SAC told him there would be no action, told the SAC that publications like *Burlesk* "were a major contributing factor to the rise in juvenile delinquency and adults' criminal tendencies." He once again asked that the FBI take action, and the SAC once again explained why it could not. Noll said he understood. In 1943 he filed a complaint against a publishing company in St. Louis, but an assistant U.S. attorney ruled that its magazine, which contained an article titled "The Tragedies of the White Slaves," was not obscene.[59]

In 1953 Noll raised another issue related to obscene literature. He suggested that the FBI investigate those who did most of the writing for *True Story* and *True Romances*, claiming that the writers were, as a publisher had told him, "Communists or Communist-bent." The argument that Communists were responsible for the spread of indecent material in America did not often appear in Catholic anti-Communist literature— there was, after all, little if any evidence for the charge—but it was a potentially explosive assertion.[60]

Noll himself pushed the argument. According to his authorized biography, "the more he studied the situation the more the Bishop became convinced that much of this printed and pictured lewdness was being produced and circulated to destroy the morals of youth in perfect keeping with Communistic objectives." The connections that Noll wanted the reader to draw between lewd literature, anti-Catholicism, and Communism were stated clearly in the very next sentence: "Frederick Collins, in *Liberty* of November 23, 1937, had expressed a similar view, quoting [Russian Communist] Gregory Zinovief's statement that 'Our party cannot be indifferent to religious questions. . . . The Communist Party says what Marx says, that religion is the opiate of the people. Of course, it is very important how your anti-religious propaganda is conducted, whether it is done shrewdly or crudely.'" By any standard of logic Noll had not proved that Communists were distributing obscene literature, as he also had asserted shortly after the Collins article appeared; but perhaps that was not his point. The threats to Catholicism were intertwined and needed to be combated as if they were one.[61]

This was also, of course, Hoover's view of the world, and he immediately ordered an investigation. Nothing apparently ever came of this inquiry or of any others into similar charges (this was one of three incidents I have discovered in which a report came to him about Communists distributing obscene literature), for had evidence been found, Hoover certainly would have made the connection public.[62]

Noll made two further requests of the FBI when he asked it to look into *True Story* and *True Romances* in 1953. First, he wanted Hoover to order an investigation of the high school sorority initiations he had learned about from a *McCall's* article. What the article revealed, he wrote, "outrages decency" and "certainly has a close relationship to the growth of juvenile crime." Second, Noll asked that the FBI back federal laws that would forbid the transportation of indecent literature across state lines. Hoover once again sent an agent—an "experienced" one this time—to explain to Noll the limits of the FBI's jurisdiction as well as that of the post office. Hoover himself wrote to Noll, telling him that the FBI could not support legislation to curb such publications.[63]

The FBI, if Noll had had his way, would have had more power and influence. As we have seen, he periodically asked the Bureau to investigate all sorts of things he considered problematic. In the course of discussing tactics for ridding "downtown" areas of "salacious" literature, Noll wished for an FBI with the power to enforce a strict moral code. But "as it is[,] the FBI can act only when somebody takes it upon himself to prosecute a retailer for selling an off-color periodical which does not enjoy the second class mail privilege." Several years later Noll wistfully mentioned to Hoover that he wished the FBI could investigate the "causes as well as the effects" of crime.[64]

I know of no publication that had a closer relationship with Hoover and the FBI than Noll's *Our Sunday Visitor*. It reprinted Hoover's speeches and routinely cited him as an authority. It regularly asked him to write articles specifically for its pages. After Noll's death these close connections continued. The newspaper chimed in with strong support during the "smear" campaign of 1958 and 1959. In 1960 the FBI cooperated with an associate editor in developing and running a series called "Communism Looks at Our Youth."

Our Sunday Visitor often invoked Hoover's authority in the course of making its own editorial points. The first time the paper's FBI file indicates this occurred was in 1937, when an editorial asserted that the Communist Party could give a signal to the "nearly 4,000,000 criminals and criminal-minded people in the United States" and get immediate action. It then quoted from a speech in which Hoover discussed the country's recent increase in crime, assuming the reader would make the necessary connection. One of the final such references to Hoover occurred in 1964, when Father Richard Ginder, a regular columnist for the paper, Noll's biographer, and the Bureau's friend, drew on a recent issue of the FBI's *Law Enforcement Bulletin*. One of the reasons why Hoover was so effective, Ginder argued, was his "firm grasp on the fundamental doctrine of original sin and the basic depravity of human nature." In the years in between, the newspaper called upon Hoover's expertise in reference to juvenile delinquency, disorder in the home, deteriorating morals on the home front during World War II, good parenting, teenage female safety, and fighting Communism.[65]

Noll's newspaper also reprinted Hoover's speeches and articles. For example, in 1939 the speech "Fifty Years of Crime in America" appeared after Hoover had first delivered it in Nashville. In 1950 *Our Sunday Visitor* reprinted an essay that Hoover had written for an Easter series edited by Norman Vincent Peale. Hoover's 1956 testimony before a congressional subcommittee on appropriations also reappeared in the paper. By 1942 the newspaper's editors had grown so confident of Hoover's approval for what they were doing that they cobbled together an article out of several of his speeches without even asking his permission. FBIHQ only discovered this when a high school valedictorian asked permission to give Hoover's address as her commencement speech. It took some time before it was discovered not only that the "Seat of Government" had never formally approved the reprinting of "What Washington Might Think of the US Today," but also that it had never prepared an article with that title.[66]

The relationship between the FBI and *Our Sunday Visitor* was firm enough to outlast Noll's death. In 1960 an editor asked the Director to contribute an essay to the May issue on Communism. He sent along "Communism—an Enemy of Human Dignity." The following year Hoover again provided a piece for the May issue: "Communism—a Menace to Freedom." In 1963 he sent along "The Indispensable Supports" and in 1964 "Obscene Literature—Threat to Our Young People."

"The Indispensable Supports," which argued for a belief in God as the keystone of America's past and present while attacking Communism as a "powerful atheistic force," brought many letters of praise. Illustrative of the relationship between the Director and Catholics was an exchange between Hoover and a seventh- or eighth-grader in a Catholic school. Every Monday, the student wrote him, the class had to bring in a *Sunday Visitor*. They were asked this time to write on Hoover's "Indispensable Supports"; students would receive extra credit if they could discover what his religion was. Hoover responded this way: "I am a member of The Presbyterian Church and I have always believed that the things which give life meaning are built on discipline, work, love, and faith in God. Especially do we need faith, regardless of the religious preference, for in this materialistic time each of us needs the reservoir of strength which can come only through the cultivation of the spiritual side of one's nature."[67]

There is more evidence that the close relationship between *Our Sunday Visitor* and the FBI continued after Noll's death. Part of it has to do with the Bureau's counteroffensive against the "smear" campaign of 1958 and 1959, while the remainder revolves around the FBI's concrete aid to the newspaper.

Father James P. Conroy, an associate editor, was "advised" of the smear campaign against Hoover in November 1958. G. A. Nease, who reported directly to Clyde Tolson, Hoover's second in command, first gave Conroy copies of the American Business Consultants' *Counterattack* and the American Legion's *Firing Line*, which "summarize[d] this situation." Then, in preparation for countering the *New York Post*'s forthcoming critical series on the FBI, Conroy was told about "the columns written by Murray Kempton containing the various criticisms of the College of Cardinals and of Cardinal Spellman." Conroy "expressed great appreciation," telling Nease that he "would do something about this." Nease assured Tolson, "We will undoubtedly be hearing further from Father Conroy."[68]

Conroy's response came in his column—"Father Conroy Talks to Youth"—of December 7, 1958. Subtitled "And Now the FBI," Conroy led off with Cushing's Communion breakfast talk, which, as we have seen, stoutly defended Hoover against the ongoing smear. He described the evidence that pointed to a conspiracy by Communists who "have burrowed like rats into every facet of American life." The subversive plot would have gone unnoticed if not "spotted" by "staunch and loyal Americans like Archbishop Cushing—and of course the FBI itself." Father Conroy urged his readers to research Communism, to initiate discussion everywhere, and to pray that through "Our Lady's intercession"—the following day was the Feast of the Immaculate Conception]—"the FBI and other branches of government occupied with internal security be given all necessary guidance during these trying times!"[69]

Conroy also counterattacked against the smear through the *High School Reporter*, which he sent to Catholic secondary schools throughout the country. Some seven hundred newspapers, according to Nease, picked up the *Reporter*'s "editorial suggestion" that "the FBI be the central topic of discussion and the communist smear campaign against the FBI be highlighted against a background of the communist efforts to brainwash American youth into the communist way of thinking."[70]

A nun signing herself Sister M. Maurice, for example, thanked Conroy for the newsletter, which informed teachers of the "trends and Catholic thought of the day on a high school level." A "busy teacher has little time to read widely," wrote the nun. Juniors and seniors at her Catholic Central High School in Steubenville, Ohio, were going to attend an assembly on the FBI. *The Dome*, a publication of the Academy of Notre Dame in Washington, D.C., stoutly defended Hoover and the FBI in an editorial titled "Can Truth Triumph?" It concluded, referring to the smear campaign: "Americans can counteract this only by learning the truth about the FBI. A few Catholic and other publications have already taken up the cause, but more must be done. Mr. Hoover and the FBI have protected and defended you all these years. Will you help them?"[71]

The FBI and Father Conroy cooperated in the struggle against Communism in several other significant ways. After Conroy read Hoover's *Masters of Deceit*, he checked with fifty of the two thousand Catholic high school newspapers he dealt with, only to discover that "very few" of them "had any positive course of instruction on communism as it is operating in the world today and few had proper reference books the students could utilize." Finding a donor willing to buy fifty copies of *Masters of Deceit* to give to the schools he had contacted was Conroy's first step.[72]

The second directly involved Bureau help: Conroy "wondered if the Bureau could help him from time to time by furnishing thumbnail ideas on which he could capitalize as being weaknesses found in daily American life which the Soviets use for propaganda value." He would then call "attention to just how the communists make propaganda weapons out of them against the Western World." He mentioned as an example a recent *High School Reporter*'s discussion of "fads." Sometimes, he observed, instead of thinking for themselves, young people become "addicted to fads." Communists, "unscrupulous politicians and social rabble rousers" were "well aware that young people are easily addicted to fads[,] which can become a habit that is carried into adult life." This propensity "makes people vulnerable to propaganda of all types and robs them of their ability to think for themselves."[73]

Inspector John J. McGuire, delegated by Hoover to talk with Conroy, told the priest that the Bureau "would be glad to be of any possible assistance we could." After giving as an example the way Soviet newspapers always mentioned "American hooliganism and undisciplined American youth," McGuire offered that perhaps the FBI could "furnish him specifics and quotations" from Russian publications that "poke fun at American youth." Nease, who accompanied Conroy during a short visit with the Director, suggested several other topics that the priest might take up in his newsletter, such as the "over-idolization" of movie stars and rock and roll singers, teenage drinking, and the "lack of American culture."[74]

Hoover approved FBI cooperation with Conroy with a handwritten "Do all we can to help" on a memo summarizing the priest's visit with McGuire. The first thing the Bureau did was to supply an article by Hoover, "Youth—Communist Target," to kick off Conroy's "Communism Looks at Our Youth" series. It then provided the priest with monthly reports of "several hundred words, each, well documented," on "specific, topical items," which he also used in his series.[75]

In one case Conroy received even greater help. In January 1959 he asked McGuire for information on the Communist Party's involvement in a world youth festival to be held later that year: "John, I am in need for some authentic data on the Vienna Youth Festival coming up this summer. Also do you know of any definite play that the Reds are making to entice any of our youth groups into going over there. From what I have been able to learn it is to be much the same as the Moscow Youth festival." After some discussion at FBIHQ, it was decided that the Bureau would furnish Conroy with a "brief public source background memorandum"—that is, on paper without a letterhead and with references only to material that was publicly available. Conroy was delighted with the information in the memo, whose only identification was "Seventh World Youth Festival." He responded, "Thanks a million for the excellent run-down," adding, "The background which you have given me will be invaluable[,] . . . especially the 'interest of the Communist Party U.S.A.' that nails it down but good."[76]

At the end of May 1959 the Bureau assessed the program, which Conroy had suspended for the summer. McGuire, who continued to handle the FBI's relationship with the priest, noted that the results were impressive: "90% of the high school press had something to say about communism and the smear against the FBI and the Director." Conroy, moreover, had arranged with the National Catholic Education Association to make the series "must" reading and discussion material for Catholic high schools. It is not surprising, then, that McGuire, "in view of the excellent results brought about by our relationship with Father Conroy," recommended that the FBI should "continue to deal with him during the fall months when the schools reopen."[77]

There is no evidence in the FBI file on *Our Sunday Visitor* file indicating that cooperation was in fact resumed in the fall of 1959, but Conroy did make a reference, in a May 1960 letter to McGuire, to "the anti-Communist projects upon which I am working with the guidance of the Director and yourself." Friendly relations between Father Conroy and the FBI continued for at least the next several years.[78]

What seems to have most attracted Noll and those who succeeded him at *Our Sunday Visitor* to Hoover and his FBI was the way in which the congruence between their values and those of a very powerful and influential non-Catholic could be brought to bear on their agenda for America. Two examples involving Noll illustrate this point.

First, in Noll's column "The Bishop's Chat" in a 1940 issue of *Sunday Visitor*, he used one of Hoover's articles—published in *Woman's Day* in 1938—to make his case about the need for religious education for children and for a revival of stern parental discipline in the home. After two paragraphs glossing Hoover and two quoting him Noll concluded, "Hoping that you will hearken to Mr. Hoover if not to me, I am . . ." The second occurs in a 1942 editorial, "We're Losing War on the Homefront." After noting that many observers had commented on the increase in juvenile delinquency since 1940, Noll argued that few non-Catholics were dealing systemically with the problem. Hoover was the exception: "Almost alone, among non-Catholics who have expressed themselves on the crime situation, J. Edgar Hoover goes to the root of the problem and points to the remedy." After quoting Hoover at length, the Fort Wayne bishop closed on the same note: "When our Nation makes up its mind to follow Mr. Hoover's advice—which incidentally is 100% Catholic—we shall have made a good start towards the solution of our problems of immorality, in sex matters, crime and juvenile delinquency. But full success will never be achieved so long as religion is barred from the public schools of the country."[79]

Another Catholic cleric with whom the FBI had a fruitful relationship was Bishop Fulton J. Sheen, the extraordinarily popular writer, speaker, and TV personality. Sheen was born in rural Illinois in 1895. After attending St. Viator's College and St. Paul Seminary, he was ordained in 1919. Noted early on for his brilliance, he received degrees from the Catholic University of America and the University of Louvain in Belgium. After having served a year in a poor Peoria parish as his bishop's way of testing his obedience, Sheen moved on to teach philosophy at Catholic University. Becoming the first regular speaker of the *Catholic Hour* radio program in 1930, he quickly became its most popular one, reaching 4 million listeners on 118 NBC stations. *Life Is Worth Living*, his TV show which ran weekly from 1952 to 1957, was seen by millions each week.

Sheen also was a prolific writer. He published more than ninety books, many of which appeared on the bestseller lists. Among the most popular were *Preface to Religion* (1946) and *Life of Christ* (1958). He also wrote hundreds of newspaper and magazine articles that seemed to appear everywhere from the 1930s to the 1950s. Sheen probably was the most influential Catholic speaker and author of his era.

He shared much with Hoover. There was, for example, his lifelong crusade against Communism. Sheen never limited himself to just this one issue, but he seldom strayed far from it. It was not merely that he believed Communism to be an unmitigated evil. Having come to maturity during a period of American history when nativism was running high, Sheen saw Catholic anti-Communism as a means of proving one's loyalty to America and also of making America a stronger country.[80]

The language Sheen used to characterize the dangers that threatened him, his Church, and his country suggests, moreover, that he and Hoover shared much more than just a militant and sustained anti-Communism. He described Communism and Communists with the identical adjectives and metaphors the Director used: Communism was a "cancer," it came in "tides," it was "slimy"; its followers were "snakes" and "rats." Just as Hoover had once described himself as a doctor diagnosing a sickness that required treatment, so Sheen declared: "My attitude is like that of a physician. He hates the typhoid, but loves the patients and tries to cure them. As a Christian, I'm committed to the solemn obligation to love the Communists. I'd like to make Americans of them." In another address, titled "Our Wounded World," Sheen identified the disease as "the slavery and class struggle consequent upon godlessness and the denial of the spirit." Or as he put it another time, "Communism is related to our material Western civilization as putrefaction is to disease."[81]

Just as Hoover focused on order, stability, and hierarchy, so Sheen highly valued all three. Part of his commitment to them came from the neo-scholastic philosophy that he learned during the revival of the Church's teaching of Thomas Aquinas's medieval theology and philosophy. Part came from his upbringing, during which he was trained as his parents' social situation and future hopes dictated. And part came from his dedication to a life of celibacy, since these were the personal characteristics that were most helpful in that regard. From all three sources came his antimodernism, which ran so deep that he condemned both capitalism and Communism as manifestations of the modernist malady. The Catholic Church, Sheen was convinced, provided the only hope for a world in headlong retreat from reason. As he once wrote, conversion to Catholicism "brings the soul out of either chaos or this false peace of mind to true peace of soul." This "true peace of soul," Sheen asserted, "is born of the tranquility of order, wherein the senses are subject to the reason, the reason to faith, and the whole personality to the will of God."[82]

Sheen's FBI file, ironically, begins with two letters that comment on his politics from two opposing perspectives. In the first, written in 1943, a small businessman from Michigan suggested how the FBI might track down pro-Nazi sympathizers in the United States. Sheen's most recent speech, he found, had so "strongly indicted" them that they must "boil with rage." An agent should contact Sheen, who could provide the names of those "public enemies" who had "[taken] exception" to the speech. "You may rest assured," the writer noted in closing, "of my full co-operation at any time." By contrast, in January 1944, a letter from Carmel, California,

charged that Sheen was a "pro-fascist speaker whose utterances were se-
ditious and designed to promote disunity." His "subversive talks" were
"particularly dangerous" because they were "put forth in the name and
with all the trappings of religion."[83]

The first evidence of Hoover's and Sheen's shared values, in a 1944 letter,
attests to their agreement on why civilizations fall. In it Sheen thanked
Hoover for passing along a speech, telling him that he had been planning
on using a quote from a newspaper account of it in a talk he was putting
together. "A very interesting confirmation of your thesis," Sheen wrote,
"can be found in Toynbee's six volume investigation of History. He reveals
that sixteen out of nineteen great civilizations collapsed from within."[84]

By 1947 Sheen had grown quite close to the FBI, for it was then that
he gave a talk at a Holy Communion breakfast for employees of the FBI's
New York Field Office. Sheen, according to Edward Scheidt, the New
York SAC, said that he had "addressed thousands of Communion Breakfasts" and this "was the finest looking group that he had ever spoken to
of this nature." It was apparent,"the SAC continued, that "he was deeply
impressed with the clean-cut look and wholesome appearance of those in
attendance." Sheen had planned on leaving immediately after delivering
his speech but "remained for the entire occasion, obviously enjoying the
affair enormously."[85]

More than a decade later, Sheen's estimation of Hoover and his men
had, if anything, increased. Upon receiving a copy of *Masters of Deceit*,
Sheen wrote a letter of thanks to the Director. He reminded Hoover of the
New Testament story in which the police, sent to arrest Jesus, come back
empty-handed, saying, "No man ever spoke as that Man." Thus, "long
before the establishment of the Federal Bureau of Investigation," said
Sheen, drawing his lesson, "there were FBI men who had such respect for
Divine justice and Divine love that they would not infringe on his bless-
ings." He continued: "You have built up a tradition toward Divine justice
in this country which has been incomparable in the life of free peoples.
The quality of the men who surround you, their excellent philosophy of
life have combined to personalize justice in what is called a Department.
May the Lord bless you and yours."[86]

The praise also went in the opposite direction. In 1950 Hoover complimented Sheen on his announcement upon becoming director of the
Society for the Propagation of the Faith: "Your statement that our present
danger lies not from the atomic bomb but from atomic men is certainly
an incisive example of the metaphysician at his best, and in the tradition
of exact thinking which characterizes the Schoolmen." In 1957 Hoover
offered Sheen congratulations on his receipt of the American Legion's

Distinguished Service Medal: "Your many friends in the FBI were most happy to hear of this honor accorded you."[87]

There were still other signs of great respect and friendship between Sheen and the Director and his men. In 1953 Sheen spoke at the graduation exercises of the FBI's National Academy. In 1956 he again addressed an FBI Communion breakfast, this time for FBIHQ employees. Just a month before this talk, some special agents had joined an audience from the Department of Justice for a special showing of one of Sheen's TV broadcasts in which he addressed the history of the Communist Party.

Throughout his career, but especially in the 1940s, Sheen received much publicity because of the large number of converts he brought to Catholicism. Many of them were quite famous: Henry Ford II, heir to the Ford Motor Company; violinist Fritz Kreisler; journalist Heywood Broun; Grace Moore, the opera singer and actress; journalist Gretta Palmer; and Claire Booth Luce, author, congresswoman, and wife of the publisher and editor Henry Luce.

What made Sheen's connection with the FBI singular was the way it interrelated with his work with converts. Sheen specialized in converting former members of the Communist Party of the United States. Among his successes he counted Bella Dodd, the high-ranking New York Communist labor leader, and Elizabeth Bentley, the onetime Communist and Soviet courier, whose defection to the FBI revealed large-scale espionage in Washington. Jack Lawrence of the National Maritime Union was one of his failures. Evidence of FBI involvement is strongest in the case of Louis Budenz, Sheen's grandest triumph.

Budenz, a baptized Catholic who graduated from law school in 1912, served as the assistant director of the Catholic Central Verein in St. Louis, publicity director of the American Civil Liberties Union, and editor of *Labor Age*. In 1935 he joined the CPUSA and thereafter held increasingly significant editorial positions; by 1945 he had been the *Daily Worker's* managing editor for several years. After his return to the Church, he had a long and controversial career as an anti-Communist speaker, writer, and government witness.

Virtually no one knew about Budenz's plans to leave the CPUSA. According to the account in his autobiography, *This Is My Story*, he did not even try to contact Sheen until two months before he was received back into the Church. His defection, then, took almost everyone by surprise— everyone, that is, except the FBI, for Sheen had tipped off the Bureau in advance about Budenz's decision.

Sheen would not have done this without having had personal contact with someone at the Bureau, and in fact we do know that some contact had occurred; we just do not know much about it. In 1944, when Sheen made headlines with his assertion that the Soviet Union was preparing to sign a separate peace treaty with Germany, D. M. Ladd, a high-ranking Bureau official, recommended to Tamm that future Boston SAC Laughlin, "who has previously interviewed" Sheen, talk to him again to see if he had any specific information to back it up.[88]

Budenz's defection took everyone else by surprise. Sheen, who had previously debated Communism with him in person and in print, received Budenz, his wife, and their three daughters into the Church on the evening on October 10, 1945. They had planned on announcing the decision the following evening, but a leak forced an announcement shortly before the service began. Those in the FBI who were not in the know heard the news sometime that day when E. E. Conroy, New York SAC, sent an "urgent" teletype to FBIHQ announcing Budenz's decision: "Resigned from Communist Party and Returned to Catholic Church Through Efforts of Msgr. Fulton Sheen." While some Communists undoubtedly heard the news the evening of the tenth, most probably did not find out until the next day, when they read the *New York Times* story headlined "Daily Worker Editor Renounces Communism for Catholic Faith." Budenz's name was still on the masthead of the *Daily Worker*.[89]

On October 12, with William Z. Foster, head of the Communist Party, attacking Budenz for "desertion" and party leadership desperately trying to figure out if they were going to see further defections, the FBI began making arrangements to interview Budenz. Ladd recommended to the Director that the Baltimore SAC "contact Monsignor Sheen, who apparently arranged for this transfer of allegiance on the part of Budenz, and endeavor through him to effect arrangements whereby two Bureau supervisors may interview Budenz." After consulting with Hoover, Tolson approved the decision.[90]

J. P. Coyne, an up-and-comer in FBIHQ's Security Division and later a staff member with the National Security Council, conducted the interview. Coyne told Sheen that the FBI wanted to interview Budenz and that it was going through him "in view of his much appreciated courtesy in informing the Bureau in advance of the fact that Budenz intended to resign his connections with the Communist Party in order to embrace Catholicism." Sheen told Coyne that while both he and Budenz favored cooperation with the Bureau, neither wanted any fanfare: Sheen had just turned down a request from the House Committee on Un-American Activities (HUAC) for Budenz to appear before it; Budenz himself was not going to lecture or write about the CPUSA in the foreseeable future. Sheen "reiterated the fact" that he favored such an interview with the FBI "because he realizes that it will be handled on a confidential basis and because there will be no publicity accruing there from."[91]

Apparently making the decision for Budenz, Sheen promised Coyne that he would be "completely cooperative in any respect." Moreover, he "twice volunteered the statement that the Bureau could be assured that Budenz will be most willing to furnish any information in his possession which is considered of interest to the FBI." Sheen promised to talk to Budenz and arrange an interview.[92]

About a month later, after visiting with Budenz for several days at Notre Dame, where he had been given a teaching position, Sheen reported to Coyne. The interview with Budenz, set for the following week, should go well, Sheen thought, since "there is no question in his mind concerning the sincerity of Budenz in renouncing his connections with the Communist Party and in embracing Catholicism." Budenz was also willing to furnish "all the details in his possession" about the CPUSA that the Bureau wanted.[93]

There was one issue, though, that required attention: Budenz, "somewhat concerned over his personal security," wanted a Catholic to interview him. Why? Since there were "leaks in the FBI," CPUSA leaders "have access to and frequently receive information from the files of this Bureau." Budenz, in fact, claimed to have seen such information. (This assertion, if it proved true, would directly connect Budenz to the ongoing investigation of Bentley's revelations about an espionage ring in the federal government.) Coyne "urgently recommended" that the FBI secretly record the Budenz interview; Hoover approved the request. Ladd recommended that Special Agents Coyne and E. H. Winterrowd—Catholics "thoroughly familiar with the Communist picture"—interview Budenz. Tamm approved the request.[94]

A snag developed, however. About a week later Sheen called Coyne to see if final arrangements had been made for the interview with Budenz, only to learn that Notre Dame officials had forbidden Budenz to talk with anyone. Expressing dismay, Sheen offered to appeal to Father Hugh O'Donnell, president of the university, "for the purpose of ironing the matter out and securing the approval which Budenz apparently feels necessary before consummating the aforementioned interview."[95]

Instead of accepting Sheen's offer to intercede with O'Donnell, Hoover had Tamm, the Bureau's highest-ranking Catholic, telephone the Notre Dame president to gain approval for the interview, which the FBI now considered vital to national security. O'Donnell explained that he had "counseled" Budenz, who had been "besieged from all sides," not "to see anyone, talk to anybody, write anything or make any public appearances for at least the next six months." O'Donnell, Tamm reported, "stated, however, he considered the Bureau and its interests in an entirely different category than he did the other requests being made of Budenz and thought it was most desirable for the Bureau to interview Budenz." When O'Donnell said he wanted to sit in on a portion of the interview, Tamm, thinking quickly on his feet, told him that Hoover would be "delighted to have him present when we talked to Budenz." This would not be a problem, he assured Hoover, since "we contemplate a week or so of interview and obviously Father O'Donnell could not give more than an hour or so to any such participation."[96]

Sheen was not present when Coyne and Winterrowd, armed with hundreds of questions, interviewed Budenz in a South Bend hotel room from December 6 to December 12, 1945. Except for allowing his house in Washington to be used as meeting place for Budenz and the special agents in April 1946, Sheen disappears from Budenz's FBI file. Budenz apparently no longer needed or wanted his help in his dealings with the Bureau.

Bishop Fulton J. Sheen, then, was close to the Bureau during those years when he exerted his widest influence in America. The FBI files that have been released provide a good overview of that relationship. Sheen shared much in common with Hoover and his men, whom he considered valiant defenders of Church and country. For both Hoover and Sheen, Communism was a significant threat, but neither ever lost sight of the fact that it ultimately was part of a larger set of dangers that had to be confronted.

Sheen's files, particularly when read alongside his discussion of the FBI in *Treasure of Clay*, also raise some important questions about the extent and nature of its help to him: Did the Bureau provide a check on each and every potential convert who was newsworthy? Did the incidents of contact with Communists that Sheen mentioned actually take place, or were they a figment of his imagination as the Bureau might have suspected? If the latter, why did the Bureau continue to view him as a trustworthy friend into the late 1950s?[97]

Francis Cardinal Spellman was born in Massachusetts in 1889, received his B.A. at Fordham, and was ordained in 1916. After nearly a decade in the Boston archdiocese, he served as an attaché to the Secretariat of State at the Vatican from 1925 to 1932. In 1939 he became the sixth archbishop of New York City and military vicar for the U.S. Armed Forces. Spellman was made a cardinal in 1946. He remained head of the New York archdiocese until his death in 1967.

The cardinal was an enormously ambitious man who eagerly and successfully sought advancement in the Church. He made connections with important people almost everywhere he went. His service on the Secretariat was the first ever for an American, as was his consecration as bishop at St. Peter's in Rome. Spellman was in many ways the public face of American Catholicism from the late 1940s to the mid-1960s. Powerful and supremely confident of not only of his own rectitude but also that of his Church and his country, he pugnaciously defended them against their enemies: immoral movies (*Two-Faced Woman* in 1941, *The Miracle* in 1951, *Baby Doll* in 1956), alleged anti-Catholics (Eleanor Roosevelt in 1949), Communists and antiwar demonstrations (in the 1950s and 1960s), and striking workers (gravediggers in 1949).

There surely was significant interaction between the FBI's New York Field Office and the Cardinal's chancery office prior to 1942, but it is not until then that material released by the FBI begins to document a relationship between Spellman and Hoover. Several events during 1942 brought the two into close contact and laid the basis for further cooperation. They are worth looking at in some detail.

First, on March 10, 1942, Hoover received an invitation from Timothy Galvin, Supreme Master of the Indiana Knights of Columbus, to participate in a radio program. Galvin explained to the Director that the purpose of the broadcast was to "make a contribution to national morale" by "bringing home" the "high, spiritual values which are involved in the present great conflict." The other speakers were to be Clarence Manion, dean of the law school of the University of Notre Dame, and Cardinal Spellman.[98]

Hoover accepted the invitation but could not make it to New York City for the March 22 broadcast and supper afterwards. Instead he participated by hookup from Washington, D.C., and sent Edward Tamm as his representative. The speech he gave, "Our Nation's Strength," was met with enthusiasm by Catholics all over the country, who sent in postcards and letters of appreciation.

In the next several weeks Spellman and Hoover exchanged letters about the program. Hoover's went out the day after. He apologized for not having come to New York—"official matters of a most urgent nature" had detained him—and praised the prelate's speech: "I want to thank you most highly for your stirring and thought-provoking address which, in my opinion, was one of the best I have ever heard." He also added that he hoped to meet and visit with Spellman in the near future. Though pro forma in tone, the letter delighted Spellman. He immediately replied,

asking Hoover for a copy of his speech and sending along one of his own.
Spellman also invited Hoover to one of the luncheons during which he
often carried out the business that earned his chancery the nickname of
"the Powerhouse."[99]

In June 1942 Hoover did have lunch at the chancery office. The cardinal,
for reasons unknown, was absent that day, but Bishop John O'Hara, Spellman's military delegate, who was himself close to the FBI, stood in ably.
Also present (Hoover noted that they should be placed on the "general
m[ailing]/list") were the archdiocese's secretary for Catholic charities,
the secretary for education, and the national secretary for the Near East
Welfare Association.[100]

Several months after the luncheon O'Hara sent Hoover a copy of his
superior's recently published book *The Road to Victory*, in which Spellman took up critical social and moral issues that also were of great concern to Hoover. The Director's enthusiastic response delighted Spellman
and cemented a relationship between the two. The central point of the
book was that the war inside the United States was as important as the
one outside it. As Spellman put it, "nations may be destroyed not only
by foreign enemies but also by internal decadence." Among those who
were undermining American freedom "in the very name of freedom" were
those who used "cursed, vicious language," the "filth column" that went
about "debauching" the "minds and bodies of our boys and girls," those
who attacked religion, and those who were guilty of "making venomous,
subversive speeches against our form of government."[101]

Religion, discipline, and an absolutist conception of truth, according
to Spellman, were essential to the country's well-being. Religion was the
"foundation of democracy," the "foundation of national good faith" and
of "national salvation." Discipline, he argued, "is an essential part of the
training of the young. Where there is no discipline, there can be no progress in education." It "should emphasize the objectivity of truth and as a
consequence the authority of truth." All truth "stems from God and therefore involves no contradictions."[102]

The argument that America's internal enemies were threatening it just
as dangerously as its external ones was a favorite theme of Hoover's. His
ideas, moreover, about the values undergirding American society were the
same as Spellman's. It is not surprising, then, that the Director responded
in wholehearted agreement: "Regardless of the numerous fronts on which
our soldiers and sailors are fighting at this time, our victories will depend
as much on the protection of internal America, our faith in God, and our
morality at home, as our winning of battles on foreign fields." Spellman
replied in a similar vein: "I've read your numerous excellent speeches and

I really feel we could pinch hit for each other as we seem to have similar appraisals on various matters."[103]

Out of this set of interactions—and without ever actually having met each other—Spellman and Hoover embarked on a working relationship that continued until the former's death in 1967. In part their association took the form of sending each other publications and speeches that each thought especially important. These exchanges—as well as those in which each man sent along his best wishes through intermediaries—ensured not only that each continued to consider the other significant but also that they went on agreeing with each other. Their association also took the form of going to the other for help in the pursuit of mutual enemies and specific institutional goals.

The tenor of the relationship between the cardinal and the Director was established immediately. Just a few days after the exchange of letters about *The Road to Victory*, Spellman sent Hoover a congratulatory letter on the twenty-fifth anniversary of his "devoted, patriotic, successful" service with the federal government. (He also enclosed an editorial from the *Brooklyn Tablet* that greatly praised Hoover's career. It took special note of his "repeated insistence on strongly family discipline and healthy family life.") Hoover thanked Spellman, writing that "one of my great sources of encouragement has been the unswerving loyalty of my good friends. I hope we will always be able to work together in the same spirit of mutual accord."[104]

One of the topics about which the two men exchanged speeches was juvenile delinquency. In 1944 Hoover sent along copies of several talks he had given about the problem; Spellman replied that he hoped to find the time to write a piece about the issue, adding, "I know that your observations will be very helpful to me." In 1945 Spellman, in presenting the Champions Award of the Catholic Youth Organization (CYO) to the FBI Director, noted his efforts to combat teenage crime. Hoover thanked him for his "kind and understanding remarks." The problem continued to be important to both. As Spellman wrote Hoover in 1963, "I am also doing what is possible to assist in the struggle which you are making against juvenile delinquency."[105]

The two men also exchanged speeches about Communism and Americanism. In 1953 Hoover sent along a copy of the statement he had given to a congressional committee on the Harry Dexter White case, a "spy" case from the 1940s that was still producing political controversy. Spellman thanked him for it and passed along a speech of his own, "America, Grateful Child of Mother Europe," in which he vigorously defended his country against criticism from overseas about McCarthyism and civil rights. Hoover, pleased that the cardinal liked the statement on White, was delighted with Spellman's speech. "You certainly did a magnificent job of presenting America," Hoover praised him, and of giving "a clearer understanding of why we are so proud of our country."[106]

Hoover and Spellman, to take just one more example, again exchanged speeches about the dangers of Communism the following year. In November 1954 Hoover received the prestigious Cardinal Gibbons Award from the Catholic University of America. His acceptance speech called for the revival of a sense of urgency about the nation's Communist problem. A "healthy, virile democracy," he said, would not compromise with those who wanted to destroy it, the "debauchers of the public mind," the "corrupters of our youth," the "poisoners of the wells of education of our children." Spellman congratulated him on the speech and sent a recent address in which he had said virtually the same thing in Iowa, "America Awake!" Hoover praised it and agreed with the cardinal that U.S. "citizens must not be apathetic to the menace of Communism and other totalitarian forms of government."[107]

Hoover also received a steady flow of reassuring news about Spellman from his men. Some of it came in on an impromptu basis. In 1946, for example, he received a note from an unidentified person, probably an agent with his own connections to the chancery office, recounting a luncheon at Spellman's residence. "During the course of this occasion," the writer noted, he "spoke of you in terms of highest praise, and indicated that he feels great affection for you." The cardinal had also inquired about the ailing SAC's health and got his home address so he could drop him a note. Other information derived from the regular contact that SACs were required to have with the most important people within their jurisdiction. In two cases SACs apparently were reporting on their initial visits with Spellman after taking up their new position. In 1952 SAC Leland V. Boardman met and talked with Spellman, who "expressed his admiration for the Bureau" and "remarked that he has a very high regard for you." In November 1954 SAC James J. Kelly not only reported on such a meeting but also passed along news about Cushing's recent operation. ("The rumor around Boston had it that his operation involved cancer, but I did not receive official word of this until I spoke to Cardinal Spellman today.") Kelly's last paragraph neatly summarizes the point of the visit: "As your representative in New York, I was received most graciously by Cardinal Spellman. He struck me as being a very big man who daily makes it a point to be humble by holding the coat of his visitors regardless of station.

I was greatly impressed by his friendliness to the Bureau and believe he is a real friend of yours."[108]

A month or so after this initial visit with Spellman, Kelly applied to have him officially approved as a "SAC Contact." Among the information the SAC provided the Bureau was a suggestion as to what the cardinal could do for the FBI: "This contact can be of assistance in furnishing information relative to bogus priests and persons claiming official relations with the Catholic Church. He also can be of assistance in furnishing information concerning prominent Catholic priests and laymen."[109]

While providing enough information to produce the desired effect—Spellman was in fact made a SAC contact—this description does not adequately describe the relationship between the FBI and Cardinal Spellman. First, what is entirely lacking is the matter of what the FBI could do in turn for the contact. In Spellman's case, as undoubtedly with most of the other of the Boss's bishops, the relationship was not just one way but rather was mutually beneficial. Second, a good portion of what appears in the FBI records documenting the relationship between Spellman and the FBI is much more interesting than this mundane description implies.

Foreign affairs was one of the areas in which Spellman provided help to the FBI. Since he knew Latin American and South American prelates, the Bureau came to the cardinal on two occasions for help in gathering intelligence. According to FBI records, in June 1944 a special agent, at the suggestion of someone whose name has been deleted, "renewed his friendship with Archbishop Francis J. Spellman." During their meeting, at which Cardinal O'Hara, who was well connected in the Southern Hemisphere, was present, "it was discreetly ascertained" that there was to be a Eucharistic Congress in Buenos Aires in October. It was unclear if Spellman or O'Hara was going to be there, but the agent used the occasion—this may have been the real purpose of his visit—to tell Spellman about the FBI's Special Intelligence Service (SIS), which operated in South America. The operation "was discreetly outlined to the Archbishop and the presence of a Bureau representative in New York City assigned to this program was outlined to Archbishop Spellman." Before leaving Spellman's office, the agent made arrangements for that representative to meet him "for the purpose of cultivating the Archbishop's acquaintance in the event that at any future time, questions might arise relative to which the Archbishop could assist the Bureau in answering."[110]

Spellman decided not to go to Argentina for the Eucharistic Congress, but Bureau representatives continued talking with him because there was

a possibility that O'Hara might go. After Hoover informed the New York
SAC that the FBI was "intensely interested" in the trip, there was yet another meeting. Spellman told an agent that although O'Hara had decided
not to attend the conference, if someone in a "responsible position in the
Government, either in the State Department or the executive branch of
the Government specifically requested" that he go, the cardinal would
"see to it" that he did.[111]

The FBI also went to Spellman in 1955 about yet another South American Eucharistic Congress. In this case someone from the Bureau met
with Spellman about the "church dignitaries" making the trip. The agent
proposed that they "stop in various South American cities to discuss with
clerical officials of those cities the necessity of making an intensive study
of Communism and using effective means to combat this menace in
Latin America." The agent also "set forth the Communist problem and his
thoughts as to how Catholic clergy of Latin America" could "effectively
combat the menace of Communism." Spellman, who "was impressed with
his survey and suggestion," told the agent that because of logistical problems, he could not participate in the program. He nevertheless thought
that two colleagues, one from Puerto Rico whose name has been deleted
and another, possibly O'Hara, of Philadelphia, "would be able to help him
and he would arrange for them to get in touch with [him]."[112]

Spellman's cooperation went even further. Apparently during that same
meeting, though the record is unclear, he told the agent that "one of the
officials of the church most knowledgeable about such matters in Latin
America" was at Catholic University. Spellman then "summoned [name
deleted] to the Woodner Hotel where he was staying." After having "outlined" the agent's program to him, he urged that person to "stay in touch
with" him, "study his suggestion, and take the necessary steps to implement if possible."[113]

One of the ways in which the Bureau demonstrated its willingness to
cooperate with Spellman just as he did with them was to extend assistance in his writing projects. In the earliest instance, during a lunch in
1944 with a special agent, Spellman discussed an article he was writing
on juvenile delinquency, "Why Blame the Children." He told the agent
that after having read the Director's recent speeches on the topic, he felt
that Hoover's "approach to the problem was in practically all effects, the
same as his." Spellman thought it "quite possible" that the FBI knew of
cases that could be used "to illustrate the necessity for the maintenance of
proper home life, school life, and church life of the juveniles of the United
States in order to prevent the rise of juvenile delinquency." He also wanted

any information the Bureau had on Communist involvement in programs dealing with juvenile delinquency.[114]

Hoover approved the transmittal of the information to Spellman through the New York Field Office. He sent to SAC Conroy a letter for the cardinal as well as information that was to be passed along verbally. The letter encouraged Spellman's efforts, told him that FBIHQ had put together some "data" for him on juvenile delinquency," and that someone (the name has been deleted) would soon be visiting him to "make it available." In the letter to Conroy, Hoover provided four examples illustrating "Communistic infiltration into youth programs," a pamphlet on junvenile delinquency, and six case files (undoubtedly in blind letterhead memoranda) on the same. "Of course, it is expected," Hoover wrote, "that the Bureau will not be considered the source thereof."[115]

Hoover did not always approve Spellman's requests for help. In 1946 someone who was ghostwriting an article for Spellman—perhaps Father John Cronin—asked Ladd to have FBI experts read a summary and give him suggestions as to how to proceed. Ladd recommended that "we do not do anything on this matter at this time."[116]

Another denial of Spellman's request for help, this one in 1956, reveals much about the relationship between him and the FBI. At 11:30 AM on February 23, Spellman called SAC Kelly and asked him to come to his residence. Kelly, who went over that same day, discovered that a U.S. senator—whose name is deleted—had contacted the cardinal, asking him if he had sent a $10,000 check to an individual (whose name is also deleted) in Minnesota as a campaign contribution. At Spellman's request, the senator provided him with a copy of the letter and the canceled check; neither the signature on the letter nor the check was the cardinal's. Would it be possible, Spellman asked, "for the Headquarters Staff at the Bureau to make a contact with the Senator so that the matter . . . could be handled quietly and without publicity." The SAC told him that he would check with Washington. Kelly, whose main goal was to help Spellman, thought that the FBI could use the fact that a "fraudulent mailing and forged signature on a check" had been sent interstate as an entrée to visit the senator and "see if he is satisfied with the Cardinal's response." If he was, "the Senator could be told of the Cardinal's hope that the inquiry could be handled quietly and without any publicity." Nichols did not oppose the idea. "If you concur," he wrote Tolson, "we will see that this is done."[117]

Tolson and Hoover, however, taking a broader view, vetoed the recommendation. Tolson simply replied, "I don't think we should do this." Hoover's handwritten comment was more revealing: "We can give no assurance as to what [name deleted] might do as to publicity." Several days later FBIHQ decided that Kelly should tell Spellman that the senator "is unpredictable[,] and since nothing has been stated by him so far concerning this matter, there is a chance that he may not use it but that if we would make contact with him it might plant an idea in his mind and then he may for sure have something to say about it."[118]

Hoover did approve help for the cardinal in another case. In 1954 Spellman received an "anonymous card" telling him about a book that was going to be published in Gerard, Kansas, "vilifying the Cardinal as well as the Church generally." An aide to the cardinal outlined what he wanted the Bureau to do: first, find out if such a book really was going to be published; second, discover the author's name; and third, provide information about the author. Spellman's thought was that "should the author have a Communist background or an unsavory background, this information could be placed by the Chancery Office in circles where it will do the most good in explaining the author's motives in writing such a book." Hoover's comment was, "See what we have."[119]

FBI files did not reveal any information about the plan to publish a book, but the Kansas City Field Office, which had jurisdiction over Gerard, suggested that the publishing firm of E. Haldeman-Julius was "capable" of putting out such a work. This firm, Hoover informed Kelly, "has in the past published various attacks on religion, especially the Catholic Church, as well as an inaccurate, scurrilous and libelous attack on the Bureau and myself in approximately 1948."[120]

Since it was now possible that an enemy common to both Spellman and the FBI was about to strike again, Hoover approved a leak: "You are authorized to advise Cardinal Spellman in a strictly confidential basis." There followed mention of not only some specific things the Cardinal was to be told but also certain documents he was to be given: (1) a "blind memorandum" exhibiting information from the 1938 Dies Committee report; (2) a photostat of a newspaper article on the indictment of the head of the publishing firm; (3) and a copy of an *America* article about the Haldeman-Julius Company. Someone at FBIHQ phoned Kelly and told him that he was to "handle this personally with Cardinal's office." This was done on January 10, 1955.[121]

Spellman's well-known reputation for being a political operator comes through in these episodes marking his relationship with the Director and his Bureau. Many bishops developed a friendly relationship—some even a genuine friendship—with Hoover, but Spellman does not seem to have done that. Outside of three brief moments—twice when the cardinal presented Hoover with CYO medals (1945 and 1963) and once when he spoke to a graduating class of the National Police Academy in 1946—the two men do not even seem to have been in each other's company. Although Spellman occasionally would join his fellow Catholics in the kind of praise for the FBI that was normally reserved for the sainted—he once noted that "FBI" stood for "faithful, brave, intelligent Americans"—he generally refrained from that kind of acclaim. Hoover's and Spellman's working relationship rested on a shared set of values, but the FBI files reveal it as primarily a pragmatic one: they were two very powerful men who had a common set of enemies.[122]

This examination of the Boss's bishops began with the conservative O'Hara but ends with the liberal Patrick Cardinal O'Boyle (1896–1987). Born in Scranton, Pennsylvania, and ordained in 1921, he served for several years as head of Catholic Charities under Spellman. In 1948 he became the archbishop of Washington, D.C., when that diocese was separated from Baltimore. Three years later a politically astute and experienced Catholic journalist and trade unionist wrote a memorandum in which he assessed O'Boyle's track record. He first discussed in great detail his firm commitment to desegregation. He then noted that as episcopal chair of the National Catholic Welfare Conference's Social Action Department, O'Boyle went "along completely with the thinking" of labor priests Fathers Raymond McGowan and George Higgins: he gave "them considerable leeway."[123]

But for O'Boyle, as for so many others, a commitment to the patriarchal family as the principle of order in society went hand in hand with liberalism. In 1953, for example, he gave the opening address to the twenty-first annual Family Life Conference, the theme of which was "the father, the head of the home." It is, he argued, "an old but unchanging truth that the father represents authority in home." Those who "learn and live by wholesome respect and authority in the home qualify as citizens who know genuine respect for public authority." In this way the "respect and authority deserved and commanded by the father are the source of respect for law itself in society at large."[124]

O'Boyle's relationship with Hoover and the FBI was unexceptional. His FBI file is, in fact, quite mundane. It consists almost entirely of invitations he and Hoover sent each other over the years. (For various reasons, each of them repeatedly had to turn them down.) There is no mention of his anti-segregation activities. O'Boyle warrants our attention because of the speech he delivered at the graduation exercises of the FBI National Academy in 1951. Established in 1935 in a successful effort to gain influence among police officers throughout the country, by 1951 the academy had graduated 2,311 officers. O'Boyle had been invited to give the commencement address in 1948 but declined because the date was Good Friday. He eagerly accepted this appearance.

O'Boyle's speech is important because of the way it demonstrates how he thought through the body. Its significance lies in the fact that O'Boyle was not so very different from any other bishop or archbishop—probably not so different from most priests—in using the body, in all its various forms, as a way of understanding the world. Somatic imagery looms large in the archbishop's talk.

The FBI, O'Boyle asserted, was "not simply the chance aggregate of individuals who pass qualifying tests for entering upon a noble work for the welfare of the country." There needs to be, he argued, "a bond and a spirit to knit men together into a powerful collective principle of action for the common good." The head of the FBI's body was the Director. "In your case," he told the graduates, "what enlivens your organization is the spirit that comes down from the head, as vital impulses flow from the brain to the heart and muscles of a man, to order a pattern of action suitable to the role and purpose of the organization."[125]

The FBI, though, was also an antibody for the larger body that was America:

> In serving these institutions of our democratic faith, the FBI is like the silent, invisible forces which are part of the biological system of vital assistance and repair to the living organism. Unless the organism contained these elements of protection, which respond to the needs of the body in injury and disease, destruction and disaster would much more frequently be the plight of men. We are the beneficiaries of these hidden and voiceless powers within us, doing their work in the silent depths of the body. Their presence and action is vital insurance that nothing goes astray in the organism without natural detection and defense. There is a parallel here with the work of the FBI, silent and alert guardian of our liberties in the health of the body politic of the citizens.[126]

CHAPTER 3

———— ∽ ————

Assistant to the Director
Edward Tamm and His
Chicago Connections

I T WAS AMERICA'S first postwar Eucharistic Congress. Honoring the
Real Presence of Jesus Christ and celebrating the centennial of the Diocese of Buffalo, it began September 21 and concluded September 25, 1947.
Among its highlights were the opening and closing pontifical Masses, attended by 15,000 and 20,000, respectively; the meeting for workingmen,
with 42,000 present; and Monsignor Fulton J. Sheen's speech before an
audience of 20,000. About 200,000 came to the congress's closing ceremo-
nies, where Francis Cardinal Spellman presided over the benediction.

"Sectional meetings" were scattered through the four days. These gatherings, seventeen in all, brought together Catholics with similar jobs to hear
speeches aimed specifically at them. More than a thousand teachers, for
example, heard Father Robert I. Gannon, S.J., president of Fordham University, tell them that they were "the last hope of saving the world from
complete degradation." About fifteen thousand "young men and women of
high school and upper elementary school classes" heard speeches by Frank
Leahy, Notre Dame's athletic director, and Father James Keller, M.M.,
founder and director of the Christophers.[1]

Edward A. Tamm, assistant to the director of the Federal Bureau of
Investigation, spoke to Catholic public service workers on the evening of
September 23. In the thorough, logical, and precise manner that had become his way of life, Tamm reminded his audience of their responsibilities
as Catholics. In words reminiscent of John Winthrop's sermon on board

the *Arbella* in 1629, he told them, "The eyes of the world are upon us." Catholics in public service, he said, were "failing the Faith," for among them there was "far too much graft, greed, dishonesty, impurity, excessive drinking, laziness, and deliberate and systematic untruthfulness." Instead of "honesty being the best policy—*policy becomes the best honesty*." In addition, Catholics who worked in the public sector overlooked or participated in "the squandering of public funds, the countless rackets, the gambling syndicates, obscene motion pictures, plays, and literature."[2]

Catholic public servants, Tamm argued, had to begin to change things in their "daily orbit." That meant starting with themselves and "working out from there." And, he continued, "it is precisely through the reformation of ourselves that we will restore all things one day in Christ. This is our responsibility as Christians; as members of the Catholic Church." Drawing on the inspiration of Keller's recently formed Christophers and rejecting political-structural change, Tamm repeated his central point: "If we improve our own moral conduct we will improve the conduct of those about us. If we improve the conduct of those about us we will improve the social order. For good people will make a good society and there is no other way we can get a good society."[3]

J. Edgar Hoover was Tamm's "example of what a public servant can do if he has the ideals, principles, faith—and lives by them." An "exemplary type of public servant" and a "man of sterling, [C]hristian, character," Hoover, though not a Catholic, put "to shame many, many Catholics who are in public life," said Tamm. He began his good efforts "as we all can begin, in his own daily sphere of work armed with Christian principles which he never lost."[4]

Edward A. Tamm was well positioned to discuss the responsibilities of Catholic public servants. After becoming a special agent in the Justice Department's Bureau of Investigation in 1930 (it did not become the FBI until 1935), he rose rapidly, gaining experience in a variety of positions and levels. In 1934 he was promoted from his post as special agent in charge of the Pittsburgh Field Office to the first in a series of key appointments at the "SOG" (Bureau shorthand for "seat of government"). Soon the FBI's third-ranking member, Tamm served as such until he resigned in 1948 to take a federal judgeship. For at least a time, he seems to have handled "Catholic matters" at the FBI. Hoover not only called him in whenever sensitive Church issues were at stake but also apparently relied on his judgment in this area, for again and again he accepted Tamm's written "recommendation for action" with a scrawled blue ink "Ok H."

Tamm's career provides an excellent case study of the advancement of a Catholic in the public sector. His early years in the FBI show what it was like to be a rising star during the formative years of Hoover's Bureau. But more specifically, Tamm developed a strong and dense set of male friendships among the Catholic clergy and laity in Chicago, connections that he would maintain even after he left the Bureau. He surely saw no tension between his role as a public servant and his religious obligations as a Catholic, but there is, as we will see, considerable evidence to suggest there was reason to do so.[5]

In 1948 Tamm told a Senate judiciary subcommittee that his request for a job with the Bureau of Investigation had originated in the fact that 1930 was "economically a very difficult year," though his application did not mention that practical consideration. "I have made application for appointment as Special Agent because of a natural interest which I feel in work of this nature," read the first line of his dictation test from his initial job interview. Tamm was quite impressive that day. His interviewer, Inspector J. M. Keith, noted his "gentlemanly demeanor and excellent appearance" and his "considerable mental alertness and sincerity of purpose." Tamm's dictation test was evaluated as "good," and his "Bureau test rating" was an 85. After receiving Keith's evaluation of "favorable consideration," Assistant Director Harold Nathan recommended that Tamm should be investigated, the next step in the hiring process. Clyde Tolson, on his way to becoming J. Edgar Hoover's right-hand man and best friend, approved Nathan's recommendation.[6]

The Bureau's examination of Tamm was thorough. It had to be, for the organization that Hoover had inherited in 1924 when he became Director was scandal-ridden, filled with political appointees and operatives trained in "old gum-shoe methods." Hoover soon had in place a "Manual of Instruction" that established strict guidelines for the behavior of special agents both on and off the job. Nothing was more important, read the 1927 version in its section titled "Applicants for Positions—Investigation Of," than researching the backgrounds of those applying for jobs.[7]

Agents interviewed acquaintances from every phase of Tamm's life. Having grown up in Butte, Montana, he went to Catholic high school in Helena, attended Mount Saint Charles College for a year, and then did two more at the State University at Missoula. Georgetown had awarded him a law degree just a few months before he applied to the Bureau. Tamm had worked several summers on the railroad, where his father, who had been employed there for years, probably helped get him the job.

Agents from the Washington, D.C., Field Office interviewed the two local references Tamm provided: the dean of the Georgetown Law School and Tamm's landlady. The dean, whose comments were highlighted by a mark in the margin of the transcript, "could not recommend him too strongly for the position." Tamm's "scholastic record" was "one of exceptional standing"; he finished fourth in his class and received the "prize in legal ethics his third year." (The dean also noted, in a comment that would not have failed to catch the attention of Hoover and Tolson, that Tamm had not missed a day of class in his two years at Georgetown.) Tamm's landlady added to the glowing report. He had stayed with her for a year, did not drink, and used tobacco "moderately." She referred to him as an "ardent Church member" and considered him to have "high morals."[8]

Investigating agents did not, however, limit themselves to interviewing Tamm's two references in Washington, D.C. Among others they talked to were railroad people with whom he had worked, his landlady in Bozeman, the father of a girl with whom Tamm had kept "company for several years," the family doctor, the principal of Central Catholic School, and several officials of the local mining company. Everywhere they found testimony to the "character" for which Hoover was looking. The president of the North Butte Mining Company, for example, whose daughter Tamm had been seeing, considered him a "young man of good reputation" and "exemplary habits" with "much energy and determination to succeed" and "a pleasing personality." Tamm made friends easily but was "careful of his associates." His personal habits were "of the very best."[9]

It is not surprising, then, that Tolson, in charge of personnel, placed Tamm's name on the "eligible list" the very same day that he received a summary of the investigation. Tamm was virtually everything Hoover and Tolson were looking for. His life's path—growing up in the West but coming east for school—was one with which they were familiar. His values— hard work, determination, and steadfastness—were theirs. His religion was not the same—they were both Protestants—but he was an "ardent Church member," and Georgetown was known to them.

Hoover sent out Tamm's appointment letter on November 11, 1930, and shortly afterwards he accepted the position. Later in the Bureau's history, training would be a much longer and more involved process, but for Tamm it lasted just a few weeks. His final grade in "Rules and Regulations" was 98 and in "Instructions" 100. The inspector in charge of the training school noted that there was an "excellent likelihood" that Tamm would develop into "a better than average field agent." He also observed "some latent executive ability" that he was certain would develop "with experience."[10]

Tamm spent little time at his first two posts—the San Antonio Field Office until January 8, 1931, and Kansas City until February 9 of the same year—but gained valuable experience and caught the eye of his SACs. At San Antonio, where he arrived for work on Christmas Eve, the SAC noted that he was the most impressive of the new men sent there for seasoning; Tamm had worked on National Vehicle Theft Act, White Slave Traffic Act, and Escaped Federal Prisoner and Impersonation cases but not as yet any National Bankruptcy Act cases, so the Kansas City SAC, probably at the request of headquarters, immediately put him to work on one. He filed two reports on the case, handling it, according to the SAC, in a "thorough and comprehensive manner."[11]

The Kansas City SAC's February 1931 "Special Efficiency Report" on Tamm was significant for two reasons. First, it brought him a supervisory position at FBIHQ. Second, it makes note of those values and personality traits that Hoover considered essential to the reformation of the Bureau, that is, its re-creation as an organization in his image. The SAC thought that Tamm "had ability considerably in excess of the average agent." Just as important, he had been "prompt" in reporting to the field office, performed his assignments in "the most careful manner," and "gave every indication of being most desirous of becoming thoroughly familiar with Bureau rules and procedures as soon as possible."[12]

Tamm's supervisory position apparently had a probationary period built in, because after about a month of supervising Motor Vehicle Theft Act cases, he was evaluated. Thomas Baughman, whom Tolson had replaced as Hoover's right-hand man and best friend, was "favorably impressed" with Tamm's "industry and ability." He "appears to be very ambitious" and "handles the work assigned to him rapidly." Any mistakes he made were due, Baughman reported, to his inexperience. He had, moreover, a "pleasing personality." In conclusion, he was qualified to "remain on one of the desks as a supervisor."[13]

The next step for Tamm, who was being tested at positions of increasing difficulty and responsibility, was one of the two assistant special agent in charge (ASAC) jobs at the New York City Field Office. Hoover and Tolson apparently wanted to promote him to SAC with a minimum of ASAC experience, but Tamm's youth slowed the process. E. J. Connelly, the New York SAC, noted these problems in his thirty-day report on Tamm. He is "an intelligent young man," Connelly wrote, and "is earnest and sincere in all of his efforts." Tamm had had little opportunity to work on his duties as ASAC, but Connelly had seen enough to conclude that "as to more serious matters or occasions which may arise," he seemed "a little immature, which possibly he can eradicate by experience." Connelly could not recommend his immediate promotion to SAC but thought he "should materially develop in the next few months." In sum, "his potential possibilities as an executive are dependent upon what he exhibits in the future in connection with his work here."[14]

Tamm spent two years as ASAC at the New York Field Office developing into the kind of special agent–supervisor Hoover wanted. During this
time he not only served under three different SACs but also was evaluated
by several different inspectors from FBIHQ. The reports on Tamm were
mixed: on the one hand, he was intelligent and hardworking and was
doing a great job; on the other, rigidity, sarcasm, and arrogance sometimes typified his supervision of the ninety agents assigned to the field
office. That Hoover never doubted that Tamm would develop into an effective leader became clear when the Boss overlooked an allegation of
alcohol use that could have ended Tamm's Bureau career.[15]

In January 1934 Tamm's life changed greatly. First, on January 19,
1934, the Director named him Pittsburgh SAC. He did so in a simple
one-sentence letter of appointment, but in response Tamm sent Hoover
a handwritten letter of about six pages in which he thanked him and told
him of his recent activities as SAC. The letter is important, for it suggests
Hoover's capacity for instilling in his subordinates the deepest level of
devotion. Moreover, it indicates the degree to which for Tamm, even at
this early date, Hoover and the FBI were becoming one and the same
thing, and he was merging with both. "I do want you to know," Tamm
wrote Hoover, "that I will give you, personally and officially, the utmost
of my efforts, energy, and ability twenty four hours a day." He continued,
"Please accept my thanks and gratitude for the opportunities which you
have opened for me, and my pledge that my entire endeavors will be to the
continued advancement and perfection of the Division under your most
capable guidance."[16]

The second life-changing event came in late January, when Tamm married. His engagement had been announced in both the *Newark Evening
News* and the *New York Times* in June 1933. Grace Sullivan, who had
graduated in 1932 from Trinity College, the "Catholic Vassar," wed Tamm
at the Church of the Immaculate Conception in Montclair, New Jersey,
on January 30, 1934.[17]

Tamm had been a Pittsburgh SAC only a few months when in May
1934 Hoover transferred him to FBI Headquarters. He immediately dug
into his duties, serving as an administrative assistant until October 1935,
when he was promoted to inspector. In both these positions he supervised
others and answered directly to Hoover. In August 1937 he became an assistant director.

Tamm's career at the Bureau had antedated the federal government's
war against crime, which was announced to great fanfare in August 1933,
but until his promotion to Washington, he seems to have been touched
little by it. While at Pittsburgh he led an unsuccessful raid in pursuit

of the notorious bank robber John Dillinger—and made the *New York Times* when he told reporters how robbers used code to guide their escape routes—but his real involvement in the war against crime did not begin until he moved back to FBI Headquarters.[18]

May 1934 was a particularly bad time to report for work at FBIHQ because of the shootout at Little Bohemia in Wisconsin's north woods that had occurred the month before. It was there that Special Agents Melvin Pervis and Hugh Clegg had badly botched an opportunity to capture Dillinger and another notorious bank robber, Baby Face Nelson. The criminals escaped, and an agent and one bystander were killed. This was just one of the most spectacular in a chain of events through which Hoover learned how ill prepared his FBI was for a major operation like the war against crime. The Director worked zealously, firing off an almost unending series of sharply written memos and terse telephone calls, to fix ongoing organizational problems.

Many of these missives went to Tamm. Some memos in Tamm's personnel file, while not tactfully phrased, were appropriate, for Hoover was, in his own way, teaching Tamm while continuing to routinize and improve operations at the Bureau. At other times, though, Hoover seems to have been dominating others for the sake of his own ego. At still other times, he was simply being mean. Nevertheless, Tamm apparently thrived under Hoover's management style.

Just a few months after he had begun his work as an administrative assistant, Tamm received a memo that illustrates this aspect of Hoover's administration. On July 25, 1934, Hoover expressed his "extreme displeasure" with how the "memorandum on the John Dillinger case was handled." Hoover reminded Tamm that he had given "specific orders several times" that there "should be maintained a current memorandum of all facts in this case." Moreover, he had brought it to Tamm's attention that this was not being done. Although Tamm himself was not responsible for preparing the memo, "it was in charge of a supervisor under" Tamm's direction. It was "imperative," Hoover told Tamm, that he "check the work" of his supervisors to make sure that it was "properly organized." Finally, he must "give immediate attention to a complete reorganization and a closer direction of the supervision of the supervisors' work."[19]

During one month alone, September 1934, Tamm received sharply worded notes concerning the absence of properly prepared press material, an inadequately prepared memo, the failure of headquarters to pass along to the field the identification of a machine gun, the absence of an "interesting case" memo on a prison escape, the failure to get out a "general letter" to the field offices on the Karpis-Barker crime gang, and the delay in sending out a circular. Nor does September seem to have been a particularly busy month in terms of the work of the Bureau. One of the lessons that the barrage of memoranda was teaching Tamm was that, no matter what pressing case was consuming hours and hours of his time, ordinary tasks still had to be done right and routine still had to be followed. Hoover's rebukes did not slow down for the next several years.[20]

In other respects, though, September 1934 was an exceptional month for Tamm. Not only was he directly supervising some of the operations in the war against crime, but also he apparently had taken over the Lindbergh kidnapping case when he was promoted. He must have been working an extraordinary number of hours per week, for Hoover graciously and profusely thanked Tamm early in October for his recent "tremendous help and assistance." Tamm's supervision of the Lindbergh case "over many long and weary months had contributed materially," Hoover wrote him, "to the successful outcome of that case," which had ended with the capture of a suspect.[21]

It was in September 1934, moreover, that Tamm, in the first of two instances, instructed operatives in the field to use rough interrogation methods to get information. The agent was "to go to work" on the prisoner since he is "yellow, and, of course, there is a way to deal with people like that." A "good vigorous physical interview" was the solution. Tamm told the St. Louis Field Office to provide a "substantially built agent" for one case, and in January 1935 he urged the use of "vigorous physical efforts" in the interrogation of another prisoner.[22]

There is some evidence that Tamm began to take the same approach toward supervising those below him that Hoover took toward supervising him. Tamm apparently had some of the same qualities in his personality—remember the comments on his managerial style when he was an ASAC in New York City—but working in such close proximity to Hoover may well have had an impact, as may the day-to-day pressures of the job. In late October 1934, for example, he held a "Supervisors' Conference" to discuss how to prepare weekly write-ups of investigations and how best to report major developments in "cases of current interest." Tamm assured Hoover that he "spent considerable time in emphasizing to the Supervisors the absolute necessity for more rigid examination of all current reports and mail passing across" their desks. If anyone committed a "major error," Tamm warned, he would "recommend" his "dismissal."[23]

Firing supervisors for "major errors" was "entirely proper," Hoover replied, but cautioned Tamm against overemphasizing punishment and fear. What was needed instead was the "proper training and supervision by you of the supervisors," since most of them were "new in their work" and "no doubt" found "many things confusing." Hoover did not want them "'rattled' or panic-stricken." These men, moreover, "have been reported as having potential possibilities for development, and consequently, I think that you should give particular care and attention to their training and development."[24]

This would not be the last time Tamm erred on the side of rigidity or spoke sharply to subordinates, but it was not his sole management strategy. When tempered, this tendency in his personality produced praise from those below. William Ramsey, who joined the FBI in 1933 and was killed in the line of duty in 1938, reportedly told a colleague: "We have some [damned] good men in the Bureau, and one of the best is Ed Tamm. If one calls him on an emergency, it seems that he knows all about the case already, or he learns right away what it is about, and he then tells you what to do without hemming and hawing. And you can depend upon it, if you do as he says, you are o.k. and there is no buck passing. We've lost some good men in the Bureau, and I hope that E. A. Tamm stays around a long, long time."[25]

Tamm's response to the former special agent who passed along this praise after Ramsey's death is worth looking at within the larger context of the developing relationship between Tamm and Hoover. Tamm sometimes responded to the regular salary increases and promotions that he received with letters that verged on the sycophantic; for example, on being promoted from one pay grade to another in July 1934, he told Hoover that he was "confronted with an actual realization of the inadequacy of printed words to properly express sincere gratification." His letter to the former special agent went even further than his thank you letter for the Pittsburgh SAC position in conflating Hoover and the Bureau:

> I feel that I, like many other men in the Bureau, am only trying to do in a feeble way what the Director does in magnificent fashion each and every hour of his all too busy career. Those of us who have achieved any degree of success in the Bureau's work I feel owe their success in its entirety to the standard which is set by the Director in his personal performance of the duties which are imposed upon him. I frankly believe that most of us are following in the footsteps of one who is much greater than any of us and consequently it is always my belief that the credit for not only the Bureau's accomplishments, but for the proper development of the Bureau's personnel is due solely to the Director.[26]

J. Edgar Hoover has since become so vilified all across the political spectrum, and so cartoonlike in the American imagination because of

rumors of cross-dressing and closeted homosexuality, that it seems virtually impossible that anyone in his right mind could praise Hoover in this
way. It has been forgotten that Hoover was a genuine leader of men and
had been so since he was a teenager. He provided both the organizational
framework and the context of leadership in which certain kinds of men
could develop their capabilities to the fullest. Tamm, like so many other
Catholics of his generation, was clearly that kind of man.

While Hoover and Tamm saw each other "practically every day" from
1934 to the latter's retirement in 1948, there is little available evidence on
their working relationship, let alone their personal one. The files suggest
such an overwhelmingly professional association between the two, however, that when evidence to the contrary appears, it seems obtrusively out
of place, but also illuminating.[27]

In September 1936, in a speech to the national convention of the Holy
Name Society, the Catholic men's devotional group committed to honoring the name of Jesus, Hoover defended the Bureau against its critics,
attacked "modern laxity" in raising children, and praised discipline in
society and the home. Tamm and another favored agent sent a playfully
formal telegram to Hoover: "Predicated upon past performances the Gold
Dust Twins expected superb presentation and delivery and are proud to
state that the speech exceeded even our most optimistic expectations.
Congratulations."[28]

Tamm's hard work, reliability, loyalty, and intelligence brought him yet
another promotion in August 1937, when he became an assistant director.
His duties at headquarters expanded as Hoover increasingly relied on him
to handle sensitive matters. Tamm, for example, played a significant role
in the Bureau's relationship with the House Committee on Un-American
Activities, which Congress established in 1938 to investigate dissident
groups on both the Left and the Right. Their political objectives were
similar, but Tamm and Hoover deeply distrusted the committee's chairman, Martin Dies, whom they considered a publicity-seeking loudmouth.
Tamm not only helped develop the strategy for dealing with the Dies-run
committee but also was the Bureau contact who handled its endless requests for information. These required sensitive handling because of the
committee's political support in Congress.

The new assistant director took care of other sensitive matters as well.
He was responsible for the Bureau's discussions with the Office of the
Attorney General about a 1937 Supreme Court decision concerning wiretapping. Several years later Tamm played a key role in Hoover's successful
efforts to get public statements of support from both the attorney general

and the White House in the face of increased criticism of FBI activities. That same year, 1940, he ran a political investigation for FDR.

Tamm also participated in what Athan Theoharis has shown to be the illegal and extralegal activities that came to be the norm at the Bureau. As a member of the FBI's Executive Conference, Tamm helped develop the "series of separate records procedures to ensure the undiscoverable destruction of especially sensitive records." Moreover, he personally approved, as part of his job, technical and/or physical surveillance and investigation of numerous targets when there was little or no basis in law for doing so. Among these were Inga Arvad, who had a wartime affair with John F. Kennedy, and Henry Grunewald, a private investigator who was politically well connected.[29]

He also continued doing more mundane work. In October 1937 he organized a luncheon at the Mayflower Hotel in Washington for members of the International World Police. Several months later Tamm arranged for the Bureau's "first annual Christmas tree." In January 1939 he went to Hollywood to consult on several movies featuring the Bureau. In June 1939 Tamm apparently helped arrange for Hoover to receive a honorary degree from Georgetown. In a "Dear Ed" letter, of which there were few, Hoover let Tamm know that he recognized the part he had played in the award: "I, of course, am not unmindful of the role you played and, through it all, I could see your loyalty and friendship." It was "rather difficult," he continued, "for one to express in words his true feelings, and so all that I shall attempt to do is to say 'thank you' from the bottom of my heart."[30]

America's entry into World War II found Tamm with a new title: Assistant to the Director. In early January 1941 Hoover successfully requested the attorney general to create this position, which recognized Tamm's standing as the FBI's number three man. As such, Tamm had responsibility for the Bureau's three investigative divisions: the Security Division, or Domestic Intelligence; the Investigative Division; and the Technical Laboratory. The assistant directors who headed these units reported to Tamm. During the war, moreover, he served as the FBI's representative to the Inter-Departmental Intelligence Conference and, of course, retained his membership, which had begun in the mid-1930s, on the Bureau's Executive Committee.

Relatively little about Tamm's wartime work appears in his personnel file. Hoover thanked him in March 1945 for the "grand job"—requiring "quick and careful decisions"—which he had done in Mexico City the previous month at the Inter-American Conference. (This work may have involved the Special Intelligence Service that the FBI operated in Central and South America during the war, which Tamm essentially oversaw.) Tamm also received praise for his month's work at the United Nations Conference held in San Francisco, where, Hoover wrote, his "planning and organization were responsible to a great extent for the successful culmination of the Bureau's assignment" (a reference to U.S. security operations).[31]

Tamm had worked and worried himself into physical and mental exhaustion by the time he returned from San Francisco. Constantly tired and under stress since January, noted his May medical report, he had begun taking a barbiturate every night because he could not sleep. Just one was ineffective, so he turned to taking a pill that was "readily soluble" and another that was "enteric coated" so as "to get [both] an immediate and [a] prolonged effect." Even so, they were "only partially effective in promoting sleep." Other symptoms were just as serious: his muscles had been aching since mid-April, and he had recently experienced a day of fever and chills. Moreover, he had been finding blood in his stool from time to time over the preceding three weeks. Since the fall of 1944 he had been alternating between diarrhea and constipation. He was tense all the time with "occasional dull headaches."[32]

Despite all these ailments, Tamm apparently had been planning on continuing work, for the doctor's notation indicates that he had come to the office simply "for a routine yearly physical examination." In mid-May he finally underwent a complete physical at the U.S. Naval Hospital. Since the war had begun, he taken just ten days off—so a doctor could attend to a problem with his arm. He was on call both nights and weekends, and usually got at least one call a night.[33]

The doctor doing the medical examination concluded that Tamm had a "fatigue syndrome that requires close attention." It should be relieved by "a rest and vacation from all Bureau activities." It was recommended that he spend a month relaxing "at a recreational spot of his own choosing," take no more night and weekend calls, and go on no more trips for the "immediate future." The doctor further advised a "general reduction in Bureau responsibilities," the elimination of barbiturates, and an examination before returning to work.[34]

Hoover, whose close interaction with Tamm must have—or should have—given him an idea that something was wrong, went further than the doctor in making his own recommendation. His "official orders"—as well as "personal wishes"—were that Tamm was to take two months off from work. Hoover, moreover, told D. M. Ladd, one of Tamm's key assistants, that Tamm was not to be told what was going on in the office. "There is not much sense in your staying away from the office," Hoover wrote Tamm, "when you keep in constant contact with it. The doctors indicate that there must be a severance by you from *all* Bureau activities and I intend to see that this is done." Hoover closed the letter, "Sincerely your friend."[35]

It is impossible to tell to what degree Tamm obeyed his doctor and the Director. (As we shall see in chapter 4, he was involved in the massive leak of documents to Father John Cronin that occurred during his time off.) Whatever the case, Tamm, who came back to work apparently well rested and rejuvenated, soon found himself and other high-level Bureau executives deciding to adopt a well-thought-out program to isolate and severely weaken the Communist Party of the United States. Although he was to leave the FBI before the completion of the program, Tamm was intimately involved in its origins and the frustrations and fears that produced it.

We know that Tamm, as a practicing Catholic, hated Communism, but beyond that we have little specific information about his attitude toward it. It was, moreover, only for a short period of time his primary responsibility at the Bureau. (As a member of the Executive Committee and the third-ranking FBI official, he would have been involved, of course, in every major decision concerning the CPUSA.) On two occasions prior to 1945, though, Tamm was significantly involved in matters related to Communism.

In 1940 Tamm recommended, in a move whose importance is impossible to exaggerate, that labor unions be investigated as part of the FBI's ongoing surveillance of "united front organizations." As a result, the FBI opened "Communist Infiltration" files on virtually every CIO union. Where there was considerable Communist activity, for example, in the United Electrical, Radio and Mechanical Workers of America (UE) or the Food, Tobacco, Agricultural and Allied Workers of America (FTA), the Bureau collected thousands of pages of information. Some of the most important portions of it, as we will see, ended up in the hands of anti-Communist activists.[36]

Merely collecting information, however, was not enough when it came to Soviet espionage. In November 1943 Tamm brought to the attention of Assistant Secretary of State Adolf Berle evidence of Russian use of the CPUSA to infiltrate the country's atomic weapons program. Tamm pressed him to "initiate a vigorous course of action," but Berle, in charge of security matters at the State Department, equivocated about how he proposed to handle this when he discussed the subject with the attorney general. Nothing, finally, resulted from this meeting.[37]

The refusal of the Roosevelt administration to take action against the CPUSA surely contributed to what appears to have been a growing sense of frustration on the part of Tamm and his colleagues. By 1945 the FBI had collected massive amounts of evidence that demonstrated the threat of Soviet espionage in the United States, CPUSA involvement in Soviet espionage, and CPUSA "infiltration" of and substantial influence in— if not domination of—numerous CIO unions. While almost all of this evidence was gathered illegally and/or extralegally and was therefore of little use in legal prosecution, its existence and implications cannot be disputed.[38]

Wiretaps (technical surveillance) and bugs (microphone surveillance) were the most potent illegal and/or extralegal weapons the Security Division employed against the CPUSA. While Ladd, the division's supervisor, normally approved their use, there is a record of Tamm's having done so at least twice before 1945. Agents installed a wiretap that Tamm sanctioned in August 1941, then, because it was "producing good info" on its target, the International Workers Order, a fraternal society led—if not dominated—by the CPUSA, the field office recommended that it be reestablished.[39]

Planting a bug was a more sensitive and labor-intensive operation than a wiretap because it often required surreptitious entry into the room in which the targeted discussion would be occurring. In one case a specially trained squad planted one with Tamm's approval. The Bureau discovered that Roy Hudson, who handled trade union matters for the Communist Party, had been deeply involved in the United Automobile Workers of America (UAW) convention. In a follow-up effort, a microphone, which was in place for more than four hours on August 23, 1942, transmitted a CPUSA meeting reviewing its convention activities.[40]

Tamm's growing frustration is obvious in two memos he produced in the year following his return to work. The first of these, written with the assumption that it would be destroyed, was addressed in early November 1945 to the Director. Tamm recommended the discontinuation of wiretaps on CIO unions in "which there is a strong element of Communist activity." Despite "our information about these Communist activities" in the unions, Tamm charged, "nothing whatsoever is done by the policy-making agencies of the Government" about it. Tamm concluded pessimistically: "I think we should, consequently, evaluate this coverage, particularly since the termination of the war, upon the basis of a realistic approach predicated upon the fact that no affirmative action is taken upon the information which we furnish. . . . When these technical surveillances are evaluated upon the basis of the question, 'What will anybody do about the information received from these technicals?,' we might as well face the fact that our effort is practically wasted."[41]

Tamm's conviction that the FBI was wasting its time continued into the spring of 1946. By then Louis Budenz, the onetime Catholic who had left the Communist Party and returned to the Church, was discussing with the Bureau whether or not he should name specific Communists and Soviet agents in America in his memoirs. That Tamm wanted to give Budenz the go-ahead was less significant than the reason why: "Despite all our coverage of Communist and Soviet Agent activities, very little practical good comes from it. It seems to me that if Budenz exposes a lot of these people and their activities, at least, it will render them impotent for future operations in the United States."[42]

What was the source of Tamm's frustration? Some of it probably came from the defeat the FBI had suffered in the *Amerasia* case—Tamm had missed the FBI's key decision-making moments because of his illness, but not the fallout—but much of it must have come out of his particular position in the Bureau. As assistant to the director, Tamm had immediate knowledge and awareness of CPUSA infiltration and spying, which produced a sense of urgency about the Soviet threat. The program Ladd suggested in February 1946 indicates that other key FBI officials shared Tamm's frustration. Worried about the outcry from "Leftist and so-called Liberal sources" should the Bureau have to arrest American Communists in the event of war with the Soviet Union, Ladd proposed a far-reaching program to counteract such a response: "It is believed that an effort should be made now to prepare education material which can be released through available channels so that in the event of an emergency we will have an informed public opinion." Creating that "informed public opinion," though, had tremendous implications and was nothing less than a declaration of war against the CPUSA and anyone who did not enthusiastically enlist in the battle under the leadership of the FBI and its allies. Ladd has been accused being rather simple-minded, but his analysis was acute and his agenda ambitious.[43]

The CPUSA's strength, which Ladd argued was "out of all proportion to the actual size of the Party," came largely from "its connections in the labor unions" as well as its support from liberals. Since Communism was in his opinion the "most reactionary, intolerant force in existence," it should be possible to "assemble educational material which would incontrovertibly establish the truth." Such material, as well as information "indicating [Communism's] basically Russian nature," would undermine the party's influence in the unions and reduce its support among "persons prominent in religious circles." He recommended that a two-day training conference for "Communist supervisors" from eighteen or twenty important field offices be held to implement the program.[44]

One important strand in the history of the post–World War II destruction of the CPUSA and those who worked with it is the recounting of the
FBI's efforts in putting this program into effect. Tamm's involvement in the
leak of documents to Cronin anticipated this program in that it provided
information that could be used to isolate the party. To this end, Tamm approved three bugs in 1947; information from one of them ended up in the
FBI office files of James B. Carey, secretary-treasurer of the CIO.[45]

The Archdiocese of Chicago was the largest and, arguably, the most important diocese in the country, so it was appropriate, from the Bureau's point
of view, that it had a special relationship with the FBI. To some extent the
connection between the two institutions was embedded in the friendship
between Hoover and Samuel Cardinal Stritch, but mostly it centered on
Edward A. Tamm, one of the country's most powerful Catholics, and the
staff of the chancery office.[46]

Stritch, born in Nashville, Tennessee, in 1887, was ordained in 1910.
Smart and talented, he quickly moved up in the Church's hierarchy. Consecrated a bishop in 1921 for the diocese of Toledo, he served there until
1930, when he was appointed archbishop of Milwaukee. In 1940 he came
to Chicago as archbishop and was named cardinal in 1946. He served
there until he was chosen for a Vatican post in 1958.

Hoover and Stritch were on friendly terms, but they had little direct
contact. Stritch's FBI "see references"—files not captioned under his
name but containing references to him—run considerably longer than his
main file. Perhaps the only time the two men met was in 1956, when the
Director spoke in Chicago to the National Council of Catholic Women.
The most important assistance the FBI gave Stritch came in the last
months of his life, when it expedited the travel of his personal physician
and a specialist to treat him in Rome.[47]

Stritch had trouble making decisions, and even when he did make
up his mind, he procrastinated in taking action. Moreover, he did not
work long hours. For all these "administrative failings," however, Stritch
was successful because he surrounded "himself with strong managerial
types and gave them virtually free rein." Monsignor Edward Burke, the
chancellor, and Monsignor George Casey, the vicar general, were two of
the managers who "virtually ruled" the archdiocese. Monsignor John D.
Fitzgerald, Stritch's secretary and vice chancellor, who joined Burke and
Casey among his closest advisers, was at the center of the archdiocese's
network of relationships with Tamm.[48]

The relationship between Fitzgerald and the FBI was mutually beneficial: Fitzgerald was a "fixer"—he connected people with jobs and with

other people—so from his side, his friendship with the Bureau was in part one piece of a larger set of connections. This comes through clearly in Fitzgerald's conclusion to a thank you note to Hoover for the FBI's help in what turned out to be Stritch's final illness: "Through the years you have never failed me or mine in the many crises in which my affections were deeply involved." From the FBI's side, Fitzgerald was the connection not only to Stritch but also more generally to Chicago Catholicism. Even after Fitzgerald had left the chancery office and taken a suburban parish, the Chicago Field Office recommended that he be designated a "SAC Contact." He was still "very close" to Stritch and had arranged for the Chicago SAC to meet the cardinal. He was, moreover, "invaluable as an entree into Catholic Circles in Chicago at all levels."[49]

Fitzgerald, who knew of Tamm through his brother, who had gotten to know his whole family while on vacation in Wisconsin, met him in 1945 in San Francisco. Stritch had sent his secretary ahead to serve as his "eyes and ears" during the nine-week period when the United Nations was being formed. The priest, whose credentials were signed by Alger Hiss, spent a good deal of time with Tamm, who was responsible for U.S. security operations. Fitzgerald gained considerable insight into Soviet espionage efforts and formed a strong bond with Tamm, "who laid an interminable mortgage on his admiration, respect, and affection."[50]

Tamm and Stritch, who must have taken to each other immediately, had a close relationship until Stritch died in 1958, long after Tamm resigned from the Bureau. On one level it was a question of business—the Church's business. Tamm, for example, wrote the cardinal in 1947 that he hoped they could soon meet to discuss the "many mutual matters of interest which are pending on our agenda." On another level it was a question of personal affection, for as early as 1946, Stritch had invited Tamm for a visit at Hobe Sound on Jupiter Island, the archdiocese's property in Florida. For Tamm, as he wrote Stritch in 1948, their friendship was "the richest page in my life."[51]

Stritch and Tamm had a multifaceted agenda. Sometimes it included European issues, for not only was the Church an international institution, but also the United States had a substantial stake in the postwar European settlement. At other times it involved domestic issues and politics; Stritch played an important role at this level because of Chicago's significance as well as his various positions in the National Catholic Welfare Conference, which represented the Church's interests at the national level. The two also took up internal Church issues, for the boundaries between the Church and the Bureau could be quite porous. Finally, local problems, though often handled by Fitzgerald, also were part of their agenda.

Two different but related twinges of conscience might have stricken Tamm as he pursued this agenda. First there was the hoary argument that Catholics could not make good public officials because their loyalty was to Rome. The second was something that Tamm himself, as we saw earlier, had spoken about in his Eucharistic Congress speech. Because the "eyes of the world are upon us," he had said, Catholics in public office had a special responsibility to be honest—that is, to act so that "honesty" was "the best policy" and not the other way around.There is no evidence, however, that Tamm had any compunctions about what he was doing. Surely he was convinced that there was no discrepancy between his obligations as a Catholic and as an American. Maturing, moreover, within an organization which assumed—as FBI files released under the Freedom of Information Act consistently reveal—that leaking documents and even lying to the public and other government entities were justified to ensure a higher good, Tamm sought the goals of both church and state. Combine this with the reality of the Communist threat and the attendant fear, and it becomes even clearer why Tamm crossed the line as he did.

The evidence for the ways in which Tamm and Stritch worked together on foreign policy is not terribly good, since the latter was often (purposely) vague in his correspondence with the Vatican's apostolic delegate. Furthermore, what was going on was sensitive, to say the least. What is clear, though, is that Tamm often served the Church, and he continued to do so after he quit the Bureau to take a federal judgeship.

That the best paper trail involves Italy is not terribly surprising. It was, of course, the Vatican's home. It also was the scene of a virtual civil war as the Allies and the Resistance overthrew Mussolini's dictatorship toward the end of the Second World War. The left was strong and articulate. The Italian Communist Party (PCI), in particular, was one of the best led in Europe and enjoyed considerable popular support.

One of the things Tamm did was to provide Stritch with information. Very likely he did so quite often, though this can be directly verified only once. Sometime in late 1946 the Chicago cardinal apparently asked him to figure out how much importance the Truman administration attached to the Vatican mission. Tamm's determination that it meant relatively little, combined with similar information collected a bit later by Gael Sullivan, a high-ranking Democratic Party official closely connected to the Chicago Church, led to a letter from Stritch to Archbishop Amleto Cicognani, the apostolic delegate, suggesting a way to turn that around.[52]

Tamm also intervened with others for Stritch and the Church. In May 1947, as political tensions increased in Italy, the cardinal had Tamm contact Charles Fahey, the State Department's legal adviser, about two distinct matters. First, "espionage services"—Tamm may have been the conduit here—had reported that Moscow was sending gold bullion to the PCI via airplane through Romania into Switzerland and from there across France to Italy. (He even knew what time the flights had arrived in Zurich.) The second bit of business that Tamm took up with the State Department was more crucial but less sensational. The Italian prime minister, by way of a priest from the Vatican's Secretariat of State, sent Stritch a message for Truman "giving in detail the urgent needs of Italy at this time." Before this priest saw Stritch, though, he gave a copy of the message to Gael Sullivan, who promised to take it up with Truman. Stritch, knowing how Washington worked, understood the necessity of getting this information to the secretary of state. He gave the memo to Tamm, who talked to Fahey, whose report on the State Department's current thinking about Italy Stritch then sent to Cicognani.[53]

Later that same year, in November, Tamm carried out another assignment from Stritch. Although Stritch's letter does not specify exactly what the FBI agent was to do, it does state that the Church was "depending" on him to "implement" the plan "as per" their "phone prattle of yesterday." Stritch wanted to be kept informed of progress on the matter. "We are further," the letter concludes, "into the enormity of our debt to you."[54]

The disposition of Libya and Eritrea, two of Italy's prewar colonies, was the subject of yet another of Tamm's tasks. These countries were important to the Vatican, and therefore to the American Church, so in April 1949 Fitzgerald sent Tamm memos offering suggestions on how to address the matter. The cardinal wanted Tamm to "have these confidential memos to place before [his] people."[55]

Tamm handled more than Italian matters for the Church. At Stritch's request he lobbied in favor of a loan to Great Britain during the summer of 1946. As part of that effort he followed up on the cardinal's visit with Senator Patrick McCarran, a Nevada Democrat, who declared himself "tremendously impressed" with his arguments. "I am continuing," Tamm wrote the cardinal, to "contact friends in Congress." He assured Stritch that he was doing everything he could as a "private citizen" to get the bill passed. A month later Stritch indicated how pleased he was with Tamm's work on the British loan: "I have been told that you did a good job for me. At least we have done our utmost."[56]

Several ambassadorships also engaged Tamm's efforts on behalf of the Church in 1946. He had been told—by whom it is unclear—that Stritch would be having a talk with the president, who might ask for recommendations for ambassadors to Brazil, Cuba, and Puerto Rico. Tamm provided Stritch with information on three men, noting that when Stritch gave someone his personal endorsement, any "subsequent misconduct will reflect upon you and the Church." In that sense Stritch's position was very similar to "ours in the FBI, because we likewise must assume a tremendous responsibility when we vouch for a man's character." Two of the men, Joseph B. Keenan and Edward P. Murphy, Tamm knew "intimately:" they "practice their religion because they believe in it." He did not know the third, Francis P. Mathews, with whom Father Cronin would soon be working, but Hoover did know him and was "much impressed with him." After suggesting which ambassadorship ought to go to each man, Tamm apologized for not having come up with other names, but added that all three men were "politically and personally acceptable" to the Truman administration. Stritch thanked Tamm for the information and told him they would discuss it during their visit in Chicago.[57]

At least once, Stritch had Tamm take care of a domestic issue. Rumors apparently had reached Duane G. Hunt, the bishop of Salt Lake City, that Bushnell Veterans Hospital at Brigham City was going to close. He went to Stritch, who went to Tamm. The surgeon general's office, Tamm was told "confidentially" by someone in the War Department, would announce the closing in four or five months. Tamm promised Hunt that he would keep in "close touch" with the situation. At some point in the next several months Tamm and Hunt met and discussed the issue. Tamm decided to approach Senator McCarran, who had been helpful previously, through Gus Vanech, a Department of Justice lawyer with whom he was quite close. Vanech talked to McCarran, who seemed to agree that abandoning the hospital was a bad idea and promised to talk to both Utah senators.[58]

Tamm and the FBI also aided the Chicago Archdiocese with a set of issues that were more local in nature. One was a personnel matter that might be referred to as "problem priests," on which they cooperated without publicity. Father Vincente Del Salto fit this category. Burke had conversations with both FBI and Immigration and Naturalization Service (INS) agents about Del Salto, who was being held for violating the terms of his visa and evading the draft. Chicago officials were unsure of his status as a priest, for he was working in a factory and not wearing a collar. The Dominican provincial thought he should be assigned to Ecuador, since there was no priestly work for him in the United States and the government would not let him stay on at the factory. He finally was deported.[59]

Father Charles van Estvelt presented a different sort of problem. The FBI had "held him under suspicion and shadowed him" because he had been in Alaska and was traveling from place to place. Van Estvelt had recently moved from Milwaukee to Chicago, but Stritch forbade him to say Mass and offered him no "hospitality." FBI agents were "watching his moves with suspicion," Stritch wrote the Apostolic delegate.[60]

The FBI's investigation of a Father Pothmann in 1946 illustrates further cooperation between the Bureau and the Church. In addition to sending along an FBI memo about Pothmann, which probably came from Tamm, Stritch told Cicognani that in their surveillance of the priest, the FBI agents had "tried to do their duty and at the same time save the Church from very undesirable publicity." They could have gotten a search warrant but preferred to work through Church authorities to keep things quiet. Pothmann was threatening to sue the FBI for illegal entry and search and seizure, but the FBI, Stritch said, had nothing to fear since it was only trying to help the Church. Stritch suggested that Cicognani have Pothmann's superiors tell him not to take any legal action.[61]

The INS similarly helped the archdiocese when, in July 1949, one of its agents came to Burke with a complaint about a Father Thomas, pastor of St. Francis "Mexican Church," who had been getting jobs for Mexicans in the United States on temporary visas. The agent told Burke that he did not want to get the priest in any trouble. When questioned by Burke, Thomas stoutly defended his actions. Hungry and without money, the Mexicans had come to him for help. He had offered assistance in only one or two cases. If he cooperated with the INS, the Mexicans would no longer trust the parish priests. Burke noted in his memo about the conversation that he thought the complaint was "not too serious," especially since the INS agent was not Catholic and a "bit prejudiced." Thomas pledged that he would not "knowingly" violate the law.[62]

The FBI and Tamm sometimes ran name checks for the archdiocese. In 1945, when a Frank E. Mason tried to get in to see him, Stritch had Fitzgerald check him out with Tamm. Mason, whom Tamm knew well, was "notorious" for being an "alarmist"; moreover, he had been "eased out" as special assistant to the secretary of the navy and failed to get work with Military Intelligence. He was now doing some work as a journalist. Tamm urged Fitzgerald to be quite cautious about anything on which Mason reported. Stritch passed along this information to the NCWC's assistant general secretary.[63]

Fitzgerald's memorandum on the check that he had run, for undetermined reasons, on two brothers, Dr. Frank Chesrow and David Cesario Chesro, tells us something about the closeness of his relationship with the FBI. When the Bureau leaked information, it normally did so in the form of "blind letterhead memoranda," which contained information from public sources; therefore there was there no indication where the memo came

from, and none of the information could be traced to the Bureau. It was
highly unusual for anyone outside the FBI, even those who were greatly
trusted, to be able to distinguish between these memoranda and Bureau
case files. Yet Fitzgerald understood the difference between the two. "The
FBI files" on the brothers, he wrote, "show nothing startling. All they
have are the usual information sheets—no case file." The blind letterhead
memorandum indicated that David was a vice president of the organization Aid to Italy and had once associated with Judge George Quilici, "who
is—as you know—the weed in our garden of posies." (Quilici had participated in what the FBI and the Church considered CPUSA front groups
during World War II.) There were rumors, moreover, that the two brothers
had helped Dillinger. Fitzgerald deemed the report "unsatisfactory."[64]

The relationship between Tamm and Catholic Chicago was not limited to
his friendship with Stritch and those in the chancery office. Nor was he
the only conduit between the FBI and Catholic Chicago. We now turn to
the other connections through which the Bureau and Windy City Catholics cooperated with each other.

An excellent window into this world is provided by a 1948 letter written
by Monsignor Fitzgerald in which he discussed the efforts of a "young
Catholic gentleman" named Stephen O'Donnell to get a Ford dealership.
O'Donnell had worked for Gael Sullivan, first in his role as assistant postmaster general and then as executive director of the National Democratic
Committee. O'Donnell, Fitzgerald wrote, "has been quite useful to us
through the years." Stritch, who had "formed a deep personal affection
and interest in Steve," had asked Fitzgerald to help him get "set up" outside of Washington. O'Donnell had applied for a Ford dealership in Chicago, but despite his excellent qualifications and assurances that it was in
the works, had not yet received one.[65]

Among the people Fitzgerald called on to help him out was Tamm.
Tamm talked "frequently" about O'Donnell with a former FBI colleague,
John Bugas, at the Ford Motor Company. (While serving as Detroit SAC,
Bugas had been lured away to head up industrial relations there during
World War II.) Bugas told Tamm that the hang-up was in Chicago. But
when William Campbell, another of the contacts Fitzgerald turned to,
spoke to the Ford counsel in Chicago, he was told that the problem was
in Detroit.[66]

Campbell was a central part of the network on which Fitzgerald depended and of which Tamm was an essential component. A 1928 graduate
of Loyola University Law School, he became Bishop Bernard J. Sheil's

closest adviser in constructing the prelate's social service empire and his personal attorney. (The bishop married Campbell in New York City in 1937.) In turn, Sheil introduced Campbell to George Cardinal Mundelein and helped connect him with the Democratic Party in Chicago. Campbell became the archdiocese's associate general counsel in 1933, and in 1935 he became the Chicago director of the National Youth Administration. Incorporating its functions into his law office, he handed out largesse to Catholic organizations, especially Sheil's Catholic Youth Organization (CYO). Extending his influence, he became a sometime intermediary between the Roosevelt administration and Chicago's Catholics. Though recommended by Sheil and Mundelein for a federal judgeship in 1938, he had to settle for district attorney for northern Illinois. In 1940 he was appointed a federal judge; from then on his political activities became more circumspect but possibly no less frequent.

Campbell's connection with the FBI originated as a result of his efforts, starting in 1931, to keep Sheil informed of Communist organizing in Chicago. Early the following year he provided the bishop with a lengthy report based on his meetings with the FBI and the Chicago Police Department's "Red Squad." The next interaction was in 1939, by which time he was district attorney. A notation appended to a letter in the FBI files from Hoover to Campbell in 1959 indicates that in 1939 the FBI "had some difficulty with Campbell in connection with some statements he made to the effect that he was incensed at the effrontery of Mr. Hoover in wanting advanced information on a tax case indictment." These troubles, though, were seemingly forgotten by 1942, when he received a friendly letter from Hoover, and certainly by the late 1950s, when Campbell's friendship with Richard D. Auerbach, the Chicago SAC, began.[67]

Auerbach performed many kindnesses for the archdiocese and also was a close friend of Campbell's. "I have become very well acquainted with him," Auerbach informed the Director, "and find he is an ardent admirer of you and of the FBI in addition to being a delightful social acquaintance." An FBI note reiterates that Auerbach was the "recipient of close personal confidences of the Judge," who had "expressed his personal admiration for the Director." Campbell, furthermore, had gone "far beyond the usual normal judicial bounds in supplying data to us," especially in a case that "was scheduled to come to trial" in Chicago in May 1959. In 1964, Campbell served on the nominating committee when Loyola University gave its first Sword of Loyola Award to Hoover.[68]

The FBI, of course, returned Campbell's favors. In 1964 it tracked down a person involved in an estate in which he was "interested," and in

1965 the Bureau helped him arrange a trip to give a commencement address in Omaha. In 1968 the Chicago Field Office twice warned him that demonstrators would be coming to the courthouse.[69]

Stephen Mitchell worked closely with all these men. Mitchell was a Catholic lawyer who had received his B.A. from Creighton and his law degree from Georgetown in 1928. He worked for General Motors for several years, then practiced law in Chicago from 1932 to 1942. After working for the government during the remainder of World War II, he came back to Chicago and set up his own law firm. Mitchell was an originator of Adlai Stevenson's "senator/governor movement" and ran Stevenson's presidential campaign in 1952. Stevenson also chose him to head the Democratic National Committee. A practicing Catholic, Mitchell served on the board of governors of the Catholic Lawyers' Guild of Chicago.[70]

Mitchell wrote Fitzgerald in 1949 that he had had a "good lunch" with Fitzgerald's uncle, and later that same year Campbell and his family spent the week of July Fourth at Mitchell's vacation home. The year before, he had helped set up a luncheon at Stritch's residence for Arthur Krock of the *New York Times* and several others, including Fitzgerald. Stritch, Mitchell wrote Krock, was "delighted at the prospect of visiting with you in an informal way."[71]

In 1950 Mitchell and Campbell worked together, at Stritch's request, to stop a World Bank loan to Yugoslavia because of religious persecution there. In January there was a meeting in Campbell's chambers, and within several weeks the operation was in full swing. Both men first went to work on their friends in the banking elite. Mitchell then talked to a State Department official, to Krock, and to his fellow journalists David Lawrence and Walter Lippman. Campbell not only used his connections with Chicago bankers to get to Allen Dulles, one of the most powerful financial men in the country, but also talked with Ben Cohen, the U.S. delegate to the United Nations. Stritch, who considered this a better strategy than "any sort of mass protests," was quite happy with the work of Campbell and Mitchell.[72]

Tamm and Mitchell, who may have known each other at Georgetown Law School, not only traded favors but also became good friends. In 1948 Mitchell wrote to say how pleased he and the other Chicagoans were with the way Tamm's nomination for a federal judgeship was proceeding: "Fitz could not be better pleased for as you know he is extremely interested in anything that affects you." Mitchell did his share, as we will see, in the successful effort to gain him this position. "Your ears should burn this noon," Mitchell wrote Tamm, "when Fitz, Bill Campbell, and I have lunch together." Mitchell apparently visited with Tamm often when he came to

Washington. By 1951 their deep friendship was a central element of the network centered on Fitzgerald, as Mitchell indicates after he spent time with Tamm: "I passed along a full report to Bill [Campbell] and 'Fitz' this morning. Bill has half a mind to go to Florida with you."[73]

The relationship of these Chicago Catholics with the FBI extended far beyond their connections with Tamm. We have seen evidence of some of this, but there is still more. While in certain cases only a little information exists—Mitchell, for example, noted in 1949 that the Chicago SAC was "well and favorably known to us"—in others, considerably more is available.[74]

The New World, the Chicago Archdiocese's weekly newspaper, consistently supported Hoover. In its longest and most pointed praise, it noted, after discussing the upcoming HUAC investigation of Communist infiltration of Hollywood, that Hoover was one of those "men in high station who are fighting this menace to the wall." A "solid American," he not only had "warned" the country that "red penetrations constitute a real threat to our community," but also had "armed the government and the people with a huge pile of facts." *The New World* printed lengthy excerpts from a speech that Tamm delivered to the Holy Name Society and later gave much attention to his judicial nomination. (Of course, none of these articles mentioned the close relationship between archdiocesan officials and Tamm.)[75]

The newspaper's most significant discussion of the FBI came in its question and answer section. Responding to an inquiry about the Spanish Inquisition, *The New World* wrote that in order to understand it correctly, one had to "envision a nation in which one faith is common to all," where "the close alliance of Church and State made unity and purity of faith essential" not only to the Church but also to "civil society." In such a society, the response continued, "heresy was an attack on the essential beliefs of the people and was regarded as a crime which the secular ruler was bound to investigate and punish." In fact, "it is the history of mankind that no individual or nation tolerates attempts to contaminate or destroy its essential beliefs," *The New World* concluded. "In this pattern, we in the United States have Congressional committees, the F.B.I., etc., empowered to inquire into, to prosecute and to punish those guilty of subversive actions against the principles and practices of democracy so dear to every one of us."[76] Could there be a more revealing statement of the relationship between the FBI and the Catholic Church? Most American Catholics had come to identify their religious values so completely with those of the American state that whatever they considered an attack on the latter was also an assault on the former.

The connections between the Chicago archdiocese and the Chicago Red Squad illustrate this conflation of church and state at the local level. The Red Squad—or "Industrial Detail," as it was officially known—gathered information on radicals and kept tabs on them. It illegally tapped phones and probably obtained information through break-ins. The Red Squad, bitterly despised by radicals, most trade unionists, and civil libertarians, was a constant presence at Chicago strikes and demonstrations from the late 1920s through the 1960s. Like its counterparts in other large American cities, this group, which freely shared its information with those who shared its values, was largely made up of Roman Catholics.[77]

Campbell went to the Chicago Red Squad in December 1931 for information on Communist organizing. He knew the captain who headed it, William Killeen, whose response to Campbell began, "My dear Bill." Campbell soon met Lieutenant Make Mills, who ran the detail on the ground. Mills provided him with a good deal of information, which he passed along to Bishop Sheil in 1932 and 1933.[78]

In December 1944 Stritch received questionnaires from Father John Cronin for the report he was preparing for Catholic bishops about the CPUSA. He asked Father Bernard M. Brogan at Catholic Charities to have them filled out and suggested that he go to Mayor Edward Kelly for Red Squad intelligence: "I think he will let you have some very valuable information which is in the Chicago Police files." Several months later Brogan returned two questionnaires. One had been filled out with the help of Mills and Police Commissioner James Allman, the other with aid from Campbell and the Chicago SAC.[79]

Other information on the relationship between the Chicago Church and the Red Squad dates from 1949. Because of a papal decree that excommunicated Catholics who were Communists but even ruled that Catholics could not read Communist literature, Chicago Catholics who worked on the Red Squad had to get special dispensation to do their work. Father Thomas Meehan, editor of *The New World*, in the course of helping them get this permission, revealed much when he declared that the members of the Red Squad, "all Catholics," he wrote, had been "most helpful to me at *The New World*." The members of the squad in 1949 were Joseph Ternes, a "practical Catholic" from St. Leo's parish; John Posvic, a "practical Catholic" from St. Ludmilla's; William H. Hayes, "a very good Catholic" from St. Genevieve's; John O'Brien, who demonstrated "practical and fervent Catholicity" at Resurrection; Thomas F. Ryan from St. Barnabas; Frank Shea, a "good Catholic" from St. Francis of Rome in Cicero; Richard Gorecki, a "staunch" Catholic from St. Michael's; John

Czaplewski, from Our Lady of Victory; and Frank J. Heimoski of St. Rita's, who headed the squad.[80]

Evidence still exists for one of the "enumerable [*sic*] occasions" on which Heimoski helped Meehan. Sometime in 1948 Stritch asked Meehan to collect information on the Civil Rights Congress (CRC), an organization in which CPUSA members and "fellow travelers" played an important role. (This inquiry probably occurred because of the CRC's efforts to gain political advantage from the Chicago run of the Jesuit George Dunne's play *Trial by Fire*.) Meehan apparently asked Heimoski to provide information on the CRC, because a folder on the group, complete with several letters from Heimoski, survives in the archdiocesan archives.[81]

Heimoski's opinion of *Trial by Fire*, which sharply condemned racism and segregated housing in its depiction of an official cover-up of the terrorist murder of a black family, is worth looking at. Heimoski considered the play, which he had seen, a "noble cause." That said, though, he had a serious criticism: the "parts dealing with the law enforcement officers and the Federal Bureau of Investigation appeared overplayed, and tending to place lawful authority in a ridiculous light." The CRC was pushing *Trial by Fire*, Heimoski wrote Meehan, because of its antiauthoritarianism.[82]

Sometime toward the end of 1947 Edward A. Tamm decided to find a new job. While the official reason given was money—the college education of his children was on the horizon—apparently he could not continue to work the long hours that he had previously put in. Stritch first tried to set him up with a job in Cincinnati. He then provided, in Tamm's words, "gracious aid" with regard to a vacancy on the U.S. Court of Customs and Patents Appeals. In the course of thanking Stritch for this help, Tamm wrote that a judicial position was especially attractive because "medical reasons" required that he adjust his "working pattern."[83]

The possibility of a judicial position came closer to reality on February 1, 1948, when President Harry S. Truman nominated Tamm for an opening on the District of Columbia's Court of Appeals. It is impossible to know precisely who played what role in Tamm's securing this nomination, but several things are clear. First, Hoover could not have been telling the complete truth when he told a newspaper that the nomination came "as a surprise," since he would certainly have been consulted before the fact; Tamm, after all, was the number three man at the Bureau. Second, Stritch probably played some part in it, and perhaps Fitzgerald and Campbell as well. The day after the nomination Tamm wrote the cardinal: "Were it not for your confidence in me, I know that I would not have been selected for this high office, and I, consequently, acknowledge my deep and lasting obligation to you."[84]

Tamm's nomination, however, quickly ran into substantial obstacles. The first hurdle was the District of Columbia Bar Association. Not only had Tamm never practiced law, but also, as it turned out, he had never even taken a bar exam. Although he had been admitted to the Minnesota bar in 1943 and allowed to practice before the Supreme Court in February 1947, his application to the District bar had been denied. This organization, which asserted that the attorney general had ignored the role it traditionally played in the process of selecting judges, polled its membership about Tamm: they voted 900 against him to 173 for him.

The second obstacle was even more serious. The day before the Senate Judiciary Subcommittee was to begin its hearings on his nomination, word got out that the Republican senators intended to try to reopen their investigation into the Kansas City vote fraud of 1946. Republicans had first made an issue of this corruption incident, which took place during a congressional election, when they held hearings in 1947. At stake was the question of who was responsible for the FBI's admittedly limited investigation, Attorney General Tom C. Clark or the Bureau? (If the former, could it be tied to Truman because of his connections to Tom Pendergast, boss of the infamous Kansas City Democratic machine? And if the latter, exactly who?) Republicans had a field day with Hoover's testimony, which strongly suggested that Clark had limited the investigation through his instructions to the Bureau. The Director then released a statement saying that his testimony had been misunderstood. Toward the end of July 1947 Senate Republicans, after a "turbulent" all-night session, gave up their efforts to force a far-reaching investigation of the matter.

Although the vote fraud issue and the District Bar Association stood in Tamm's way, he had powerful supporters. Some of them appeared as his witnesses during the hearings. Others, however, worked behind the scenes. Stritch had "Junior" (Bishop William D. O'Brien) get unidentified bishops to write letters on Tamm's behalf. Mitchell apparently busied himself working for Tamm's nomination in a variety of ways, though there is firm evidence only for his efforts with Irving Dilliard, a *St. Louis Post-Dispatch* editorial writer. He apparently worked on Dilliard to have the paper's Washington correspondent write a favorable story on Tamm's nomination. Mitchell never found out if his "St. Louis friend got into action," but his efforts—as well as those of Stritch—suggest some of the ways in which the Chicago Catholic network functioned.[85]

FBI personnel also actively worked for the nomination. Just a few days after it was announced, the St. Louis SAC called Tamm and asked if he should contact, through intermediaries, a Missouri Republican senator, Forrest C. Donnell, who was on the subcommittee. Tamm reported to Hoover that he told the SAC not to do this or "anything else which could be construed by any hostile persons as any activity or action on the part of the Bureau officially to influence my nomination." The most important thing was to avoid action that "might result in any criticism of the Bureau." Hoover, not so scrupulous, scrawled on Tamm's memo, "If he knows someone well enough there is no objection." A few days later Donnell invited the St. Louis SAC to breakfast to discuss the nomination. The senator gave him some information about the upcoming hearings and then asked for copies of Tamm's articles and speeches. Louis B. Nichols, the head of public relations for the FBI, asked permission to collect the material and have the SAC pass it along to Donnell. Tolson approved the request and sent it on to Hoover, who wrote: "Yes & do *at once*. H." (This effort to swing Donnell's vote backfired; he not only voted against Tamm but also outwitted Hoover, for he developed a line of questioning based on both the subject of and the audience for Tamm's speeches, referring to the speeches by title, date, and venue.)[86]

The Bureau had not yet finished promoting Tamm's nomination. The Atlanta SAC was given qualified approval when he asked permission on February 16 to get his predecessor involved in helping Tamm. An internal memo on the request reads, "I told Mr. Foltz [Atlanta SAC] that we in the Bureau considered Mr. Tamm's nomination to the Judiciary as a high honor and that, of course, any action that Mr. Smith [former Atlanta SAC] wanted to take would be entirely up to him." The next day Nichols had a conversation with a Michigan senator during which he provided him with important Department of Justice inside information and brought up the Tamm nomination.[87]

The first day of Tamm's confirmation hearing was February 18, 1948. More than a dozen witnesses testified for him, and he won great praise from Clark and Hoover. Tamm began his testimony toward the end of the day, when he "admitted" to a questioner that he had personally directed the Kansas City vote fraud investigation. He was the sole witness during the second day's three-hour hearing on February 19, when the only topic of discussion was the corrupt election.[88]

Tamm, who stood up under intense scrutiny, took responsibility for the Bureau's failure to do a complete investigation of the vote fraud. He felt, as he told the subcommittee, a sense of "personal shortcoming and dereliction." Tamm refused to be trapped into blaming either of his superiors, Hoover or the attorney general. He publicly apologized to the former—"I probably am responsible for embarrassment of Mr. Hoover which should not have been his"—and testified that the latter had not put any restrictions on the investigation.[89]

Access to internal FBI communications via the Freedom of Information Act provides private confirmation of Tamm's public testimony. In a memorandum to Hoover dated June 18, 1947, Tamm says exactly what he later told the Senate Judiciary Subcommittee. He informed Hoover that he had approved the "memoranda submitted to you by the Security Division concerning handling of the Kansas City election fraud case" and "the preparation of the brief for your testimony before the Senate Committee." (These memoranda did not tell Hoover that the investigation was incomplete.) Referring to D. M. Ladd, who headed the Security Division, and a supervisor who worked under Ladd, Tamm wrote, "To summarize, therefore, I feel that the responsibility in this matter is a three-fold one and that any responsibility in the case should not be directed solely to Mr Blakesley but should be rather directed to Mr. Blakesley, Mr. Ladd and myself."[90]

The hearings held on March 2 and March 18 focused on the glaring reality that Tamm had never practiced law. The testimony of Austin F. Canfield, past president of the District Bar Association, was particularly devastating. Although Tamm was "one of the cleanest, most decent, most intelligent men" he knew, and there was "none firmer or of more capability," Canfield opposed his appointment. He had no experience, while the last ten or eleven judges to be appointed had come from the Department of Justice. Other testimony looked into why Tamm had not been admitted to the Minnesota bar.[91]

The Senate Judiciary Subcommittee did not meet again until the first week in May, when it voted 2–1 (Donnell voted against Tamm) to send his nomination to the full Judiciary Committee. The decision was shrouded in secrecy—none of the subcommittee members had anything to say when they emerged after voting—but word soon leaked out. Mitchell, for example, reported the vote to Dilliard, noting, "This is the best that could be expected." Tamm responded stoically when his nomination expired without action by the Senate Judiciary Committee. He thanked Stritch for his support and told him that he thought a committee vote would have gone 10–3 in his favor. It had been a long five months, during which he had been under "every possible type of attack," he wrote, but the experience "had made him a better person."[92]

While there were particular reasons why senators were uneasy about Tamm's nomination—the obvious interpretation was that the judicial nomination was a payoff to Tamm for taking the blame for the botched Kansas City investigation—in the end it failed for reasons having nothing to do with him. Republican senators had blocked eleven of Truman's nominations, either refusing to consider them or else rejecting them outright. The Republican Party, convinced that it would win the presidential election in November, believed, according to the *New York Times*, that "it should have the plums to offer candidates of its own choosing."[93]

Truman, never one to back away from controversy, made recess appointments of all eleven, including Tamm, on June 22, 1948. Although this was something of a gamble—he would have to be renominated and then approved by the Senate—Tamm quit the FBI on June 25 after twenty-eight years of service and with 702 hours and 30 minutes of vacation time owed him. In his letter of resignation he wrote that it had "been a pleasure and privilege to serve under" Hoover's "magnificent direction through the years." In response, Hoover thanked Tamm for his "intelligent, loyal and successful work" and noted that he had "handled a great many matters of importance in a very skillful manner." Tamm, with his two children and wife looking on, was sworn in on June 28 in a robe presented to him by the FBI Executive Committee, on which he had so long served. On being installed as a judge in late June, he received flowers from both Stritch and Hoover.[94]

Controversy, however, continued to dog Tamm. (It had even permeated his swearing-in, from which local lawyers were conspicuously absent. A Washington newspaper wrote that "seldom has there been so cool a ceremony.") Critics raised several questions about his appointment. First, should the number of days allotted to his temporary term begin with a thirteen-week vacation, since the District Court was now in summer recess? Second, how long was his recess appointment for? Third, would he have to be reappointed during the special session of Congress that would soon begin? And fourth, was he eligible to receive pay?[95]

Two occurrences ended Tamm's problems. First, toward the end of August the controller general ruled that the three federal judges serving recess appointments "could continue to serve and draw pay" until after the new Congress began in January. Second, Truman's victory in November meant that a permanent appointment for Tamm, as the *Washington Times-Herald* asserted, could now be "rated a certainty," since Republicans had been primarily responsible for the Senate's earlier non-action. The prediction was accurate: Truman renominated Tamm for the position which he currently occupied, and a Senate judiciary subcommittee differently composed than the previous one held several hearings, which attracted little attention. On March 29, 1949, the Senate unanimously confirmed Tamm's appointment as a federal district judge.[96]

"Judge Tamm's Many Interests Span Fishing, Poetry, Sports Cars," read the headline in a Washington newspaper in 1958. In great detail a reporter examined Tamm's hobbies and enthusiasms. He owned several sports cars, including the Jaguar he was currently driving; showed his horse about thirty times a year; had owned a prizewinning bulldog; and was an "incurable fan" of the Washington Redskins. (He had been following a Redskins game in 1941 when he was called by the Honolulu SAC, who held the phone out the window so Tamm could hear the sounds of the Japanese attack on Pearl Harbor.) "I've always believed," Tamm told the reporter, "that fatigue is nothing more than boredom." This story affirms what one senses in the material that exists on Tamm's life after he retired from the Bureau: life was good; leaving the FBI had been the right thing to do.[97]

During the seventeen years that Tamm served on the U.S. District Court, several of his judicial decisions found their way into the *New York Times*. In a delicious bit of irony, Tamm issued an injunction in 1954 preventing the National Labor Relations Board from decertifying the Fur and Leather Workers Union as a collective bargaining agent because Ben Gold, its president, had been convicted of filing a false affidavit that he was not a Communist. Gold praised the decision as a "victory for the democratic rights of labor and a defeat for official lawlessness."[98]

The *Washington Post* returned to the issue of Tamm's original judicial appointment when President Johnson named him to the U.S. Circuit Court of Appeals for the District of Columbia in 1965. It noted editorially that there had been legitimate reasons to "challenge" the original appointment, but that Tamm's service had been "an overwhelming response to that challenge." He had "won general recognition as a trial judge of great fairness and firmness," whose "devotion to the law and his understanding of it" had been "enriched by his experience on the bench." There was every reason to think that Tamm would be a "discerning and dedicated appellate judge."[99]

Tamm lived up to the *Post*'s expectations. The Circuit Court of Appeals became during his tenure a "leading force in the protection of defendants' rights." While Tamm did not always vote with its "liberal wing," he was "seemingly guided," the *Post* said, "by a common-sense approach to the case at hand." In 1977 he set aside a Federal Communications Commission ruling that the "seven [dirty] words" could not be spoken on the radio. The FCC, he wrote, had entered into the "forbidden realm of censorship."[100]

On leaving the FBI, Tamm had accurately predicted in his resignation letter that he and Hoover would continue the "happy relationship" they had "built up through" the years. Elements of Tamm's relationship with Hoover and the FBI after his retirement present an interesting contrast with the *Post*'s analysis of his years as a judge.[101]

Tamm's commitment to protecting defendants' rights could not have come easily. Only the very deepest veneration of and respect for the law could have overcome his traditional views on the relationship between the individual and society and the criminal and society. These views, at least as Tamm privately expressed them to Hoover, did not change over time, as he consistently praised his former boss's continuing promulgation of the values and morals they had espoused as FBI officials. In 1958, for example, he applauded a speech Hoover gave before the American Bar Association and hoped that the "very substantial sentiments expressed by you will be taken to heart, especially by the Judiciary." The "pendulum of judicial action has swung about as far as society can tolerate it," Tamm wrote. A "more realistic appraisal of the rights of society, especially in criminal cases," was a necessity.[102]

The praise Tamm extended to Hoover for this speech is only one example of the dozens of letters he sent Hoover over the years. Even though Tamm knew that the Director wrote relatively few of his speeches and articles himself, he extravagantly praised them and Hoover in a way that is embarrassingly reminiscent of the sycophantic letters he wrote when climbing the bureaucratic ladder in the 1930s. In 1960, for example, he told Hoover that he had been "tremendously impressed" with his testimony before the House Subcommittee on Appropriations. Later that same year, in the course of praising another speech, he wrote, "Your views are so sound upon this subject—as they are on so many other subjects—it gives me a great sense of pride in your intellectual integrity when you place principle before self." In 1966 he told Hoover that the FBI National Academy—where law enforcement officers from around the country came for intensive training—"constitutes a living monument to your farsightedness and courage."[103]

There is something almost creepy, however, about the apparent ease with which Tamm transferred his allegiance from Hoover to Clarence Kelley, who became FBI director after Hoover's death. In 1974, referring to a profile that had recently appeared, he told Kelley: "Most certainly this biographical sketch, which will reach literally thousands of government lawyers and judges, will add substantially to the high esteem to which you are universally regarded." In a near-blasphemous excerpt from another letter to Kelley, Tamm wrote: "I once felt that while a successor would undoubtedly be appointed to replace Edgar Hoover, no one in reality would take his place. The excellent manner in which you are conducting the

Bureau's diverse and difficult operations has caused me to think that you are actually taking his place."[104]

Mutual assistance typified the relationship between Tamm and the FBI after his retirement. From the surviving evidence, apart from significant efforts by an American embassy official in Paris to get the judge's son a job, Tamm benefited primarily by receiving travel assistance for both himself and his friends. In 1952, for example, agents in Paris and London, at Tamm's request, helped friends of his with their travel. In 1954 the Boston Field Office extended Tamm and his wife "courtesies," and two years later, an agent arranged, on behalf of a friend of the judge's, "to expedite clearance with the customs and health inspectors." In 1958 the San Francisco Field Office gave Grace Tamm "an extensive tour of the points of interests" in the city and the "surrounding area." The Tamms reeceived help during a twenty-fifth wedding anniversary trip to Mexico and similar aid on a trip to Tamm's hometown in 1970.[105]

What did Judge Tamm do for the FBI in exchange? One thing he did was to provide Hoover with bits of information about judges and the judicial system that, when combined with other bits of information, could be significant. For example, in 1952 he sent along a letter that a district court judge in Portland, Oregon, had sent to his colleagues concerning an FBI matter. In 1958 he passed along rumors and a newspaper clipping about a potential judicial vacancy in Honolulu.

At other times, however, his help was more substantial. In 1961 he acted as an intermediary with the FBI for MGM's proposed television series on the Bureau. In 1965 he informed Hoover about a reported meeting between Congressman Don Edwards, a former FBI agent, and three radicals closely associated with the CPUSA, during which they supposedly wrote a bill, later introduced in Congress, to abolish HUAC. Tamm did not want to give Hoover the name of his informant, a former assistant United States attorney, but would do so if it later became "essential." In 1968 he told Hoover that judges were talking about a *Georgetown University Law Journal* article that discussed the FBI's role in the pre-trial investigation of jury panels. Tamm, convinced that the article was mistaken, asked Hoover for the correct information so he could inform the judges. Hoover not only provided Tamm with a long memo but also sent a letter to the law journal.[106]

Tamm's aid in a least two cases was even more substantive. In 1958 Hoover sent Tamm six copies of a memorandum on Michigan Supreme Court Justice George Edwards. The memo, which contained only "public source material," accused Edwards of having been a socialist in his youth. Edwards had introduced and successfully fought for an "Advisory Council of Judges, National Probation and Parole Association" resolution criticizing Hoover. The Director clearly intended that Tamm pass along copies of the memo to judges to let them know about Edwards's background. It seems safe to assume that Tamm complied with the implicit request.[107]

In January 1971 Tamm telephoned Hoover to alert him that Chief Justice Warren Burger would be calling about a plan to place former FBI agents in the federal and state court systems as "court executives." Tamm explained what Burger would propose so Hoover could be better prepared to respond when he called. Tamm thought that, in addition to their executive responsibilities, "they could be a tremendous force for keeping some of these stupid appellate opinions from coming out." Hoover, who agreed with him, also noted that there was "the opportunity for the man to ultimately become a judge." For Tamm, however, the most "important thing was to bring a sense of realism into some of these [judicial] deliberations."[108]

"The eyes of the world are upon us," Tamm told Catholic public service workers in Buffalo in 1947. We will be judged, he said to the assembled men, not only by how well we do our job but also by how well we meet the "superior requirements expected of us as Christians; as Catholics who have a rational philosophy, a holy religion and the use of the sacraments to make us better people." He urged them to "keep in mind that we claim to have something of enduring values—the pearl of great prices. Is it any wonder then, that others observe us to see if we succeed or fail; to see if we are good or bad; to see if we are better or worse than those who do not make the unique claim that we make? How are we measuring up today to our responsibilities. In what manner are we keeping our trust; our bond with God?"[109] Tough standards. Harsh word to live by. Tamm, though, set the terms. How, then, to judge him as a *Catholic* public servant?

The issue, of course, is who applies the standards and who does the judging. By the standards of the time and by his own criteria, Tamm was not only a fine public servant but also a fine Catholic public servant. He worked in an extraordinarily dedicated fashion to defend his country and its laws against those criminals and subversives who intended it harm. By his criteria and those of his Church, he surely lived up to the FBI's motto, which he once said had been his idea: "Fidelity, Bravery, and Integrity."[110]

From a different perspective, though, Tamm's dedication exemplifies the ways in which American Catholicism had come to conflate its own morality and interests with those of the American state. Tamm later claimed that it was on his advice that Hoover decided not to spy on Wendell Willkie for President Franklin D. Roosevelt in 1940, but there is no evidence that he ever advised against the blatantly illegal wiretapping of FDR adviser Thomas Corcoran which went on from 1945 to 1950. There is no evidence that Tamm spoke against the "Do Not File" procedures that high-level FBI executives put together in 1942 to hide illegal and immoral activity. Tamm himself had ultimate responsibility for the "maintenance of records on technical surveillances."[111]

Tamm's work at the Bureau grew out of the belief of the Catholic Church in the 1920s that it was the country's only major religious body that still believed in America as both reality and potential, as John Winthrop's "citty on a hill." Tamm's work at the Bureau, more significantly, laid the basis for an even less critical and more magisterial triumphalism in the 1950s. Tamm, and those Catholics who cooperated closely with him—such as Stritch and Fitzgerald and Campbell—identified the needs of the Bureau with those of the Church and those of the country. "We were ambitious," Tamm told an interviewer about his generation of FBI men; "we not only wanted to do it right, we wanted to do it better." Perhaps it was appropriate that as American Catholicism entered the mainstream and lost its ghetto-like identity, it was the Protestant Hoover who determined what both "right" and "better" meant. Perhaps it was the ur-Protestant American John Winthrop who gave Tamm the phrase "the eyes of the world are upon us."[112]

CHAPTER 4

⌒⌇⌒

Father John F. Cronin
and the Bishops' Report
on Communism

Father John Cronin, S.S. (1908–1994), was as significant to his church's anti-Communist activities as it was to the anti-Communism movement as a whole. After a bruising two-year battle with Communists in the Baltimore shipyards, he persuaded the U.S. Catholic hierarchy to finance a year-long study of subversion, which resulted in his "The Problem of American Communism in 1945: Facts and Recommendations." That document, known as the bishops' report, was a Trojan horse inside which was hidden Cronin, who as a result became an assistant director of the Social Action Department of the National Catholic Welfare Conference in February 1946. His appointment on November 12, the same day the administrative board of the NCWC approved his report, began a policy shift there that eventually resulted in the Church's retreat from a pro-union and anticapitalist social Catholicism. "The Problem of American Communism in 1945" also launched Cronin's career as an anti-Communist of national importance. Having made the right contacts and achieved the right position in the right place, Cronin played such an important role in the anti-Communist movement that it is difficult to exaggerate its significance.

The most immediate outcome of Cronin's report was the series of pamphlets he wrote for the U.S. Chamber of Commerce: *Communist Infiltration in the United States* (1946), *Communists within the Government* (1947), and *Communists within the Labor Movement* (1947). Francis P.

Matthews (1887–1952), who received Archbishop Samuel Stritch's permission to read the report, was the connection with the Chamber of Commerce. A committed New Dealer, former Supreme Knight of the Knights of Columbus, and future secretary of the navy, Matthews chaired the Chamber's Committee on Socialism and Communism, under whose auspices the reports appeared. By spring 1947 more than 1 million copies of the three pamphlets were in print. They were something, Cronin's mentor argued, of which he could be proud: "Your long months of research in the field of Communism have officially borne fruit by way of a big harvest." All three, moreover, played a crucial role in the increasing salience of Communism as an issue in congressional politics.[1]

There was still more that kept Cronin busy in 1946 and 1947. Well connected to various anti-Communist networks, Cronin was intimately involved in organizing, financing, and establishing the magazine *Plain Talk* and then the newsletter *Counterattack*. The former published for only about a year but the latter lasted for more than two decades. American Business Consultants, publisher of *Counterattack*, also did research for corporations that had a "Communist problem" and vetted artists, actors and actresses, and radio and TV personalities. *Red Channels*, the blacklisters' bible, was its work.[2]

Cronin pursued Alger Hiss from the moment he learned about Hiss's role as a Soviet agent in September 1945. He discussed Hiss at numerous points in "The Problem of American Communism" and passed along to journalists documents attesting to his activities. Most important, however, was the help Cronin gave the freshman congressman Richard Nixon in his battle against Hiss. Using contacts developed during his research for the bishops' report, the priest fed Nixon FBI investigative reports leaked to him by Bureau agents. Nixon used this information to great effect as a member of the House Committee on Un-American Activities, which held the hearings that led to Hiss's ultimate conviction for perjury. Cronin went on to write speeches anonymously for Nixon during his vice presidency.[3]

Cronin's report for the bishops laid the groundwork for other actions as well that cannot be discussed here because of space limitations. Suffice it to say that without the report, Cronin could have not done what he went on to do. No one has told its full story. (This is so in part because historians have neglected the Catholic archives, but also because Cronin did not want anyone to know everything. "I have consistently covered sources during this report by giving misleading indications," he stated. Why? "I could not risk the jobs of my informants by giving any indication of their identities.") This account is almost certainly not the final one, but it is more complete than any other to date.[4]

Father John Cronin was born into a devout Irish American working-class family in Glens Falls, New York. His father, who had an eighth-grade education, worked in a paper mill his whole life; a "union man," he kept the books for his local. His mother, who must have had some education since she taught school for one year in Ireland, was sickly and seldom left the house except to go to Mass. The Cronin family lived in a section of Glens Falls called the "Swine District," which was inhabited almost entirely by others like themselves; there was only one Protestant family on their block.[5]

Cronin, the eldest of eight surviving children, graduated from St. Mary's Academy, the local Catholic school, and entered the College of the Holy Cross at fifteen. After graduation he became a member of the Society of St. Sulpice, a group of diocesan priests primarily dedicated to educating and training Catholic clergy. Ordained in 1932, he joined the faculty of St. Mary's Seminary in Baltimore and worked on his doctorate at Catholic University. He not only completed his dissertation in 1935— on the epistemology of Cardinal Newman—but also produced a set of mimeographed lecture notes on economics for his students' use.[6]

Cronin was apparently led to the unlikely study of economics for public as well as personal reasons. The unprecedented unemployment and misery during the Great Depression surely must have played a role, as did the fact that working-class Americans, many of whom were Catholics, increasingly were turning to unionism as a solution to their problems. On a more personal level, studying economics was a way not only to make sense of the world but also to master it, to create order out of the chaos he saw all around him. Here, as in whatever he did and wherever he went, Cronin sought unity and order.

From 1935 to 1940 Cronin spoke, lectured, and taught on social Catholicism on the East Coast and through the industrial Midwest. He also published several pamphlets, numerous articles, and a textbook, *Economics and Society*. By 1940 his credentials as a Catholic social theorist who could handle technical economic questions were well established.

Cronin was not, however, a "labor priest," as those clerics were known who gained much public attention in the late 1930s and beyond because of their commitment to working-class struggles for unionization and dignity. There had always been priests who worked closely with the American Federation of Labor as chaplains. There had even been a few whose support for a particular strike made headlines. What set these "labor priests" apart was their unclerical activism, their audacity, and their unhesitating willingness to enter into controversy, if necessary, to support union drives. They also set up labor schools, wrote column after column for the newspapers, and helped establish chapters of the Association of Catholic Trade Unionists (ACTU). Perhaps most important of all for our purposes, their very presence on the cutting edge of working-class struggle diminished the efficacy of accusations of Communism as well as anti-union sentiment among Catholics.

There were several reasons why Cronin did not qualify as a labor priest. First, he was an intellectual for whom the illumination of economic theory through Catholic social theory was paramount. Second, he had devoted little energy to supporting union drives and walking picket lines—partly, one imagines, because it did not suit him temperamentally, but also because of the relatively few opportunities available in underorganized Baltimore, with its conservative bishop, Michael J. Curley.

That said, Cronin was a well-known and respected colleague of the leading labor priests east of the Mississippi. He had also done a bit to support union drives. In 1939 he gave a talk at the state convention of the Maryland CIO and was a featured speaker in the labor schools that the Baltimore archdiocese set up in 1940. He spoke at organizing rallies for two Baltimore shipyard locals as well as for the Steel Workers Organizing Committee. The Industrial Union of Marine and Shipbuilding Workers of America (IUMSWA) used a statement of Cronin, along with those of other Catholic priests and Protestant ministers, in support of a 1941 union drive. The following year the Men's Clothing Manufacturers of Baltimore and the Amalgamated Clothing Workers chose Cronin as their permanent arbitrator.

Father John Cronin's life changed forever in July 1942, when Francis O'Brien came to visit him at St. Mary's Seminary. O'Brien, who headed the "All American Ticket for a Democratic Union," had just been defeated, along with the rest of his running mates, in a union election for the presidency of Local 43 of the IUMSWA in Baltimore. He went to the offices of the Baltimore archdiocese to seek help in fighting what he correctly considered to be a Communist Party faction which had just defeated him. The chancellor, Monsignor Joseph Nelligan, advised him to visit Cronin, who, according to his later accounts, did not take O'Brien's accusations seriously. He did, however, pay more attention when an FBI agent came to him several days later and sought his assistance in obtaining information about CPUSA infiltration of the Baltimore labor movement.

Later that year, in the fall, a member of one of the two opposition groups that had been formed to fight what they considered CPUSA domination of Local 43 came to the Sulpician for help. This time Cronin, spurred to action by Nelligan, who was disturbed by the increasingly public Communist presence in the shipyards, agreed to help and plunged into the fray. For the next two years, with his heart, soul, and body, Cronin fought the Communists in the shipyards and other wartime factories in Baltimore.

What motivated Cronin to work twenty hours a day for months on end? What led him to take so many risks? What caused him to leave his study and classroom at St. Mary's? Ideas, moral commitment, and a deep belief in God, of course, drove Cronin, but he configured these things in a way that, while recognizably Catholic, was also distinctly his own.

Unity was an overriding concern for Cronin. Before the war, much of his research and writing had revolved around what he considered the absolute necessity of producing a "unified and complete program of Catholic social reform." While the social encyclicals—*Rerum Novarum, Quadraggesimo Anno,* and *Divini Redemptoris*—"set up standards, moral imperatives, which are based on eternal truth," Cronin realized that implementing them was not so simple and often produced disagreement. In the absence of a unified position, Catholics were "passive and inert in an age of social upheaval." At the very moment, he felt, when the nation needed Catholic leadership and Catholic solutions, such inactivity prevented non-Catholics from seeing the Church's truth and contributed to a "wave of sullen discontent, even of anti-clericalism."[7]

"To act we must agree," said Cronin, and so he set out to produce the intellectual basis for unity in his vast scholarly output of the late 1930s and early 1940s. He first worked at characterizing the nature of contemporary American capitalism. He then critically discussed ongoing Catholic reform efforts as a way of offering an approach to the solution of current problems. Out of this work came a set of economic positions that, as we will see, Cronin was convinced could provide the basis for unity among Catholic social theorists.[8]

Cronin increasingly argued that the nation had to be one just as the Church had to be unified. Over and over again he asserted that individuals and groups had to put aside their own interests and focus on winning the war. As he succinctly summarized this reoccurring theme, "At all costs and at whatever sacrifice, we must become one nation, united and free." In the fall of France in June 1940 he saw an important lesson for the United States. The "spirit of man is still the first line of defense," he declared. But instead of discipline, there was "unleashed individualism." Rather than cooperation, there was "class strife." France fell because "patriotism yielded to selfishness, and unity to partisan strife."[9]

The war, for Cronin, held both promise and peril. The path of national unity and the submersion of self-interest would lead to a military victory that would ensure the survival of America and a free world and prevent the Axis from closing off the markets necessary to resolve the continuing crisis of unemployment and underemployment in the postwar period. But selfishness and conflict would divide the nation and open the door to its initial moral defeat and ultimately an Axis military victory. In a very "literal sense," Cronin argued, America was "on trial." Before it lay "the way of life or death."[10]

The trade union movement was central to Cronin's hopes and fears. While he stoutly defended it, he also argued that it had serious obligations and responsibilities. It was time for labor leaders oriented toward class struggle to give way to labor statesmen: "The fighter who pulled the union through its days of strife must be replaced by the responsible executive who sees the entire picture and who seeks the general welfare of all." The "fighter" might "well be pensioned off" and given a "decent job" away from "negotiations and policy making." His replacement, a "labor executive," ought to be "quiet, soft-spoken, persuasive, informed, tactful." Labor statesmen would view capital not as the enemy but rather as a "partner" and adjust to "economic realities." In making industry as "productive, as efficient, and as profitable as possible," they would lay the foundation for postwar stability and unity.[11]

He strongly believed that Communists, and to a much lesser degree racketeers, were the kinds of leaders that labor ought to avoid. Cronin devoted most of a July 1941 article to a discussion, aimed at Catholics, of how to identify Communists in the labor movement and what to do once they had been revealed. He recommended reading official Communist publications to discover the political positions of Communists and those whom they favored. Not every leader praised was a member of the CPUSA, nor was every organization whose political positions coincided with those of the CPUSA a front group; a careful investigator, Cronin argued, would soon develop a "nose" for the problem. A more direct approach was to go to anti-Communists in the labor movement for information.[12]

For Cronin, Communists were the fly in the ointment of unity, military victory, and national rejuvenation. In a 1940 radio address he cautioned unionists that those who "open wounds[,] long since healed, by preaching the fatal message of class hatred" were "no friends of labor." The path "to the left into the valley of revenge" enters the "unhealthy swamps of national discord to emerge into the burning desert of civil war," while the road of labor responsibility "passes through green fields and smiling forests of national unity to emerge into a vision of peace and prosperity."[13]

Cronin's solution to the problem of Communism is suggestive of the ways in which he was thinking through the body: "Here we must be mercifully harsh like the doctor who removes a festering limb, lest life itself be snuffed away by its contagion." In this somatic and medical metaphor Cronin was positioning himself as the expert/doctor and the labor movement/nation as the body. There were other points when the pressure of the oncoming war seems to have led him to the same sort of thinking and feeling. In one article, for example, he described poverty as "broad festering sores" that "brought to the body politic the disease of sickness, crime, and vice"; a "growing cancer" was how it was characterized later in the same piece. At another point Cronin invoked the body, even the (Mystical) body (of Christ), when he described the unanimity he fervently desired: the "organic unity" which America required needed to be as "permanent as the union of the cells and tissues and nerves which make up the human body." Americans needed to work together as brain, muscle, and heart to "foster the welfare of the entire body." The "evil germs of rebellion and communism" had to be eradicated, as did self-interest, a "cancer which eats into the vitals of a country."[14]

Communism, then, threatened Cronin at several levels. First, for him it was an atheistic and diabolical force that menaced Catholicism in particular and Christianity in general. Second, it was at war with his country, whose very existence was at stake. Third, it could destroy any possibility that Americans might create, through the process of winning the war, a society in which unity and harmony would rule. Finally, Communism appears to have threatened Cronin at the core of his very being. The metaphors that he used to described its menace were somatic ones, suggesting that Cronin felt endangered by forces both within and without the margins of his body. The very unity that was so central to his vision of the world and so seemingly essential to him as a person was being undermined.

Cronin joined the battle with the CPUSA in wartime Baltimore with serious responsibilities in mind: he took upon himself nothing less than saving his country, his Church, even himself. The Catholic Church, he wrote his fellow priests, faced a task "no less sobering" than when it had kept alive "the flickering flame of human culture" from the fall of Rome to the Middle Ages. In "self-protection," the Church had to "undertake the temporal mission of saving society." It was, Cronin admitted, "a new and weighty burden" to add to the priests' primary task of saving souls.[15]

The Sulpician's two-year battle with Baltimore's Communists, the details of which are now well known and readily available, reveals much about Cronin personally and how he went about his business. It helps place him, moreover, within the larger community of Catholic social activists. Finally, it was this experience that led to his work for the bishops in 1944 and 1945. There are five main lessons here.[16]

First, and indicative of Cronin's personality, was the tenacity, energy, and sheer willpower that he brought to an extraordinarily difficult and complex situation. Despite his almost nonexistent previous contact with the working class, despite public attacks that called his patriotism into question, despite periodic setbacks that would have discouraged the most confident of men, Cronin kept after the Communists day after day, week after week, and month after month. He ran caucus meetings at St. Mary's Seminary, worked up leaflets, wrote numerous letters to union and Church officials, and at one point directed the work of ten priests doing anti-Communist organizing at six different worksites in Baltimore. (He also continued his seminary teaching, ran his annual summer institute at Catholic University in Washington, D.C., and had at least a hand in the rebirth of Baltimore's labor schools.) It is not surprising that by the spring of 1944, a doctor told Cronin, who wrote a priest friend that he was working twenty hours a day and sleeping four, that he should "take a good rest now, or later in a pine box."[17]

Second, Cronin was willing to work with virtually anyone in his battle against Communism. As he soon learned, his allies in the shipyards were among the most backward of Baltimore's working class. Anti-Semitism, racism, dishonesty, and a fondness for alcohol and violence typified more than a few of them. Cronin expressed little but contempt for many of them, whom he thought too stupid to lie. (He seems finally to have respected his left-wing opponents more than his allies.) It was distressing to him that Baltimore's employers could only "with difficulty" be "enlisted to aid the decent elements against the subversive." In attempting to organize workers at Glen L. Martin Aircraft Manufacturing, he considered help from the company for crucial to "fostering a decent union," but the owner would not cooperate because he "believe[d] all labor leaders are communists." Cronin admitted that such "support would violate the National Labor Relations Act" but thought that "this difficulty could be handled."[18]

Third, although both Cronin and the CPUSA considered unity to be the number one priority during the war, they defined it differently. For the Communists, unity meant assembling a broad alliance of disparate groups around a common program. For Cronin, this was a false unity; real unity required sharing (or at least accepting without question) certain underlying beliefs. Those who did not have these beliefs or who opposed them had to be isolated and rendered powerless, even if that meant, as it did in

Baltimore, temporary disorder. Cronin's negotiations about the shipyards with two high-ranking Communists in October 1943 revolved around the implementation of these competing definitions of unity.

Fourth, there was the issue of where anti-Communism ranked in Cronin's priorities and what kind he would espouse. Those in Baltimore who opposed Communism also fought labor-management cooperation during the war, so when Cronin joined them, he was, without explicitly saying so, downgrading what labor priests and Catholic labor activists considered to be primary: support for the principles of Philip Murray's 1941 Industry Council plan. Defeating Communism, according to most Catholic laborites, was merely the first part of the process of building a trade union leadership that would fight to "restore all things in Christ," a reconstruction that had come to be largely embodied in Murray's plan for the joint sharing of industrial power and responsibility. For Cronin, however, all this took a backseat to the struggle against Communism; his anti-Communism took on a decidedly negative cast as it became an end in itself.

This was not the only place—and this takes us to the fifth and final point—where Cronin broke with existing thinking about clerical involvement in the labor movement. In assuming public leadership of the movement, he had virtually supplanted the laity in his role as organizer and director. By failing to create a group of stable and mature union leaders, he helped set the stage for a possible Communist return to power. His mistakes—inevitable given the situation and his lack of experience—incurred anti-Catholic publicity. In short, little of what he had done in Baltimore was of a positive nature.

All this notwithstanding, Cronin could not have functioned in the context of the Baltimore social situation without a willingness to jettison existing Catholic wisdom. There were far too few Catholics in the city's defense plants to produce the basis for a stable Catholic union leadership, as there was in other industrial cities. Probably nowhere else did a priest lead such a heavily non-Catholic faction within a CIO union. It was Cronin's personal traits more than his clerical status that allowed him to do this. In Baltimore's extremely unsettled wartime conditions there was a great deal of room for the kind of heroic individual action of which Cronin was capable, but at which most Catholic social activists looked askance.

Cronin learned in Baltimore both the desirability and potential of what might be called ecumenical anti-Communism. There it had been a necessity, for the Baltimore workforce was heavily Protestant, and Jews were prominent in the anti-Communist leadership Cronin found in the shipyards. A rarity in the pre-Vatican era of "ghetto Catholicism," he was

comfortable working with non-Catholics and continued to do so on a
variety of anti-Communist projects well into the 1950s.

Cronin's relationship with the FBI would wax and wane from 1946 on,
but since the moment when an agent first approached him in 1942, he was
quite friendly with FBI agents, who provided him with much information.
It was the FBI's files that initially confirmed for Cronin that Communism
was a growing threat in Baltimore. For Cronin, those files would remain
an almost sacred source of information and a guide for action. As I will
show, he returned again and again to the FBI for this information.

Cronin also learned the caution that he felt was necessary for a priest
who wanted to become active in the battle against Communism and for
sound unionism. With his Baltimore experience undoubtedly in mind,
Cronin argued in 1945 that prudence dictated a concern with "not merely"
what was done but *how* it was done. Without that sense of caution, a priest
(was he talking about himself here?) might "bring doubt and suspicion
upon the entire Catholic Social program." After Baltimore, Cronin always
tried to act and speak judiciously. Yet there remained something reckless,
even if conspiratorial, about Cronin's anti-Communism. Fighting Communism, especially in the way he did, put into play to certain aspects of
his personality that astute observers would notice again and again.[19]

An army intelligence officer who interviewed Cronin in the summer of
1943 was, as far as I know, the first to remark on these traits. He found
the priest "highly intelligent, well-informed and sincere in his attitude in
connection with removing Communists from labor groups." Yet he feared
that Cronin might be "inclined to talk too freely concerning" his contacts
and the information he had received from them. "This was noted," the
officer continued, "particularly in his statement that he had had contacts
with the FBI." Several other factors might "affect his reliability as an informant." One was his pro-labor position; another was Cronin's operating
assumption that the ends justified the means—or, as the officer saw it,
the "informant's willingness to utilize dissimulation in connection to his
dealings with subversive groups."[20]

The Social Action Department that Cronin would join in 1946 was an
original and integral part of the National Catholic Welfare Conference
founded by the American bishops in 1919. Its purpose was to educate
American Catholics on social questions, particularly about the progressive Bishops' Program of 1919. For the first time liberal Catholics had a
national platform that was both relatively free of local pressure and in a
position to influence federal legislation. That this voice for social Catholicism was institutionalized meant it was able to survive the reactionary

1920s to be of significance during the depression and into the next two decades.

Liberals, led by the indomitable Monsignor John A. Ryan (1869–1945), directed and staffed the Social Action Department (SAD) from its inception. Ryan almost single-handedly created a Catholic social ethic and reform program out of papal teaching, moral theology, midwestern populist-progressive thought, and a commitment to understanding capitalism as it actually existed. A strong supporter of unions, he also worked to pass minimum wage laws for women in Wisconsin and Minnesota. In 1915 he joined the faculty of the Catholic University of America, where he trained scores of priests in social Catholicism. Ryan published numerous articles, pamphlets, and books, including the seminal works *A Living Wage* (1906) and *Distributive Justice* (1916), and wrote the 1919 Bishops' Program of Social Reconstruction.

Father Raymond McGowan (1892–1962) worked alongside Ryan as the assistant director to create the SAD's "one-sideness," as the conservative Bishop John Noll considered its political perspective. Upon Ryan's death, McGowan became director and remained so until his retirement in 1954. The son of a railroad worker, McGowan may have been more radical than Ryan. He also published a great deal, including *Toward Social Justice* (1933), and was running the SAD on a day-to-day basis by the mid-1930s.[21]

Ryan and McGowan were convinced that federal legislation was necessary to solve the country's most pressing social issues. But with the exception of the federal child labor amendment—here the SAD's support incurred the wrath of Boston's William Cardinal O'Connell—they had little opportunity to implement this conviction in the 1920s. The SAD did what it could. It defended unions and fought the open-shop movement at every opportunity. Until the 1919 program became hopelessly unrealistic, the SAD used it as a yardstick by which to measure ongoing changes in capital-labor relations. Each issue of the NCWC's official publication, *Catholic Action*, contained department news and commentary on current social issues.

The SAD seldom shied away from controversy. Monsignor Ryan was constantly in trouble. In 1921 employers responded to his attack on the open-shop movement by sending a rejoinder to every priest in the country. In 1937 Archbishop Curley threatened to take away Ryan's faculties to say Mass in his archdiocese. In 1941 he got into hot water for publicly attacking the archconservative Father Charles Coughlin. Two years later Ryan's support for public health care found him opposing the National Catholic Hospital Association. Conservative Catholic irritation at his firm support for President Franklin D. Roosevelt never waned, nor did that of several of his ecclesiastical superiors who considered him to be far too liberal and much too public in his opinions.

McGowan sometimes equally angered his superiors. Curley actually removed him from the SAD in 1937 and appointed him to a parish, though he backtracked once national pressure was applied. In 1944, at a closed meeting of Catholic newspaper editors, he attacked Montgomery Ward, which was then locking out some of its employees, as well as the *Chicago Tribune* and several other newspapers as a "lot of dogs" that were trying to destroy unions and "bring about fascism." Later asked for his side of the story, McGowan could not remember having named the *Tribune* but admitted that he might have since he had mentioned other papers. He also could not remember having made the "dogs" comment, either, but agreed he might have "because I use it, with a smile, for reactionaries generally in private." McGowan received the sharpest rebuke for this incident.[22]

The Social Action Department took on new importance and a somewhat different role when the NCWC led the Church in an institutional turn toward the immediate interests of its working-class constituency in the mid-1930s. In November 1936 the annual General Meeting of Bishops approved Ryan's plan to establish a series of "Priests' Social Action Schools." These schools, which generally lasted four weeks, with classes five days per week, had three purposes: to study the social encyclicals, to investigate local industrial and labor conditions, and to discuss the "principles and methods of priests' participation in economic issues." Milwaukee, Toledo, San Francisco, and Los Angeles were the sites of the schools in 1937; Chicago and Buffalo in 1938; and Cleveland, Pittsburgh, and Chicago in 1939.[23]

This was just one of the many ways in which the SAD acted as a clearinghouse and center for the organizing and training of labor priests who supported the ongoing union drive among industrial workers. Almost all of the direct work in this organizing and training went on at the local level, but the SAD helped set up the meetings, provided personnel when it was able, and connected one activist cleric with another. It performed a similar function with regard to the Catholic labor schools that were set up all over the country. (The SAD had little if anything to do with the establishment of the ACTU.) Perhaps most of all, the SAD, which wore the NCWC's mantle of respectability, provided legitimacy for Catholic labor activists, both clerical and lay.

In 1939 McGowan's request that another priest be assigned to the SAD was honored. Father John Hayes (1906–2002) was the only priest McGowan apparently ever seriously considered for the position. Hayes was well read in the social encyclicals and had experience in working with the CIO's organizing drive in Chicago. Moreover, he had helped form a chapter of the ACTU and was on good terms with key Chicago activists. Hayes's primary task at the SAD was to work with other priests on what McGowan euphemistically called "industrial relations." He warned Hayes that there would be some difficulties with his work, but "none that will be placed by our Dept."[24]

Hayes edited a newsletter titled *Social Action Notes for Priests*. Originating as a one-page sheet sent to about two hundred priests, it soon grew to four—and sometimes six—pages; by 1945 about a thousand were receiving it. One of the first things that Hayes did was to circulate a questionnaire in which he tried to get an idea of clerical activity in the labor field. The answers he received provide an approximate idea of what labor priests—to use that term quite loosely—were doing. Of the sixty-two who responded, three-quarters replied that they had lectured over four hundred times, and about the same percentage had given sermons over four hundred times on social questions. Almost two-fifths said they were involved in labor schools, while about the same number were regularly meeting in study clubs with other priests. Almost two-fifths had union contacts; about one-quarter had helped form an ACTU chapter.[25]

"Here is another SOS," wrote an anxious Cronin to Hayes in November 1942. "I hate to trouble a busy man, but I do not wish to make any mistake in the trouble I am starting." Hayes was but two years older, yet Cronin turned to him as the expert, for he was the much more experienced man when it came to complicated labor situations like the one Cronin was facing in Baltimore.[26]

Hayes and Cronin exchanged many letters over the next two years as the Baltimore battle raged. Sometimes Cronin asked for more help; sometimes he wanted Hayes to intercede with high-ranking Catholics in the CIO's National Office. Hayes's advice partook of the existing SAD–labor priest paradigm about how to fight the CPUSA: focus on a positive program; do not preempt the role of the laity; concentrate on laying the foundation for a stable set of local leaders. Cronin often ignored this counsel and then asked Hayes how to get out of the mess into which he had got himself. For his own part, Hayes began—even if only in the most tentative ways—to move away from the prevailing wisdom. (It was not so much Cronin's work in Baltimore that influenced him in this direction but rather the more successful and less publicized efforts of Father Joseph Donnelly in Connecticut.)

Chance entered the picture late in 1943. After returning from the ordination of Monsignor Francis Haas as bishop of Grand Rapids, where there was "quite a crowd of the Church's leftist wing," Hayes entered the hospital with what turned out to be tuberculosis. By the early summer of 1944 he had gone to Texas for rest and recuperation. He never returned to Washington. Not only did Hayes's illness create an opening in the SAD that Cronin would fill but also it removed an experienced opponent of the viewpoints he brought with him.[27]

While Cronin was fighting the CPUSA in Baltimore, he also focused on yet another goal: to increase the Church hierarchy's awareness of the dangers of Communism and persuade it to act. There is no indication that any of these attempts became public, but there also is none that anyone in the SAD or in labor priest circles knew what Cronin was up to.

There were several reasons why Cronin began this campaign with Detroit's Edward Cardinal Mooney. The most important was that Mooney was the chairman of the NCWC's administrative board, which ran the NCWC between the bishops meetings, and thus the first among equals. There were other advantages to beginning with Mooney. He always had been pro-labor and encouraged the growth of a vibrant group of labor priests in Detroit. It was under Mooney's reign, moreover, that the Detroit ACTU and its influential newspaper, *The Wage-Earner*, originated and grew to national significance. If he could convince Mooney, it would be harder for those who downplayed the Communist threat or wanted to fight it differently to respond.

The "growing power of the communist party which is making hay while Stalingrad shines" was the first of two separate but distinct concerns that Cronin raised in an October 1942 letter to Mooney. His evidence was increased fund-raising, revived recruiting efforts among youth, and a heightened Communist presence in trade unions. Cronin's second worry was that the Church was losing workers because of "inadequate facilities" for Mass and the sacraments as well as the fact that laborers often worked on Sundays. In Baltimore and elsewhere, workers were being lost to "indifference." Were "factory Masses" an answer?[28]

Cronin's letter apparently coincided with information that Mooney was receiving about growing CPUSA influence in Detroit, for he asked Cronin to have something ready to present to the bishops' November meeting. Cronin's report, "Communist Activities," is a significant document not only because of its eventual impact on the bishops but also because it anticipated most of his later arguments.

It began with what was for Cronin the most important point: there had been a "notable and alarming resurgence of Communist activity throughout the United States in recent months." He then used examples drawn from his observations about events in Baltimore to buttress his argument. The CPUSA, in Cronin's analysis, was taking advantage of three things.

One was the wartime alliance with the USSR, which had created an "aura of respectability" within which Communists could operate. The second was the vast inexperience of most Baltimore union leaders and members. Sixty-seven Communists—the number is almost certainly the FBI's—had already taken over a shipyard local of thirty thousand workers and were working on another. Third, the reactionary labor position of Baltimore's employing class was being used by Communists to their advantage.[29]

That the CPUSA might well "capture many [more] unions" created both short-range and long-range dangers. The short-range dangers were significant. Although it certainly was not the Party's goal, growing Communist influence could produce a "slackening of the war effort" because of factionalism and division. Furthermore, if Stalin was forced into a separate peace, the CPUSA might well support him. The "remote dangers," according to Cronin, were even greater. The CPUSA could come out of the war both "well-financed and in a dominant position in the industrial field." It could systematically exploit the issue of racial discrimination and "recruit great numbers of malcontents [i.e., blacks] to their side." Finally, the Party might even recruit large numbers of white members if the Russian army's success continued in the face of no substantial anti-Communist opposition.[30]

The remainder of Cronin's letter proposed a "counterattack" against the CPUSA. There were, he wrote, three general ways to proceed. The first was to place an "exclusive reliance upon denunciation": this was the negative way to fight Communism. The second was to focus on eradicating the injustices that led people to join the CPUSA: this was the positive way to fight Communism. The third method, focusing on counterorganization and disciplined tactics, would work best, Cronin thought, "where the problem is that of a highly organized minority taking over a union." The primary goal is not to convince people that Communism is wrong but rather to teach them "the technique of fighting an enemy whose viciousness they realize."[31]

The positive and negative methods of fighting the CPUSA were well known in Catholic labor circles; they encapsulated, respectively, the liberal and conservative positions toward Communism. Cronin had derived the third method from what he called "signal success[es]" in Chicago and Detroit, but it was actually Detroit's development of the trade union "conference" on which he drew. Detroit's ACTU, locked in a desperate struggle for the hearts and minds of the city's working class, had adopted the Communist organizational technique of the "fraction," in which CPUSA members of a local assembled before its regular meeting to hammer out a set of positions for its members to work toward in a disciplined way.[32]

Cronin was soon implementing this method in Baltimore, in combination with the negative approach, but with one major innovation: he
himself replaced, as Donnelly also did for a shorter period of time in Connecticut, the working-class leader that he noted was the responsibility of
the Catholic labor school to produce. This model, then, as reworked by
Cronin to fit the local circumstances, brought the priest from either the
negative or positive sideline directly onto the field where the contest was
occurring. It was, as Cronin was soon to discover, a risky undertaking.

The November 1942 bishops' meeting took up Cronin's report, but there
is no record of any discussion or any decision being made. He continued
to push, however, for a reassessment of the Church's national position on
Communism even while he fought the Party in Baltimore. Using recent
CPUSA boasts about its recruiting successes to illustrate his point, he
warned Archbishop Stritch in May 1943 about the "increasing Communist menace," which was growing in "prestige, power, and influence to
a dangerous degree." It was not too late for a "counterattack," provided
that priests and seminarians were trained for the battle. Cronin therefore
urged Stritch to send priests to his Institute of Catholic Social Studies at
the Catholic University of America: "Your need for their services is great,
but the need for a crusade against Communism is urgent," wrote Cronin.
He may have been disappointed at Stritch's apparent refusal to commit
students, but he must have been delighted at his recognition of the seriousness of the problem when the archbishop agreed, "Indeed there is need
to be on guard and to use all proper means for the defense and widening
of our *culture* in the face of insidious attacks made against it."[33]

On April 19, 1944, about seventeen months after Cronin had raised the
alarm about Communism with Mooney, the administrative board of the
NCWC decided that it would address the spread of Communism at its next
meeting in November. Just a few weeks before, Monsignor Michael Ready,
the NCWC's general secretary, had spent a "long time" in discussion
with William Bullitt, the former ambassador to Russia. Bullitt had told
Ready that President Roosevelt and his secretary of state, Cordell Hull,
"felt helpless in the face of [the] well-organized pro-Russian bloc in the
Government." While Ready was somewhat suspicious of Bullitt—who he
thought was trying to draw Catholics into a battle for ulterior motives—he
wrote Mooney a long letter about the conversation. Ready also reported to
the administrative board on the Bullitt conversation, as well as one about
Communism with the secretary for Latin-American affairs at the British
embassy.[34]

Was there a connection between the Bullitt conversation and the decision to take up the issue of Communism? Here, as in so much of what follows in this chapter, it is impossible to draw causal connections between events that may well have been merely coincidental. My guess is that the conversation influenced the bishops to a certain extent because of their concerns about who was making the decisions in the State Department and who had the president's ear.

The administrative board decided on November 12, 1944, to finance a "factual study of the spread of Communism" in the United States. It was the sense of the board, which was dominated by the liberal wing of the Church hierarchy, that a "constructive program to meet the danger" ought to come out of the study. Stritch moved that the episcopal chair of the SAD establish a committee to study Communism and come up with a "program of constructive action for combatting its effects." Francis Cardinal Spellman of New York, seconding the motion, offered to "make available much useful data in his possession." The motion carried, and $10,000 was allocated for the study.[35]

The minutes indicate that Monsignor John O'Grady of the NCWC came up as someone who might write the report, but there was never any doubt that Cronin was the man the bishops wanted. It was not just that he was on good terms with Mooney, who chaired the board. It was not just that he had raised the issue of Communism when no one else in the liberal wing of the Church was doing so. Cronin also was Bishop Karl J. Alter's man. Alter (1885–1977), the bishop of Toledo from 1931 to 1950, was well read in neoclassical economics. He and Cronin had met in 1936 and corresponded on and off about the subject for the next seven or eight years. Under Alter's influence, Cronin moved further and further away from Keynesian economics—Alter was conversant with the *General Theory*—and closer to a purely monetary analysis of the origins of the depression.

Alter, who was the Social Action Department's assistant episcopal chair from 1936 to 1942 and its chair from 1943 to 1948, must have been unhappy for a long time with the ideological cast of the department. It apparently was not until July 1944, though, that he made his opinions known to Ready. The question was how to fill Hayes's slot in the SAD. An obvious choice was Father George Higgins, a priest from the Chicago archdiocese who was finishing his dissertation at Catholic University. "I have high regard" for Higgins's scholarship, wrote Alter, but "am inclined to agree with the Archbishop [Stritch?] that a little seasoning by way of parish work would be desirable." Appointing Higgins, moreover, would "merely [extend] the same line of thought already dominant in our Department."

Might not Cronin or Father Wilfred Parsons, S.J., be "a more helpful addition to the present staff?"[36]

Cronin and Alter moved quickly to establish the broad outlines of the study. Although Cronin was to be temporarily assigned to the SAD for the duration of the research (about five months), his office was to remain in Baltimore; he was to have complete authority over the product and would submit the final document to Alter. Monthly reports would go to Alter, Ready, and McGowan. Cronin hoped to hire Paul Weber, a Detroit ACTU leader, as a research assistant; he could be especially useful in contacting secular anti-Communist groups. He also planned on getting information from Catholic activists familiar with Communist infiltration in their fields. In the immediate future, though, Cronin was going to concentrate on putting together questionnaires that would go out across the country.[37]

There was virtually no examination of what Cronin referred to as the "positive" part of the report in his letters to Ready and Alter—the portion where the recommendations for changes in how the Church conducted its social action would be made. He discussed it a little more in his letter to McGowan, noting that the administrative board, wanted "an emphasis on appropriate positive remedial action," but even at this stage of the process, the positive part was taking a back seat.[38]

Cronin accomplished a great deal in the next month. He hired "reliable" part-time secretaries for "confidential work" and consulted with priests, "government investigators," and labor leaders. During a previously arranged lecture tour, he discussed the project with people in Detroit, Grand Rapids, and St. Louis. As a result of these consultations, as well as research into published material such as Eugene Lyons's book *The Red Decade* and Dies Committee reports, Cronin had drawn up and sent out questionnaires to all the bishops and about three hundred priests.[39]

The reference to "government investigators" was, as we will see, purposely vague. In fact Cronin had gone, less than a week after the study officially began, to the Baltimore Field Office of the FBI for information. The Baltimore special agent in charge asked FBI Headquarters what to do. He was told to talk to Archbishop Curley and determine "what he thinks of him [Cronin] and of his request to the FBI." If Curley "says they [the Church] are interested in this project, [name deleted] will handle the interview here." The archbishop, of course, approved Cronin and the study: "Any assistance the Bureau could give [Cronin] or his survey would be appreciated." Curley told the agent that he knew Hoover "very well" and "was very appreciative that the Director thought of coming to him."[40]

Late on the morning of November 29, 1944, therefore, Cronin spent time with a supervisor from D. M. Ladd's Domestic Intelligence Division.

Some of the most important parts of the memorandum reporting on the conversation are deleted, but its main points are clear. Cronin tried to get quite specific information; the supervisor refused to provide it. The latter did, however, suggest to the priest certain angles for approaching his research. Cronin had apparently told the supervising agent that he would be going to the Baltimore Field Office for more discussion but "was discouraged from doing this" and was told to go instead to FBIHQ if he wanted to talk things over.[41]

Three main lines of investigation would be pursued in the coming months. First, the information obtained from the questionnaires would be collected and assessed. Second, Cronin hired Harry Read to do the specialized research on Communist infiltration into labor that would reveal the "approximate strength of the Party in the various unions, mainly CIO." (Read, a former Chicago newspaper writer, Newspaper Guild activist, and ACTU leader, was editing the Michigan CIO paper.) Finally, Cronin would conduct an "independent investigation," creating his own files from information gathered by "reliable outside investigators," "spot checks" in cities such as Chicago and Detroit, and "special reports" from about forty priests who were "experts" in their fields.[42]

This was not, however, the whole story as several letters demonstrate. One, written by Stritch, indicates that intelligence agencies also were going to be involved in the bishops' report at the local level. The Chicago cardinal sent along his questionnaire to Father Bernard M. Brogan, an official at Catholic Charities. Stritch suggested to Brogan that he get help from the Chicago Red Squad, where, as we have seen, the archdiocese's connections were quite good. If you go to Mayor Edward Kelly, the cardinal wrote, "I think he will let you have some very valuable information which is in the Chicago Police files."[43]

Another portion of the story takes up Alter's and Cronin's continuing concern about accessing reliable intelligence sources while protecting their identity. A letter dated December 26, 1944, indicates that Alter considered Cronin too optimistic about the potential value of the questionnaires "I would suggest therefore," he told Cronin, "that you depend . . . on the authentic sources of information available in the Dies Committee Reports, Bureau of Intelligence and FBI." In a letter written December 30, Cronin, who had not yet received Alter's, told him that although the FBI, the Civil Service Commission, and "similar agencies" had been explicitly omitted from his accompanying report, "I have established excellent contacts [with them]," but "their pledge of secrecy is so strict" that "I felt I couldn't mention" them. Nevertheless, "as a result of their advice and information, I have confidence that we will get the facts on this problem."[44]

Alter was pleased with Cronin's progress and delighted with the news about his actual sources. He did, though, want to tip off his fellow bishops in some way about them:

> I am very much pleased to know that you have had such satisfactory contacts with the government authorities. We shall do everything in our power to respect the pledge of secrecy so that we will not refer to any specific department or to any individual by name in the government. I hope, however, that we shall be able to use the phrase "public authorities" or "government authorities" or something equivalent so as to support our statements and give them something more than the character of mere personal opinion.[45]

Cronin pursued two main lines of inquiry once he returned to his "piled-up" work after his father's funeral in January 1945. First, he carried on much correspondence about the questionnaires and began processing those that came in. (Cronin expressed no surprise at the "very sharp cleavages of opinion, particularly among priests," that appeared in these first returns.) Second, he worked on setting up "an independent investigation" to "supplement" and "correct," if necessary, the findings of these questionnaires. The general plan, he reported, was to get a "comprehensive study" of New York City, Detroit, Chicago, Cleveland, and the West Coast.[46]

Here the emphasis again was on finding reliable sources of information. Cronin first went to Spellman, who, he had been told, claimed to have "valuable sources of information." Spellman referred him to Bishop John F. O'Hara, C.S.C, the former president of Notre Dame, who, as military delegate, assisted Spellman, who was serving as military vicar of the U.S. Armed Forces. O'Hara, as we have seen, was quite conservative, a firm anti-Communist, and well connected. He "arranged the various contacts" for Cronin, including a "private research organization" that had spent $200,000 to build its files, as well as individuals, "both private and government," who had contacts with informers inside the CPUSA.[47]

The actual research, Cronin reported, was to be done by Hazel Huffman. Cronin investigated Huffman before he interviewed her and found that she not only had much experience in researching Communism but also possessed "valuable personal files." On the negative side, his sources told him that "excessive zeal on the subject might influence her judgment." Cronin's interview, though, convinced him that she was able to distinguish between a liberal and a Communist. He hired her at $250 per month for three months. (What he did not report was that Huffman had testified, as part of the "weirdest collections of evidence ever permitted," before the

Dies Committee on the Federal Theater Project. She later worked as an investigator for the committee.)[48]

Read, who had been fighting Communists within the United Auto Workers since 1941, was an excellent choice to research their infiltration into labor. His agreement with Cronin that the situation was critical—as Read put it in a letter to Higgins, "we are rapidly approaching the cross-roads on internationalism and what should be the policy"—lent an urgency to his work. (In a move that could not have pleased Higgins, Read turned down his request to write a pamphlet on the annual living wage because of his research work for Cronin.) By the end of the month he had put in about twenty hours and collected much information. Read was convinced that the CPUSA was trying out a new strategy of using Protestant clergy as "fronts" in Detroit. This corroborated rumors Cronin had heard about Communist Party plans to attack Catholics through the publications *The Protestant* and *Converted Catholic*.[49]

Once again, though, what Cronin did not include in his official report was at least as important, if not more so, than what he did: he had discovered that the Hearst Corporation was the source of Spellman's files and that the information was better than he thought it would be. He made contacts with three different intelligence agencies. One was the FBI, where Cronin now had contacts in the Baltimore and New York field offices. The second was the Office of Naval Intelligence, the New York City branch of which high-ranking fellow travelers in the military had, Cronin claimed, "dismantled because it was so effective" in collecting information on the CPUSA. The final intelligence agency in which Cronin had made contacts was the New York City Red Squad, or "secret squad" as he called it. It was running "plant informants" in the Party and had access to FBI files. Cronin concluded by noting that he would not be surprised if Father Hugh Donohue, a San Francisco labor priest who was writing the West Coast report, had similar contacts.[50]

How the Chicago diocese handled Cronin's questionnaire illustrates his argument that, with "some exceptions," the best diocesan reports "on the basis of internal evidence were compiled from information obtained from government officials, local, state, and federal." Someone there decided that the Red Squad's help with the questionnaire was unsatisfactory, so the FBI was approached. When Spencer Drayton, the Chicago SAC, asked FBIHQ how to handle the request, he received specific instructions on how to answer the questions. Drayton and Special Agent James York were accordingly judged "most cooperative." Judge William Campbell also was helpful in producing a second version of Chicago's questionnaire.[51]

Sometime in March, Alter decided that Cronin should make a preliminary report to the April meeting of the bishops' administrative board.
Although he therefore spent much of March working on this document,
Cronin found time to increase his contacts with intelligence agencies. He
met with J. B. Mathews, the former fellow traveler turned anti-Red and
chief investigator for the Dies Committee, who was "working on material"
for the report. Someone provided Cronin with a copy of the New York
City Red Squad's two-volume report. Father William J. Smith, S.J., an
important labor priest in Brooklyn with excellent intelligence contacts, introduced him to two "fine" FBI agents and spoke of an additional one was
an "old friend." An agent in Baltimore, moreover, told Cronin that he had
been "authorized" to help him with the report. His "excellent contacts"
in the civil service, who previously had worked with him on "subversive
matters," also had "offered to help" on this report.[52]

What was going on here? Was Cronin playing to Alter's desire for contacts with intelligence agencies by exaggerating the number he had? Was
he unconsciously and repeatedly going back over the sources of information he had developed? My guess is that both these suppositions, while
quite reasonable, are inaccurate. Instead Cronin was purposely multiply-
ing his sources—even within the same agency—for several reasons.

First, not only were Cronin and his sources operating on a "need to
know" basis, but also many of them decided personally whether or not to
provide Cronin with information. Putting these two facts together, it becomes clear why Cronin would multiply sources even at the same agency:
he might get information from one that another would not give him.
Moreover, he could do so on the safe assumption that none of his sources
would reveal the fact that they had been leaking documents.

Second, some sources had access to better information than others.
Kenneth Bierly, one of the former agents involved in founding the group
that would eventually publish *Counterattack*, could well have been one of
Cronin's sources. He spent most of his six-year FBI career in the New York
Field Office, where he worked on the subversives desk from 1943 until he
left the Bureau in 1946. Bierly had "assisted in the development of several
paid Confidential National Defense Informants" and had contacted a
"rather large number of confidential National Defense Informants" about
the CPUSA. He also had been used on several technical surveillances and
a "large number" of "physurs" (physical surveillances). A close relationship with Bierly, therefore, would have been much more advantageous
than one with an agent who did less politically sensitive work.[53]

Cronin had so far done little on the positive side of the report. He had
asked Higgins for the names of priests who were experts in social action

so that they, as well as the dioceses, could be polled about its future direction, but as of the middle of February he still had not received the names. (The responses about the positive program finally came in too late to be included in the interim report.) In February he did take up the positive program with unspecified SAD personnel as well as a Catholic University professor. Cronin ended up, then, writing the scant positive part of his interim report almost entirely out of his own experiences and intellectual study.

In March, though, Cronin wrote several letters that reveal not only how he conceptualized the relationship between the positive and negative parts of his report but also what he was thinking about the SAD and its brand of social Catholicism. In a letter to Higgins, who must have been growing increasingly uneasy about the direction of his research, Cronin pointed out the good that would come of the report. Using the conservative O'Hara as an example, he argued that bishops would be recruited by his negative program to his positive one: "The most interesting development of late is Bishop John O'Hara, who keeps very close track of C.P. developments. Since he is close to Archbishop Spellman, and since several other important forces are already convinced of the importance of social action, we may get results in the way of concerted support for a positive program."[54]

The second letter, perhaps inspired by a meeting with Higgins the week before, tells us even more. First, we learn that Cronin and Alter had previously taken up their disagreements with the SAD: "Furthermore, as we discussed last November, I fear lest some of the followers of Monsignor Ryan are driving up a few blind alleys." Second, although we have no indication of what these "blind alleys" were, we do learn that Cronin, as he had been doing since 1940, was thinking hard about how to get Catholics to agree on a common set of social principles. (These positions, of course, were his and Alter's.) The "practical problem" was to gain "agreement along these lines, without doing anything which would appear to be coercion or interference with personal opinions and legitimate disagreements." Perhaps the solution was "a well-balanced commission reporting to the Bishops," followed by a "temperate letter from the Hierarchy putting things in their correct perspective." The roadblock to getting such a letter from the bishops, though, Cronin noted, would be two outspoken liberals: Archbishop Robert Lucey of San Antonio and Bishop Francis Haas of Grand Rapids. He ended the discussion in a quandary: "It is a difficult dilemma to achieve unity without regimentation. It is better to convince people than to coerce them. But until we have a definite program, Catholic Action is bound to be hindered."[55]

Alter was delighted—a "wonderful job" he wrote—with the first draft of Cronin's interim report. He must have been assured, moreover, by those whom Cronin had lined up to check its veracity. In New York, the FBI and "other sources" were going to review it; in Washington, the civil service, military intelligence and, "hopefully," the FBI.[56]

The evidence on how FBIHQ responded to Cronin's request for help in checking over the first draft is murky because of numerous deletions, but it is safe to say that he did not get as much assistance as he wanted. On April 5, 1945, Ladd wrote Tamm a lengthy memo in which he both summarized the priest's draft and told his superior how a supervisor working under him had responded. Cronin, it seems, had made some accusations with little evidence, had got some statistics on Communist Party membership wrong, and had implied that the FBI had approved several assertions. What should Ladd have his subordinate say when Cronin called the next day?[57]

Every point Tamm wanted made to Cronin is deleted but for one thing: that "the Bureau was neither approving nor disapproving of the report in whole or in part and that under no circumstances did the Bureau want any impression created that it was approving or disapproving of the report in whole or in part, inasmuch as its relations with [Cronin] . . . had been on a strictly confidential basis." This was stated again when Cronin dropped off a copy of the final draft.[58]

After having the report checked, Cronin spent the first week of April on revisions and preparation for the meeting of the administrative board. On April 8 he sent twenty-two numbered and labeled copies by registered mail to the general secretary of the NCWC "so as to take maximum precautions against leakage or unauthorized use." The "publication or even circulation" of the report, Cronin wrote, might "cause considerable trouble."[59]

On April 10 he presented a "brief oral summary" of the progress of the project and gave each board member a copy of the interim report. After Cronin was congratulated for his work, it was moved by Stritch, seconded, and carried that he should look into setting up a permanent office in New York City with a "trained research assistant" and an "investigator" to "carry on and supplement" the research work on the CPUSA. Although it is not mentioned in the minutes, the board decided to continue the investigation and have Cronin prepare a final report for the bishops' meeting in November.[60]

The issue of setting up a national research office was related to the problem of Huffman. The evidence is especially fragmentary and one-sided, but Cronin probably had allowed what must have been his overwhelming conviction of the need for a research office located in New York City—home of CPUSA national offices, and a place where Cronin frequently traveled—to cloud his judgment about her. It apparently was a report submitted by Huffman, without any documentation, that both greatly upset Cronin and led to a meeting between Alter and O'Hara in New York. At this meeting Alter discovered that while Cronin's opinion of Huffman was "a bit reciprocated on her part," O'Hara perceived her work to be important enough to assume its funding. (O'Hara did agree that Huffman should make her documentation available to Cronin.)[61]

But during the first week in April the Huffman situation changed, and here we learn just how much was at stake for Cronin in the outcome. O'Hara decided—Cronin's "sense" was that he had further investigated her—that she ought to be dropped owing to "lack of funds." Cronin, obviously relieved, then revealed to Alter the nature of his real worry: he had been warned away from Huffman by an unnamed agency—undoubtedly the FBI—because of her "lack of discretion and judgment," but thinking her files (which turned out to be "badly dated and almost completely deficient in many vital fields") and contacts might help, he had hired her anyway. But then he began to worry that his "few contacts with her"—here he was forgetting that the FBI may have known what he had done—might "lead to the cutting off" of his "most valuable sources of material."[62]

The recommendation for a research office on Communism, which Cronin—erroneously or strategically—attributed to O'Hara, remained in the interim report. If it was taken up, Cronin argued, several specifications ought to be met. First, money enough to hire a "first-class investigator, preferably a former FBI agent," had to be allocated. Second, the office should not be located in a public office building, "since some of my sources of information have rifled too many such offices to place any trust in them." Finally, the office needed to be national in focus; otherwise it was possible that another situation would develop as it had with Bishop James McIntyre "sending down baskets of [local] material for investigation."[63]

The Huffman problem was finally resolved in early May when she was let go, she was told, for "lack of funds." She demanded a healthy severance check, to which Alter gladly agreed. (He even went along with paying a final padded expense account and giving her two extra weeks' salary.) The New York office was being closed, in Cronin's words, in "an atmosphere of friendliness and good will." He hoped it remained that way, because if Huffman talked, it would hurt "us."[64]

Cronin's "Tentative Confidential Report on Communism," as he titled his interim effort, was quite long, amounting to forty-eight pages and several appendixes. Its key assumptions and basic assertions were the same as those of the final report. The recommendations for fighting the CPUSA, which included what he called the "positive program," also were essentially the same. The significant difference between the interim and the final reports was that the former offered considerably fewer specifics than the latter. Cronin was right when he noted that the November report would be "more detailed, more thoroughly documented, and more adequately criticized."[65]

This basic distinction between the two reports can be tied directly to the nature of the sources to which Cronin had access. He relied on two general kinds: "Church sources" and "outside sources." The primary component of the first was the questionnaire mailed to every diocese and to about two hundred priests. Its purpose was to provide information about the CPUSA as well as a basis for assessing the quantity and quality of Catholic information on it. At the time of the interim report, Cronin had received sixty-eight replies to the diocesan questionnaire and about one hundred to the clerical one. A secondary—but still essential—aspect of "Church sources" was the use of investigators. Here Cronin mentioned Read—"whose experience in the labor movement and whose careful scholarship led to results of high value"—and noted that reports from investigators in New York City and San Francisco had not come in.[66]

Cronin's discussion so far was relatively straightforward and remained so when he discussed the printed portion of his "outside sources" category. He noted that he had used, albeit with much care and qualification, the infamous Dies Committee reports. Read also had studied CPUSA publications. His comments on his "inside information," though, reflected his need to protect his sources. Cronin first made it clear that intelligence agencies—both city and federal—gathered their information in a way that made it tremendously reliable: "Police and government agencies can make direct inquiries, cover meetings, and use other means for obtaining direct information. Naturally material of this sort is more complete and more accurate than any other." After noting that "such information is rarely if ever made available to outsiders," Cronin assured his readers that his findings did not contradict those gathered by intelligence agencies: "The director of the survey has reasons to believe that the facts and conclusions presented here are not at variance with these accurate and detailed studies."[67]

The phrasing was brilliant: Cronin told those readers who wanted (and needed) to know where the best information was, that he had (at least indirect) access to it, and that he had to hide its availability. What he did not tell his readers was that at every point he had relied on intelligence sources not only for information but also for a review of his data and analysis.

He did not, however, have as much access to FBIHQ information as he would soon have, and he had not yet talked with Ray Murphy of the State Department. From the former would come quite specific and fairly complete information on the CPUSA; from the latter, concrete assertions and/or information on Communist infiltration of the federal government.

Cronin seems to have planned on spending most of his remaining research time on the positive program. Clearly there needed to be some "filling in [of] details," but "it was felt" generally that the report was "substantially accurate." Things changed dramatically in May, though, when a directive from Moscow, delivered through an article in the theoretical journal of the French Communist Party, produced in the CPUSA a sharp lurch to the left. Cronin thought that Party members' new militancy would make them easier to identify and "thus reduce confusion within Catholic circles." Paul Weber, however, who was closer to the ground in Detroit, was convinced that a "more vigorous Communist policy" would "win recruits within the ranks of labor" because working people were "restless and dissatisfied."[68]

The Communist Party's new approach forced Cronin to reopen sections of the reports and ignore the positive program. He believed that the investigative work could be kept to a minimum because he was getting "unofficial help" from "some of the best-informed persons on this subject." His "most important activities" during the month, in fact, had "consisted of taking steps to make the contacts" he had hinted at previously.[69]

Cronin never mentioned him by name, but the person who apparently provided the final go-ahead for the FBI's help—with, of course, J. Edgar Hoover's approval—was Edward A. Tamm, the third-ranking Bureau official and its highest-ranking Catholic. On December 2, 1944, just after Cronin had begun work on the report, Tamm had noted that he was "afraid" it was to be "once over lightly," but he apparently was coming around to the idea of helping the Sulpician.[70]

On May 1 Cronin informed Alter that the amount of investigative time he would have to spend depended on "certain delicate negotiations which are now going with *our main source of information*." He thought he had a good chance to get the "extra help" because he had heard through the "grapevine" that "they"—the FBI—were pleased with his "approach." About two weeks later Cronin wrote a letter in which he provided the information needed to identify Tamm: "My own request for even greater co-operation from my sources is going well, but must await the return from SF of the man who will give the final answer."[71]

Tamm was then in San Francisco handling security for the United Nations meeting. After a doctor's examination upon his return to Washington, he went on sick leave until August. Hoover ordered Tamm not to be in contact with his office, but if we can believe Cronin—and there is no reason not to—he clearly was. In early June, Cronin informed Alter that he had learned some important news through Father Robert S. Lloyd, S.J., the director of the Jesuit retreat program at Manresa House in Annapolis. Lloyd, who was extraordinarily close to the FBI, had informed him that the "high official I wished to see had recovered enough to get his assistants working on the program which I sent you earlier this week." Cronin continued: "More details will be available later, but it now appears that the top levels of this particular group are doing my research for me. If this goes as expected, the results would be far superior to any obtainable by previous techniques." Several weeks later the "grapevine" had it that the FBI's research project for Cronin was "tremendous": ninety-one typed pages of material had been gathered for just one section of one question.[72]

That the FBI was now doing Cronin's research substantially changed the way he and Alter decided Cronin should use his time. He was now able not only to return to his plan to work primarily on the positive program but also to do some of his own writing. In May he arranged to have the NCWC's education department do a survey on current Catholic educational efforts on social problems. He also attended an ACTU policy meeting in Detroit and discussed its particular way of fighting Communism.

Cronin spent the month of June at Rosary College in River Forest, Illinois, working on a book that the publisher wanted by July and studying social action in nearby Chicago and other Midwest locations. (He could do this because the help from the FBI was "most extensive in quantity and quality.") In July he met with the NCWC's Commission on American Citizenship as well as Louis Putz, C.S.C., an expert in Catholic lay action who taught at Notre Dame. He also attended a meeting on Catholic adult education with Father Reynold Hillenbrand, the central figure in the development of liberal Catholicism in Chicago. Cronin's immersion in what has been called "Chicago-style Catholicism" was virtually complete, as his roommate at Rosary was none other than Father John Hayes, almost recovered from tuberculosis.[73]

Cronin, his mind freed from investigative work and focused on Catholic social theory and the positive program, now turned his attention to the unity in Catholic social thought which he considered "necessary to permit the drawing up of a successful program of action." His strategy apparently was two-pronged. He began by corresponding with, and then visiting, Father Bernard Dempsey, S.J., "the leader of a school which stresses the economic rather than the ethical aspects of social problems." But he also approached the other group with which he was most concerned: the followers of Monsignor Ryan, who stressed ethics and human welfare rather than "economic law."[74]

Cronin and Higgins had been discussing exactly what the former was intending with the bishops' report and how its purpose was related to the SAD and its mission of promoting Catholic social ethics. You and I both agree, Cronin wrote at the beginning of his letter of July 1945, that the issue is the "complete and balanced truth. With none of us is there any question of half-truths, presentations so partial as to be false, and so forth. Here there is no room for difference." But there could be "disagreement" on "factual matters and their relevance. There can also be differences in emphases in presenting the truth." With these "principles" in mind, Cronin wrote, "we can catalogue differences."[75]

The "questions of Communism, faults within the labor movement and the preceding Administration, and similar problems are first of all factual questions," he continued. And here "we liberals have missed out on some of the facts." He proceeded to cite chapter and verse regarding Communist infiltration into the federal government: "The point is that a lot of middle-of-the[-]roaders know these facts, and similar facts about the brethren [CPUSA] in labor and about abuses within the labor movement, and we gain nothing by denying facts." The "crowd I have in mind," Cronin continued, "have excellent sources for their information, not just the Dies tripe." So "when we deny these situations [Communist infiltration] because the Dies Committee offered ridiculous 'proof' we become labeled a faction just as much as the Brooklyn *Tablet* and the *Sunday Visitor*. In our positions we are supposed to know a little more than either Dies or Bishop Noll." His point was "that an accurate picture of these situations is the very best answer to the reactionaries."[76]

The issue might be, Cronin conceded, as he continued to try to back Higgins into a corner, the "significance of the facts." A Communist takeover in the United States was of course not a possibility, but there were places in the world "where some well-placed propaganda could do a lot of harm." Here Cronin specifically named the possibility of Communist armed revolt in Italy and Yugoslavia and asked what would happen in China if the United States did not support Chiang Kai-shek to the degree it ought. If the "worst happens, and Western Europe and Asia both go Red[,] I would not feel easy about the fifth column groups in North and South America."[77]

Cronin began his analysis of how best to fight the CPUSA with a criticism and an admission: "I feel that we (with myself the greatest sinner, as can be seen from *Economics and Society*) have tended to oversimplify the problem of how best to handle the brethren." He now believed that "social justice" was not "the all-inclusive weapon" but rather "one of several." In some cases "counterorganization" was "vital," while in others "counter-propaganda" was needed. Finally, there "may be a place for occasional direct attacks on Communism."[78]

Cronin concluded his letter with a lengthy discussion of the positive side of his program. On the one hand, his "immediate objective" was to "simply prepare a balanced, factual report, with an adequate study of remedies." On the other, he believed that the report could be a "powerful stimulus to our whole program." He closed by listing "four objectives" for which he had received approval. All this might be a "pipe dream," he admitted, but the objectives had been approved at the April 10 NCWC administrative board meeting. By November, when the final report was to be presented, he thought the argument would be put together in an even better form.[79]

Stritch's efforts in July to help Cronin with his investigation are revealing about his relationship with the local FBI as well as the degree to which both Cronin and Tamm operated on a "need to know" basis. As we have seen, Cronin had sent, as a result of the CPUSA's turn to the left, yet another questionnaire to the Chicago archdiocese sometime after the April 10 meeting, but Father Brogan reported to Stritch in July that it had not yet been filled out. The "local FBI," said Brogan, which "furnished such excellent cooperation in our first study," had promised to provide all the "factual data" he needed. The Chicago Field Office told Brogan, however, that FBIHQ had to approve the information it was going to release. After the field office forwarded the material, FBIHQ replied that Baltimore had sent in the same information and that the answers to the questionnaire would be sent directly to Cronin.[80]

We learn several important things from Brogan's letter. First, Cronin had cast a wide net within the FBI in his efforts to obtain information. He had official and unofficial contacts with the Baltimore office and at least unofficial contacts with New York, as well as both official and unofficial contact with Tamm. According to Stritch, moreover, he also "spent a good deal of time" at the Chicago field office. Second, Cronin was compart-mentalizing his sources. It was one thing for Brogan not to know about the cooperation that Cronin was getting at the highest levels of the FBI, but it was another for Stritch not to know. Not only had Tamm apparently not told Stritch about the help, however, but also Cronin revealed little when he was informed of Brogan's discovery. "As you suggested," he told Stritch, "I am receiving extraordinary help *from Washington*. I was not sure of getting this until recently, hence my earlier request for help."[81]

Cronin did relatively little work on the report during August, but what he did do was extremely significant. In his account of activities for that month he reported: "It has been definitely ascertained that an American Communist M.P. [Party member] stole the full formula for the atomic bomb and delivered it to the Soviet Union. State Department veto has thus far prevented prosecution or publicity. It is requested that this fact be given no circulation prior to its public release, if such a release is finally cleared by the State Department." The question for us is the same as that asked by someone, probably Monsignor Howard Carroll, who had replaced Ready as the NCWC's general secretary, in a handwritten note next to this paragraph: "data—evidence?"[82]

This assertion is astounding. By the date of Cronin's report on his August activities, which he sent out with a cover letter dated September 6, the Soviet Union had in fact received significant information concerning the development of the atomic bomb. The problem, however, is that we have only recently been able to come to this conclusion. It was not until 1949 or 1950, moreover, that the FBI had the information.[83]

What Cronin told Alter but did not include in his official report is even more interesting. He had known about the Communist theft of the "atomic bomb formula" as early as February but only recently learned that it had been smuggled out of the country. (He would later write Carroll that a "recheck" indicated the USSR had obtained a "formula, nearly complete," but not everything.) We know now that it was in fact February when Klaus Fuchs passed atomic secrets to Harry Gold.[84]

There was yet another startling revelation in Cronin's August report, another paragraph beside which Carroll expressed his skepticism ("proof?"). Cronin wrote: "It is known that the Democratic candidate for mayor of New York has had direct contact with Communist emissaries, who flew to California to pledge endorsement to him. At present his contacts with the Party arise through his brother, who meets regularly with Bella V. Dodd, political director of the New York State Communist Party. Thus, [William] O'Dwyer, a Catholic, is working hand in glove with the Communists, while [David] Goldstein, a Jew, is fighting them."[85]

From where had these stories come? From where was Cronin getting the information?

My hunch is that Cronin, who made several references, as we have seen, to a "grapevine," had access to two different sorts of rumor mills within the FBI. The first consisted of the informal exchange of information that occurred in the normal course of the Bureau's work. Agents, after all, were regularly transferred between field offices. It is hard to imagine that they did not bring the latest news with them. The second sort comprised those agents who were more politically aware than their colleagues, those who put their work within a larger national and international context.[86]

While there is good evidence to support one of Cronin's assertions and indirect evidence for the other, their significance goes beyond their origin and the means by which Cronin heard about them. From his perspective, he had reliable information that the USSR had stolen his country's atomic secrets. The State Department, moreover, was the bad guy in his account, for it did not want to publicize the theft. The O'Dwyer story was an equally frightening domestic counterpart: a Democrat—and a Catholic at that!—was in bed with the CPUSA.[87]

Cronin's mindset seems to have shifted at this point in the investigation. Whether it was the secret meetings or the enormous amount of Communist infiltration he was discovering or the sensitivity of the FBI documents, he increasingly adopted a cloak-and-dagger approach to his research. He told Alter that he had had some information sent him through an "intermediary"—Lloyd—rather than directly. Anticipating the bishop's skeptical response to the subterfuge, Cronin added: "All this sounds as fantastic as a detective story, but this work has to be done in such an atmosphere. That is why quacks flourish on the subject." Then came the explanation for the "intermediary": "But the data being furnished is as accurate as a microphone and camera can make it."[88]

A sizable proportion of the FBI material—perhaps all of it—for which there is a record of Cronin's having received it did indeed come to him via Lloyd. One of the FBI's blind memoranda, on the Communist Party's "financial resources," was dated June 13, and several others, on religion, July 11, but much bore an August date. More arrived through Lloyd in September and October. A good deal of this information, as we will see, wound up verbatim in the final report.[89]

The cloak-and-dagger business continued into September 1945, as Cronin's work on the bishops' report wound down. While he mainly spent September reviewing material at hand, he found time to meet with two "government officials on Communism in government and in the international scene." One of those two probably was Benjamin Mandel, an ex-Communist turned HUAC investigator. The other, with whom we know he met, was Raymond E. Murphy.[90]

Murphy, who was born in Maine in 1896, graduated from Bates College in 1920 and received a Georgetown law degree in 1922. After beginning in the Eastern European Division of the State Department in 1925, he moved to European Affairs in 1937, where he specialized in Communist matters, especially in debriefing defectors. He worked closely with Jay Lovestone, the Communist turned anti-Communist and future CIA agent. Murphy, who exuded self-righteousness and arrogance, "saw himself as the lone professional anti-communist in the State Department." From another perspective, though, that of "old line State Department personnel," he was "psychopathic with reference to Communist matters." According to FBI sources, he "has stated often that his life is in constant danger as the knowledge in his possession is of such a detrimental nature to the Communist movement that they, the Communists, would not hesitate to end his life."[91]

In late September, Cronin had Carroll set up a meeting with Murphy to "discuss the matters we talked about earlier." Cronin's account of the discussion indicated that Murphy would be a "very good source, complementing the group [the FBI] which he dislikes so much." He "is as vocal as they are reluctant on the subject of infiltration within the government. So I can use each source for what they will furnish." Or as Cronin wrote Alter, Ray Murphy "has quite a bit on Party penetration into government offices."[92]

Alger Hiss, the State Department official who would be found guilty of perjury—actually treason—in a widely publicized 1950 trial, was the most prominent among the many about whom Murphy talked to Cronin. Murphy, who had heard about Whittaker Chambers's accusations concerning Hiss, was worried about Hiss's loyalty. In March 1945, after the FBI had sent Chambers's 1942 interview to State Department security officers, Murphy talked to Chambers about Hiss and other members of the spy ring with which he had worked.

Sometime in September, Cronin bought a five hundred–pound office safe for "certain material received during the past month, and to be received next week." The information, which could not be duplicated, was "given on condition that it be adequately protected." It therefore necessitated a safe that was "too heavy to be removed easily" and "strong enough to resist ordinary burglary." The data he had gathered during the investigation "made him cynical regarding the safety of locked doors and locked files."[93]

Cronin began writing the report in October, but there was still research to be done for the section on Communist infiltration of government, the "weakest of the whole lot," as he told Carroll. He had been hoping that Murphy would provide him with good information, but as it turned out, Cronin decided that was not the case. Playing both ends against the middle, Cronin had the FBI check his information. The review confirmed what he suspected: "Murphy has been disappointing, mainly because he is hard to pin down. An expert [FBI] cross-check on his data showed many suspected Reds to be merely liberal." (It could have been at this time that the Catholic agent William C. Sullivan provided Cronin with access to the FBI's report on Chambers. If so, Cronin had yet another Bureau connection.) Cronin's meticulous research methods had already prepared him for this eventuality; earlier that month he had begun to seek an alternative source of information.[94]

A "very delicate favor" was what he wanted from Carroll. He had been told by "competent informants" that the best information on Communist infiltration of government was in the FBI reports to Congress on possible violations of the Hatch Act, forbidding federal employees to engage in partisan political activity. Since the FBI would not permit him access to these reports, Cronin wanted help in getting them a different way. "Might it be possible," he asked Carroll, "through Mr. Butler [Eugene Butler, assistant director of the NCWC's legal department] or otherwise to approach some senator on the Committee which receives this report." The "right senator could be told in a general way and in confidence what we are seeking." Cronin gave Carroll "a personal guarantee" that the material would be used carefully, "in an analytical rather than a sensational way." Furthermore, "where I have prior information of my own, as in the case of Alger Hiss (State Dept.) or Harold Young (secretary to Henry Wallace), I shall make an advance reservation using my own material."[95]

Carroll took Cronin's request seriously and got right to it, but Butler apparently was going to be of little help. Cronin therefore came up with another idea: he wanted Carroll to get him a list of the senators who had access to the "Hatch Act data." He would then "call around" and see if he could "make a connection" himself. Yet another possibility, Cronin suggested, was to have the latest government manual sent to him. With those names and sources, I "may be able to work something better myself than is now available." Butler, meanwhile, had contacted the clerk of the Senate Committee on Privileges and Elections, who was checking to see where the report was. Carroll finally wrote Cronin at the end of October to say that the clerk could not find the report and that Carroll should see him the next time he was in Washington.[96]

Both Cronin's cautiousness and his reliance on the FBI continued during the next few weeks before he presented his report. He sent an advance copy to Stritch and asked him to have his FBI "contacts" look it over. Expecting trouble at the meeting where he would present the report—presumably from the liberal wing of the episcopacy—he told Stritch that it "would be a great help if it could be said that it was read over by extremely well-informed sources and they found it substantially correct." Stritch wrote Cronin that he had "confidentially" asked the Chicago FBI field office to go over it and was told that the review would be done in

Washington in about a week. Cronin also sent advance copies of the report to five other members of the administrative board. While he did not list them by name, he noted that "each of these bishops, except possibly Archbishop McNicholas, has ways of checking on the Report." So did another recipient, Richard Cardinal Cushing, since "Soucy of the Boston FBI, is a Catholic."[97]

Finally, Cronin, apparently at Alter's request, traveled to South Bend to have Louis Budenz check the report. Budenz, as we have seen, was the former high-ranking CPUSA member who returned to the Church and immediately went into seclusion at the University of Notre Dame. Cronin's access to Budenz indicated the importance that members of the hierarchy attached to his project. It was not until early December that FBI agents came to South Bend to interview him.

On November 12, 1945, Cronin presented a "rapid summary" of the study to the bishops' administrative board and handed out mimeographed copies. Several days after the board expressed "great satisfaction" with the work, he also reported to the General Meeting of the bishops, who, we can assume, were just as happy as the board.[98]

One final task needed to be accomplished: getting the report to all the Catholics who needed to see it. After discussion the board decided that a copy should go to every bishop, but that a cautionary letter, which was drafted by Cronin and signed by Alter, ought to precede it. "Our investigator," the letter read, "was fortunate enough to obtain access to highly accurate sources, with the result that the report is replete with detailed information, much of it not known to the public." The "most valuable of these sources are so confidential," however, "that they cannot be used to substantiate the statements made in the report." As a "protection against inadvertent deception on the part of the investigator, several of the bishops and Archbishops submitted the report to some of the best-informed sources in the country. Their verdict was that the document was accurate and well-balanced." The administrative board, the letter continued, had approved circulation of the report as long as it was kept confidential. The document should not be shown to any "laymen," and only with the ordinary's permission to priests who were editors, teachers in labor schools, and the like. The report would be sent first class and by registered mail.[99]

Father John Cronin's report "The Problem of American Communism in 1945: Facts and Recommendations" is an impressively bulky document. Much of it single-spaced on legal-sized paper, it is 146 pages long and includes three indexes (subject, name, and organizations/publications). There are, as far as I know, only four copies extant: at the Archdiocesan of Det... of Detroit, the University of Notre Dame, Catholic University, ar... larry S. Truman Library.

...e ...d) of Cronin's document followed a four-page "introduction and summary." Then came four chapters that addressed the subject of Communism, worldwide (chapter 1) and in the United States (chapters 2, 3, and 4). Chapter 5, on how Catholics should respond to the threat of Communism, concluded the report. Four appendixes, running more than fifty pages, followed: they covered public sources of information about Communism, the CPUSA's internal structure and personnel, "selected" CPUSA front groups, and the Communist infiltration of labor.

"World Communism and the United States," chapter 1, provided the moral and political foundation for the remainder of the study. Cronin's starting assumption was that the CPUSA was a "disciplined organized movement, seeking primarily to foster Soviet policies." Not only was its "present policy" one of "complete subservience to the Comintern," but also, in a showdown with the USSR, it would "act as a Soviet Fifth column."[100]

That battle, Cronin thought, was closer than most Americans believed because of "Soviet imperialism," a "program of encirclement and aggression fully as ambitious as that envisioned by the Axis." In Europe, the USSR had taken Latvia, Lithuania, and Estonia, "installed puppet governments" in Poland, Romania, Bulgaria, Albania, and Yugoslavia, and "seriously infiltrated" governments in Czechoslovakia, Hungary, Austria, Finland, and Soviet (East) Germany. Its "influence" was "great" in Italy, France, and "possibly" Belgium and the Netherlands. In Spain and Portugal the Soviet Union was "agitating through front groups." Among the "major nations" in Europe, only "Britain, Sweden, Norway, and Anglo-American controlled Germany" enjoyed "relative freedom from [Soviet] control." In Asia, where Communists were "fostering the independence movement among colonial peoples," Soviet influence was growing. (This did not mean that the independence movement was "Communist inspired or dominated," but "merely that [the Communists] seek to use it for their own purposes.")[101]

This examination of "Soviet imperialism's" progress revealed, Cronin argued, two "reoccurring points": Soviet control or infiltration of a foreign nation, and the CPUSA's either direct or indirect "propaganda campaign within the United States to justify the existing situation." Cronin then re-surveyed the same territory, encroaching Soviet imperialism, to illustrate the interrelationship between the two recurring points.

Part of his argument here was that there existed an intimate connection between the CPUSA and "Soviet imperialism." As he put it, "American Communism would be unintelligible unless it were viewed against the background of Soviet Imperialism." Another point he v shed to about the CPUSA's organizational threat: "the real menace of mmunist movement lies in its disciplined organization."[102]

Chapter 1 drew two conclusions. First, not only had Soviet imperialism "expanded greatly the number of persons and nations under the rule of atheistic communism," but also, within the next twenty years, it could sweep away Europe and be well along in doing the same in Asia, raising the specter of "Europe completely sovietized and Asia on the road to total subjection." In each case "the wisdom of American foreign policy will probably be the deciding factor." Therefore—and this was his second point—"American Communist fronts are striving mightily to influence American policy." Their "maximum objective" was to "win support for or at least acquiescence in Soviet policy." Their "minimum objective" was to "becloud issues and confuse the public and interested groups" so that no "positive policy will develop."[103]

Chapters 2, 3, and 4 provided an immensely detailed and acute discussion of the current status of the CPUSA. According to the report, while there were only about 75,000 card-carrying Communists in the United States, numerous other Americans—consciously or unconsciously—accepted its goals and carried out its purposes. Whether they fell into the category of "fellow traveler," "concealed communist," "opportunist," or "dupe," they were part of the Communist apparatus. "Front groups," that is ostensibly non-Communist organizations founded to pursue apparently noble aims, were one of the chief avenues through which the CPUSA pursued its goals: "No matter how laudable their professed purposes, one can be sure that in practice their activities will be directed toward strengthening Communism." Specific discussions then followed under the headings "Foreign Language Front Organizations," "Negro Fronts and Programs," "Communism among Jews," and "Communism and Youth." (Appendix 3 provided detailed information on the fourteen leading organizations and lesser data on dozens of other groups.) Cronin's conclusion was sobering: "The Communist Party appears as a well-disciplined although small group, which multiplies its effectiveness enormously through the use of front organizations and controlled publications. By these methods, relatively large sums of money can be obtained for propaganda and agitation. Furthermore, pressure behind any given issue can be built up enormously through the enlisting of 'innocents' and the cumulative effect of publicity by interlocking front organizations."[104]

Chapter 3, which discussed Communist influence in the labor movement, was potentially the most significant section of the report. Not only did Catholics constitute a large section of the working class, particularly those organized in the CIO's industrial unions, but also clerical support for CIO organizing had been instrumental in its success. There were, moreover, many important Catholic labor leaders, including the devoutly religious Philip Murray, CIO president, and the talented but erratic James B. Carey, CIO secretary-treasurer.

In this chapter Cronin assessed the extent of Communist influence in the American Federation of Labor (AFL) (negligible) and the CIO (extensive in some unions and certain positions). A long and complicated appendix, summarized in the text, provided a list of Party-controlled union locals in the AFL; a list of prominent "Communist," "Fellow Traveler," and "Opportunist" labor leaders; and a lengthy discussion of Communist strength in the CIO. This appendix, the only "really original" section of the report, according to Cronin, was based on Read's work. Read, Weber, and several FBI agents had provided the labeling of the individual labor leaders.[105]

Next he took up Murray's relationship to the Communist Party in the CIO as well as the related problem of the extent of Communist influence in the CIO's Political Action Committee (PAC). Both issues had been a source of tremendous debate among Catholics, especially labor priests, beginning in 1943. Cronin judiciously adopted an "on the one hand"/"on the other" approach to these problems, but his judgment seemed to be that there was relatively little that Murray, having inherited the problem, could do to solve it, and that the Communist Party had much more influence in the CIO's PAC than most liberal Catholics were willing to admit.[106]

A third issue that Cronin discussed was the degree to which the Party controlled the unions that made up the CIO. He rehashed the appendix material at length in an attempt at precision but finally concluded that "it is not possible to answer simply whether or not the Communists have controlling power in the CIO." Much, he argued, "depends on the issues which arise." They could not, for example, "depose Philip Murray and replace him by a known Communist." Nor could they "win any issue where the overwhelming majority of workers were definitely opposed to their stand." But "where issues can be confused so as to salve the consciences of opportunist or fellow-traveling union officers, where questions arise about international matters, political problems, or other situations only indirectly connected with labor," they "can usually have their way." The "technique of obfuscation, so successfully practiced with front groups, works equally well here."[107]

His conclusion? The CPUSA had a "strong political interest in capturing the labor movement." The Communists' strength in the CIO was "greater than is often realized." Yet "all their achievements rest[ed] upon the shallow foundation of mass indifference and ineptitude." When workers "have been trained and inspired to fight for their rights"—and labor priests and the ACTU had often done that—they have "put down this disruptive minority."[108]

While chapter 4, "Communism and the Public," dealt with a "miscellaneous set of subjects," no matter how carefully its findings were camouflaged, it contained explosive material. It was here that Cronin addressed "Communism and Government." And it was here that he dealt a decisive blow to the viewpoint that the question of Communist infiltration was an irrelevant one.

During the past decade, Cronin argued, "Communists did penetrate into key positions of government." While neither Franklin nor Eleanor Roosevelt (nor any other of their "close advisers") "consciously sponsored Communists as such for government posts," they "belonged to that school of liberals" who did not "think the question of Communism was very important." Those "close to" the Communist Party therefore gained influence with them and were able to get Communists into important positions. On the one hand, Communist infiltration "was not so serious as Mr. Roosevelt's enemies charged, but it was much more extensive than his friends were wont to admit." Communists tended to "gravitate to positions most suitable for aiding the Communist line." In the 1930s these had included "reform agencies" such as the Departments of Labor and Agriculture. During the war they had been the "propaganda, price control, and foreign policy groups." Now communists could be found wherever they "might have the power to influence American foreign policy"—for example, in the State Department.[109]

The State Department was, Cronin argued, the CPUSA's "greatest objective." Michael Greenberg and Allen Rosenberg of the Foreign Economic Administration, which had been moved to State, were labeled "left-wingers," while Alger Hiss was declared a "Communist." The priest implied that John Carter Vincent and Archibald McLeish were Communists as well but left the description at "has instigated many of the attacks on MacArthur [*sic*]" for the former and "has aided their [the Communists'] propaganda policy" for the latter. Three others were named in the paragraph on the State Department.[110]

There were problems in other departments, too. Five officials in Immigration and Naturalization had "leftist views," and there was a "mild infiltration" at the Treasury Department. Three in the Budget Bureau, including the assistant director, were accused of either "gullibility or left leanings." The priest then moved on to Congress and those figures close to Roosevelt.[111]

Cronin's assessment of his own work was remarkably astute. This section, which undoubtedly relied greatly on Murphy's investigations and his access to other departments' security files, was "weaker than the rest of the report." Except for the material on six specific individuals whom he named—Hiss among them—"the information obtained was not from sources of unimpeachable accuracy." He was nevertheless convinced that the "data given" were correct but "general rather than circumstantial." (Four of the persons who were named, in addition to the group of six, showed up on Elizabeth Bentley's espionage list.) The material on the war agencies and the State Department was better than the rest but still not what the author would have wished or what he thought he had presented in the rest of the report.[112]

Then came an astounding discussion of "Communism in the Armed Services" that was derived mainly from "a former official of the Foreign Economic Administration, who had contact with high military sources." Using a sleight of hand seldom found elsewhere in the report and which may have been unconscious, Cronin implicitly attributed to Communists a lengthy list of grave sins that he, in the next paragraph, indicated originated at the White House as "part of the general campaign to please the Soviet Union."[113]

An examination of "Communism and the Liberals" followed. In a convoluted discussion Cronin first defined liberalism, its attitude toward Communism, and the judicious way in which their relationship needed to be treated. After the assertion that the Communist Party's "real use for liberals today" was for "publicity," a lengthy discussion of the "press and magazine," "authors and writers," Hollywood, radio, and teachers followed. This evidence, combined with that in his previous chapters, he argued, "begins to explain the success of Communist propaganda, particularly in regard to Soviet foreign policy." In view of all "these influences and pressures, one need not be amazed at the success of Communist propaganda."[114]

In the concluding chapter of the report, titled "Communism and Catholicism," Cronin offered a judgment of the problem and suggestions as to how Catholics ought to respond. There was no chance that America would go Communist or even that the CPUSA would gain "large numbers" who believed in Communism as a doctrine or accepted its discipline. If, however, the Red menace was defined in terms of the world and America's role in it, Communism was certainly a threat. A "weak stand" in the face of Soviet imperialism, Cronin argued, "would probably be the equivalent to the appeasement polices of the Allies before Germany broke forth with the invasion of Poland." It "would appear," he asserted, "that the maximum objective of the Soviet fifth column" was "the winning over of the United States to an acceptance of Soviet polices."[115]

Cronin then argued that, given this assessment, neither the negative way of fighting the CPUSA, through denunciation, nor the positive way, through social reform, was wholly appropriate. The remaining seventeen pages of the report recommended the specific steps the hierarchy ought to take to join the battle against Communism in a specifically Catholic way.

Cronin proposed, first, that he maintain his contacts and remain familiar with Communist Party literature so he could present semiannual reports to the bishops. (He thought, however, that he should spend most of his time on the positive program.) Second, the present report should be turned into a brochure for the clergy, who also should be encouraged to subscribe to the *New Leader*. Third, the Catholic laity ought to become involved, along the lines that the future founder of the Christophers, Father James Keller, M.M., had recently suggested, in the battle against Communism. The goal was to teach the "glorious truths of our Faith to a world which too often knows not the truth." Or as the Sulpician put it a bit later, "To do all this, we must abandon the 'foxhole' position of being merely defensive, negative, and critical, and go forth with the supernatural confidence of a St. Paul or a St. Francis Xavier."[116]

Cronin gave over the remainder of the report to a discussion of his positive program for defeating Communism. The first stage of his two-pronged plan was education in "social problems and Catholic social principles." The majority of the clergy should receive a "minimum understanding of objectives," while a few should attend highly specialized schools. Textbooks needed to be produced for priests and seminarians, while a "Catholic social manifesto," which could be the basis for the unity that Cronin so desperately desired, also needed to be written. "Social education" in Catholic primary and secondary schools had to be initiated, as did the beginning steps to instruct sisters for that work.[117]

From education would come the "trained cadre" to direct the struggle for Catholic social values. Since priests would initially lead the labor movement, Cronin next discussed how they ought to handle Communists in the ranks. (A related discussion of the ACTU was included in this section.) These clerics, Cronin argued, ought to establish schools for social action at the diocesan level and work together at the national. The NCWC's Social Department could play a coordinating role in all these efforts.[118]

In concluding his report, Cronin once again focused on the positive nature of the struggle against the CPUSA: "With these steps as a beginning, the rest will come in due time, God willing. Such a program should strengthen the Church in America and in the process remove the danger of Communism."[119]

Cronin and Alter, as we have seen, had long been unhappy with the Social Action Department's political trajectory. Monsignor Ryan's death in September 1945 provided the opportunity to make a change. The person to replace Ryan, Alter noted, "should have better grounding in economic science than any present employee of the dept." Such knowledge, he noted, "would help to create a better balanced policy in public statements." Since Cronin had decisively rejected Ryan's brand of social Catholicism, he was the perfect ideological choice. At its November 12 meeting the administrative board of the NCWC appointed McGowan director of the SAD and Cronin and Higgins assistant directors.[120]

As important as this decision was, however, more significant were the duties Cronin was to perform and the way in which those responsibilities were determined. He and Alter discussed them shortly after the administrative board heard a summary of his report and appointed him to the SAD. The next day, November 13, Cronin put together a memorandum outlining his responsibilities. Since they were going behind the backs of those in the SAD and wished to conceal their collaboration, Cronin asked Alter to have his suggestions retyped since his "typing style" was "bad enough to be distinctive." The intent of Cronin's memo, which became more or less his job description, was to provide him with "freedom" from detail work so that he could concentrate on the positive program recommendations in his report. But there was more to it than this. The terms that Cronin set were meant to allow him the time to act as an ideological counterweight to McGowan and Higgins. As he wrote Alter, "we should be firm in insisting that the necessary writing be done."[121]

There was the issue, of course, of Cronin's being moved into the department without consultation with McGowan, and the issue as well of Cronin's increasingly obvious disagreement with Monsignor Ryan's social Catholicism. For his part, Cronin promised Alter that he would work with his "colleagues in a spirit of friendliness and harmony." As for them, Cronin thought that McGowan's appointment as director would "remove the suspicion which I believe was the real cause of the flare-up last summer."[122]

One last set of letters between Alter and Cronin reveal more still about the depth of their disagreement with McGowan and Higgins. Cronin's most basic criticism of an article that McGowan had recently published was that it should not be called "Catholic," since it represented one school of thought, not the Church's "universal truth." This was a "serious error" that "had pervaded the entire thinking of the Department under the late Monsignor": the SAD advertised its programs as "Catholic social teaching" when they were "merely informed opinions as to *means* for attaining ideas espoused by the Church." Individuals, Cronin continued, were going into fields where "they do not have advanced training, either formally or through self-education." How to solve the problem? The solution was not, Cronin argued, Bishop James McIntyre's: "repressive criticism." Neither was it to require all three priests to agree, with recourse to the episcopal chair if there was no consensus. What if Haas became chair? "I might find myself pretty thoroughly gagged" and have to resign, wrote Cronin. The solution, rather, was the continued pressure of facts from the outside the SAD and continued discussion inside it. In addition, a set of instructions should be issued to the department specifying that: (1) not everything issuing from the department could be called Catholic; (2) members must distinguish whether they were writing as an individual or as a SAD member, and in cases of highly controversial material the episcopal chair must be consulted; and (3) the *Social Action Notes for Priests* and weekly "Yardstick" column that currently were advertised as coming from the SAD must be reidentified as the work of individuals.[123]

Alter had so much confidence in Cronin that he readily accepted his suggestions as to his duties as well as his advice on limiting the influence of the SAD. He considered the latter recommendations "a clear and quite comprehensive exposition of what would be a sound policy for our dept." He would follow Cronin's advice "with the sincere hope that it meets not only a verbal but also a convinced acceptance of what should be the policy of the dept." Late in December, after receiving a letter from Cronin's superior officially releasing him, Alter told Cronin that he had sent McGowan a memo "outlining your special duties" as "contained in [your] previous letters."[124]

Cronin's report and the work that went into it were first-rate. We now have a considerably fuller picture than ever before of its writing and of the varying sources that contributed to it. It is clear that the FBI more or less wrote large chunks of it and provided a good deal of the most accurate information. Murphy's contribution, though, particularly on Hiss, was essential. Because of all this help, Cronin was able to provide the hierarchy with extraordinarily detailed information on Communist strength in the United States. There are clearly points where Cronin's ideology led him to see Party members where there were only liberals and to conflate events that proved useful to the USSR with a conscious effort to aid it. In the main, though, Cronin got it right. There were Soviet spies in the federal government and elsewhere. Secrets about the atomic bomb had been passed along to the USSR. Alger Hiss was guilty. Julius and Ethel Rosenberg were guilty. Elizabeth Bentley's stories were more true than false. The CPUSA did have good deal of power in some CIO unions. It is hard to argue, for the most part, with Tamm's assessment of the report: "It is conservatively presented and rather fundamentally sound."[125]

Recent scholarship supports Cronin's assertions about the extent of Communist influence in the United States. His judgment that there was no chance of it gaining significant power on its own, let alone making a revolution, seems both judicious and accurate. Research into the origins and early development of the Cold War suggests, however, a considerably more nuanced interpretation than his understanding of "Soviet Imperialism."

Cronin's analysis was sometimes more sophisticated, but his was essentially a zero-sum understanding of the world which antedated NSC-68, the important National Security Council document of 1950 that encapsulated and codified the viewpoint that had been developing since the end of the war: that there were only two camps in the world—the United States (which was intent on preserving freedom) and the Soviet Union (which was intent on extending totalitarianism)—in the world, that when the United States won, the Soviet Union lost, and that when the United States lost, the Soviet Union won. Every event in the world, the argument went, could be fit into this bipolar analysis.[126]

Cronin's zero-sum vision of international relations seemed reasonable because it was on its way to becoming the primary mindset within which Washington policymakers functioned. This vision, however, excluded contradictory evidence. Just as President Truman was developing a tendency to do, Cronin "riveted" his "attention on the Kremlin's ominous conduct and overlooked signs of Soviet moderation." Stalin was quite willing to deal with the United States as long as it agreed to his "basic territorial demands": restoration of the 1941 borders and "a sphere of influence in Eastern Europe."[127]

Dealing with Stalin in this way, of course, would have left Polish Catholics and other Eastern Europeans at his mercy, but that was no more than what was happening anyway. It also was something that U.S. foreign policymakers cared little about. Cronin, at one point in his report, used conditions in Eastern Europe to critique the positive path of fighting Communism: "It is hard to see how social reform in the United States will restore liberty to Poland or free Hungary and Czechoslovakia from Soviet economic domination." Although he would not have seen it this way, Cronin was merely posturing. Short of starting World War III, the

United States could do little in the short term about Stalin's incursions in Eastern Europe.[128]

Cronin's report had its greatest immediate impact on the SAD, long a thorn in the side of Church conservatives. For one thing, it strengthened the conservatives' hand. Noll is a good example here. In April 1945 he wrote Cronin, as he would Bishop Bernard J. Sheil, an "I told you so" letter: "I feel particularly interested in the results of your investigation, because everything I wrote from 1936 on is verified by your findings. I was regarded as seeing 'Red' when there was no 'Red.'"[129]

In addition, it brought Cronin to the SAD, for without the report he would not have been appointed to the department, no matter how closely his economics agreed with that of Church moderates and conservatives. Cronin's appointment signaled the beginning of a reconfiguration of Catholic social action and social policy that produced an all-out war against American Communists and those who worked with them and ultimately the jettisoning of it's the NCWC's vision of "economic democracy."

Neither of these things occurred immediately, but Cronin's appointment set off shockwaves in Catholic labor circles. In a letter that was undated though written before Cronin's appointment but during his ascent to power, Father John Monaghan, the chaplain of the New York ACTU, offered Higgins this assessment: "Your good friend John Cronin is getting to be the l'enfant terrible of Catholic social action. His latest articles, his Communist complex, his megalocephalia which I believe includes taking John Ryan's mantle are very dangerous. I read lately a letter he sent to Roger Larkin the other day and it was bewildering. I think he would like to be Joseph to our Richelieu and the Josephs are the more dangerous, for they are always doing the right things for the wrong reasons."[130]

The comments of Father H. A. Reinhold must be seen in light of his outspoken opposition to Hitler, his subsequent exile from his native Germany, and his run-ins with the FBI and U.S. Church authorities. He wrote in December 1945 after he had heard (erroneously) that Cronin would be appointed SAD director: "Cronin in McGowan's place is typical: it paralyzes all the good and isolates George H[iggins] completely. After the asinine things I've heard about Cronin, I would not be surprised to see him help plot a fascist overthrow. His methods are perfectly fitted for it and the lack of conscience in him makes him a perfect tool for something senatorial. Anything smacking of cloak and dagger will fascinate him and make him do the strangest things."[131]

Strong words from Monaghan and Reinhold, yet not without truth. What the army intelligence officer had noticed in 1943 had apparently intensified, as Cronin seems to have become increasingly focused on ends rather than means and increasingly convinced that only the most heroic effort on his part could save the world from Communism. Along with this came paranoia and a sense of self-importance that led him to do "the strangest things."

For some months Cronin lost much of his sense of proportion. In correspondence with his superiors, he fretted that Communists in the Treasury Department would get at him through his tax returns, named the date for the Communist Party uprising in France, and worried that Communists might break into his office. In July 1946 he notified his superiors that "confidential sources" had told him that a Party member had enrolled at the National Catholic School of Social Service. Although she had withdrawn, Cronin, who lived at the school, wanted his letter kept "for the sake of the record," since "the possibility of obtaining information or of compromising a person by these methods are obvious."[132]

He apparently convinced himself, for a time at least, and as Ray Murphy had, that his actions alone could save Christianity and the United States. In early February he informed Alter not only that the Communists, "through their tendrils in the Budget Bureau," were trying to "take over" the FBI, but also that the Soviet Army was preparing to invade Western Europe. The "present picture," he argued, seems to "threaten the very existence of Christianity through much of the world, and the security of this last great haven of freedom, the US." He was willing to "take personal risks"—"even to the extent of being disclaimed and rebuked publicly"—to launch a "major attack" on those who were pro-Soviet.[133]

Out of this sense of crisis came a Communion breakfast talk by Cronin in which he asserted, according to a *Washington Post* headline, that "2,000 Reds Here Hold U.S. Jobs." The Communist Party was affecting policy in the State, Treasury, and Budget departments; Russia had atomic information. Cronin's superiors were sanguine about the press he received, but Hoover thought he had "popped off too prematurely."[134]

The very day that the *Post* reported his speech, Cronin approached the FBI with a plan for getting to the atomic scientist J. Robert Oppenheimer, under suspicion of being a Soviet agent. Father John O'Brien, at the Sulpician seminary, was "well acquainted" with Oppenheimer's secretary, who, Cronin thought, could be persuaded to turn informer. At a meeting with Cronin and O'Brien, however, she refused to do so. Cronin went back to the Bureau seeking "derogatory information" on Oppenheimer "that could be used in giving a 'pep talk' to the girl." His Bureau contact declined to help.[135]

Two years later Cronin proposed to Congressman Francis Walter, a member of HUAC, a series of nasty, dirty schemes to manipulate a grand jury into indicting Edward Condon, a scientist then under attack by anti-Communists. Those to be involved included an informant on the grand jury; several HUAC investigators; Alfred Kohlberg, a financial backer of *Counterattack* and a key member of the China Lobby; and New York governor Thomas Dewey, who was clearly going to be the Republican nominee against Truman in that year's presidential election.[136]

Monaghan and Reinhold, however, did not get at the whole truth. Cronin was quite ambitious and had become entranced with conspiracy and secrecy. He also was drifting further from reality and deeper into ideology. (His attack on Truman's choice for secretary of state, Dean Acheson, as a pro-Soviet appeaser was to him the logical and absurd place to wind up). Yet Cronin was onto something that the pro-Ryan SAD had ignored: the CPUSA had a great deal of limited, but still real, influence in America, and there were Soviet spies in the federal government.[137]

Perhaps it was these "facts"—as well as the USSR's ongoing solidification of its defense perimeter in Eastern Europe—that brought McGowan and Higgins increasingly around to Cronin's position. Cronin had seen "startling changes in a year." These were especially noticeable in Higgins, who, Cronin claimed, now said that Father William Smith, S.J., the vehemently anti-Communist labor priest with whom Higgins had fought for several years, was "99% right." In light of the way "Smith has been excoriating Philip Murray and the CIO," Cronin continued, "that is a remarkable statement."[138]

CHAPTER 5

⬥

A Jesuit Informant

Father Edward A. Conway, S.J., and the National Committee for Atomic Information

T HE HEARINGS that resulted in the well-publicized decision not to renew Robert Oppenheimer's security clearance began on April 12, 1954. A week or so into them Father Edward A. Conway, S.J. (1902–1965), wrote a brief memo to his superior: Conway wanted him to know that he had played a part in the prehistory of the drama going on at the Atomic Energy Commission. "In view of the excitement over Dr. J. Robert Oppenheimer and the atomic scientists," Conway began, "the attached memorandum may be of interest." Prepared for Archbishop Samuel Stritch of Chicago, the Jesuit explained, and presented orally to the spring 1946 meeting of the administrative board of the National Catholic Welfare Conference, it led to Conway's authorization "to continue as finance chairman and treasurer of the National Committee on Atomic Information [NCAI], with weekly contact with the FBI, which eventually caught up with our 'Executive Director.'" As a result, "we fired him," the memo concluded, "and 14 of the 15 office workers, whom he had hired, resigned 'in protest against our undemocratic procedures.'"[1]

Conway's connection of the firing of Daniel Melcher (1912–1985) in July 1946 with the Oppenheimer hearings suggests more than his flair for drama and his penchant for self-promotion. Melcher was a minor player compared to Oppenheimer, but to his detractors, his directorship of the NCAI provided him with the opportunity to advance the USSR's position or even to betray his country. In Conway's mind, the Melcher and Oppen-heimer matters both involved national security, loyalty, the atomic bomb, Communism, and patriotism. Catholicism, of course, was implicated too—not just the Jesuits, not just the U.S. Church, but the "holy, Catholic, and apostolic" Church, for this was how Conway positioned himself. From his perspective, he had done his duty for country and Church when he played a central role in purging Melcher.

The story of Conway's cooperation with the Bureau takes us deeper into the relationship between the Church and the FBI. In this case both sides took their shared values for granted and set to work, with no apparent equivocation, to intervene directly in the workings of a citizens' group of no small importance. That each was convinced—and there is consider-able evidence on their side—that the stakes were quite high should not keep us from recognizing the undemocratic and deceitful nature of what they did.

The situation, though, was a complicated one, for Conway—and through him the FBI—had several significant allies. Working closely but surreptitiously with Michael Amrine, public relations man for the FAS (Federation of Atomic Scientists, subsequently the Federation of Ameri-can Scientists), and William Higinbotham, the executive secretary of the organization and its liaison with the NCAI, Conway accomplished his task with few having any idea of what had gone on. Without Amrine and Higinbotham's agreement with Conway that Melcher and his staff were significant security risks, and without the enormous pressure created by the earliest months of the Cold War and the enormity of the atomic bomb, it is hard to imagine such a purge having been pulled off.[2]

There was nothing in Conway's career before 1943 to suggest that he could—or would—perform the part he did on the national stage. He re-ceived his B.A. from Holy Cross, his M.A. at St. Louis University, and his Ph.D. from the Gregorian Institute in Rome. Ordained in 1936, he was teaching at Regis College in Denver, where he had been since 1938, when he began the ecumenical peace work that provided him with the experi-ences that not only gave him the necessary qualifications for the NCAI job but also equipped him to play an extraordinarily difficult and complicated role there.

From 1943 through 1945 Conway participated in the drafting, publica-tion, and promulgation of "Pattern for Peace" (October 1943), an ecu-menical peace statement that gained considerable national attention, as well as *Goals for San Francisco* (April 1945), a set of recommendations for world government. He also served the Church at the founding conference of the United Nations; while he had Catholic News Service credentials, his primary purpose was to keep the highest levels of the U.S. Church informed. These activities positioned Conway for his NCAI work in a number of discrete but related ways.[3]

First, he learned how to get what he wanted from his superiors, both Jesuits and non-Jesuits. He was on leave from his Jesuit community (Regis) and province (Missouri) from 1943 until the end of 1946, which gained him the freedom to go about the important work he had undertaken. In obtaining this leave, he had impressed his provincial, nationally known Jesuits (Fathers John LaFarge and Daniel Lord), NCWC officials (Bishop Karl Alter, Monsignor Howard Carroll, and Father Raymond McGowan), and high-ranking members of the episcopate (Edward Cardinal Mooney and Samuel Cardinal Stritch).

Second, Conway learned how to organize his work and his time. Despite his self-promoting tendencies—a key ingredient in his success—the Jesuit does seem to have carried a large burden of the paperwork necessary to each of the projects. Moreover, he had the vision to see how each part and each person fit into the larger work. While coordinating all his projects, he also gave lectures to Catholics in dozens of cities and wrote a newspaper column, "Days of Decision," that appeared in numerous Catholic newspapers.

Third, "Ned," as his friends called him, gained experience in working with non-Catholics. This set him apart from most other Catholics, who did little ecumenical work in this era of "ghetto Catholicism." He worked closely with Jews and Protestants—147 leaders from all three faiths signed the "Pattern"—and drafted *Goals* with the ranking official of the Federal Council of Churches' Committee on a Just and Durable Peace and the Committee on Peace of the Synagogue Council of America. Early on he addressed the Carnegie-funded Church Peace Union, which decided to secretly fund much of his work. He also impressed influential people such as Clark Eichelberger (1896–1980), founder and chair of the Commission to Study the Organization of Peace.[4]

Finally, Conway had on-the-job training in balancing conflicting loyalties, roles, and responsibilities. He was functioning as a Catholic and as an official of his organization, as a Jesuit and cleric, and as a U.S. citizen and member of a universal Church. Advancing Catholic values and Catholicism was Conway's top priority, but that could occur only if he was willing to subordinate this goal for long periods of time.

The waters in which Conway was swimming were deep, dangerous, and uncharted, not just for him but for the Church as a whole. Despite his reports to those above him, despite seeking approval for his biggest moves—"particularly reassuring" for his provincial—Conway was largely working on his own. His success at doing so left him well positioned to take up the even more difficult job in the NCAI.[5]

The announcement of the dropping of the atomic bomb on August 6, 1945, was a "psychic event of almost unprecedented proportions." From it came enormous fear and a felt need to act promptly and decisively, which resulted in the formation of the two organizations that would be the scene of Conway's activities for the next year: the FAS and the NCAI. For both, the question was the same: Who would control atomic energy domestically and internationally?[6]

Atomic scientists had begun organizing even before August 6. Led by scientists in Chicago, where work on the bomb had finished earlier than anywhere else, they announced the formation of the Federation of Atomic Scientists in early November 1945. Although its name would soon to be broadened to the Federation of American Scientists, those involved in the Manhattan Project remained at its epicenter for many years. A month or so later a meeting of representatives from about fifty national organizations established the NCAI. The FAS was technically NCAI's parent, but the lines of responsibility were never made clear.[7]

Conway's hard work from 1943 through 1945 earned him a position as temporary treasurer of NCAI. On December 18 he was named permanent treasurer and financial chair at NCAI's founding meeting. Within a month the Jesuit also established a connection with the FBI that was formalized in March 1946. Since all of this required the approval of his various superiors, Conway laid out in a series of memos, two in December 1945 and one each in January and April 1946, the reasons why he ought to take the position, work with the Bureau, and continue to be away from his province.

The memo that apparently gained NCWC approval for Conway to accept the NCAI position was dated December 12, 1945. The situation was dire, the Jesuit argued, since what happened in Congress and the Senate as they went about determining who would control atomic energy could decide the fate not simply of the United States but of the entire world. He was well situated to affect the outcome. He already had helped Senator Brien McMahon, a Connecticut Democrat, write a speech and elsewhere referred to himself as the senator's "informal adviser." It was on McMahon's Special Committee on Atomic Energy, which had been created in late October, that the FAS focused its hope of defeating those who advocated military control of nuclear power. As an official in the NCAI, which was essentially the "civilian" arm of the FAS, Conway was in a position to be greatly influential.[8]

The reason Conway gave for being allowed to take the position was the specter of Communist manipulation of issues surrounding atomic energy. Although he acknowledged that "various groups" were "trying to turn [atomic] policy in the direction of their own interests," his primary concern was the Communist Party of the United States and its supporters. As he noted at the end of the December 12 memo, those who "follow the Communist line have been especially active" in using the scientists to raise money for their own purposes and in trying to "capture" the FAS. The scientists, Conway noted, "with a few exceptions," were "entirely sincere" and filled with a "profound sense of public responsibility." They were, however, "politically rather naïve."[9]

A follow-up report on December 20 was even more alarming as to what the Communists were doing to gain influence within the NCAI. At the December 18 founding meeting, Conway wrote, organizations had worked "tooth and nail" to gain membership on the seventeen-member executive committee, and "those with communist leanings were especially active." Conway himself could not be on the nominating committee, since the interim steering committee had slated him for permanent office, but he made sure that Catherine Schaefer of the NCWC staff was made a member. She then blocked the nomination of Martin Popper, the national executive secretary of the Lawyers Guild, an organization in which the CPUSA played a leading role. Some of those who ended up on the executive committee were from "organizations of leftist tendencies," but not enough, Conway thought, to "dominate" it.[10]

Conway's next report, dated January 14, 1946, focused on the Communists' effort to gain control of the NCAI. He had discovered that "their favorite device is one of infiltration in the form of voluntary office assistance and the doing of odd jobs for the group they want to capture." The Jesuit, though, was fairly sanguine about the threat, since he had moved into an "active voice" in NCAI leaders' policymaking. He believed that "if I am of sufficient service to them I will later be in a position to speak frankly if they are in danger of succumbing to the blandishments either of vested industrial interests or communist saboteurs." Conway also reported on the continuing meetings of the Dublin Conference, a group of internationalists in which he participated. The priest was worried about the political complexion of some of its members, noting that he was "checking with friends in the FBI for information."[11]

By this point, then, Conway had begun, with the apparent approval of Father Raymond McGowan, his immediate Social Action Department superior, the relationship with the FBI that would continue for the next year. Conway had a "close personal friend" from Milwaukee who worked in the Washington, D.C., Field Office. It was to him that he probably turned after receiving McGowan's permission. These rather informal meetings, several of which are noted in Bureau records, continued into February and early March. By then, however, Conway wished to resign his NCAI position, according to Father John Cronin, S.S., his SAD colleague. Cronin wanted him to stay, so he asked several FBIHQ agents to come to the SAD offices on March 9 to talk to him.[12]

Conway's relationship with the Bureau became "official" with this meeting. One of the agents present was Conway's Milwaukee friend, the other from FBIHQ's Internal Security Section. After talking with Cronin, they interviewed Conway from about 10:20 A.M. to 12:45 P.M. He was "extremely cooperative" and gave them "considerable information." They were particularly pleased with the "names of approximately 25 individuals who" had "aroused his suspicion in connection with agitation and pressure activities aimed at influencing the control of atomic energy and the dissemination of technical and other information concerning it." Conway, convinced "that a carefully organized [Communist] campaign" was "under way to influence the control of atomic energy and the pertinent information concerning atomic experimentation and the utilization of the results thereof," agreed to "furnish the Bureau any assistance possible."[13]

Because of "the obvious cordial relationship between the two," Conway's Milwaukee friend was designated to "continue the contact with [Conway] for the present." This arrangement apparently did not last long, but the Bureau then assigned a Catholic graduate from a Jesuit school to the task.[14]

The information that Conway provided the FBI agents was relevant to two on-going investigations. One pertained to the USSR's successful efforts to use the CPUSA to obtain atomic energy secrets. In April 1943 the Bureau had discovered that the NKGB, the "Soviet security and political police" and predecessor to the KGB, was working through a high-level CPUSA functionary to get information from scientists in the Manhattan Project. Relatively little was discovered on this front, however, until Igor Guzenko, a Soviet code clerk in the Russian embassy in Ottawa, defected in early September 1945. His revelation of extensive Soviet spying in both Canada and the United States provided information for—and a sense of urgency to—the Bureau's investigation known as CINRAD. The other investigation had begun when, in November 1945, Elizabeth Bentley walked into the New York Field Office, initiating a process that culminated with her giving the FBI the names of dozens of persons in Washington, D.C., who had provided information that went to Moscow. Some worked for the government, some did not. The extent of the spying was wide reaching and of great significance. The FBI began a full-court press on this investigation, which it code-named GREGORY.[15]

Both CINRAD and GREGORY must be kept in mind in any consideration of Conway's cooperation with the FBI. On the one hand, what he was doing was duplicitous and underhanded: from March 9 on, he was an informer for the FBI. No one with whom he was working—at least not until June, if at all—knew that Conway was regularly reporting to the Bureau. He would, as we will see, provide the FBI with considerable information it could have received nowhere else and engineered, with its cooperation and encouragement, the firing of the NCAI's director. On the other hand, he was acting from honorable and patriotic motives. The Soviet Union was using the CPUSA and those close to it to spy on his country. It was becoming increasingly clear how fragile the wartime alliance with the USSR was, and conflict with Russia appeared to be in the offing.

Two events in the month leading up the March 9 meeting undoubtedly gave Conway the sense that his work would be significant. First, in a radio broadcast on February 3 the influential journalist Drew Pearson revealed Guzenko's defection. Until this point both Canadian and U.S. officials had been able to keep the news secret. The reaction was immediate and sharp, particularly when Canadian officials arrested thirteen citizens on charges of espionage. Second, on March 4 British officials arrested the physicist Alan Nunn May, who almost immediately confessed to violating the Official Secrets Act. Nunn May, who had worked on the British portion of the Manhattan Project, had provided the Soviets with much atomic information.[16]

The FBI's primary focus of interest was FAS. In 1946 there was not an atomic scientist of any note who did not visit its offices, which it shared with NCAI. Among them, as we will see, were a few with CPUSA backgrounds, and many more who espoused the kind of politics that readily fit the Bureau's understanding of what a party-liner's position on atomic weapons would be. NCAI's importance to the Bureau, though, should not be underestimated, for here, as we will see, was a director and staff with significant connections to the subjects of the GREGORY investigation. Several, moreover, were very close to, if not actually in, the CPUSA.

Conway's "constant contact" with the FBI took the form of meetings and telephone calls with the Washington Field Office. There are references in Bureau files to one in April, two in May, and another in June. There is little in the records to indicate exactly what was discussed, but from a report Conway sent Stritch, we can get an idea of what his thinking was on FAS and NCAI as well as what the FBI was telling him. Conway's long memo, written at the end of April, bears extended discussion.

It was necessary to go into such detail, he explained, to "at once justify" his "fears and provide illuminating sidelights on Communist and fellow-traveller methods."[17]

He began with the November 16 meeting that established the basis for NCAI. The Jesuit could not discover who had sponsored the meeting but "saw familiar people very busy at the door." Among them were Michael Straight, the owner and publisher of the *New Republic*; Helen Fuller, the magazine's Washington correspondent; Freda Halpern, secretary of the Independent Citizen's Committee for the Arts, Sciences, and Professions (ICCASP); Joy Falk of United Church Women; and Rachel Bell, the Washington representative of Americans United for World Organization.

The information that Conway had on these five, which probably came from the FBI agent with whom he was working, scared him. Straight, who had bankrolled the meeting, was a liberal who had been "taken in repeatedly by the left-wingers," according to the priest. Falk was a member of the CPUSA club of New York City's eleventh district. Halpern, whose organization had just been denounced by the *New Leader*, was "almost certainly a Communist." Bell was a "Communist party member." Fuller was a "Liberal" with close connections to Harold Young, Vice President Henry Wallace's secretary, who was "reported to be a Communist."[18]

Falk and Halpern wound up on the NCAI's executive committee, Falk then being elected secretary. Halpern, Conway reported, "has worked very closely with Bell," who "in turn is very close to Helen Fuller." Both Bell and Fuller were "adept at organizing pressure on Capitol Hill." All three had "worked mightily for the nomination of Wallace as vice president and were in daily touch with Sydney [*sic*] Hillman [labor leader Sidney Hillman], during the Chicago Convention."

Conway was worried about two others on the seventeen-member committee. One was Olya Margolin, executive secretary of the National Council of Jewish Women, who "meets surreptitiously, after mysterious telephone calls[,] another party[,] who is a frequent visitor to the Soviet Embassy, Robert Lamb, CIO, about whom there is considerable discussion." Another was Gardner Jackson: "There is doubt about him, although after having been beaten up by Communists some years ago he is supposed to have turned into a bitter anti-Red." Jackson had denounced Daniel Melcher when he was proposed for the job of NCAI director, but someone—probably his FBI contact—had told Conway that it might have been an act, "just a devious Communist plot."

Melcher himself, said Conway, was a "radical," but there was no confirmation that he was Communist, although all his contacts were with "the ultra Liberals." The six female staff members he appointed were "so-called liberals." (Here Conway named just one person, Edith Marzani, who edited *Atomic Information*, the NCAI's newsletter. She came from "Press Research Associates, a left-wing propaganda outfit, closely tied in with the Nation and New Republic.") Melcher, Conway concluded, was "easily taken in by the Communist line, which he follows thinking it is nothing more than Liberal."

If we accept, for the time being at least, Conway's—or, perhaps better, the FBI's—analysis of the politics of those involved, here is what we have: of the seventeen members of NCAI's executive committee, there were two who were Communists (Falk and Halpern), one who was in touch with a person who visited the Soviet embassy, and another who might have broken with the Communist Party.

It is hard to tell if this Communist sympathizing bothered Conway in and of itself or if it worried him because of the organization's access to scientists with atomic secrets. Because both NCAI and FAS had offices in the same building and NCAI maintained constant intercommunication with the scientists, Conway's agent had told him, "those offices would be an excellent listening post for anyone who wanted to keep abreast of developments." Moreover, because atomic scientists took turns in coming to Washington to work with the permanent staff of FAS, "the latest information from the sites is always being discussed in the offices."

The way to control the FAS, Conway wrote, perhaps thinking of his own actions here, was "helping [it] in every conceivable way." Only left-wing liberals and the Communists," however, were doing anything to assist the scientists in their fight for civilian control of atomic energy. Here Conway pointed to the example of Bell. "The guiding genius," she had organized the Emergency Committee for Civilian Control which produced "terrific pressure" at a key point in the Senate debate. The "net result" was that the scientists were "beholden to no one but Rachel Bell, a Communist party member, and her left-wing assistants."

Two senatorial aides also concerned Conway. Herbert Schimmel, secretary to Senator Harley Kilgore's "anti-cartel committee" (a subcommittee on war mobilization of the Senate Military Affairs Committee), was "generally believed to be a Communist." In the priest's judgment, he had the West Virginia Democrat, "who addresses left-wing demonstrations" at his request, "completely under [his] domination." At a meeting at his house where William Higinbotham, FAS chair, was invited to discuss strategy, Schimmel "gave out with the party line in the most bald-faced manner" the "whole evening." McMahon, who thought Schimmel a "menace," was "helpless in the face of this situation." It was only the left that aided "him in his fight against the other ten members of his committee." It was, moreover, "widely believed that his own secretary[,] a Mr. Calkins[,] is a party member."

Conway was unsure about "a number of the key scientists." Melba Phillips, important because she served on the FAS staff, was "definitely Pink." Oppenheimer's background was worrisome: "He was said to have once held a card in the Party. He was president of the Teacher's Union in California." Harold Urey and Leo Szilard, despite the fact that he had "yet to catch them in a slip," also had Conway worried. The "arresting and disturbing thing about this uncertainty is if they are Communists," then the "jig is up." Edward U. Condon's case was "was even more disconcerting," but the FBI was "aware of the situation."

Conway provided Stritch with this information because he desired the cardinal's approval for what he was doing. The Bureau—Conway's agent as well as the "head of the FBI international espionage section"—wanted him to continue at the NCAI since the priest was providing them with "an inside picture of developments." They were "especially concerned" to have "the names of all those who show special interest in the scientists, and who were circulating around them." Conway already had "given them a number of leads for which they have appeared grateful" and had provided "scores of names for examination." His analysis of the state of affairs was dire: "I may say here that the situation in Washington with reference to the atomic bomb is ten times as bad as it ever was in Ottawa. The difficulty comes not from Red agents, who are pretty well identified, but from U.S. communists and fellow-travellers, who are much harder to handle." Conway thought the "next months would be critical." He concluded with a question: "Shall I continue my intimate association with the scientists as Treasurer and Finance Chairman of the Atomic Information Committee or shall I withdraw?" He had the FBI's "encouragement" but wanted "to have the approval also of the Administrative Board, at least through its chairman, Cardinal Stritch." No formal response, as far as I can tell, has survived, but Stritch clearly approved.

Was the situation at NCAI as dire as Conway thought? Either his information was terribly flawed, his political sensibilities were not terribly acute, or he was seeing things through a very special lens. Perhaps it was a combination of the three. Some of his assertions are clearly false, such as his claim "on good authority" that California congresswoman Helen Gahagan Douglas was "a Party member" (a charge that Richard Nixon would repeat when he ran against her for the Senate in 1950). So too his assertion about Calkins. Conway's implication that Hillman was left wing enough to taint Bell, Fuller, and Halpern is also wrong. That Andrei Gromyko, the USSR's ambassador to the United States, who became its

UN delegate in April 1946, used material from the Kilgore Committee in a speech does not, of course, imply anything sinister. Nor was it particularly significant that the *Daily Worker* and the "whole leftist press recently denounced the cut" in the committee's appropriation. Why a U.S. senator in charge of an extraordinarily important committee would be "helpless" in the face of the Schimmel situation is impossible to fathom. If the secretary was a "party member," moreover, why didn't McMahon have him fired? Why would he even have been hired in the first place?[19]

There is relatively little to support other of Conway's assertions as well. He flatly asserted that Rachel Bell and Joy Falk were members of the CPUSA. Bell, a crackerjack organizer, was active in world government organizations. Her husband, George L. Bell, was the Commerce Department's director of foreign trade. (She, ironically, would become, according to Melcher, one of Conway's most important allies.) There is no evidence in the secondary literature or the House Committee on Un-American Activities hearings to support Conway's charge. There is none for Falk in this material either, but the Jesuit's assertion about her appears in an FBI file. The ICCASP, which would play a significant part in Wallace's presidential run in 1948, was a front group, but I have found nothing on Freda Halpern.[20]

The evidence is better for Helen Fuller. Walter Steele, in Ellen Schrecker's words a "professional patriot," testified before HUAC about Fuller's popular front–left politics in 1947. The FBI opened a "100" file on her in 1941. By 1945 the Bureau had determined that she was not a Communist but had, as Steele asserted, participated in numerous front groups, including the Southern Conference for Human Welfare, the League of Women Shoppers, and American Peace Mobilization. The Bureau closed its file on Fuller that year; she served as the *New Republic*'s Washington editor 1946–1948, political editor 1948–1951, and managing editor 1952–1962. Conway considered her a "Liberal."[21]

FBI phone taps and surveillance probably were the source for the assertion about Lamb and Margolin. Lamb was fired as legislative director of the Steelworkers' Union in July 1947, at the same time as Len DeCaux and several other left-wingers, so Conway may have been onto something here. Irving Richter, the legislative director of the United Auto Workers, remembered Lamb as being "close to, but not of, the left." Helen Lamb, a writer for the *New Republic* and perhaps his wife, was in close contact, according to the FBI, with several key subjects in GREGORY.[22]

Jackson and Straight are in categories of their own. There was no reason for the FBI or Conway to doubt Jackson's sincerity as an "anti-Red." Left-wingers did beat him up. He did become anti-Communist. "Pat"

Jackson would become, within a few months, one of Conway's most important allies—albeit an indirect and inflammatory one—in his battle against Melcher. Straight, who had numerous meetings with Soviet intelligence prior to 1940, spent much time with the FBI during its GREGORY investigation. He had readily admitted to those contacts while working for the State Department. Surely the Bureau was concerned about his having anything to do with atomic scientists, but there is no mention of this in Conway's memo.[23]

That leaves Melcher, the NCAI director, about whom Conway did not seem terribly concerned when he wrote this memo on April 29. Matters would change greatly, however, as the months went on and the Jesuit learned more and more about the political complexion of the NCAI's executive committee and the office staff. There are, however, several other main characters in our story, primarily William Higinbotham and Michael Amrine. Without their commitment to firing Melcher, Conway would have been unable to accomplish what he did.

Melcher, whose tenure as NCAI director lasted from January through late July 1946, had a significant career prior to it and a grander one after. There were accusations that he was a CPUSA member but no direct evidence to support them. Conway thought that he was "easily taken in by the Communist line," but Melcher was not a gullible man. The Jesuit was much closer to the mark when he later asserted that the NCAI director had "proven connection[s] with subversive elements": Melcher was close to some who were CPUSA members and even more whom Conway identified as fellow travelers. Many of his friends and some he hired at the NCAI offices, moreover, were tightly linked to individuals who spied for the Russians. Melcher once wrote—somewhat disingenuously—"I'm not a communist. Neither am I a red-baiter." "Fellow traveler," as we will see, probably was closer to the truth.[24]

Daniel Melcher grew up in a privileged and cultured environment. His father was Frederick G. Melcher (1879–1963), co-editor of *Publishers' Weekly*, president and owner of its parent corporation, R. R. Bowker Company, and originator of the Newbery and Caldecott medals in children's literature. His mother, Marguerite Fellows Melcher (1879–1969), was a playwright and author. Melcher's favorite sports, which he had to give up during World War II, were flying and skiing. He belonged to a yacht club in Washington, D.C., and he and his wife employed a part-time maid.[25]

He graduated with an A.B. in economics from Harvard in 1934 and held various publishing positions overseas and in the United States until 1942. Classified 4-F, Melcher worked in the Treasury Department's War

Finance Division until he resigned to take the NCAI job. He moved up quickly there, going from publishing consultant to national director of its education section. According to the assistant to the secretary of the treasury, Melcher, who originated the "Schools at War" program, which focused on selling stamps and war bonds in schools, "turned in one of the best jobs of any of the section chiefs" who served during the war. Twenty-six people worked for him at one point, and the Office of Strategic Services (OSS) tried to lure him away.[26]

Melcher's publishing career post-NCAI topped his father's. He founded *Books in Print, American Book Publishing Record,* and *School Library Journal.* The International Standard Book Numbering (ISBN) system was his creation. While serving as head of Bowker for many years, he ran at least one other publishing company, which specialized in reference books. In addition, Melcher was an inventor and author.

Some evidence for Melcher's politics prior to 1946 suggests a popular front perspective—a solid, tough liberal who did not Red-bait—but considerably more indicates that he was further to the left than that. In early June 1941, before Hitler's invasion of Russia, he participated as a panelist for a League of American Writers' session on juvenile literature. Founded in 1935 by the CPUSA, the League lost many members and much support because of the Stalin-Hitler pact but still attracted some talented young writers and professionals in the publishing business. In December 1946, after the NCAI had fired him, Lewis Merrill, president of the United Office and Professional Workers of America (UOPWA) and a member of the CPUSA, offered Melcher the politically sensitive job of editing *Technical America.*[27]

Melcher's political and personal friendships with Rose Segure and Betty Bacon suggest a similar political perspective. Segure, who was close to the CPUSA if not in it, was working for the National Negro Congress, a front group, in 1946. Her correspondence with Melcher begins that year—although they clearly had known each before this—when she was handling the singer Paul Robeson's West Coast tour. She later ran Henry Wallace's presidential campaign in New Mexico. Bacon, a lifelong CPUSA member, initiated a postwar children's book series for International Publishers, the CPUSA press. Melcher not only supported her personally during the earliest stages of the project but also more or less wrote the business plan she presented to International.[28]

The FBI files that resulted from the Bureau's GREGORY investigation confirm that Melcher was close to the CPUSA. The relationship was ongoing during and after his NCAI directorship, so it is impossible to know exactly what the FBI and Conway knew and when they knew it. There is material in GREGORY not only about Melcher but also about the staff he hired, and it is extraordinarily illuminating.

First, Melcher himself. He was close enough to Philip Keeney, who was working, along his wife, Mary Jane, for the KGB and Russia's main intelligence unit, known as the GRU, to serve as a witness on Keeney's passport application. Melcher also mentioned him in his family's form letter that went out in August 1946. Mary Jane Keeney was contacted by Ursula Wasserman, "a strongly suspected Soviet espionage agent," about staying with her when she came to Washington. One of the things Wasserman wanted to do there was to get in touch with Melcher. He was among several important figures in the GREGORY investigation whose contact information appeared in Wasserman's address book.[29]

Melcher, the FBI noted, had "been in contact with a number of persons who have figured" in that investigation, several of whom he hired to work in the NCAI office. One was Rose Alpher, whose husband, Dr. Isadore Alpher, provided false medical information for Maurice Halperin, who, as an employee in the OSS and the State Department, spied for the USSR. A member of the American Peace Mobilization (APM) and a local sponsor for three committees that supported the Spanish Loyalists, Isadore also was in contact with Mary Jane Keeney. Rose, a member of the APM and the League of Women Shoppers, was an assistant supervisor of the Federal Emergency Relief Administration in 1941. Rose Alpher was NCAI's office manager.[30]

Cynthia Dierkes was deeply implicated in GREGORY. She and her husband, John Dierkes, who had worked at the Treasury Department, were friends—in fact they spent considerable time together one summer at the Jersey shore—with Helen and Gregory Silvermaster, who ran one of the spy rings in Washington, and their roommate, William Ludwig Ullman, also a spy. The Dierkeses, moreover, were close to Robert Miller III and Jenny Miller, who were probably spies. They and the Melchers seem to have each rented a floor in the same house. Cynthia Dierkes, in early June, was setting up the new offices for NCAI.[31]

There were more leftists and/or fellow travelers on the staff; probably one and possibly a second were CPUSA members. In the former category was Edith Marzani, whose husband, Carl, would go to prison in 1947, convicted for lying about his past political affiliations on his application for government employment, as he admitted in his autobiography. Another staff member, Doris d'Avila, had been the "research girl" for Richter, the left-wing UAW representative in Washington, D.C., when she resigned to go to work for NCAI. Her husband, Fred D'Avila, the assistant editor of the *CIO NEWS*, was fired in 1947, along with others, as Philip Murray began moving against the CPUSA members and/or fellow travelers on the CIO staff.[32]

Nancy Larrick, also an NCAI staff member, is in a category all her own. She had succeeded Melcher as director of the education section of the Treasury Department's War Finance Division. Larrick, though, served for only a short time before leaving to become assistant director of the NCAI. She was one of the many staff members who resigned when Melcher was fired. It is impossible to tell what her politics were before she came to NCAI, but they clearly were left-liberal afterwards. Larrick, the author of a pathbreaking article on racism in children's books, was one of the founders of the Council on Interracial Books for Children in 1965.[33]

There is little reason, then, to dispute Carl Marzani's characterization of Melcher as "a smart, progressive, excellent editor." Melcher certainly hired people associated, in one way or another, with the CPUSA and its causes. There is the "progressive" part and we will see much of that. But he also was a very good editor and manager, and we will see evidence of that as well.[34]

William Higinbotham—or "Willy," as he was known to one and all—started out thinking quite well of Melcher, but that opinion changed gradually, and then dramatically, as the months wore on. By late June or early July he was prepared to get rid of him for the good of the FAS and NCAI, though he finally plotted to do so for trumped-up reasons. If we are to understand how Higinbotham got to that point, we must begin with a look at his career prior to the NCAI.

The son of a Presbyterian minister, Higinbotham was born in 1910 and considered Caledonia, New York, his hometown. He graduated from Williams College in 1932, but, as he put it, "there were no jobs looking for a fresh BA from Williams," so he went on to graduate school at Cornell. Willy spent the next eight years there working on a physics degree. He supported himself throughout his graduate career at Cornell by playing the accordion in square dance bands. (He continued playing on Saturday nights for the rest of his life.) The physics department's search for a technician coincided with Higinbotham's long-standing interest in electronics. He began there full-time in 1935, then in 1940 he went to MIT, following Robert F. Bacher (1905–2004), to work on radar. The next move came in December 1943, when he went to Los Alamos with Bacher, who would remember him as "one of the best circuit experts" in the United States. There he was a group leader in the electronics division.[35]

Higinbotham's post-NCAI career was substantial. He stayed on in Washington as the FAS executive secretary until December 1947, when he moved to the Brookhaven National Laboratory. He retired as its senior physicist in 1984 and died ten years later. His early interest in the control of atomic weapons turned into a lifelong pursuit; much of his interview with the Columbia Oral History Research Office is devoted to this topic. He remained very active in the FAS, which renamed its headquarters in Washington, D.C., for him in 1995.

It is not easy to pin down Higinbotham's political views. He got along with everyone and was doctrinaire about little, so there is a familiarity toward individuals and organizations in his correspondence that can be deceiving. He also was not afraid of associating with Communists and leftists: Higinbotham, for example, spoke at the Win the Peace Conference in 1946, which had heavy Communist participation, and the Communist-dominated Waldorf Conference in March 1949. He understood the difference between capitalism and socialism, he took seriously enough Mike Gold's critical article in the *Daily Worker* analyzing why the United States dropped the atomic bomb to query Oppenheimer about it, and he offered a sophisticated critique of the Marshall Plan. Perhaps the best way to characterize him is as an old-fashioned American dissenter.[36]

There was, though, a hard edge to Higinbotham when it came to the scientists' movement. This came out quite early in his tenure as executive secretary of the FAS. In late November or early December, on "about the day" when he came to Washington to stay permanently, he received two reports that "Susie," the organization's full-time secretary, was a "card carrying member" of the Communist Party. One report came from the office of General Leslie Groves, who had overseen the Manhattan Project, and the other from the FBI. So, as Higinbotham later told an interviewer, "I had to fire her. And look around and get somebody else."[37]

The issue, at least as he remembered it in that 1980 interview, was not her membership in the CPUSA but rather concerns over the possible theft of secrets. Did he fire her, his interviewer asked, "because it wouldn't look good for the organization? There wasn't anything wrong with being a Communist?" To which Higinbotham replied: "No—well, but the point is, . . . if you are closely associated with the Communist Party, then you're bound to have somebody say, 'yeah but you know they're stealing secrets,' and you just wanted to—well, I explained to her, you know painfully, that we just couldn't have her. We had to stay as clean as we possibly could." There was, as Higinbotham surely knew, plenty more to this story. Some of what he left out—intentionally or not—indicates that Chicago scientists were implicated in Susie's firing.[38]

Michael Amrine (1918–1974), whose legal name was Milton F. Amrine, is the final central actor in this story. A novelist, science writer, and editor, he began his newspaper career, at the age of sixteen, for the *Emporia*

Gazette in Kansas. He went on to work for the *New Orleans Item*, the *Kansas City Journal*, the *Baltimore Sun*, and the *London Daily Herald*. During the war he was with army censorship and the Alsos mission, "an American scientific intelligence combat unit whose main objective was to determine German progress in developing an atomic bomb."[39]

Amrine, like Melcher and Higinbotham, had a significant career after working at the NCAI. He directed public relations for the Advertising Council of America for a year and then freelanced, including ghostwriting for atomic scientists. In 1953 he went to work for the American Psychological Association as "in-house science writer and media relations contact." He stayed there for many years but also wrote reports for the National Academy of Sciences and the National Institute of Health. In 1959 he published a book on the making of the atomic bomb, and the following year one on Hubert Humphrey.[40]

Amrine went to work part-time for FAS in mid-January 1946. From the scientists' perspective, they were getting a professional journalist. He was, according to Higinbotham, a "very good writer": his work on Harold Urey's article "Atomic Terror Tomorrow," which appeared in *Collier's*, was quite impressive. Amrine was to assist in getting articles placed and in following the organization's press coverage.[41]

The journalist, however, did not see his employment with FAS and NCAI as simply a job. What comes through in a side agreement between him and Higinbotham is something very different. It is worth quoting that statement in full because it provides an indication of how important Amrine thought the work of controlling atomic weapons was and how deeply he was committed to it. "He is embarking on this fantastic crusade," reads the agreement, "taking risks and hoping for results beyond that of the ordinary employer-employee relationship, and it is recognized internally that he should have reasonable right to be consulted or informed of basic policy decisions. In other words, responsibility and access commensurate with risk." This starting point explains much about Amrine's role in Melcher's firing. He went into FAS and NCAI hoping to accomplish great things in facing down the tremendous danger to humanity the bomb had unleashed.[42]

There is little hard evidence for Amrine's political views prior to his work with the scientists. The FBI turned up nothing during two security investigations. It is tempting to work backwards from what is revealed here—to assume that he had a history of anti-Communist activity—but my sense is that Amrine's politics were developing as he went along. He apparently was the first of the three key players—the others being Conway and Higinbotham—to have become decisively opposed to Melcher. The development of this animosity is worth examining in some detail.

A "lengthy deposition" for the FBI, dated July 22, 1946, gives us Amrine's explanation of why he had turned against Melcher. (He dictated the narrative at Conway's urging, which in turn came at the "instigation" of the Bureau.) His "first intimation" of Melcher's "political sympathies," Amrine remembered, came when he, Higinbotham, and Alfred Cahn attended a "private party" at Herbert Schimmel's house. Schimmel had grown up in an Orthodox Jewish family and received his early education in Palestine. His advanced degrees in physics came from the University of Pennsylvania. Jobless, he did a stint with the Works Progress Administration and finally ended up working for several congressional committees. He connected with Senator Kilgore in 1942; Schimmel suggested the formation of what would become known as the Kilgore Committee on war mobilization. Their association grew into "a partnership between the two men." Schimmel was also on friendly terms with four or five of those who, the FBI discovered during GREGORY, were spying for the Russians.[43]

Barry Commoner, who had a Ph.D. in botany from Harvard, also was present. In the navy since 1942 and a lieutenant, he had been assigned to the Kilgore Committee to get the views of scientists on legislation affecting them. By the time of this meeting he may have completed his military service since Amrine described him as working for "Science Illustrated," though he was wearing a navy uniform.[44]

The "stated purpose" of the gathering was to explain some of "the workings of Senate Committees to help the scientists in their work with the Federation and NCAI." What Amrine quickly figured out, however, was that Schimmel's and Commoner's analysis of both domestic and international affairs was "not only identical with the Communist line, but planned for the purpose of twisting the course of the Scientists' campaign to bring it closer to the ideas of the extreme left-wing."

At some point in the evening, before Schimmel and Commoner finished speaking, Amrine got a chance to engage Melcher "in a private conversation." He told Melcher that "world cooperation ran two ways," and that Schimmel and Commoner "had said much about our national policy and every subject under the sun but that they had not said anything about Russia." Melcher "became very agitated," Amrine remembered: "I put him down at that time in my mind as the kind of fellow who swallows everything that the Communists say out of a misguided desire to be fair to Russia and to the Communist Party."

Amrine, the deposition continued, recalled a "late night conversation" with Melcher about the damage that could be done to NCAI if anyone in it "could reasonably be accused of being a Communist sympathizer." He came clean about his own past in the Newspaper Guild and "student peace movement" and asked Melcher if "he had ever at any time engaged in activities which would give him the name of being radical or a "'Red.'" Melcher's response, according to Amrine, was that "he had never done anything whatever to give him that name, never joined any organization that might be considered Communistic in tendency, signed any petition, nor given any other evidence of being left-wing."

Melcher may technically have been telling Amrine the truth—except for, perhaps, his participation in the American Writers' Congress. Amrine in turn seems not to have doubted him at the time; if he did, there is no expression of it. Months later, though, at the time of his July 22 deposition, here is how he interpreted this conversation: "I now consider this important because in view of repeated comments I have heard from all kinds of people, I know that he must have done *many things* to give this impression and that, therefore, thus early in the game he was lying."

It is possible to see a similar sort of rendering in another incident discussed in the statement. Shortly after the Schimmel dinner party Commoner, Higinbotham, Melcher, Amrine, and some scientists were discussing "copy for an ad" and the "exact line to be taken." They disagreed "over what was to be or ought to be said on the subject of war." Commoner and Melcher wanted to "promote the line that the atom bomb made war impossible, and that there was, therefore, no need for any national defense—armies or navies were completely obsolete etc." They "were in accord while the rest of us were honestly trying to think out what could or should be said."

Although Amrine did not say so explicitly, he clearly thought that Melcher and Commoner were following the Communist Party line. There is, though, no evidence of that in his recounting, other than his explanation that "the line of the Communists and of informed scientists and others on identical issues is sometimes very close together and perhaps indistinguishable to the average citizen, but the line can be distinguished and the points of difference are in fact crucial."

It is apparent, then, that by March or April Amrine had become quite suspicious of Melcher's politics—according, that is, to his FBI deposition. There is no way of knowing the degree to which he was reinterpreting events in terms of later information, but it is safe to say that he went into the summer with an anti-Melcher disposition. Conway, of course, was suspicious of virtually everyone. Higinbotham alone seems to have been completely supportive.

Melcher stood up to Higinbotham's initial characterization of him as a "very live wire." For months he worked extraordinarily long hours for little pay and persuaded his underpaid staff, almost all female, to do likewise. The NCAI, under Melcher's leadership, had accomplished a great deal by early summer, but several espionage scandals—one in Canada and the other in Great Britain—established the context within which his enemies could begin the process of purging him as director.[45]

The NCAI surely fulfilled its mission of "education for survival." During its first five months it grew from nothing into a $10,000 a month operation and had the funds to expand to $20,000. Its office space, which it shared with FAS, expanded from four rooms to eleven. More than seventy national organizations had joined as constituent members, and about 450 speaking engagements had been arranged under its auspices. A two-day "Institute on World Control of Atomic Energy," held in July, attracted 985 delegates from thirty-eight states and seventy-four organizations. It put out a monthly newsletter, *Atomic Information (AI)*, and distributed reprints of speeches and articles by FAS members.[46]

Melcher turned himself into a fund-raiser after the staff "missed two pay-days" in April and May and only money borrowed from "friends" was keeping NCAI going. His campaign, which featured Albert Einstein, brought in $60,000 "as a result of a single telegram to 830 people who had given at least $100 to other progressive causes." The list of those who contributed is quite impressive.

NCAI had many projects that by late June or early July either were in the crucial beginning stages or would start soon. Philadelphia FAS members had raised money for a film that was in the works, while Amrine had got the Ad Council to send out about 300,000 pieces of literature. NCAI tied the professional fund-raiser it had hired in to its support from the "March of Time" newsreels. It had also committed to hiring "a radio promotion man" who would work with the "radio industry" on its July 16, August 6, and fall programs.

On June 4 the NCAI executive committee, in recognition of what its chair called his "outstanding leadership, untiring energy, and efficiency," raised Melcher's salary 50 percent; this restored the pay cut he had taken when he left his treasury job. Within a matter of days, however, things began to fall apart. Numerous events established the framework within which key figures shifted from mistrusting Melcher to deciding to fire him, but the two spy scandals seem to have been most significant.[47]

The revelation that the Soviet Union had spies in Canada, which came out at the beginning of February 1946, reverberated throughout the nation. Its impact was especially pronounced in Washington, D.C., where it drastically transformed the debate in Congress about civilian versus military control of atomic energy. In alliance with Senator McMahon, the NCAI,

FAS, and key members of the academic-intellectual-technocratic community had defeated the May-Johnson bill, which would have established military control. A new bill, much more to the liking of FAS, was moving its way through Congress under the direction of McMahon's special committee. General Groves and his congressional supporters were nursing their wounds.[48]

The spy scare, though, as Higinbotham wrote on March 1, "completely changed the picture." The opponents of civilian control "capitalized" on it and garnered enough support to get the May-Johnson bill another hearing. Groves testified in both open and closed hearings before McMahon's committee despite the senator's determined opposition. Higinbotham, who was very pessimistic, even feared that the committee might report out something "like the Johnson bill or worse." He warned the FAS chapters to be careful with Groves: "It is perfectly alright [sic] to attack the statements of the General. However, I urge you to be very cautious in all public statements."[49]

The response of the FAS national office to those groups that used the spy story to "discredit scientists" was to remain silent, except to "state that we do not believe in unilaterally giving away vital information." On the one hand, this seems to have been a principled response, but on the other, it was "difficult," in Higinbotham's opinion, to know what to do when the FAS was "smeared. As he wrote to another correspondent, "We could not think of any adequate way of fighting back at the time and I believe our silence in this case was the best thing that we could do." (He would follow the same course again in 1950; when Senator Joseph R. McCarthy attacked him and the FAS, a spokesman said that he "had no comment on the McCarthy assertions.")[50]

In early March 1946 espionage again was front-page news when British authorities arrested Alan Nunn May for spying for the USSR. His confession intensified the spy scare and added to the political pressure against FAS and NCAI, the two most effective organizations fighting for civilian control of atomic energy. AI's coverage of the Nunn May affair would become one of Amrine's key charges against Melcher.

Higinbotham thought that the espionage uproar had peaked about March 1, but Conway, who returned to Washington after several weeks away, found the situation dire. "There is a terrific spy scare going on and the military are taking full advantage of it," he told his sister. Senator Arthur H. Vandenberg, a Michigan Republican, had introduced an ominous amendment to McMahon's bill. According to Conway, the "scientists claim it means virtual military domination while Vandenberg claims it means nothing of the sort." Groves had scored several more significant victories, and Conway "fear[ed] that the scientists' cause" was "finished."[51]

Rachel Bell and her people, in close conjunction with FAS and NCAI, set to work arousing public opinion against military control, particularly the Vandenberg amendment. She was extraordinarily effective. By the end of the month "there were signs that the atmosphere was clearing." The primary focus of the struggle for civilian control moved largely behind closed doors.[52]

The revelation that the Soviets had been running espionage rings in Britain and Canada was one of the signs in the first half of 1946 that the "grand alliance" between the USSR, Great Britain, and the United States was disintegrating. Other warnings of this deteriorating situation included the eight thousand–word telegram (the famous "long telegram") sent to the secretary of state by Moscow-based Kremlinologist George Kennan arguing that "Stalinist Russia was a totalitarian regime bent on expansion"; Winston Churchill's "Iron Curtain" speech, in which he "said publicly what the professional diplomat wrote privately"; the crisis in Iran; and the declining fortunes of the Chinese Nationalists.[53]

FAS—like, to some degree, NCAI—often was on the defensive during the period leading up the attack on Melcher in June. NCAI kept a folder of Canadian and U.S. newspaper clippings that followed the spy scare. FAS not only followed suit but also, at the suggestion of Lamb and the journalist Al Friendly and with the approval of the FAS national council, put together a ten-page summary and analysis. In early May the FAS office sent this memo to its member associations, various scientists, journalists, and other interested parties saying that it was doing so because of the "unfortunate effect of the Canadian spy scare on our atomic energy in this country."[54]

HUAC began its own investigation into atomic espionage in late March. It announced that it had concluded its investigation at Oak Ridge and would soon hold closed hearings in four other research centers. The FAS memo drew its readers' attention to what HUAC was up to and warned of its impact on the congressional debate and the morale of atomic scientists. It also suggested that Ernie Adamson, HUAC's chief counsel, was working with Groves. In early June the FAS national office warned the Chicago group that HUAC investigators might be visiting and advised it on how to handle requests for records. FAC officers did not think that hearings would occur because they were "pulling all the right strings," but Chicago had to be prepared if the congressmen tried to pull a "fast one." This specific hearing, and hearings more generally, never came off, but the threat hung over the FAS offices all summer and beyond.[55]

The first step toward firing Melcher was taken at the June 9 NCAI executive committee meeting, where the so-called Baruch report was discussed. Five months earlier, in January 1946, the United States and the Soviet Union had agreed to establish a United Nations Atomic Energy Commission. Truman chose a special committee to draw up a position paper that would guide the Americans in their work on this commission. The committee produced a document, known as the Acheson-Lilienthal report, inspired by Oppenheimer, its only physicist consultant, which laid out a plan for international control of atomic weapons and atomic energy. The hopes that this report produced for genuine cooperation were at least diminished, if not destroyed, when Truman appointed Bernard Baruch, the Wall Street financier, to handle the presentation of the U.S. proposals to the UN. Baruch, as many scientists realized, was not the right person to convince the Russians of the Americans' good intentions. His social position and personality were all wrong. Baruch, moreover, had little sympathy for international control.

There are two accounts of this June meeting. Melcher, who supported Acheson-Lilienthal, was, Higinbotham wrote, "for editorializing on the Baruch proposals," but most of the others were "for a straight report." Another meeting was called for June 23. According to Larrick's memo, there was much that Higinbotham left out. "There had been," Gardner Jackson asserted vigorously at the meeting, "serious criticism of NCAI publications." He admitted when questioned, though, that he had not read any of them and had not challenged the critics, nor would he produce their names, but said only that the matter was "serious and deserving of a special meeting." The executive committee agreed, Larrick wrote, to gather on June 23, even though Melcher already was committed to an FAS meeting in Chicago.[56]

It is unclear why Jackson chose this moment to go after Melcher, but he probably had discussed the political tenor of NCAI's material with Amrine. As we have seen, there were numerous episodes in the first few months of Melcher's directorship that made Amrine wary of him. His apprehensions seem to have increased during the spring. It is best to hear things from his side, as he explained it in his July 22 statement for the FBI.

Throughout late winter and spring, said Amrine, he paid close attention to the Communist Party position on atomic energy so he could "be very careful that the program of the Federation did not inadvertently fall into the traps of the Communist line." What he discovered while "checking this over" in July was that "on each one of these points I have had vigorous expressions of opinion from Mr. Melcher and I cannot think of a single instance in which he has deviated from the Communist line." More than this: "I will stand unequivocally on this statement that the evidence to me so far as our discussions are concerned are that the line of Mr. Melcher and the Communists are identical."[57]

Three other incidents, the journalist attested, provided additional evidence of Melcher's fellow-traveling. First, Melcher "jumped" Amrine in the office one day about his "expressions against the Communists and said that he did not know what the Communist attitudes were, but that so far as he had observed, their viewpoints were identical with those of the scientists." When Amrine vigorously disagreed but was not able to continue the discussion because he was too busy working, Melcher "lost his temper and left the room." Amrine thought that Melcher was trying to "smoke" him out to see if he was "hep to what was going on."[58]

The second incident involved an interview with Einstein. Melcher, according to Amrine, horned in on the trip to Princeton and then tried to sit in on the interview. He "attempted to argue" with Amrine "about what should be in it. His points were without exception along Communistic lines." When this did not work, Melcher tricked the NCAI executive committee into not using the interview. Higinbotham later wrote that he had no idea why Melcher did this, but Amrine clearly thought it was because it did not follow the Communist Party line.[59]

Third, Amrine noticed a disturbing correspondence between the views of Larrick and the *Daily Worker* about the Baruch plan. He was concerned not with the "merit" of her criticisms but rather with their origin, and thought that Melcher "echoed" her points "very strongly." The day after he talked to Larrick and the morning he spoke to Melcher, Amrine bought a copy of the *Daily Worker* and "found the lead editorial expressing" their arguments "in *exactly the manner and tone*" they had used. "This was much more than coincidental," Amrine believed, "and could not be dismissed as a mere accident." Walter Lippman, he admitted, soon made the same points about the Baruch plan, but he could not see how, since the proposals were not made public until Friday, "on Sunday Miss Larrick could so accurately forecast the Communist line."[60]

Again, this might be hindsight on Amrine's part. We do know for sure, though, that on June 4 he voiced concerns that FAS was taking positions that coincided with those of the CPUSA. "Warns on future possibilities of losing out because of Red scare—avoid making statements which tie in with policy of *Daily Worker* & *New Masses* if possible," read his handwritten notes on a memo to the organization's officers.[61]

Jackson, in preparation for the June 23 meeting, had Amrine put together a lengthy analysis of *AI* which indicated that Melcher and others on his staff supported "political beliefs and procedures beyond our common search for information and our understanding of atomic problems." Neither Amrine nor Higinbotham could be at the meeting, but Conway, whom Amrine had seen several days before, told him that he had Higinbotham's proxy. Not yet convinced that Melcher had to go, Higinbotham, as he noted in his diary, saw the problem primarily as an administrative one: "The red scare again about Dan. I can't supervise everything, but now we that have dough, someone has to do it. What I'd give for more help!"[62]

Amrine was convinced not only that Melcher was dangerous and was setting up NCAI and FAS for a fall, but also that the situation was getting increasingly dire. He wrote Jackson two days before the June 23 meeting that his "heart" would be with him: "We may have a tough fight ahead, but it will be the most important of your career." Amrine then recounted a discussion between him and Melcher about editorial control of *AI*. Melcher argued that he would "clear everything with Higinbotham[,] but primarily for scientific accuracy not politics." This convinced Amrine that Melcher was trying to put himself beyond supervision: "In other words, he has got his start and is cutting out on his own. But you can bet he will throw around the fact that his organization was instigated [by] and cohabits with the scientists." The NCAI newsletter, Amrine argued, needed an editorial board; if he could not serve on it, he wanted "absolutely to have the right to attend and speak." The issue, though, had become personal. After noting how many readers his *Collier's* piece with Urey had had and how many important people had come to him for advice, he closed his memo: "I'll be goddamned if I'll put up with being by-passed in an organization for which I've done so much and I'll be more goddamned if I'll stand by and let them sabotage it. Yrs still getting madder."[63]

Melcher's version of the discussion that so angered Amrine was considerably different. On the same day that Amrine wrote Jackson, June 21, Melcher wrote Higinbotham, who apparently had participated in the conversation about editorial policy, to set up procedures for reviewing copy. Melcher asserted that NCAI had checked every publication with an FAS officer at some stage and would continue to do so. "It seems to me," he wrote, that this has worked pretty well. You and I haven't disagreed on anything yet." Melcher admitted that he had not given Willy enough time to review the "Freedom in Science" issue, but Higinbotham had assured him once he had looked it over that there were no problems. The NCAI director promised Higinbotham that he would check "final copy" with him or with another FAS officer if he was not there.[64]

The June 23 NCAI executive committee meeting that featured Jackson's attack on Melcher was bizarre. Amrine, Higinbotham, and Melcher were away from Washington on FAS and NCAI business, and Jackson also was absent. Ralph McDonald, the NCAI chair, originally invited Larrick, according to her account, to the meeting but then changed his mind. She, however, using information from McDonald and, we can assume, others present, provides considerable detail that is missing from the official minutes.[65]

Jackson, despite his absence, played a critical role in this meeting. Sometime beforehand he sent a 516-word telegram to McDonald which "hinted that his charges against Mr. Melcher would be serious." He also noted that he could "document them." The evidence, in the form of Amrine's memo, materialized, however, only after an executive committee member was asked to go to Jackson's office to get it and then reveal the identity of the author. Both Jackson's telegram and Amrine's memo were read at the meeting.[66]

Amrine's memo raised eight specific examples of Melcher's political agenda at work in *AI*, but several references are too vague to be identified. Two of the remaining six had to do with Spain. One news item repeated what Amrine accurately called a "wild assertion" by Oscar Lange, Poland's Communist UN delegate, about the number of German scientists working on the atomic bomb in Spain. The other noted that the anti-Franco government in exile had provided the UN with additional information about German atomic scientists working in Spain. The original copy of the article had referred to its charges as "substantiated," but Conway got the wording changed to "submitting" additional charges.[67]

Two of the remaining examples concerned atomic spying. At several points *AI* had commented on the Nunn May case in a way, Amrine argued, that set it apart from mainstream U.S. scientific opinion. (Most scientists avoided the issue because Nunn May had voluntarily confessed.) It, moreover, had quoted the British Association of Scientific Workers as if the group represented commonly shared English scientific sentiment. In the case of the Canadian spy story, *AI* noted that one of the defendants had been acquitted but neglected to report that others had been found guilty.[68]

Amrine, in what was perhaps the most damning piece of criticism, observed that *AI* had quoted extensively from Frederick Joliot-Curie, the French physicist, but failed to indicate that he was a member of the French Communist Party, trying instead to pass off his views as those of a disinterested scientist. Melcher, more significantly, planned on scheduling Joliot-Curie to speak at the upcoming NCAI institute.

The memo's final criticism concerned an "Opinion-Round-Up" that showed a "slant observed in other selections of opinion and news round-ups, which reminds one strongly of the technique used by propagandists to slant ostensibly impartial compendiums." The piece approvingly quoted

Senator Claude Pepper, who had described the United States holding the "atomic bomb like a Damoclean sword" over Russia, and two well-known conservatives who had made "possibly the two most extreme and worthless comments on atomic subjects made by anyone at any time." Amrine admitted that he did not have any "evidence outside of these writings to prove in court or to the satisfaction of a reasonable man that the persons being discussed belong to the Communist Party." He was convinced, however, that "a representative of the Unamerican Committee" could work this material "into an extremely damaging attack."[69]

There is no official report of the NCAI executive committee's response to Amrine's charges. McDonald told the absent Larrick that it "laughed [them] off" but did bring up Melcher's nonpolitical mistakes. According to the also absent Higinbotham, and confirmed by the minutes, the executive committee "decided it had not paid enough attention to its responsibilities," so it set up publications, finance, and policy committees to provide "closer and more effective supervision."[70]

Conway has slipped far from view in our story, and that is how he wanted it. He informed a superior that he "had no part in preferring the charges against Melcher" at the June 23 meeting. "I restrict all my observations," he continued, "to questions of efficiency, prudence, administrative ability, etc." Melcher had to go, but Conway did not want to take a leading role in the deed. (It is impossible to know for certain whether or not he was secretly meeting with Jackson and Amrine.) He continued to play this behind-the-scenes part as events began to move toward Melcher's purge.[71]

The Jesuit remained in close communication with the FBI. At the end of May he wrote the NCWC general secretary, saying that his "FBI contact [had] just left." The agent had told him that the Bureau kept "two men on Oppenheimer always" and that "eighteen members of the House are Commies." Several weeks later Conway reported that he was "continuing his contacts with the FBI." This time his agent had informed him that after the June 23 meeting Melcher "phoned the man considered by the FBI to be the head of the Communist underground in the District of Columbia, and told him about being charged with being a communist." A week later the New York Field Office inquired of the Washington Field Office what it knew about Melcher. Washington agents "had word that a foreign agent whom they had been watching for months had a date for dinner with Melcher in Washington at a certain apartment." Conway later learned that "she had come down to negotiate for a position" with the NCAI.[72]

How do we evaluate this? Because the assertion about Congress is so blatantly wrong—within the realm of possibility only if "Communist" is defined so loosely as to be absurd—it is tempting to rule completely out of hand the rest of what the agent told Conway. Given, however, the FBI's months-long surveillance of Ursula Wasserman and what the Bureau discovered, undoubtedly through a wiretap, about her effort to contact Melcher, there seems little doubt that she was the "foreign agent" Conway's contact mentioned. Another FBI document also suggests that the assertion about Melcher's telephone call was correct.[73]

Things moved fairly quickly from the executive committee's June 23 meeting to its July 7 one, when all new NCAI activity was suspended and the decision was more or less taken to fire Melcher. New people got involved in the action, and there was considerable plotting. It is difficult to sort out exactly what happened when and who did what to whom. Nevertheless, this is what appears to have occurred.

Melcher continued to provide ample support for Amrine's argument that he had to be let go. First, he brought in a journalist to handle NCAI's press relations for its national institute on atomic weapons. The problem was not only that Melcher hired someone when there was an understanding that the job could be handled internally but also that the person was George "Slim" Engerman. Amrine knew Engerman from the *Morning Sun* during his own days as a reporter in Baltimore. There "and now among Washington newspapermen," said Amrine, Engerman "has a reputation of being a Communist, not an extreme left-winger but a Communist." Engerman (his name is also spelled "Engleman" and "Engeman" in the documents) was telling people that he recently had been fired from McGraw-Hill for "red-baiting reasons." Amrine, who had talked with him several times since he had come on staff, was "convinced that he was a very dangerous man to be associated with our educational campaign."[74]

It is with the Engerman hiring that we begin to see evidence that Amrine was discussing his fears with Conway and Higinbotham. The former knew—surely from Amrine—about Engerman's reputation in Baltimore. "I have called the FBI's attention to his record on the Baltimore Sun," Conway reported, "where he was generally believed to be a Commie." Amrine also brought his concerns to Willy, who noted in his diary, "Mike aroused because Dan hired George Engleman for a couple of weeks."[75]

Dan Gillmor also played a part in Amrine's indictment. Melcher, who "spoke quite highly of him" (there is direct evidence from Melcher for this), told Amrine that he "had once been instrumental in hiring Gillmor for the Treasury Department although he was considered to be a Red and was said to have been fired from other Government agencies for that reason." Amrine had "previously heard from friends" that Gillmor, "formerly a magazine editor, was a Communist sympathizer if not a Communist." Only a few days before, Amrine wrote, "I accidentally noticed Mr. Melcher's name on a letter from Gillmor." (This suggests—indeed, probably indicates—that Amrine rifled through Melcher's desk.)[76]

Matters heated up as the July 7 meeting approached. On July 3 Amrine came to Higinbotham "all upset" with "more evidence." He had heard— erroneously, since it would not happen until December—that Carl Marzani had been "kicked out" of the State Department. The problem here, of course, was that Edith Marzani, Carl's wife and probably a current Communist Party member, had worked for NCAI almost from its inception. Higinbotham's diary entry is a written sigh of relief that he did not have yet another Communist personnel problem to handle: "Edith had to quit anyway" (because of illness). There were also concerns about a woman who worked for Congressman Hugh DeLacy who was also doing the news clippings for NCAI, FAS, or both. Higinbotham did not think there was a problem ("Can't see any trouble here"), but he did not know what Amrine may have been aware of: DeLacy was secretly a member of the CPUSA. "Things," Higinbotham noted, "are kind of tense." Amrine, though, had raised yet another reason why the NCAI director had to go, for after this diary notation Higinbotham wrote, "Dexter Masters?"[77]

Melcher had hired Masters—who, like Engerman, had recently been fired from McGraw-Hill for reasons "in which 'Red-baiting' featured largely"—to put together a "press book for use by newspapers" on the dropping of the atomic bomb on Japan. Despite the fact that he and Higinbotham wanted it to be "factual," the book that Edith Marzani had compiled was not only "sloppy and inaccurate" but also, Amrine argued, "as obvious a sample of propaganda in the guise of fact as I have ever seen." A more recent version, done under Masters's direction, he considered just as bad: it "contained distortions of the atomic situation—and to me was quite significant of the concealed purposes of the authors."[78]

On July 4 Amrine and Conway, probably working in concert, had lunch with Higinbotham. The "long talk" that ensued surely was part of their effort to convince him that Melcher had to be fired immediately. Higinbotham was perplexed. "I can't figure this all out," he confided to his diary. "Somebody thinks I am an F.B.I.!" (This, Higinbotham noted in the marginal comments that he seems to have gone back and made from time to time, was "Dan's rumor.") Flummoxed, he took the afternoon off and went to a movie that evening.[79]

The next day Conway and Higinbotham had lunch again, but the latter's diary gives no indication what they discussed. He had learned that John Simpson, FAS's representative to the NCAI executive council, whom he expected at the meeting, was not coming. Simpson (1916–2000), a Metlab scientist active in the Atomic Scientists of Chicago, had worked closely with the McMahon committee and became the senator's "private science adviser and speech-writer." In a long, forceful letter he had pressed Higinbotham to take action again Melcher and assert FAS direction of NCAI. But now he was going to miss the meeting and had given Leo Szilard his vote. Willy, frustrated, commented: "What a system. Also he should have given us warning."[80]

The Sunday, July 7, meeting, held at the Sheraton Hotel, began at 1:00 P.M. and lasted, without a break, until about 11:00. Melcher, "on advice" from McDonald, ignored Jackson's and Amrine's charges. He merely presented his report on the first six months of NCAI activity and recommended five specific programs of expansion. "No interest was shown," Larrick noted, "almost no questions were asked, and Mr. Melcher was requested to leave the meeting." After that, just two topics were discussed. The first, of course, was Melcher himself. Second, fundraising had become, partly because of Szilard's involvement, a serious matter of contention. As with the Melcher situation, trouble over funding had been brewing for days. The money issue took time to discuss; it is impossible to know exactly how much, but we do know that when it came up, everyone was already exhausted. The meeting, as we have seen, resolved to suspend all new NCAI activity for a month.[81]

This was a well-attended function. Almost every organization on the NCAI executive committee was represented, either by the regular member or, in several cases, by a substitute. McDonald, the NCAI chair, introduced those who were there, since a number of them had not been at a meeting in awhile. Jackson's second consecutive absence was significant, though it goes without explanation in the surviving materials.[82]

Few charges of Communism and/or fellow traveling were mentioned in reference to Melcher. Instead there was an "extended discussion of NCAI staff needs." Helen Reid (1901–1965), who directed international affairs for the American Association of University Women, "expressed much dissatisfaction" with Melcher and wanted him replaced immediately. Others also criticized "aspects of his work," but there was no agreement about what made a good director and the "desirable procedure" for "correcting staff deficiencies." Criticisms of Melcher were limited, according to another official account, to "the field of organizations." NCAI, after all, had been created for this very purpose, and those present were "certainly the most competent judges of this sort of activity." To some extent the problem, the executive committee confessed, was its own fault because it had not adequately supervised Melcher. Everyone present agreed, though, that he was not "competent enough" to direct the NCAI, so they decided to tell him of their decision "to get another more competent director. They would ask him to keep his present position" until he was replaced.[83]

These, of course, were not the real reasons why Melcher was fired. As Conway reported a day after the meeting (he was present but apparently said little and certainly did not take a leading role), his dismissal was blamed "on other grounds than" politics. Or, as he put it about a month later, "the arguments used in this matter at the meeting dealt with everything except the real reason[,] which is his proven connection with subversive elements." (The Jesuit noted that only Falk, of whose Party affiliation Conway was convinced, brought up Communism.) "Any red-baiting," Higinbotham remarked, was "regretted."[84]

Higinbotham's diary entry for July 7 is as much about the deep background of the decision to fire Melcher as about the meeting itself. "For the record," he wrote, "I should say that Pat Jackson was opposed to Dan at the start and has always been very leery of him." He continued: "Conway & Dan have always clashed personally." McDonald, the chair, "is honestly just worried and trying to do the right thing." Turning to the meeting, he noted that Reid "felt strong about wages & hiring for every job." Falk "carried much of the self criticism." Higinbotham reproached himself for his passivity during the meeting. He, of anyone present, had worked the closest with Melcher. He, because he was FAS chair, had the responsibility of overseeing Melcher's work. There were many reasons, as we have seen, and as Higinbotham noted in his diary, why he did not or could not do so. Yet in the end, none of this mattered: "I am guilty for not standing up to defend Dan and making this [other?] clear."[85]

On Monday, the day after the July 7 meeting, McDonald and Melcher had a four-hour session in which they discussed the situation. McDonald then described the meeting to Higinbotham. McDonald, who Willie considered the "fairest and most decent person I have ever seen," was convinced that Melcher was not "the man for the job of director or that he is very good for the job he has—principally because of [his] personality and desire to run the whole show." Melcher, according to Higinbotham's account, "kept asking what's the matter with him?" while McDonald "kept trying to see under what circumstances Dan would take a subordinate position," but "there didn't seem to be any." Instead Melcher seemed "to think he should be, indeed, the director and that the committee and scientists should assist *him*." Melcher "suggested a knock down session and expulsion of the people with whom he couldn't get along," Willie reported. "Conway, Reid and I were included!"[86]

Larrick's version of the July 8 meeting is—once again—considerably different from the official one. First, she noted that she was present, something left out of Higinbotham's recounting. Second, Larrick asserted that McDonald "expressed his continuing confidence" in Melcher and stated that he would resign from the executive committee if it "forced action" to oust the director.[87]

Melcher, fighting to keep his job, went over the heads of the NCAI executive committee. He visited Einstein on July 10 at Princeton and "told him there was a lot of red baiting going on." ("This is a hell of a note!" was Higinbotham's diary entry.) On July 12 Melcher wrote Oppenheimer asking him for "counsel and guidance if the NCAI's potentialities for good are not to be wrecked." He wanted "Oppie" to read an enclosure and tell him if he was "sizing up the danger to the NCAI correctly." Melcher did not send this note until about a month later, nor did he send the enclosure, a long memo to McDonald dated July 8.[88]

This letter to McDonald is worth examining in some detail. Not only is it the fullest discussion—rivaled only by a letter to Einstein after his firing—of Melcher's thinking, but also it gives us a good sense of his politics. It was this letter, moreover, that led Conway, who obtained a copy, to move decisively and aggressively against Melcher.[89]

It opened, "I have been surveying the wreckage after yesterday's 10-hour Executive Committee closed session (July 7)." Melcher offered seven examples of the "results" of the "order to suspend all activity for the next four weeks," then outlined his fall from grace since the June 4 executive committee meeting. He had learned "through roundabout channels" that he had been "severely criticized" at the June 23 and July 7 meetings. "Unfairly," he thought, no one had brought the problems to his attention: "None of them has ever voiced his criticisms to me." Yet "outsiders" with whom he worked knew about "the critical discussion" of him.

Melcher then discussed four complaints that had "reached" him. He confessed to all of them but asked if they were serious enough to warrant "arresting the whole campaign in mid-stride." Melcher knew that three or four executive committee members thought he wanted to "run a personal show," yet he did not think there was any evidence to support this assertion.

The letter continued with a rundown of what Melcher argued were the actions that had led to the previous day's meeting. First, FAS "discovered, apparently to its surprise," that he considered himself "ultimately responsible to the NCAI Executive Board regarding the content of NCAI publications—though checking everything with the FAS as a matter of policy." Second, Conway was unhappy with an *AI* "news item critical of Franco['s] Spain." Third, "after consultation with Father Conway and Higinbotham," Amrine had prepared for Jackson "an analysis setting out to show that several NCAI issues of *AI* displayed 'pink' tendencies." Melcher assumed that this complaint was "laughed out of court" by the executive committee "with some feeling of censure for Jackson for bringing disruptive and unfounded charges on the basis of evidence he admitted he had not seen. (He even admitted he had never read any NCAI material!)" The positive side of this for Melcher was that it "brought out into the open the frank desire of Higinbotham, Jackson, and Father Conway to get rid" of him.

Melcher then moved on to an analysis of the balance of forces on the NCAI executive committee. He thought that there was a "solid minority" against him: Conway, Jackson, Reid, Higinbotham, and Bell (who usually stood in for Straight). There was a "minority" who were Melcher's defenders, and there was a "group in the middle" who had been allowed to hear the criticisms of him without his presence or response.

"This a political situation," he headed the final section of the letter. Here Melcher focused on Conway, Jackson, Amrine, Reid, and Higinbotham. Conway "seems to follow the 'Holy War against Russia' line of the Catholic Church," while Amrine and Jackson "are obsessed with the idea that impartiality means uncritically opposing anything that the Russians are for, even if they turn out to be for 'freedom of science.'" Reid, whom Melcher later identified as Jackson's close friend, had "[opposed] inclusion of the Russian viewpoint" in the upcoming NCAI institute. As for Higinbotham, he "goes along with all of them—though not[,] I'm sure, with the support of members of the Federation."

The eight-page letter concluded with political and personal testimonies. First came the political: "I submit that the hate Russia psychology has no place in any honest program of education to prevent an atomic war. Criticism, yes. Blind hatred, no." Then came the personal: "I would be glad to bow out, if a better man can be found to do an honest job. As you know, I can easily make more money with less grief by yielding to my father's urging (I'm an only son) that I enter his business—he owns and edits *Publisher's Weekly* and R. R. Bowker Co Publishers."[90]

The reading on July 11 of an HUAC report on the Oak Ridge national laboratory to the House Rules Committee considerably raised the political stakes and temperature. Aimed at the scientists' movement as well as those who favored civilian control, the Adamson report, as it was called (after the committee's chief counsel, who led the investigation), condemned the Oak Ridge scientists for supporting world government, international control of atomic energy, and civilian control of the laboratory. They, moreover, "not only admit[ted] communication with persons outside the United States, but in substance say they intend to continue this practice." While the report indicated that there had been contact with scientists, Oak Ridge security officers were its primary authority.[91]

The scientists' response revealed disagreement about how best to answer such charges. The Atomic Scientists of Chicago immediately released a statement that strongly attacked Adamson's charges as "'naïve and unfounded.'" Joseph Rush (1911–2006), the Oak Ridge physicist who was on the FAS administrative committee and served as its first secretary-treasurer, sent a telegram to Chicago after the protest appeared in the *New York Times* urging the group to take no further action "except in consultation with this office. Situation difficult. Must rely on advisers here." There was some second-guessing in the FAS office about this strategy, but Higinbotham was convinced that FAS was "right to take it easy." Schimmel and Kilgore were doing the "usual name calling," but Higinbotham thought if "we play ball we can help [the McMahon bill] along. We have nothing to lose. . . . [W]e should try to straighten this out from the inside—anyway can fight it out later. We must do all we can do to get a bill."[92]

HUAC was hounding the scientists. The McMahon bill was in trouble. The World War II alliance with the Soviet Union was rapidly crumbling. The Melcher problem had been simmering for a long time. It was in this context that Conway moved decisively and secretly behind the scenes to get rid of Melcher once and for all. As a Jesuit superior wrote in an earlier but similar context, doing "work that is largely hidden" is "in our best tradition."[93]

Conway, though, had much help and inspiration. First, in July alone he met at least nine times with the FBI agent who was handling him. Second, the FBI took several specific measures to push along Melcher's firing. "By some means unknown to me," wrote the Jesuit, it "secured a photostatic copy" of Melcher's letter of July 8. The FBI apparently did not give Conway his own copy but let him read it and take notes on at least a portion. He repeated in his report what Melcher had written about him—"the Vatican's Holy War against Russia"—commenting, "It is obvious that Mr. Melcher has received orders to do everything possible to hold on to the key position he now has." Second, the FBI confirmed for Conway that Edith Marzani was a member of the CPUSA.[94]

These two developments led Conway to take "drastic steps." The most important of these, he reported, were "several consultations" with

McDonald and Higinbotham, in which "I revealed enough of the information in my possession to convince them that immediate action should be taken." Implicit here, I think, is that Amrine already was in agreement with moving decisively against Melcher. It also suggests that Conway and Amrine, as Melcher asserted, had been working together, but that is uncertain.[95]

McDonald, who must have been increasingly worried about the situation, went to an assistant attorney general for information. On July 14, almost certainly after that meeting, McDonald called Higinbotham. "He has heard bad things about Marzani," the latter noted in his diary. Conway must have been relieved: McDonald was now committed to taking action.[96]

The anti-Melcher drive ran into a temporary roadblock on July 16, when the FAS administrative committee, at Leonard I. Schiff's instigation, met with Higinbotham. The committee sent a letter to McDonald that praised Melcher's work and pledged "complete confidence" in NCAI "policies." Its final sentence supported Melcher: "We would be very unhappy to see any interruption in the work the committee is doing."[97]

Melba Phillips (1907–2004), Oppenheimer's first Ph.D. student at Berkeley and a leftist, probably was secretly working with Melcher at this point. Phillips sent her own letter, dated July 17, to McDonald. Supposedly a report on the administrative committee meeting, it not only went further in its endorsement of Melcher than the official letter but also implicitly criticized Higinbotham's oversight of the NCAI. (Melcher drew in part upon this letter when he wrote Einstein about the support he was gathering.) It "reported opinion" from various FAS chapters that NCAI material had been "steadily improving." Moreover, Phillips claimed, the FAS administrative committee found it "very shocking" to hear of the NCAI executive committee's "internal dissension" and "regret[ted] the personal and personality discussions" that had taken place.[98]

Higinbotham was not happy with his performance at the administrative committee meeting of July 16. "Tired" and with "no time to prepare," as he noted in his diary, he did a "very poor job of telling the story." At the time he thought Phillips's letter was "harmless enough," but clearly he had not thought through its implications. Two days later he was convinced that "Melba pulled a fast one that day." The comment he made about the letter some time after the original diary entry was, "Caught hell from Conway for this."[99]

McDonald and Conway, in an effort to "neutralize" the "apparent vote of confidence" in Melcher, persuaded Willy to write McDonald a letter disputing the FAS's assertions. It would have, according to the Jesuit, two purposes: first, it would give Higinbotham "a chance to more fully explain his attitude toward Mr. Melcher," and second, it would provide "justification for appealing to the FAS council against Mr. Melcher."[100] Higinbotham's letter was a reluctant but ringing anti-Melcher pronouncement. It took its readers, in considerable detail, through the events leading up to the July 7 meeting, downplayed politics wherever they had emerged, and laid the responsibility for Melcher's firing at his own feet, attributing it to "his personality and desire to run the whole show." This was, of course, a cover story. Politics had everything to do with Melcher's firing. In a way, Higinbotham tipped off his readers as to what had really gone on when he launched into an extended discussion of his "feelings on the subject of communist infiltration." His letter never mentioned Melcher, but he clearly could not have been far from Higinbotham's consciousness or that of the reader who had heard anything at all about the conflict.[101]

Higinbotham was not worried, he continued, about infiltration of the FAS, but the NCAI was another matter. "There was no question" in his "mind that the FBI is watching us closely." If agents ever got "anything at all on us they and the Un-American Affairs Committee would go to town." He then discussed the "Susie" case and why he had fired her: "This I believe is the only possible course if there is any real evidence [of Communist association]." Higinbotham was keeping careful watch over the situation. "I am sincerely worried," he said, "because I believe this is a very real danger."[102]

Amrine figured prominently in the letter as well. It had been through his connections that Higinbotham had discovered the political complexion of the Win the Peace Conference at which he spoke. (Amrine had helped him write a speech that set FAS apart from the Communists and fellow travelers who played a prominent role in the meeting.) Amrine's dependable and excellent work for FAS was contrasted with that of the NCAI staff, in which Willy "did not have the same confidence." So far, he wrote, "I don't have anything specific but I do feel a great responsibility to keep informed."[103]

July 19 and 20 were the key decision days. On the nineteenth Higinbotham met with Amrine, Conway, and McDonald until 5:30 in the afternoon and with McDonald until 6:30. This may have been the occasion when, according to Melcher, Conway threatened McDonald "with a red-baiting attack" unless Melcher was "dumped." Such a threat would, of course, have "scared [the] hell" out of McDonald. There is no corroborating evidence for Melcher's surmise, but it does explain Larrick's account, which consistently showed McDonald to be going out of his way to be fair until about this point.[104]

Higinbotham's diary entry about the meeting reads: "This is it. All have evidence. Action will be drastic in the next few days." On the twentieth Higinbotham met with Conway and McDonald for about an hour. "Decided about the only way for a quick job would be for me to round up support and say I didn't have confidence in Dan," he noted. Or as Amrine put it in a letter to Simpson later the next week: "Present plans call for dropping Melcher promptly. There is no longer any doubt of his dangerous potentialities, in the minds of Joe [Rush], Will, or myself. This will be voted on at the meeting, but the hottest issue will of course not be raised. Fortunately he has given many other reasons for wanting to oust him." Higinbotham—because of the information Conway had given him, the priest thought—decided on July 19 that he should go see Tom Clark, the attorney general. On July 20 he called Clark and made an appointment.[105]

McDonald, probably as part of this strategy, sent a long letter on July 20 to the FAS administrative committee that sharply disputed the July 17 memo "clearly impl[ying] a vote of confidence in Melcher." The NCAI chair argued that he had "leaned over backward to be fair" to Melcher. He was "one of the last of the Executive Committee members to" to agree that Melcher had to go, "so anxious" had he been to treat him justly. McDonald's remarks reflected what had become the cover story for the firing: Melcher could not work with people; he was overbearing; he had neglected the business of NCAI organizations. Never once did McDonald raise politics as the reason for getting rid of him.[106]

It must have been quite a week at the NCAI office leading up to the meetings of July 27 and 28. First, Melcher's situation had undoubtedly created considerable tension. On the one hand, he seems to have carried on with at least some of his work, writing memos and making plans. On the other, Higinbotham appears to have noticed (was he keeping track?) when he was there and when he was not. There was a related, ongoing dispute about the content of the press book on the atomic bomb and atomic energy that was due to go very soon to the printers. Amrine and Masters were the main contestants, but Conway also got involved. Higinbotham tried to cool off the situation but failed.[107]

Second, the issue of Communist infiltration into the scientists' movement was in the air again. Nat Finney, a Washington correspondent for several newspapers, a Pulitzer Prize winner in 1948, and a friend to Higinbotham, did some checking in Congress and discovered that the "Republicans feel Russian issue [is] good propaganda." They were therefore trying to "stop or louse up" the McMahon bill. The scientists had made some mistakes with the McMahon committee, but the Republicans, Higinbotham wrote in his diary, were "not so much against us as our allies." On July 25 Willy, perhaps in hopes of reining in his troops, went back over the Adamson report, minimizing its importance and maximizing the significance of the FAS office's having ignored it.[108]

Third, the plotting of the anti-Melcher forces continued to include outside authorities. On Wednesday, July 24, noted Higinbotham, McDonald came "in to talk about [the] meetings for [the] weekend. Guys above very interested in our job." The next day Amrine wrote Simpson and told him of their strategy. He warned him that they would be inviting him to a meeting on July 28 and wanted him to let Willy know where he could be reached "on a private phone." The day before Amrine had spoken about the situation with Leon Henderson, the former head of the Office of Price Administration. "He shares our concerns," Amrine informed Simpson, as did "many others around town." The journalist clearly was convinced that Melcher's presence on the NCAI endangered the scientists' movement and more. "The Federation was never in such danger," he warned Simpson, "and unless everyone rallies around and is alerted[,] the damage to the reputation of the scientists, to the principles for which scientists have fought, and even to the course of international negotiation will be terrific." On Friday, July 26, Rush and Higinbotham met with Attorney General Clark.[109]

The reply from Rush and Higinbotham on July 26 to McDonald's letter of July 20 put an FAS stamp of approval on what the NCAI policy committee and executive committee aimed to do. They informed the NCAI chair that the administrative committee's letter of July 17 "was not intended to be a vote of confidence" in Melcher. Not only did Rush and Higinbotham have "very little confidence" in him, but also Urey, Simpson, and Lyle Borst, among "other leaders" in FAS, shared their "serious dissatisfaction." They concluded, "We are glad to hear that you are pressing for prompt action, and you may count upon the support of the Federation of American Scientists."[110]

There was still support for Melcher, though. The official opposition of the Association of Oak Ridge Engineers and Scientists to his firing was important, but not as significant as Phillips's. On July 26 Higinbotham "phoned Melba who doesn't agree with us & wants to talk to McDonald." (In adding, "She was in N.Y. all this week," he was probably implying that she was either staying out of the fight or avoiding taking responsibility for her opinion—or both.) Later that day he discovered there was reason to suspect that she had sent a letter of her own along with the FAS administrative committee letter of July 17, which he felt "stated some untrue things in general." These letters had been "sent out through Dan's office and to Einstein & God knows who else!"[111]

Phillips, as we have seen, had sent her own letter to McDonald. Her interpretation of the administrative committee meeting, moreover, had wound up on Einstein's desk via Melcher's letter. He had also attached the official committee letter to McDonald and a letter of support from Norman Cousins, the editor of *Saturday Review*. There is no indication that Einstein intervened in an effort to save Melcher, who continued to try to gain his support.[112]

The NCAI policy committee apparently shared the latest information about Melcher's efforts to keep his job and/or protect his reputation. The "rumors are really going," read Higinbotham's diary entry. Someone, probably Melcher, had "persuaded" Mrs. Edward U. Condon to write to Einstein. And someone, perhaps Melcher again, had told "the head" of PAC [the CIO's Political Action Committee] that "we were railroading Dan because he took part in PAC school!" Dan was "spreading the red-baiting business even though he knows its [*sic*] not that. I expect repercussions from our groups."[113]

The policy committee met on July 27, though it was only nominally a meeting of that that committee since, if Larrick's account is accurate, it was really a gathering of the anti-Melcher leaders whether they were on the policy committee or not. After some discussion, the members asked for Melcher's resignation. Reid was to take his place, and what Higin-botham called a "real search for a new director" was to begin.[114]

The next day, Sunday, July 28, the NCAI executive committee, with everyone present, or at least with an alternate in place, had a "killer" meeting. Once it had adopted the policy committee's recommendation, Melcher was called in. He laid out his record, defended it, and "demanded to hear objections." He then "read Mike's letter to Jackson, accused Father C. of being antisemitic[,] and generally loused things up." After about forty-five minutes, Higinbotham apparently put an end to the proceedings when he forcefully (and gleefully) attested to Melcher's incompetence. "I really flattened him by strong statement of *no* confidence," he confided to his diary. Higinbotham was delighted with how the meeting went. "This is a *great* committee," he wrote. "They came through this more united than ever. Celebration at Al's." The only thing that marred everyone's satisfaction was the worry that Melcher would commit some act of "sabotage" that night, so the office locks were changed.[115]

This euphoria was premature. On July 29 Larrick, "after a long talk" with McDonald, quit. The staff then met, and McDonald "explained everything" to them. Higinbotham thought it a "straightforward job," but the staff members, according to Larrick, had some things to say about

Melcher's dismissal; the NCAI chair interrupted them, however, because he "clearly wanted to do the talking instead of hearing a defense of Melcher." Willy tried to talk some of them out of leaving, but "without success." By noon, twelve members of the staff of fourteen had quit. At some point Phillips showed up. She put the "blame on Pat Jackson & Mike," wrote Higinbotham. "Says after that she saw it was inescapable that this happen." Larrick accused Melcher's critics of "Jew baiting." A "truly miserable day," Higinbotham concluded.[116]

The problems continued on Tuesday and Wednesday. There was "more picking up" in the NCAI and more conversation with Phillips. The Oak Ridge scientists' letter of support for Melcher arrived, as did a correspondent from the *Washington Herald*, who had heard "about a rumor we had fired 19 communists." This was, Higinbotham noted, a "helleva [*sic*] way to change directors—it will be some job to pick up the threads." The next day there were "more troubles" but "nothing serious." Willy's appraisal of himself and the other anti-Melcher partisans, however, was completely different from before: "I'll never forgive myself for the way this was done, although I'm certain we had to get rid of Dan & Nancy."[117]

Most of the mass resignations came via one letter, completely taking Higinbotham and others by surprise. None of those who quit, eight women and one man, had known Melcher before coming to work for him, but they were "deeply impressed with his sincerity of purpose and his outstanding ability to put into effective action the plans and policies of the NCAI." The firing of Melcher, "at a time when the broad and vital work of the NCAI is reaching fruition," they wrote, "shatters our confidence in the executive committee and in the future of this work." The signers had therefore chosen "to disassociate" themselves from the organization. Two other staff members wrote individual letters of resignation.[118]

The letter from Nancy Larrick states that she quit in "protest" over the executive committee's "undemocratic procedures" of the previous five weeks as well as the "vicious and unscrupulous statements and acts" of "several" of its members. As a member herself of some of the organizations making up the NCAI, she was "alarmed that such proceedings" had been "carried out in their name without their full knowledge of the political forces at work and without their direct consent." Marian Hale Britten's letter raised similar issues. She was "more disappointed" than she could "find words to express" that "certain members" of the executive committee had been "misled by others, whose motives I have every reason to distrust." (Here she remarked on the drinking of one of those who were doing the misleading.) Britten had nothing but good to say about Melcher

and nothing but bad about the procedures used to oust him. It particularly
upset her that some individuals had "put their own interest ahead of the
peace of the entire world."[119]

The FAS staff and McDonald spent part of August responding to criticisms of what they had done. Most of the scientists first heard of Melcher's
firing when the FAS executive council received Higinbotham's letter of
July 31, in which he laid out what had happened and why. (There was no
mention of the politics involved.) The office answered their letters by repeating the standard line on why the firing had occurred.[120]

Some of the critics received the news from either Melcher or his staff:
They were not going quietly. "Melcher & friends," Willy wrote in his diary
on August 5, "have written & sent what is supposed to be a copy of Mike's
letter" (the letter of June 21 to Jackson). "Of all the pissassed tricks!" was
his comment. Melcher himself wrote a long letter to Einstein that laid
out, in an analysis very similar to his July 8 memo, the reasons for his
firing. McDonald's response, including a refutation of the charge of anti-
Semitism, convinced the renowned scientist that Melcher's behavior was
"abnormal and even pathological." Larrick's letter about "political issues,"
Higinbotham noted, was "upsetting a lot of people," including, apparently,
someone from the Socialist Party, whom Willy "straightened out." Mc-
Donald handled the letters from the Fellowship of Reconciliation's John
Swomley and A. J. Muste.[121]

Then there were the newspaper reporters. Higinbotham did not say
anything in his diary about how the conversation went after the reporter
from the *Herald* showed up at the office, but Conway reported to a superior
about the effort—and dissembling—it required to cool her down: "It took
two hours of explanation, with liberal doses of mental reservation, to convince her that we had simply undergone an office reorganization." Finney,
writing for the *Minneapolis Tribune*, was another matter. His story about
the firing of Melcher appeared in his newspaper on August 4. It is unknown if Higinbotham tried to persuade Finney not to write the article;
perhaps he was not worried because it was a Midwest paper, not an East
Coast one. His diary entry is laconic—"Today Finney's article showed
up"—but what he crossed out is suggestive: "He got much of this dope
independently—FBI etc."[122]

Willy reported back to the attorney general on the day Finney's article
appeared. Since Melcher was gone, he wrote, it was not "necessary to ask
for your assistance at this time." The FAS had a "pretty good idea" which
scientists needed watching, and it did not seem "that any of them are in
a position where they can do any harm." He concluded with a pledge of
assistance "at any time."[123]

Conway knew, whether through Higinbotham or the FBI is uncertain, about this contact between the two scientists and Clark. He reported that Clark had "promised" the scientists "all the assistance necessary." The Jesuit's agent contact told him that Higinbotham could have just called the Bureau. "We have been in close touch," Conway noted, "during these times."[124]

After Melcher's departure the executive committee set about finding the people necessary to get the organization going again. Conway, who received a final extension of his leave of absence, despite Stritch's refusal to get involved, was in Washington to participate in the committee's hiring of a new director. The NCAI was determined, he reported, to "get a man of high caliber whose work we will not have to subject to daily scrutiny." The committee decided on Livingston Hartley, a "writer on foreign affairs," as editorial director, particularly of *AI*, and A. E. Casgrain, formerly head of group liaison for the United Nations Relief and Rehabilitation Administration, as acting director. In mid-September, Conway reported that NCAI was "forging along with a new spirit."[125]

The executive committee hoped that Casgrain could take over permanently, but that would not be the case. Part of the problem was that the committee was rethinking the organizational structure of NCAI and considering hiring a nationally known figure to become director. But part of the problem was Casgrain. At the end of October, Higinbotham noted that his staff thought him "an awful dope." Less than a week later he made a laundry list of Casgrain's deficits and mistakes; by the middle of November there apparently was a consensus that he was not the right person to become the permanent director. His relations with his staff seem to have been especially bad.[126]

Casgrain, of course, did not see it this way. In letters to Conway he laid out his frustration, his disappointment, and finally his anger at his situation. In March 1947 the executive committee offered the directorship to another candidate, who turned it down. Casgrain's staff found out about the offer and wanted to protest, but he stopped them: "Such things should not happen twice!" Finally, in May 1947 George L. Glashen, who had worked in the Retraining and Reemployment Administration, became the NCAI's permanent director. He inherited, he wrote Conway, considerable personnel and financial problems.[127]

The NCAI apparently regained some of its vibrancy under Casgrain, and maintained it for a time under his successor, but became increasingly inactive in 1948. At the end of the year the NCAI's annual meeting voted to dissolve the organization.[128] It had been a short but significant run.

Each of Melcher's three main antagonists—Amrine, Conway, and Higinbotham—had connections to the FBI. Conway's was primordial: he was the only one opposed to Melcher from the beginning and the only one whose connection to the Bureau was organic and ideological. For Conway and Amrine the evidence is direct, and for the former it also is substantial. This is not the case for Higinbotham, but it is hard to imagine that he did not at least know what the other two were doing. (Remember the case of "Susie," whom he fired because of reports from the FBI and Grove's office. Remember, too, that he and Amrine went to see the attorney general.) For Amrine and Higinbotham, opposition to Melcher and the connection to the Bureau developed over time as Melcher's politics became clearer and the price of keeping him on as director grew higher. Both developed inversely in relation to the breakdown in the wartime alliance with the Soviet Union.[129]

Conway's fixed and unshakable attitude toward Russia, which we have seen again and again, is made plain in a memo on the Bernard Baruch–Henry Wallace blowup that he produced for Alter. Wallace's critique of the Baruch report's proposals and the growing hostility toward the USSR led to Wallace's being fired as secretary of commerce in mid-September. From that point on Wallace spoke out vigorously against anti-Sovietism and U.S. imperialism.

The Jesuit's analysis of Wallace's position was part and parcel of the way he had been approaching the battle in the NCAI. (There, though, the issue was spying, not foreign relations.) The key to understanding Wallace was Philip Hauser, his adviser. From the FBI Conway had learned that, though not himself a Communist but rather an "opportunist," Hauser had brought Communists into Wallace's circle. (Two of the four men named, Harry Magdoff and Edward Fitzgerald, had been providing information to the Russians.) At the end of September, David K. Niles, one of President Truman's administrative assistants, had called Conway in for a meeting, during which Conway told Niles that some atomic scientists were worried about Hauser's influence on Wallace. By "attacking the American proposals from the rear," Conway argued, Wallace was helping the Russians, who were "waiting for the Americans to soften their defences."[130]

Joe Rush had a different attitude toward Wallace and his position on Russia. Rush has appeared rarely in this chapter, but my sense is that he played a considerably more important role in almost everything I have discussed than is possible to document. He was, Higinbotham remembered, "quiet, very excellent at thinking things through and writing things up." Rush handled HUAC for FAS. He "got acquainted with some of the

Congressmen who were most active on the House Un-American Activities Committee, and convinced them that we were legitimate," Higinbotham recalled. As a result, "we never got picked on by them."[131]

Wallace's Madison Square Garden speech of September 12, 1946, Rush thought, "balled things up in fine style." Although, in the scientist's "private opinion," it was an "excellent statement of the situation in most respects," in attacking the "good faith of Baruch and his advisers" and in delivering his speech "before a strongly Pinko crowd," Wallace displayed what Rush called "exceedingly poor judgment." Moreover, the speech made the work of men like Rush—by implication Amrine and Higinbotham but not Conway—much more difficult. As Rush put it, "We're hugging the barroom floor until the shooting stops."[132]

Rush was able to listen to what Wallace had said and honestly, at least in private correspondence, evaluate it for what it was. He did not take the USSR to be evil personified as Conway did, nor did he take the United States to be good personified. Neither did Higinbotham. Furthermore, the interests of the USSR as nation-state did not necessarily begin and end with Communism.

In November 1946 Mike Gold, who wrote a regular column for the *Daily Worker*, took up the use of the atomic bomb against Japan. In the course of asserting the congruence between Hitler's foreign policy and U.S. imperialism, Gold argued that the bomb, "in an allegorical manner of speaking," was "used as much against the Soviet ally, as against the Japanese enemy." Since then, the "atombomb [sic] and American fascism" had become "linked inseparably." Higinbotham not only read this column, in and of itself an assertion of independent thought in this context, but also took Gold's assertion seriously. It was, he wrote Oppenheimer, an "extreme statement of a point of view," but he thought the main argument—that the United States used the bomb to end the war before the USSR could get in—worth considering. He wanted Oppenheimer's opinion: "I would like to know, sometime, if there is any basis for this idea."[133]

That Amrine's thinking about these issues coincided with Rush's and Higinbotham's rather than with Conway's is clear in his correspondence with Philip Morrison at the end of July 1946. Amrine and Morrison, who had been a member of the Young Communist League and CPUSA from 1938 to the end of 1941, found themselves in surprising agreement about much. What they disagreed about was the difference between avoiding giving "unnecessary aid to Red-baiters," as Amrine put it, and Morrison's commitment to saying "what we believe right without coloring it to avoid criticism from people who will criticize anything that works in the right direction." That was, indeed, a very fine line.[134]

Higinbotham and Amrine, then, were neither Joel Kovel's "black-hole anti-communists" nor Richard Gid Powers's "countersubversive anti-communists." Their anti-Communism and cooperation with the FBI grew out of their experience and the developing Cold War. Conway was considerably closer to doctrinaire anti-Communism than either of them. His Catholicism and Jesuit training established the foundations of an anti-Communism that required relatively little evidence, let alone all that the NCAI situation provided him.[135]

Where does Melcher fit in here? While not a "card-carrying" Communist, he willingly—and surely knowingly—allied himself with the Party. The fellow traveler and/or Communist perspective of more than a few of those who worked for him at NCAI was characteristic of both the kinds of people willing to put in long hours for little pay and Melcher's eagerness to fill the positions with those who had similar politics. Such people were, as the GREGORY investigation showed, his friends and confidants.

He was not, as he claimed, like "the proverbial sparrow who strayed into a badminton game by mistake." Melcher continued to be politically active long after he was fired. His conversation with Wallace after his dismissal led to his drafting a speech in an apparent tryout for a job. Melcher and his wife strongly supported Wallace in 1948 and remained active in the Progressive Party long after that debacle. It is telling of the times that one reason why they had the "general reputation in the neighborhood as being pro-communist" was that they had "frequent meetings in their home attended by members of mixed races."[136]

At the same time, Melcher's consummate professionalism was evident throughout his life, including during his directorship of NCAI when he oversaw Edith Marzani's work on *Atomic Information*. At one point, after carefully going over the copy for a forthcoming issue, he wrote a lengthy memo in which he tried to help this intelligent but untrained woman perform well as a journalist. Among his comments to Marzani: "Don't mix editorializing with news, as in the last paragraph of League story."[137]

Conway had won a major victory for his country, his church, and himself. With the firing of Melcher and the resignation of most of his staff, the work of the NCAI could go on without fear of guilt by association. Conway accomplished this without revealing much of his hand. Melcher's actions and the growing tensions between the Soviet Union and the United States created a situation in which Higinbotham and Amrine thought it essential that they take action. That two men of considerable talent and integrity did so without shirking responsibility for their actions suggests how necessary they thought such action was. It would have been quite easy to shift the blame to Conway, but there is no evidence that they did.

The Jesuit just missed having his role revealed, though, as Melcher increasingly zeroed him in on him—and to a lesser degree Jackson—as the ringleader in the conspiracy that got him fired. In October he sent Kenneth Leslie, the fellow-traveling editor of *The Protestant,* several documents that laid out Conway's "efforts" to "get the NCAI aligned with Vatican policy." Disturbed by what he considered to be Conway's anti-Semitism, Melcher referred Leslie to Falk, who could provide information on NCAI. Leslie, however, mired in his own problems, did not run with the story.[138]

Finally we come to the FBI. Scrambling to follow up on every lead that Elizabeth Bentley had provided in November 1945, the Bureau discovered what it considered good evidence that Melcher was just a circle or two away from the USSR's spy rings in Washington, D.C. Whether the agent who was working with Conway acted on his own in instigating Melcher's firing or on orders from above, the mission was accomplished without revealing the Bureau's role.[139]

CHAPTER 6

———————— ∽ ————————

Anti-Communism in the CIO
Monsignor Charles Owen Rice
and the FBI

"MIGHT HAUNT HIM from the grave if I get the chance," wrote Monsignor Charles Owen Rice (1908–2005), referring to me, in his contribution to a symposium on his writings that I organized. There was good reason for Rice to feel this way: I had interviewed him in 1986, published an essay in which he figured prominently in 1992, and planned the 1999 symposium. During that same time I also had given several scholarly papers in which he was discussed and another, at a conference organized by the Pennsylvania Labor History Society, entirely devoted to an assessment of his career.[1]

I was just one among many, as biographers and historians besieged Rice in the 1980s. In 1983 Ronald Schatz's *The Electrical Workers* came out. Although Rice was not its main focus, the work provided a large historical context within which to place him. Patrick McGeever extensively interviewed Rice in 1982 and 1983 for a biography that appeared in 1989. There was yet another biographer at work, about whom Rice was concerned, "if she ever gets around to writing the thing." For "awhile" he was "furious" at all of us.[2]

The monsignor, though, had only himself to blame for all this scholarly attention. He began giving interviews to historians in the late 1950s and donated his massive collection of papers—as far as I can tell unexpurgated—to the University of Pittsburgh in 1976. Just as important, I suspect, was his continuing evaluation and reevaluation of his anti-Communist activities. Not content to live an unexamined life or to sit back and let historians have their way with him—although he surely tried to shape the contours of his life in the oral histories—Rice intervened repeatedly in the telling of his story.[3]

It is fitting that the final chapter of this book is on Rice. Trained as a historian of colonial and Revolutionary America, I began drifting away from that field when I directed Toni Gilpin's senior thesis on the Farm Equipment Workers. Since the union was led by Communists, I sent Freedom of Information/Privacy Act (FOI/PA) requests to the FBI for its records on this CIO affiliate. A co-authored article on using FBI records as a source for labor history resulted from those requests. I was on my way to the research that has culminated in this book. My 1986 interview with Rice confirmed my decision.[4]

There are still other reasons why this chapter on Rice is the appropriate way to end this book. Like him, I am a practicing Catholic, one moreover raised in the pre–Vatican II Church in which Rice came to maturity as man and priest. There are nuances in his thinking and phrases in his speech that resonated deeply for me. I, too, have been thinking and re-thinking many things, including the way in which I view the history of Communism and anti-Communism in the CIO. As will become clear, I no longer think in the same way that I did about these issues when I published *The CIO's Left-Led Unions* in 1992.

One of the problems with zeroing in on just one part of a person's life is that the rest gets lost. Many historians have done that with Rice. He was heavily engaged in anti-Communist activities in 1939, 1940, and 1941 and then again from 1947 through 1950; but he was born in 1908 and was still alive at the time I drafted this chapter. That leaves many years for which there is no accounting. It is possible that what he did during these six anti-Communist years was so significant that it overshadows all the rest, but that can be determined only if one studies his whole life. While I will not be doing that in this chapter, I do spend a good amount of time on his pre-1940 activities. I also have a bit to say about his post-1950 career.

This chapter is different from the others, more detailed and more heavily documented. Perhaps it is in one sense less user-friendly, but it may also be more in tune with current sensibilities, for it includes more "I" statements. Rice and I made a journey together. Let us begin.

During the steel strike of 1919, Father Adelbert Kazincy, pastor of St. Michael's in Braddock, Pennsylvania, was one of the few priests in the country who stood by his parishioners. It was not surprising, then, that in August 1936 he again outspokenly supported the right of steelworkers to organize. "Be men," he told a rally. "Have courage. Only through unity have you strength." Much had changed. "Pharaoh has not let his people go," *Steel Labor* editorialized in its coverage of the meeting, but "organized labor has more strength than in 1919." What also was dissimilar was that Kazincy was not alone in his support for Catholic steelworkers.[5]

The difference that the Church made in the drive to organize steel probably was the greatest it made in any industry. Other priests actively supported the Steelworkers Organizing Committee (SWOC), but none more fervently and energetically than Rice. From 1937 on, Rice spoke to and met with SWOC union members throughout Pennsylvania and Ohio. He did so at a time when many mill town pastors, unlike Kazincy, were still hesitant to support the CIO. A brief look at Rice's speaking engagements suggests the breadth of his activity.

Rice spoke at least twice to SWOC lodges in 1937. Early the next year he gave a presentation in Altoona, Pennsylvania, and in the summer of 1938 to the SWOC summer educational camp. In February 1939 he delivered a speech to Lodge 1330 at the Carnegie-Illinois plant in Youngstown, Ohio, addressed a Reading, Pennsylvania, district SWOC convention in June, and spoke in July in Warren, Ohio, to a SWOC picnic of more than three thousand, where he, according to the lodge president, "went over big." In August 1939 he again spoke in Youngstown and also in Farrell, Pennsylvania, where the "boys" were "very anxious" to hear him. Yet another speech in Youngstown rounded out his 1939 SWOC engagements. In early 1940 Rice again spoke to the Reading district SWOC convention, in April helped out in a SWOC election in Cincinnati, and in July spoke to the annual SWOC picnic in Bethlehem, Pennsylvania. Finally, in September 1940 Rice supported a controversial strike at Hubbard and Company in Lawrenceville, Pennsylvania. He not only put the Association of Catholic Trade Unionists (ACTU) on record as supporting the walkout but also received publicity as one of three signers of an application for a gun-carrying permit for William J. Hart, a SWOC staff member. A photograph appeared in a Pittsburgh paper of a smiling Rice bailing out joyful SWOC members who had been arrested when they tried to prevent scabs from crossing the picket line.[6]

It is impossible to overestimate the significance of Rice's pro-SWOC activity: here was a priest, in clerical garb, publicly supporting the right of workers to join unions that would bargain for them. For a church that had always been deeply embedded in the lives of its working-class constituency but cautious about advocating that which seemed the least bit radical or beyond the immediate, this was virtually revolutionary. The mere appearance of Rice at a SWOC meeting broke with years of history, experience, and past habits.

Why was Rice able to do this? Partly it was because he was young and brave. He, after all, had just been ordained in 1934 at the age of twenty-six. And partly it was because Rice was a born fighter who enjoyed conflict, combative, passionate, and fearless. He always gave as good as he got and expected nothing less in return. As he wrote in 1990: "When they hit back, I did not take it personally. If you hit, you must expect to get hit."[7]

To understand fully how Rice could pull off what he did in his support of SWOC, it is necessary to look beyond him to his bishop, Hugh C. Boyle. Boyle, who came from the Pittsburgh working class, was extraordinarily pro-labor. As a result there was considerable freedom in the Pittsburgh diocese for pro-labor priests to act. From the early 1930s on, they publicly pushed—and sometimes led—efforts for economic justice. In 1936 Rice joined with several other clerics—particularly Father Carl Hensler and Monsignor Barry O'Toole, both of whom sometimes accompanied him on his SWOC speaking engagements—to form the Catholic Radical Alliance. One of its first activities was to support the Heinz strike; Hensler and Rice even joined the picket line. Boyle did not retreat when he received complaints about the two priests.[8]

Boyle fostered Rice's pro-labor activity in yet another way. One of the things that the Social Action Department of the National Catholic Welfare Conference discovered in its organizing efforts with priests was that it did not take long for newly ordained assistant pastors to become so overwhelmed with day-to-day responsibilities that social action was neglected, if not entirely forgotten. Father Francis Gilligan, a longtime professor at St. Paul's seminary in Minnesota, noted a recurring phenomenon: his seminarians not only were interested in "social problems" but also were "critical of the failure of priests in parishes to be concerned." Within five years of their ordination, however, they had become "so preoccupied with the preaching of the Gospel and sacramental administration" that they "neglect entirely the social gospel." Detroit's Father Clement Kern remarked on the same thing. He and a colleague had begun a study club for priests: "We are trying to hook the boys just out, the ones who were red-hot in the Seminary and now that they are out are very busy and are liable to forget their interest in social action."[9]

Rice did not succumb to this dynamic during his four years as an assistant pastor at St. Agnes in Pittsburgh. His pastor there had to have been sympathetic—by choice or directive—to Rice's labor activity, for he could have stopped it simply by refusing to allow him to travel. In 1940 Boyle appointed Rice resident director of St. Joseph's House of Hospitality, loosely patterned after the Catholic Worker houses. This position, which Rice held until 1950, provided him with all the opportunity he needed for his

labor work. Like his fellow labor priests Father Raymond Clancy of the
Detroit archdiocese, who was director of archdiocesan cemeteries, and
Father Joseph Donnelly of the Hartford diocese, who served as an orphan-
age chaplain, Rice took full advantage of the latitude his superior had
given him.

Boyle could count on Rice's loyalty and obedience. Like other labor
priests, Rice was a faithful son of the Church. As far as I can tell, he never
addressed meetings in another diocese without first asking permission
to do so. If he had not sought permission or had gone ahead and spoken
after the request was denied—as it was in several cases—Boyle would
surely have come down hard on him. For Rice there was no contradiction between his temperament and political views and his commitment to
obedience. He very much wanted to join the armed forces as a chaplain
but ended his letter asking permission to do so in this way: "I put this matter in your hands. You are my Superior under God. Whatever your decision I shall carry on in the way you want with a light heart and complete
acceptance."[10]

Rice could, in turn, count on Boyle's support. I know of no instance
in which the bishop ever publicly criticized Rice, no matter how bad the
press or how many irate letters he received. Boyle in fact trusted Rice
enough to allow him to draft responses to letters complaining about him.
The two of them also seem to have worked out an understanding whereby
Rice took the "insults and slanders" that in other circumstances would
have come Boyle's way.[11]

Rice found the time and energy to support numerous other CIO unions
besides the SWOC. In 1938 he spoke at a Utica, New York, Textile Workers
Organizing Committee rally; later that year he made appearances in the
same diocese on behalf of the Amalgamated Clothing Workers of America.
He addressed a convention of the Maryland and District of Columbia Industrial Union in 1938 and visited a Utility Workers Organizing Committee local in New York in 1939. Rice lent his name to an organizing drive of
the United Office and Professional Workers Union in 1937 and advocated
CIO affiliation in Gloversville, New York, before a group of independent
leatherworkers the following year.[12]

Through all these battles Rice and his fellow labor priests publicly identified working-class goals and the Church's as one and the same. These
aims, furthermore, were the same as America's. Rice spoke for the SAD,
labor priests, and many in the hierarchy in his benediction at the 1938
CIO convention. "O Lord and Savior," he began, "You who were a worker
Yourself." He concluded: "We pray for the victory of the worker in this
country, Almighty God, because his victory is Your victory, his cause is

Your cause. A victory for labor in its struggles for decent conditions is a victory for Americanism and for Christianity."[13]

Since virtually all Catholics, including Rice, were against Communism, it surely was never far from Rice's consciousness as he went about supporting the CIO. Not all Catholics, though, opposed it in the same way. For the most rigorous, the mere presence of Communists was threatening and contaminating. For that reason they considered almost any social and political agitation to be dangerous, for it suggested the possibility of Communist infiltration and influence. Whether as a reasoned argument or not, these Catholics felt that the best way to fight Communism was by supporting the status quo. Therefore they more or less opposed the CIO from its very inception because it provided a possible site for Communist "penetration" and "infection." Perhaps the best example of this position is Bishop John F. Noll of Fort Wayne, Indiana, and his publishing empire, anchored by *Our Sunday Visitor*.

Other Catholics may have agreed in principle with this rigorous anti-Communism but for numerous reasons—social or ecclesiastical position, temperament, political sophistication—refused to throw out the baby with the bathwater. For them it was not the CIO that was the problem but rather the presence of Communists within it. The best way to oppose them was relentless denunciation and exposure. Perhaps the best example of this position is Father Francis X. Talbot, S.J., editor in chief of *America* from 1936 to 1944.

These two positions, however, often ended up being one and the same in practice, for even the most rigorous Catholic anti-Communists seldom couched their arguments explicitly in terms of support for business as usual. Not only were many Catholics working class, at least in origin, but also the demands of the Catholic social justice tradition pressed heavily on them. Therefore they most often fought Communism in the same way the second group did: by denunciation and exposure. The proponents of both positions, then, battled Communism in what a third group called a "negative way."

This final group thought that the best way to combat Communism was to eliminate those conditions that produced it: poverty, discrimination, poor working conditions, inadequate wages. Communism flourished only when social conditions deteriorated to the point where those suffering had nowhere else to turn. This position, which its proponents called the "positive" way of fighting Communism, dovetailed not only with Catholic teaching on the labor question but also with what came to be called more generally "social Catholicism." The Social Action Department of the NCWC best personified this position. Headed by Monsignor John A.

Ryan but run by Father Raymond A. McGowan during this period, the
SAD fought hard to build Catholic support for the CIO. As part of that
campaign it had constantly to confront the issue of Communism within
the CIO. It argued repeatedly that the best way to deal with the problem
was to support the growth of "sound" trade unions and the development
of competent leadership.

Labor priests belonged to this third group. If necessary, they responded
vigorously and sharply to charges—especially from Catholics—that the
CIO was Communist inspired or Communist dominated, but they spent
as little time as possible doing that. Their main objective was to support
industrial unionism. If they knew of any Communists in the CIO, they
said little or nothing about them.

Rice, as in so many other cases, did not fit into any of these groups. On
the one hand, he was a sworn enemy of Communism who often pointed
out its intrinsically evil nature, vociferously attacked local Communists,
and led campaigns against them. On the other, he consistently defended
the CIO against its Catholic critics and tried to educate them in the realities of Communist labor activity. He also knowingly endorsed at least one
Communist trade union leader. Charges that the CIO was "communistic,"
Rice argued, especially when coming from Catholics, were "ill-advised
and asinine." In excerpts from what probably originally was a radio talk,
Rice first identified himself as a priest so his listeners would know that
his words were "coming from a person who has not the slightest touch of
Communism in his system." By and large, he said, the CIO was a "good
and healthy thing," an appropriate response to a "social system that was
Godless, unjust, and unChristian." His major disagreement with the CIO
was that it did not go far enough: it did not have a "completely adequate
social philosophy back of it." The way to combat Communism was not by
"red-baiting and flag waving." It was by "striving tooth and nail for social
justice."[14]

Rice, however, could not ignore—even if he wanted to—the fact that
there were Communists in the CIO. The CIO was not "honey-combed"
with Communists, he observed; their number was "surprisingly small."
Still, Rice's conversations with "many CIO officials" convinced him that it
would be "extremely difficult to weed them out without harming the organization." Since the CIO was "fragile," it did "no good to adopt an extreme
attitude and go swinging about one hammer and tongs," for "unthinking
red-baiting by responsible people" could "wreck" it.[15]

At the same time, Communists found no more inveterate a foe than
Rice. One of his favorite venues was the debate, where he could indulge
his agonistic tendencies. In February 1938 he took on Martin Young, a

Pittsburgh Communist Party leader. Communists could not be trusted in unions, Rice argued, because for them, the "union is always second," the "party is first." They will "turn on us when it suits them." In another debate later that same year, attended by about 2,500, Rice engaged Clarence Hathaway, the *Daily Worker* editor. Hathaway's plea for a "broad democratic front" against "fascist barbarism" was rejected. "We will accept the outstretched hand of Communists," Rice declared, "only when it ceases to be Communist and relinquishes the doctrine and tactics that have put it beyond the pale of normality and ethics."[16]

Rice carefully picked his battles, though, paying close attention to the local context. This was evident in two speaking engagements in the Albany diocese in the spring of 1938. The first was in Schenectady, where he reported that the "Marxist element" was "unusually strong." The leader of the unemployed workers' movement was "decidedly Red," while one of his colleagues who was "pro-Red in sympathy" told Rice that he still practiced Catholicism. Deciding that merely "red baiting" would be "fatal," Rice first laid out his pro-labor position, then "took a sock at Communists with all the power" he "could command."[17]

The situation was different in Gloversville, New York, where Clarence Carr, a Communist Party member, was fighting to affiliate his Independent Leather Workers Union of Fulton County with the Fur and Leather Workers Union, headed by the Communist Ben Gold. Despite knowing full well that Carr was a Communist and the union was in his camp, Rice supported CIO affiliation in a rousing speech. The CIO, he argued, was winning the support of many priests and bishops. Not only was there nothing in its principles to indicate that it was "subversive," but also Rice himself personally knew all the CIO leaders, and it was not "possible for anyone to show they are unAmerican." He was as anti-Communist as anyone else, but he refused to condemn the CIO as a whole because of the presence of some Party members. He urged his listeners to vote for CIO affiliation and then thwart the Communists by being "sincere" Christians.[18]

Why had Rice taken this stance? First, as he explained to the Albany bishop, Carr was a good leader and "something of a book communist." Second, he had not used his position to help the Party. Third, Carr's opponent, a nonpracticing Catholic, had made "puerile" arguments against affiliation with a national union. Finally, it was essential to demonstrate that the Catholic Church was not anti-labor.[19]

Although Carr's local narrowly voted down CIO affiliation, Rice's speech was a success. His listeners, who finally approved affiliation in 1940, could not have come away with anything but the knowledge that the

Catholic Church supported labor. At the conclusion of the speech Rice told them that they had inherited the mantle of the American Revolution, which had been fought not "for the economic royalist, but for the workers." He also identified himself and his Church with his working-class audience when he asserted the need to go beyond the CIO: "We must go a step further and serve notice on the old economic order that it must be wiped out. The workers must be protected. We are fighting for Christians and Christianity."[20]

Rice understood, as Chicago's Bishop Bernard J. Sheil did in his 1939 support for the Packing House Workers Organizing Committee, that Communism had little or nothing to do with the central issue: Did the Catholic Church support the CIO or not? To attack Communists in the CIO without vigorously defending the organization, let alone to attack the CIO as communistic, would have been a disaster for the Church.

The most significant outpost of Communist Party power and influence in the Pittsburgh area was the United Electrical, Radio and Machine Workers of America's (UE) flagship Local 601 at Westinghouse's East Pittsburgh plant, where about twelve thousand men and women worked. The left-wing leadership of Local 601—Communists and those who willingly worked with them—were fit opponents for a man of Rice's temperament, energy, and commitment. He first wholeheartedly engaged them in 1939, 1940, and 1941 and then again from 1946 to 1950. He wrote leaflets, interceded with fellow priests for support, and frequently met with oppositionists to plan strategy. He may even have been directly calling the shots—the UE thought so—but there is no way of knowing with any certainty what role he played within the leadership caucus.[21]

Rice brought a good deal of outside support to his and his church's side of the struggle. At one time or another he acknowledged aid, but often in such a way as to obfuscate the issues. Before moving on to a discussion of Rice's relationship with the FBI, let us take a look at several other instances in which he received help from outside the labor movement.

The first case of outside assistance that Rice brought to his battle against the UE Communists and their allies involves a Chevrolet that he received in 1948. For several reasons I am personally quite entangled in this matter. First, I not only discovered the letter in which Rice thanked General Motors but also pressed Rice on the issue in a 1986 interview. Second, my allegations about the gift entered the public record when another scholar mentioned them without my permission in *Labor History*. Finally, the memo itself became public when Rice introduced it in the same issue of that journal.

The subject began with my coming across, in Rice's papers at the University of Pittsburgh, a copy of a three-sentence letter in which he thanked R. A. Kersten, at the "Chevrolet–Central Office," for his "assistance in obtaining a Chevrolet." Rice assured him "that this car will be used in important work for the welfare of this country and sane industrial relations." He closed by complimenting a local car dealership for "handling their end of the matter."[22]

I was still looking at that point in my research for "smoking guns" that would prove that Rice and others had conspired with the "bad guys" to destroy the UE. Having found what I was looking for, I went to the interview with Rice ready—eager is perhaps the better word—to confront him. Here is a transcript of that portion of the interview:

STEVE ROSSWURM: Can I bring you up two cases that I found from your correspondence that disturbed me a lot and I wanted to give—I wanted to hear what you thought about them. I found two letters, one of which is where you thank the General Motors for a Chevrolet.

CHARLES OWEN RICE: That was not General Motors—Oh, I'll tell you how that happened.

SR: Can I—

COR: I know the whole situation.

SR: Well, you say, "I can assure you this car will be used for the welfare of our country and sane industrial relations."

COR: Yeah, I know. That was Herman [Kamen]. I don't think we got a car. We got a reduction. And I don't think they gave us a car. Herman's son, Saul, had a Chevrolet dealership.

SR: Well, you say that dealership took care of their end of the deal, okay, but you write a letter into central, into GM Headquarters.

COR: I don't think we got a car from them.

SR: Hmm. Well, you say thank you for the Chevrolet.

COR: I don't know that we got a car from them. And in that particular case, it wasn't sinful. But I—

SR: But it's from the enemy, right?

COR: Well, at that time, in the automobile thing [three or four words unintelligible], and Reuther, who was on our side, was an enemy and he did wring concessions out of General Motors and he did fight them. And, I would not . . . I'm sorry that happened. I'm sorry. It was not sinful. It was not sinful.

SR: But the UE—

COR: It was dealing with the enemy.

SR: The UE would have just made—

COR: [unintelligible] But I would have had to accept it. It would have
wiped me out. Or I would have . . . You notice in these things I
haven't lied. If they find them and something happened, I would
accept it.[23]

I came out of this interview convinced that Rice had gotten the car
from GM and that he *had* acted sinfully, so I referred to the car incident
in a scholarly paper I delivered the next year. I did not try to get the paper
published, but I did ask several scholars for their comments and sent it out
to a couple more. I did so with the confidence that the contents would not
be made public because the paper carried the standard stipulation, "This
essay may not be reproduced or quoted from or summarized or referred to
without express permission of the author."[24]

Confession and repentance were a significant and recurring part of
Rice's life. It is difficult, as we will see, to determine exactly what motivated him to do so in each case, but in this instance, two factors seem to
have been at work. First, he had turned eighty the year before; thoughts
of how long he had left to live must have been on his mind. Second,
there were at least four people doing research projects that involved him.
How history would remember and God judge him, then, were consider-
ations that probably led him to publish, in 1989, "Confessions of an Anti-
Communist" in *Labor History*.[25]

At the time I paid little attention to this essay. Not only had I moved on
to another aspect of the project, but also I was weary of the whole Rice
issue. I had spent the previous two years talking and corresponding with
other scholars and labor activists about Rice. Skimming the article, moreover, left me with the impression that it was a form of damage control.

My reaction to an attack on Rice by Sigmund Diamond, which appeared in *Labor History* the following summer, was quite different, since it
contained material lifted from my unpublished conference paper. Against
my instructions on the paper's title page, Diamond had summarized the
Chevrolet incident, using the passive voice: "It has been said that Father
Rice once received a free automobile, an embarrassment if his opponents
had known about it." Diamond moreover, in an apparent paraphrase from
the paper, noted about Rice, "While admitting error, he has stressed that
he has not acted sinfully."[26]

I considered what Diamond had done a breach of trust. A full professor
with an endowed chair at Columbia, Diamond (1920–1999) had been a
pioneer in using the FOI/PA. At the time he had just published an essay
on James Carey and the FBI and would soon bring out a book on universi-

ties and surveillance agencies. He and I had corresponded and exchanged work for several years, but what he had done produced several weeks of acrimonious letters back and forth.[27]

Rice's irritation at being accused of misdeeds on the basis of an interview of which he had no transcript was clear in his response to Diamond. He assumed—without mentioning my name—that I had given Diamond a copy of the interview. "I work at a disadvantage," he wrote in a letter to the editor of *Labor History.* "There are four, including Professor Diamond, on my case. They have some intercommunication. One has notes, or a transcript, of an extensive interview with me to which I have not been given access." Rice now offered another explanation for the car which he did not provide during my interview: Cars were still in short supply because of "war time scarcity." GM Central added a car to the dealer's quota so that Rice could get one for John Duffy of the UE. It was paid for out of the money that Philip Murray, the CIO president, was giving Rice to fight the UE's Communist leadership. "I received special treatment," he acknowledged, "but not a free car."[28]

What really happened?

We of course will never know for sure, but I am convinced that Rice did receive a free car. The interview itself was enough for me, so I went public with the assertion in an article published in 1992. Rice's subsequent explanation is simply not convincing. His letter to GM actually is dated 1948, not 1946 as it appears in *Labor History* or 1947 as Rice says in the accompanying letter to the editor.[29]

John M. Duffy, the man who got the car, is the key to understanding what happened. Duffy was a "very conservative Catholic"—in fact a Republican—and an ex–coal miner from Scranton. During the war he moved to Pittsburgh and went to work at Allis-Chalmers. There he became Local 613's vice president, the position that ran the local. He was, according to Rice, a "tough, tough union man." The local had to buy him a suit so he could represent it before the War Labor Board in Washington; he would ride the train all night and go off to his appointments as soon as he arrived there in the morning. "Very anti-left," he had been fighting the Communist leadership from his base in Local 613 before he came to the Pittsburgh priest in 1946.[30]

Rice had more or less stayed out of union affairs during the war. He continued as chaplain of St. Joseph's but, more important, worked for the Office of Price Administration, in McGeever's words, as "rent czar." Beginning in 1946, though, Rice got back into the battle against the UE Communists. In St. Louis, New York, and Dayton, working-class

anti-Communist opposition to the UE leadership began springing up
where it had not previously existed and solidified where it had. To what
degree this agitation inspired Rice is unclear, but Duffy's arrival had a
great impact on him.[31]

For more than three years Rice and Duffy organized anti-Communist
opposition in the Pennsylvania UE. Duffy did some of this work while continuing as vice president of Local 613 and some while on a leave of absence
from the local, but in 1948 District 6 expelled him because of his part in a
rowdy disturbance at the Fort Pitt Hotel. From that point on he no longer
received a salary from the UE. For a time Rice supported him out of his
own pocket and let Duffy use his car for organizing, but Duffy wrecked it.
It is at this point—Rice needed a car, and sharing with his friend clearly
was not working out well—that the deal with GM came about. It was
about this time, too, that Murray began secretly giving money to Rice to
support Duffy while he did his anti-Communist organizing.[32]

If I am right—and I am pretty confident here—Rice took quite a risk
with Duffy in general and with regard to the car in particular. The UE
knew that someone was paying Duffy, but they did not know who. Fun-
neling Murray's payments was bad enough—the CIO president, after all,
was funding the undermining of the duly elected officers of one of its
affiliates—but accepting the car was much worse, for as Rice admitted, it
amounted to "dealing with the enemy."[33]

Why did Rice take this chance? My hunch is that he had several reasons. First, he probably figured that no one would ever find out. If he had
destroyed the letter to GM Central and never revealed Murray's funding
of Duffy, no one would have found out in either case. Second, he considered the battle against the UE Communists of such critical importance to
his church and country that it was worth taking the chance. Third, Duffy
was central to his whole postwar operation. In hindsight, it is hard to see
it succeeding without his cooperation.

Finally, Duffy was not just the perfect man for the job; he was also
Rice's kind of man. As the priest remembered in a column written after
Duffy's death in 1961, he "was the ideal man for the fight: unmarried,
dogged, competent, fearless and unselfseeking. Very importantly, he was a
good trade unionist who had battled it out with a tough company and who
had led difficult strikes." Almost certainly unaware that he was describing
how he himself would have liked to be portrayed, Rice continued, "While
he was not a bully and not an expert rough-and-tumble fighter[,] he had
no fear of fights of any kind, possessing boundless physical and moral
courage—a very rare combination."[34]

Rice took a similar sort of risk at GE's Erie, Pennsylvania, plant, where UE Local 506 bargained. While on a trip there he talked to Peter Macosko, a factory superintendent, but not "much because it might have made a bad impression." Rice wrote to Father Andrew Dzmura, who I assume was Episcopalian because he was married, to ask for Macosko's address and telephone number so he could "contact him" the next time he was in Erie. Rice wanted the priest to mention the letter to Macosko if he had the chance.[35]

Did he ever meet with the superintendent? No, he told me, because the companies "did not trust me." What did he want from Macosko? A worker's name, he said, because they "had no names in Erie." Astonished by this willingness to "cooperate," as I phrased it, I pushed Rice. He would not have cooperated with management, he told me, but would have "used" them if they had been willing to give him names, "because in a Communist-controlled plant, management and the Communists generally worked together."[36]

Rice's willingness to use whatever means available in his battle against Communists in the UE can be seen in yet another incident. This one, better known than the previous two, involved working with a conservative Democratic congressman, Francis E. Walter of Pennsylvania, to use the House Committee on Un-American Activities to influence an election in Local 601 which was being held to choose delegates to the UE national convention.

The UE's September 1949 convention was, as it turned out, the last time the union met as a CIO affiliate. It also proved to be the most contentious convention in the UE's history. Some anti-Communists thought they had a chance to defeat the union's leadership. Some even predicted victory. As it happened, and as Rice later claimed to have foreseen, the incumbents defeated the insurgents by about a thousand votes on every substantive issue. That was still in the future, however. In the meantime, the elections for convention delegates were bitterly fought. This was nowhere more the case than at Local 601.

Local 601 was Westinghouse's largest plant. Although its workforce had declined since its wartime peak of 23,000, the plant still employed 17,500 workers in June 1947 and 16,000 on June 1, 1948. By the following June that number had again dropped, to 12,500, yet it remained one of the largest factories in the world. Local 601 would choose eleven delegates to the UE convention, who would cast about 150 votes, in an election in which 15,000 would be eligible voters. The sides were pretty evenly matched going into these elections. In 1947 the pro-administrative forces had elected all nine delegates to the UE national convention and also had won the majority of the local's offices. The following year, though, the anti-Communists had won.[37]

Rice's intervention in this election became known to contemporaries first because of Walter's inability to keep his mouth shut. On July 31, 1949, about two weeks before the election, the *Pittsburgh Post-Gazette*'s Washington correspondent reported that the congressman had told her that, according to a Pittsburgh "clergyman," whom he would not name, Local 601 was being "converted" to Communism by "out-of-town Communists," who were moreover trying to undo the anti-Communist election victory of 1948. According to Walter, then serving on HUAC, subpoenas would be delivered soon.[38]

The Left in Local 601 immediately identified Rice as the unnamed clergyman. Tom Fitzpatrick, the group's enormously popular leader, sharply attacked him the day after the subpoenas came out as "an ambitious power-hungry priest who makes a career out of meddling in union affairs." Rice had much to say in response—two paragraphs' worth in the *Post-Gazette*—but did not deny the charge that he had arranged for HUAC to intervene. The Left kept up the attack on him for the next several weeks in its newspaper, in leaflets, and in mass meetings held at various gates of the huge plant. A reporter described a noon gathering attended by about 1,500 on Cable Avenue: "With oratory that sometimes approached hysteria, the left-wingers denounced the inquiry and viciously attacked Reverend Charles Owen Rice."[39]

Rice continued to finesse the issue. In a form letter he handled it this way: "Expect a new barrage of vilification against me. The Communists in Local 601 are being investigated by the Government and they are blaming me for it. They brought this on themselves by being Communists. They have brought shame on the whole union by that fact. The Communists around Pittsburgh blame me for everything including the weather." In denying that he had arranged the HUAC subpoenas, he never actually lied outright. For example, when a reporter from the *Daily Worker* asked him for a yes or no, "Rice sputtered, 'I won't answer that question!'"[40]

"UE District Council Called Red" blared the *Post-Gazette*'s banner headline of August 10. The day before HUAC had heard the testimony of four friendly witnesses who asserted that a Red conspiracy was at work in the Westinghouse local. The next day the committee went after four left-wingers from Local 601. It particularly focused on Robert Whisner, who had traveled to Russia in 1934 but neglected to include it as destination on his passport application. He had gone there under the auspices of an organization called the Friends of the Soviet Union and had written an article for *Soviet Russia Today* in which he argued that U.S. workers should support Russia. Whisner denied that he still held those beliefs, but the damage was done.[41]

Two days later, with the hearings still ringing in their ears and Catholic clerical opposition to the UE leadership fully apparent, the members of Local 601 voted to choose their delegates to the convention. In a clear rejection of the left wing they picked seven anti-Communist delegates. Despite having appeared before HUAC, though, Fitzpatrick and Frank Panzino were elected as well. Tom Quinn, also hauled before the committee, was elected to the District 6 council. Although more than double the number of votes were cast than was normal in a delegate election, only about three thousand members turned out, of about fifteen thousand who were eligible. Others apparently wanted to vote but were frustrated by the long lines and lack of parking.[42]

Rice, despite his obfuscations, had in fact played a central role in arranging the HUAC hearings that had helped produce this anti-Communist victory. He more or less admitted it in a 1958 interview and again in 1963, when he added that it was a case of "the wrong thing turning out right." By the 1980s his account had changed slightly. In a letter to his biographer Rice wrote that he had been "suckered" into going to see Walter. In an interview with me he gave a variety of explanations, including that he had been "used" and "set up," while essentially admitting his involvement. The editor of a collection of Rice's writings notes that he "collaborated" with HUAC in its 1949 hearing "on the eve of crucial union elections in East Pittsburgh."[43]

While we probably will never be absolutely certain about the degree to which Rice was involved in HUAC's successful efforts to influence the 1949 delegate election in Local 601, we do have some detailed information from someone directly involved in the matter: William Peeler, an Afro-American foundry worker who was in the anti-Communist caucus until he broke with it in 1952. Once he had done that, he wrote a revealing, notarized sixteen-page statement.[44]

As Peeler remembered it, "around February, 1949," he received a call from Alvin Stokes, a HUAC investigator, who was staying at the William Penn Hotel. Once Stokes admitted who he was, Peeler called Duffy and Charles E. Copeland, Local 601's business agent and a key anti-Communist leader. Copeland and Duffy "presented the investigator" with "documentary evidence of the actions of certain UE leaders to take back with him" to Washington. The right-wing group figured that HUAC's help would make it easier to defeat the Left "on any issue as well as to defeat them for office.."[45]

Rice and Ernest Vida, another leader of the right-wing caucus, then went to Washington "to urge action from the committee." (Peeler gives no date for this visit but says simply that it was in preparation for the delegate elections.) About a week later Louis Russell, a former FBI agent and senior investigator for HUAC, called a meeting at the William Penn Hotel. Ten Local 601 right-wingers and four HUAC investigators met to plot their strategy. (Rice "was not present," remembered Peeler, "although he had made the arrangements.") Once HUAC agreed to their proposal for the hearings, said Peeler, "we picked out the people that we thought would be the biggest threat to us in the election" to be summoned for questioning. They unanimously chose Fitzpatrick, Panzino, and Quinn. Whisner was their fourth choice, "even though he wasn't any real threat to the leadership or officers of the union."[46]

Peeler and the three other anti-Communists who would serve as witnesses against them went to Washington a day early to get some coaching. Peeler was given committee files to look at, and they all were shown the questions they would be asked. They even went through a trial run. "We were well rehearsed," said Peeler. At some point during this meeting, the UE's Washington representative discovered the men "conferring cosily with the UnAmerican Committee Staff. It wasn't apparent to the naked eye whether they were briefing the UnAmerican Committee or the Committee was briefing them." These four stayed in Washington during the remainder of the hearings and "were observed frequently" talking with Russell and other HUAC investigators. The Pittsburgh news coverage of the hearings appeared to be spontaneous, but according to Peeler, the fix was in at that end as well. As he remembered it, "the newspapers and radio commentators, all by pre-arrangement, had a field day."[47]

The UE figured out most of this pretty quickly. In the August 22 issue of its newspaper Betty Goldstein, latter Betty Friedan, published a long article in which she exposed the plot. She had even discovered—how is an interesting question—the date, July 25, when Rice and Vida went to Washington to meet with Walter. Amidst the details of the conspiracy, Goldstein reported not only that Rice was secretly directing the right-wing leadership group but also that his goal, as the headline of the piece also implied, was to "maintain his grasp on the local."[48]

The UE ran an editorial about this conspiracy that is worth examining. What was at stake, it said, was the "control" of the union: the opposing parties were the "membership of the UE" and the "outside forces." The "[James] Carey-ACTU group" was the "puppet of the outsiders trying to take over." These "outside forces," the editorial asserted, annually brought in "some anti-labor, reactionary governmental committee or agency to buttress them in their fight." The HUAC hearings would be, the UE predicted, "only the opening gun of a whole series of efforts by reactionaries in government to help the outsiders take over the union." The UE leadership was apparently arguing that the goal of the Catholic Church was to seize control of the union, and "reactionaries in government"—one assumes for their own purposes—were determined to help the Church do that. The "Carey-ACTU" group was working on behalf of the "outsiders," including the Church.[49]

This is, of course, a preposterous, even ridiculous, charge. Nevertheless, there is a good deal of evidence that might be seen as supporting the UE's accusations, if they are defined broadly rather than specifically. Many in the anti-Communist group were in fact willing to get help from virtually anyone in their battle for leadership of the union. Much of the evidence is concentrated around Carey, whose office functioned sometimes and somewhat as an organizing center for the UE anti-Communist group. The kinds of connections that Carey and others used were not those, it needs to be remembered, that could be created out of whole cloth. There was a history behind them. It is not possible to dig it out, but its existence must be kept in mind as the connections are discussed.

HUAC provided even more direct help to UE anti-Communists than that given those in Local 601. In November 1949 Harry Read, a Catholic journalist and ACTU veteran who was Carey's executive assistant, met with HUAC's lawyer and had dinner with him five months later. In 1949 and 1951 HUAC provided information on the political background of UE officials and organizers to Les Finnegan, another of Carey's assistants. In 1950 Joe Hawkins, a leader of the International Electrical, Radio and Machine Workers of America (IUE)—as we will see, the UE's non-Communist-dominated rival—used HUAC data in a campaign in Ohio.[50]

The Atomic Energy Commission (AEC), which had barred General Electric from recognizing the UE as the bargaining agent for its new atomic energy labs in Schenectady, New York, also helped the IUE. In 1949, before the UE convention, Finnegan got information from Oscar Smith in the AEC's Labor Relations Office. The connection continued in 1950 and 1951 as Carey and Smith remained in contact.[51]

Carey's contacts with Immigration and Naturalization probably fall into this category of connection too. There were several UE officials, including James Matles, it's the union's president, whose status as citizens could be questioned, so the telephone calls that went back and forth could well have been political in nature.[52]

It is hard to know what to think about Carey's contacts with Charles E. Wilson, the president of GE. Wilson called him in June and again in

December 1950. Several days after the December call, Carey, Walter Reuther of the United Auto Workers, and presumably Murray met with Wilson in Murray's hotel suite. The UE's accusations that Philco had been helping out the IUE in November 1949 cannot be verified, nor can the charge that Westinghouse paid half of Hawkins's and another person's salary in exchange for not taking up grievances during working hours.[53]

Then there was the political pressure that the anti-Communists brought to bear in their battle with their enemies. The IUE was able to round up plenty of political support in its quest to get elections held as soon as possible at as many UE-controlled locals as it could. In addition to lobbying the Democratic governor of New Jersey, who pushed the state courts to give priority to several cases that were blocking elections, Carey's people used their contacts in Congress to press for swift elections at Westinghouse.[54]

There is a pattern here, but for our purposes it is not a solely Catholic one. First, those bureaucrats and politicians with whom these anti-Communists worked were not all Catholics; many of them in fact were not. Second, many of the IUE founders—the "Committee of Ten" and the "Forty-niners"—were not Catholic either. Finally, there was a distinct absence of Catholics among the Dayton UE leadership and membership, a key component of the coalition that supported Carey. Yet Catholic or not, they all engaged in the same sort of activity. Oakie Wornstaff of Local 768, who grew up a Pentecostal, accepted help from the president of a company in order to bring a local into the IUE. Most important, he and two other leaders of the Dayton anti-Communist leadership were on good terms with local FBI agents and worked with them in their battle with the UE leadership.[55]

The issue of Rice's relationship with the FBI is as messy as everything else having to do with his anti-Communist years. For one thing, without Rice's discussion of the FBI in 1958, 1968, and 1977, scholars would have had no idea that he worked with the Bureau. For another, without Rice's willingness to allow researchers to look at the FBI material he received through the FOI/PA, they would not be able to discuss the relationship at all; because of the Privacy Act, no one could have access to Rice's FBI files without his notarized permission.[56]

I do not think, however, that this is all there is to the story. My hunch is that Rice, having once made a public confession about his relationship with the FBI, decided to frame its interpretation. His very openness, I am convinced, was a smokescreen.

The FBI files that Rice permitted researchers to examine are, intentionally or not, a small fraction of what he received from the FBI. In 1977, he got 126 pages from FBIHQ and in 1978, 926 pages from the Pittsburgh Field Office. I saw probably twenty-five to thirty pages at his office in 1986 and received copies of another ten or so from a researcher who had seen them there. His biographer, who, with Rice's permission, filed his own FOI/PA request, received considerably fewer pages than Rice did. I do not think any researcher has seen all of Rice's FBI material. It is quite possible that, because of the way the implementation of the FOI/PA changes under each new presidential administration, no one will ever see the complete files.[57]

Rice, not proud of his FBI connection, minimized it. The accounts in his essay published in 1977, his interview with me in 1986, his article published in 1989, and his letter to the editor in 1990 are all about the same. His story was that some local FBI agents were friendly with him, and he did receive some information, but the Bureau never really trusted him and provided no information after 1941 or perhaps a bit later. For a time Rice would have "three or four young Irish fellows" from the field office over to St. Joseph's for dinner and Ping-Pong. After that, he says, because he repeated information that James B. Carey, the soon-to-be anti-Communist about whom I will have more to say later, had received from the Bureau, whatever relationship the FBI had with him was both wary and formal.[58]

Rice admitted to me that the FBI gave him information but was vague about exactly what kind. I asked him specifically if, in the 1940–41 or 1947–1950 campaign in Local 601, he was able to get information from the FBI. He responded, "They wouldn't tell me." I replied, "They wouldn't tell you?" Rice answered: "They would yes or no me. But . . . all they would do was conf[irm], they didn't need to give me any information." Instead "old-time Socialists who were very bitter" had provided Rice with his "biggest information on the Communists."[59]

What is to be made of this? Is there enough evidence to make a judgment about Rice's connection with the FBI? An assessment of Rice's retelling of the connection? I think so. The evidence, scant as it is, suggests a more complicated and drawn-out relationship with the FBI than Rice himself later remembered.

The main file that the Bureau kept on Rice is among the FBI material at which he allowed researchers a look. The first three serials, though, are gone, and in the absence of that material alone, it is impossible to know the date when the file began. Since, however, the first serial in Rice's file was processed as a "see" reference for my request for the ACTU file, we know it is dated May 26, 1947. (Without access to that item, one would think the file began in 1967, with serial four, recording Rice's attack on Hoover in a speech over the radio and summarizing Rice's antiwar record, after which the Pittsburgh assistant special agent in charge paid a visit to the priest's bishop.) Serial six, a "correlation file" which summarizes the references to Rice that appear in other FBI files than his own, allows us to get at Rice's relationship with the Bureau before and after 1947.[60]

The references, primarily drawn from newspaper clippings, in this correlation summary for the period from 1937 to 1943, deal with Rice's pro-labor and anti-Communist activity. An example of the former, filed under the caption "Activities in Maritime Industry," contains information on Rice's speech at a 1937 meeting of the American Radio Telegraphists Association held in New York City. Rice's upholding, as an arbitrator, the Communist Carolyn Hart's dismissal from her job is an example of the latter.

That there is only one leaflet extant for this early period suggesting help from the FBI does not mean Rice received no help or that he erroneously remembered that his FBI friends would "yes or no" him. What it probably means is that Rice used the information as background rather than specifically to tag someone as a Communist. The relationship, moreover, probably was as informal and as off-the-books as Rice's description of the Ping-Pong games suggests. (This would fit with the kind of connection that William J. Smith, S.J., had with the FBI.) It might mean, however, that the connection was recorded in the 926 Pittsburgh Field Office files Rice received but which no one, as far as I know, has ever seen.[61]

Beginning in late 1942, however, Rice's relationship with the FBI, as evidenced in the correlation summary, changed. Agents began regularly going to him for information on individuals, and Rice routinely provided it to them. They asked him about Jack Barry, a man whom Rice said he had not seen for several years, but who "used to be connected with the Communist Party." The priest also "furnished information" about Harold Ruttenberg's "association with liberal groups and his activity in the labor field." (Ruttenberg, described by the FBI as a "close friend of Rice's, was the research director of the SWOC.) Stanley Glass, who later would work closely with the priest in the UE anti-Communist leadership caucus, was, Rice advised, a socialist, not a Communist. The next interaction for 1943 is deleted.[62]

So far the FBI seems to have initiated the conversations with Rice. This is not the case for the last entry for 1943, when Rice sent a letter to the field office about Dr. John Torok. Torok, according to the FBI summary, "claimed to have acquired confidential, inter-office memos of the OPA [Office of Price Administration]." He also "frequently made reference to investigations by the FBI and Civil Service Commission which had cleared him for a responsible Government position." The FBI shortly interviewed Rice about this matter.[63]

The year 1943 was something of a high point for this kind of contact between Rice and the FBI, but it continued on into the 1950s. In 1944 he "furnished information" on the "Cominfil of the CIO, Industrial Union Council" and told the Bureau that Father Casmir Orlemanski was not a Communist. In 1954 he informed the FBI that the charges of Communism concerning Harold Lavine were untrue. The following year he did the same for Morris Swimmer.[64]

What we have seen so far of Rice's interaction with the FBI provides us with some important information. Over a period of a decade FBI agents regularly went to him for information. That they did so means that they assumed not only that Rice would not publicize their visit but also that the information he provided would be valuable. Already, then, the relationship is different from what Rice suggested it was. But there is more—considerably more. The key period began in 1946. On June 2 Rice talked with the FBI about the "communist tendencies" of Lee Pressman, the CIO's lawyer and one of Murray's key advisers. Rice "showed concern over the influence which Pressman exerted upon" Murray. He "suggested" that the Bureau talk with the CIO president about the problem.[65]

Catholic labor activists, both clerical and lay, had been troubled about Pressman's relationship with Murray for some time. He was, as they correctly suspected, under CPUSA discipline and regularly consulted with Party functionaries about CIO matters. In 1943, working secretly under Roy Hudson's direction in a hotel room, he changed several CIO convention resolutions to correspond with the current Communist line.[66]

According to Rice himself, he may have been the only labor priest who directly discussed the issue with Murray. He could do so because of their tremendously close relationship. They had become friends in late 1940 or early 1941 and saw each other frequently when Murray was in town. Rice also was Murray's confessor. Even so, Rice remembered that he had to be "careful" in talking with Murray because he was "very fond" of Pressman and depended on him for advice.[67]

For reasons that are unclear but may have had something to do with Murray's attack on the Franco regime in Spain in late 1945, Catholic pressure on him increased in 1946. Whatever was going on, Rice responded as well, for it was then—it is unclear whether before or after he talked to the FBI—that he and Murray "went into every phase and angle" of the Communist Party issue. At the time Rice did not think he "did much good," since the CIO president "parried my every argument."[68]

Rice's pessimism about the conversation with Murray, which had evaporated by the time they talked again, seems to have been the prod for him to go to the FBI. My hunch is that what he wanted the Bureau to do was show Murray evidence that Pressman was operating under CPUSA discipline. What he did not know, ironically, was that in effect this already had been done.[69]

There are five serials, all dated 1947, from the FBI's main file on the ACTU that contain much information on Rice as well as the Pittsburgh ACTU. The first item, formally written and dated April 7, provides an introduction to the association, discusses the Pittsburgh chapter, and tells of an upcoming meeting on April 15. The second one is a report on that gathering, attended by more than two hundred. Within it are verbatim quotations from speakers as well as what appears to be a transcript of Rice's demagogic remarks. This suggests that the gathering may have been bugged, but if it was, the report is unlike any other I have ever seen. Rice's speech, though, was clearly not written out beforehand. The third and fourth items are reports, apparently by someone present, of another ACTU meeting held on May 20, 1947; thirty-five people were in attendance.[70]

The final serial is, for our purposes, the most important one because of what it asserts about Rice's words and actions at an ACTU meeting with seventy-five in attendance. Communists, the priest said, should not be "driven underground. They should be left as they are so that the FBI can watch them[,] for the FBI knows all the Communists in the country and can put their finger on them any time they choose to do so." He then apparently produced evidence, saying, "Here are the photostat copies of the Communist Party cards of Thos. Fitzpatrick of the U.E. District #6 Council, George Bobich and Clyde Johnson of #610."[71]

Rice denied that he produced these photostats. There is some reason to think that he lied. For one thing, he apparently did not deny the statement when he saw a preliminary copy of an article by Diamond in which the incident was discussed. Also, there is plenty of evidence to indicate that Rice was close to the Bureau during this period. Finally, the FBI did know Fitzpatrick's membership number.[72]

There are four different pieces of evidence that indicate Rice's coziness with the FBI. The first is quite simple and is from Rice himself. It is also mentioned in an interview in 1968, long before the priest had developed an awareness of how history might see him. Rice volunteered to an interviewer that the FBI had told him that John Nelson, a leader at UE Local 506 in Erie, was a Communist. The other three proofs require lengthier discussion.[73]

In 1948 Victor Riesel, the anti-Communist labor journalist, contacted Louis Nichols, an assistant to Hoover, to set up a meeting between Rice and the Director. Well respected by Catholic labor activists and disliked in the same measure by Communists and their allies, Riesel apparently had a good working relationship with Nichols. Rice, who must have known this, came to him to set up the meeting. Riesel did not know what Rice wanted but thought it must be important. There were three possibilities: Rice might just wish to meet "persons in important places"; he might be seeking aid for his battle against the Communists; or "it is conceivably possible that Rice is being sent to the Director as an intermediary from Philip Murray."[74]

Rice agreed to meet with Nichols instead of Hoover, so Riesel and Nichols set up a lunch meeting for the three of them. (If he decided that it was important enough, Nichols was going to contact Hoover if he was in the building.) As it turned out, however, Rice could not leave Pittsburgh, so he and Riesel asked for a "rain check." They apparently never collected.

In a 1949 radio broadcast Rice had some praiseworthy things to say about the Bureau: "The FBI is a terrific organization. It is an investigative body that is no danger to Democracy. It is a model of what a Democracy can do to protect itself from spies and other subversives without sacrificing or injuring any of our freedom." Having read of disagreements between the White House and Hoover, the priest came down on the side of the latter: "I hope they leave Hoover alone[;] he has done a good and necessary job. He has shown that he knows how to care for the safety and internal security of the country."[75]

Finally, in March 1950 Rice had lunch with a special agent to discuss Communist issues. Rice warned him about William McCabe, a local leader in the Brotherhood of Locomotive Engineers. The priest said that McCabe was "definitely tied up with the Communists," but Rice was, according to the report, "unable to give any specific information showing the relationship between McCabe and the Communists, although he did say that McCabe gave public statements demonstrating his sympathy for the 11 Communist Party leaders who were tried in New York."[76]

The next thing Rice and the agent discussed had to do with the former's campaign at UE Local 610, Westinghouse Airbrake, in Wilmerding, a few miles from East Pittsburgh, the home of Local 601. Rice, as we will see, had turned his attention to Local 610, "which was being neglected." There he gave "considerable advice, and managed to procure some money from a proper union source." He also tried to use the FBI.[77]

At stake was the "close relationship" between Westinghouse Airbrake and the UE. The charge of coziness between the companies and the UE, which Carey had publicly made in testimony before the House Committee on Education and Labor in September 1948, became a recurring theme of the anti-Communist forces and the IUE. Some thirty-five years later, as we have seen, it came quickly to mind when I pressed Rice about his efforts to contact GE management at the Erie plant. The charge was, of course, ludicrous, but that did not prevent it from being repeated again and again.[78]

The outlandishness of these accusations is demonstrated by the evidence Rice produced. The UE had received a pension from Westinghouse in collective bargaining; it was not a "favorable one from the standpoint of union members, but the UE as well as the Communist Party" had "made capital use of this maneuver." Through "confidential contacts," Rice had also discovered that John Bosser, controller of Westinghouse Airbrake, who was "responsible for the close relationship that apparently exists between the [company] officials" and the UE, "had a mistress" who used to work for the company. Rice had other information "with regard to activity of the Communists in the labor field" and wanted "to discuss the matter with an Agent of the office familiar with the labor situation in Pittsburgh," but there was no time to do it. Several days later an agent contacted him, but Rice "could furnish no info not already known t[o] this office."[79]

Rice was not alone in his connection to the FBI. Many Catholic labor activists, both lay and clerical, had working relationships with the Bureau. Some of them are easier to find out about than Rice's; others are harder. There is no one in the CIO whose working relationship with the FBI mattered more than James B. Carey's, but to focus too much attention on him is to miss the ubiquity of the connection. Before moving on to Carey, therefore, I want to give some sense of this pervasiveness.

Jesuit priests, committed to winning the Catholic working class from the twin "evils" of exploitive employers and "subversive elements," pioneered in the establishment of labor schools in the 1930s and continued to operate several of the leading ones until the mid-1950s. It was through this work that numerous Jesuits developed connections to the FBI. Father William Smith's relationship was the most significant because of the influence he wielded within Catholic labor circles, but I have discussed him elsewhere. Instead I want to look at three other Jesuits: Philip Carey, John McAtee, and Dennis Comey.[80]

Carey, whose father was a trolley motorman in the Bronx with whom he went out during the 1916 strike to paste up leaflets, became director of the Xavier Labor School in 1940, a position he held until its closing in 1988. (There he played an important role in helping Catholic members of the Transit Workers Union defeat the Communists in their locals.) At least twice Carey's connection to the FBI significantly influenced his position on important strikes. In 1944 he wrote a letter to the *Wage Earner*, the Detroit ACTU paper, in which he disagreed with its coverage of the Philadelphia transit workers' "hate strike" of 1944. He was critical of the strikers but did not want the newspaper to get "sucked in by the Party line." That the FBI had investigated the strike, Carey argued, strengthened his position. He similarly assured another Jesuit labor priest that Communists had not been involved in a recently concluded longshoremen's strike: "I can say not only on my own authority but on the connections we have with certain security agencies, which may not be identified, that the Communists had no part in this longshore strike."[81]

Carey's "certain security agencies" probably refers not only to the FBI but also to the New York Police Department's industrial squad. I doubt that the Jesuit would have made the categorical denial of Communist Party involvement without FBI confirmation; he had too much respect for Hoover to do that. Carey, though, was also close to two police officers who worked on the industrial squad.[82]

Father John McAtee, S.J., who also was pro-union, saw the FBI as an ally in his battle against Communism in the CIO. McAtee, while pastor at Sacred Heart in Tampa, gained some notoriety when he defended not only unions but also the closed shop. Formerly a member of the Boilermakers' Union, he vehemently championed the right of priests and ministers to speak out on economic issues: "When God's representatives cease to cry havoc against threats to the rights of man, they cease to represent God. They become the paid hirelings of capitalism or the mute connivers at rank injustice."[83]

Three years later McAtee came to the aid of Robert McNally, a Catholic leader of Transit Workers Union Local 500 in Miami, who was quite upset about the Communist affiliations of some TWU officers. McNally, bewildered, wrote to Rice in April 1947. "I have been rather confused" for the past several months, he told Rice, and "[have] spent a lot of time in mental analyses" of the CIO. On the one hand, McNally, a worker who had helped organize the local at Pan American Airlines, was a committed trade unionist. Not only had he just been elected to his local's executive board, but also he had previously served as shop steward, secretary, and chief section officer of his local. "As you can see from my record," he proudly wrote Rice, "I might be called an ardent CIO-er!"[84]

On the other, however, McNally had "many doubts" as to the "ultimate underlying intentions of our organizer and some of our elected officials." He was convinced that Charles Smolikoff, the organizer for Local 500, was "either a Communist or at least affiliated with them to some extent." He thought the same of Mike Quill, TWU president. The answers of

Maurice Forge, TWU vice president, to direct questions about his politics at a Local 500 meeting also made him suspicious.[85]

His next letter to Rice, in August 1947, indicated that McNally had enthusiastically, but carefully, followed the recommendation to begin fighting the Communist Party in his union. McAtee was running a "study club" for McNally and his five closest allies. Those five had been chosen out of a larger, secret group of thirty-five that he had put together. McNally and the priest also had visited the FBI and given agents the "names & organizations that are creeping into our union." McNally "told them what we are doing etc. *speaking out of school*," he wrote Rice; "they agreed with it and also with the ACTU and said to keep this matter quiet and [not] tell anyone of this meeting." He had told the agents that he would "keep in touch with them from time to time." It is unclear who originally decided to approach the Bureau, but McNally did discuss it with a "few" of his "trusted men," presumably those in his "study club." They knew he was going to the FBI and "agreed that it might be best if we let them know about us etc."[86]

Dennis Comey, S.J., was closer to the FBI than either Carey or McAtee. Several things probably account for this. First, he not only played a major role in countering the TWU's organizing efforts in Philadelphia during World War II but also participated in the 1944 "hate strike." Second, he had much experience in working with Philadelphia longshoremen and served as arbitrator for the ports of Philadelphia during the 1950s. Finally, Comey's handling of the docks and the TWU suggests a set of values more aligned with that of Hoover and his men than with Carey's and McAtee's.

The FBI regularly went to Comey for information—first on labor and security issues and then on waterfront matters—in the 1940s and 1950s. By 1945 he was close enough to the Philadelphia Field Office that he participated in the retreat its Catholic members made in May. In a letter to the Director reporting on the event, Comey reveals something of the depth of the Jesuits' admiration for their fellow warriors against evil. "Their whole attitude impressed," he said of the participants. "*And my reaction to their earnestness is a conviction that serious responsibilities have been placed in very capable hands.* I dare to suggest that you have ample warrant to be very proud of your men. It pleases me to be bracketed with you in such enthusiastic pride."[87]

Comey's friendliness with the Bureau did not diminish in the next decade. In May 1955 he accepted the invitation of Philadelphia FBI employees to speak at their Communion breakfast. The Philadelphia special agent in charge glowingly described his professional relationship with the Jesuit: "Comey has been most cooperative with this office for several years. In his position of Port Arbitrator at Philadelphia he obtains a great deal of information of interest to the Bureau and other intelligence agencies." (One of the other agencies undoubtedly was the Office of Naval Intelligence, for in February 1953 Comey told Carey that "Navy Intelligence" had called him the week before to check on the "rumor that the anti-Quill people were preparing to wildcat.") In view of the cooperation he had received, the SAC urged Hoover to write and thank Comey for his breakfast talk. The letter would be appreciated, he said, and "would serve to increase his relations with this office." Hoover obliged, thanking Comey both for his speech and for his "excellent cooperation in other matters over the years."[88]

The FBI also developed a close relationship with Catholic laymen, but it took until 1943 for the Bureau to figure out that it ought to develop friendly relations with the most important Catholic labor group, the ACTU. One of the reasons it took so long was that early investigations of both the organization and it members turned up what the Bureau considered damaging information.

The FBI file on the ACTU begins with St. Francis House in Seattle, which "numerous complaints" alleged was a "gathering place and hiding place for Communists in the Seattle area." Associated with Dorothy Day's Catholic Worker movement until it broke with her over the issue of pacifism, St. Francis House began publishing a monthly newspaper and formed an ACTU chapter in May 1942.[89]

Everything the Bureau discovered about St. Francis House seemed suspicious. First, Bishop Gerald Shaughnessy had apparently refused to allow the establishment of a chapter for several years. His approval finally came in June 1941, but the bishop did not appoint an official chaplain until all the parish reports on its charter members had come in. Less than a year later Shaughnessy told the chaplain to stop performing his ACTU duties. That was the end of the Seattle ACTU.[90]

It was bad enough, from the Bureau's perspective, that the group was in disfavor with local authority, but the specifics were even worse. "Confidential informants"—almost certainly the Seattle Chancery Office—told the agents that its leaders "had absolutely no understanding of Pope Leo's encyclicals and that they were not mentally qualified" to be doing what they were doing. The articles in the newspaper were "so poorly written as to easily confuse Christians and others into believing they were Communist inspired." St. Francis House was in no way "representative of the Catholic Church."[91]

The involvement of Father H. A. Reinhold in St. Francis House also was a problem. Reinhold was a refugee from Nazi Germany whose firm antifascism made him suspect in the eyes of the U.S. Church hierarchy, especially Shaughnessy, who blamed him for everything he found wrong with St. Francis House—including its "anti-clericalism." It was during the investigation of the Seattle ACTU that the FBI also began looking into Reinhold. While it is impossible to be sure, it appears that Shaughnessy exiled Reinhold to a parish in Yakima, Washington—"where he is to all practical purposes confined"—because he complained to the attorney general about the threats made by the FBI agents who interviewed him. The bishop, according to one source, undoubtedly the chancery office, had "the greatest admiration" for the FBI: a "mere request by the organization for the disbandment of any of the subject organizations, would result in his immediate curtailment of their activities, insofar as his power could attain."[92]

The Seattle Field Office clearly was mistaken about the political sentiments of both Reinhold and the Seattle ACTU. Detroit had similar problems coming to grips with Paul Ste. Marie at the same time the Seattle investigation was going on. Ste. Marie, a devout Catholic and a founder of the Detroit ACTU, worked as a toolmaker at Ford's River Rouge plant from 1927 to 1938, when he was fired for union organizing. He went to work for the UAW but lost his job, according to both Ste. Marie and the Detroit ACTU, when socialists and Communists opposed his commitment to Catholic social principles. After regaining his position at River Rouge, Ste. Marie immersed himself in plant politics and was elected president of the local in 1942. A radio endorsement of the Republican candidate for governor of Michigan played a significant role in his defeat in the next election. He died in 1946 and was buried in the brown robe of a Third Order Franciscan. Ste. Marie was forty-one years old and left behind a wife and ten children.[93]

The Paul Ste. Marie described here bears little resemblance to the one depicted in the Detroit SAC's letter to FBIHQ in 1942. Ste. Marie had talked with John Bugas for "several hours" about his "nebulous" plans for "mobilizing a select group" at the River Rouge local to investigate sabotage. Bugas, who thought Ste. Marie had a "suspicious record," concluded that he was untrustworthy and that he was "at the very least a fellow traveller" of the Communist Party when it "suits his purposes."[94]

The Bureau similarly misjudged Harry Read, whom we have already met. A founding member of the Chicago ACTU, Read played a leading role in the 1938–1940 Hearst strike and would go on to work for the Michigan CIO as the editor of its newspaper before moving to Washington in 1945. In July 1941 the Chicago Field Office actually initiated an investigation of him on the basis of a complaint that he was "acting as an undercover organizer of Negro Youth for the Communist Party and traveling extensively in this capacity."[95]

By May 1943, though, the FBI had altered its opinion of ACTU. Its file does not provide anything definitive about why this change occurred, but it apparently grew out of the ability of field offices to develop informants among ACTU members. "Many Field Offices," Hoover noted, "have found its officials cooperative in making information available in connection with the [Communist] infiltration cases." The Director gave the pertinent offices the necessary information to contact ACTU officers in their jurisdiction.[96]

It took some time, but the Detroit Field Office developed several top ACTU leaders into informants. In October 1944 it notified FBIHQ that it would "interview Paul Weber and/or Tom Daugherty" of the ACTU for "any information they may have concerning Communistic Activities" on the part of a subject under investigation. Weber was a founder of the Detroit ACTU, a member of the Newspaper Guild, and the editor of the ACTU's newspaper, the *Wage-Earner*. Doherty, as his name was correctly spelled, was the first recording secretary of the UAW's Chrysler Local 7 and another founding member of the ACTU. By June 1945 both men were collaborating with the FBI. Weber, according to Father John Cronin, was "now working with my friends, to their mutual gain." The Detroit Field Office notified FBIHQ that same month that it would maintain an unidentified contact "in order to ascertain whether Daugherty is successful in obtaining further information regarding the Subject's activities in connection with his employment in the UAW-CIO."[97]

Nineteen forty-three was a key year for Read as well. It was then that the Bureau considered using him as "a possible source of information." That same year Read's worries about the social impact of the war came to the fore when he interpreted the effort to establish day nurseries for married women as a Communist Party plot, the "initial step in having the state take over the function of the mother and the family." Read, "suspicious of the personnel in some of the existing nurseries," advised his correspondent that "someone might want to call the attention of government officials to what is going on. It might be better to do this quietly." But there was more. Read combined FBI statistics and personal assumptions in a letter to a monsignor noting that not only was juvenile delinquency up, but so was misbehavior among teenage girls, with dangerous implications: "You will recall the recent FBI statement that moral lapses among young girls are greatly on the increase with a resultant rise in illegitimacy and, no doubt, abortions. I am on the Mayor's Committee on Youth Problems and these are the facts."[98]

The FBI made its first move toward Read in August 1946, after he had gone to Washington, D.C., to take a job with the national CIO. Something or someone—it is impossible to tell—made FBIHQ review its material on him. In a four-page memo to Edward A. Tamm, the third-ranking man at the FBI and the highest-ranking Catholic, Bureau official D. M. Ladd laid out Read's career. After summarizing the original investigation, the memo indicated that the Detroit Field Office "subsequently" learned from the ACTU that Read "was considered a loyal American with anti-communist sentiments." He "was described by that organization as a Catholic and, as such, was believed by the organization to be dependable and opposed to Communist activities."[99]

There were, though, some suspicious facts that required explanation. Read served on the executive board of the Chicago chapter of the National Religion and Labor Foundation in 1940. It paralleled in some ways the Communist Party program, but there was no evidence "that the group was ever under Communist control." Read also participated in a complaint against racial discrimination at a hotel during the 1944 Michigan CIO convention. There was again, though, "no indication" that "there was any attempt on the part of Read to support a Communist cause."[100]

It pleased the FBI that the Communists were attacking Read. He got into a nasty verbal brawl—important enough to be mentioned in the *Daily Worker*—with well-know Party members from a "Red" UAW local in 1943. The Detroit Field Office, moreover, picked up a Communist Party discussion highly critical of Read in one of its wiretaps.

The pertinent information is deleted, but it is clear from what remains of the four-page memorandum that Ladd recommended Read be developed as a source of information. Five days later arrangements were made for the Washington Field Office to talk to him. It took some time to be arranged, but by late January 1947 the office had had two and maybe three meetings with Read. We do not know what was discussed, nor do we know if these were the only meetings between them. But what we do know points in the same direction: Read was working with anyone he could to defeat the Communists in the CIO.

First, we have some information about Read's activities in the late 1940s and early 1950s because his appointment books have been preserved in his collection of papers. Page after page, though, has been neatly removed, probably with a razor blade. Read—or someone else—was hiding something. Second, the pages that remain document numerous meetings with government and military officials at, for example, the Department of Defense, the State Department, the Department of Justice, the Federal Trade Commission, and the Immigration and Naturalization Service.[101]

In February 1948 Read had lunch with Father William Gordon, O.S.A., and Congressman Charles Kersten, a Wisconsin Republican who served on the House Subcommittee on Education and Labor. Gordon, a recently ordained priest who had received a Ph.D. from Catholic University, was on the fringes of the labor priest movement. He was therefore a perfect confidant for Carey, who, Rice noted, had "many priest friends" but did not "like those who actively work in the unions." Gordon would give an invocation at the first IUE convention. It is unclear how he and the congressman met, but Kersten would claim in 1953 that he had requested parole for a "convicted New York labor extortionist" at Gordon's request.[102]

About six months later Kersten and his fellow committee member John F. Kennedy met in New York City with Carey, Gordon, and a third person, probably Read, identified only as "one" of Carey's "other righthand men." One of the things they discussed, since the subcommittee was preparing to resume its hearings on the UE, was "what material" could be used against its "known Communist members."[103]

The congressmen had checked with the FBI before consulting with Carey and Read. Several days before the meeting Manley Sheppard, secretary to the subcommittee chairman, Congressman Fred Hartley, called the Bureau and asked for "any information" it had on the CIO secretary-treasurer. He said that the subcommittee hoped to "use him in connection with the breaking down of some of the stories of the [UE's] Left Wing Group since Carey is considered to be a right-winger." The FBI provided the subcommittee with a seven-page blind letterhead memorandum.[104]

That Carey would wind up in this position could not have been predicted at all in 1941, let alone 1937 or 1938. He was born in Philadelphia on August 12, 1911, of liberal Democratic Catholic parents. One of eleven children, he attended parochial grade school in Glassboro, New Jersey. His first trade union experience came during a projectionists' strike when he was a teenager working as a helper in a New Jersey movie theater. Upon graduation from the public high school, he went to work at Philco Radio in Philadelphia, going to night school at Drexel University and the University of Pennsylvania's Wharton School. He played a key role in the formation of an independent union at Philco in 1933.

From this point on Carey rode the rising wave of working-class insurgency. In 1934 he took an organizing job with the American Federation of Labor and became president of its group of workers producing radios and related products. In 1936, when the UE formed out of this federation and a number of independent unions primarily from machine shops, Carey was elected president at age twenty-four; he served as such until he was defeated for reelection in September 1941. In 1938 Carey, who had developed a close relationship with John L. Lewis, president of the United Mine Workers and of the CIO, was elected the latter's first secretary. When the office of treasurer was created, he also took on that responsibility, serving in that joint capacity until the CIO merged with the AFL in 1955.

CPUSA members had played a critical role in the organization of the UE, particularly in putting together the independent machine shop locals. Some of the most gifted, hardest-working, and most dedicated organizers and leaders were either Party members or labor militants who knowingly worked with them.

Carey fell into the latter category. He worked alongside communists in the UE and also in the American League against War and Fascism, its successor organization, the American League for Peace and Freedom, and the American Youth Congress. He held official positions in these organizations, never denouncing them as Communist infiltrated. Finally, he was arrested along with the well-known Communist William Sentner in 1938 during a strike at the Maytag plant in Newton, Iowa. Both were charged with syndicalism and sedition. The FBI consistently received reports that Carey not only belonged to "Communist-dominated organizations" but actually was a Communist Party member. In April 1941, when he began working in the Office of Product Management, the Bureau conducted "an applicant-style inquiry" into his background, and in late 1941 and 1942 it carried out a "Hatch Act Investigation." It found no evidence to substantiate the charge that he had been a CPUSA member.[105]

In May 1942, undoubtedly at his request in an effort to clear himself, the FBI interviewed Carey under oath. He denied that he had "ever been a member of any organization which advocates the overthrow of the federal government" or "disloyalty to the federal government." He also denied that he had "ever been a member of the Communist Party" or the "Young Communist League." After answering several other questions about specific organizations and specific meetings, Carey was asked a final question: "Have you ever been a member of any organization which you have reason to believe was dominated by the Communist Party?" Since the question depended, as he pointed out, on the definition of "Communist dominated"—which Carey defined as "requir[ing] loyalty or subservience to the policy of the Communist Party"—he hesitated, surely thinking of the "front" groups to which he belonged, but finally answered, "I have never been a member of an organization that I found dominated by the Communist Party."[106]

The interview concluded with Carey accepting the FBI's offer to make his own statement. Here he primarily focused on the 1941 UE convention when, he argued, the Communist Party defeated him for reelection.

Again and again Carey would use this claim as proof of his rebirth as an anti-Communist, but as with so much else having to do with Carey, the truth was not this simple. Carey's disagreement with the antiwar and anti-Roosevelt positions of his fellow (CPUSA) officers made a difference, but just as important—if not more so—were three other factors: his neglect of his UE duties, his temperament, and his support for an interpretation of the UE's constitution that would have permitted locals to bar from membership those proven to be Communists, Nazis, or fascists.[107]

This is not to say that the issue of Communism was not involved in Carey's defeat, but rather that the matter was not *simply* Communism. For our purposes, moreover, it suggests one reason why Tamm would have been so leery of getting involved with Carey even when they both shared the same objective. In the long run, as we shall see, Hoover and his third man were both right: Feeding information to Carey *was* effective. Carey *was* unreliable.

It did not take long for Carey to go to the FBI for help. On July 3, 1943, he visited the Bureau and asked for assistance in "clear[ing] the UE of communist control." Specifically, he wanted "to have a Bureau check made of all persons to be supported by the CIO." He promised that such help "would of course be off the record and he would treat such information obtained in the strictest confidence."[108]

The Bureau turned him down with its standard line about not sharing information, but that did not stop Carey from trying again in March 1944, this time at the Philadelphia Field Office, where he may have known someone. Everything in the two-page memo on his request to the Philadelphia office has been deleted except for one sentence: "Briefly, it has to do with the fact that James B. Carey, National Secretary-Treasurer of the CIO, wants to get the Director, together with Philip Murray, to clean the Communists out of the CIO."[109]

Carey's second effort—within less than a year—to enter into a working relationship with the FBI produced a flurry of memos at FBIHQ. The first came the very next day from Tamm, whose status as the highest-ranking Catholic at the Bureau may have made him more cautious than usual in his evaluation. While admitting that it was "probably unfair to question the sincerity" of Carey's request, he did just that: "I think this is probably fundamentally a desire on Carey's part to further his own interests." These interests, Tamm thought (erroneously), included becoming CIO president. He advised that "we should tread very, very carefully in this situation."[110]

Hoover agreed, but cautioned Tamm to keep the larger goal in mind: "Maybe so, but Carey is right in his concern. The Communists will only be a menace to the U.S. if they can seize labor control & this they are gradually doing." Maybe for the record, but perhaps not, Hoover added another point: "Of course, I cannot make anything in FBI [files] available unless A. G. [Attorney General] or President direct."[111]

A final memo produced by Carey's request was intended to help Tamm and Hoover decide what to do about him. It laid out his background, his labor organizing in the 1930s, and his union positions. After discussing the accusations that Carey was a Communist or Communist sympathizer and giving Carey's explanation, Ladd noted that the FBI had "developed no definite proof" that he was a Party member. He had "broke[n] sharply with the Communist element" over the Hitler-Stalin pact, and "since that time Carey has been militantly anti-communist and has lost no opportunity to injure the Communist Party in any way possible." Several excised paragraphs then follow.[112]

There is nothing in Carey's file to suggest Hoover's reasoning, but a tiny handwritten notation—not in the Director's hand—gave his decision: "Memo to Mr. Tamm[.] March 23, 1944[.] ACT." From this point until 1953 Carey worked side by side with the FBI to purge Communists and those who worked with them from the UE and the CIO. Just the outlines of this relationship provide much evidence for the UE's assertions about what was at stake in the battle.[113]

There was considerable interaction between Carey and the Bureau from 1946 through 1948, but most information pertaining to it is excised in the CIO leader's file. Several documents dating from this period that survive in Carey's secretary-treasurer files are suggestive, though, of how the FBI might have been helping him. Both are derived from an eavesdropping bug that Tamm authorized on January 8, 1947. It was installed at 6:50 the next evening in the hotel room of an official of the Food and Tobacco Workers (FTA), a union led—dominated is more accurate here—by the CPUSA. Deactivated at 2:45 A.M. the following day, the bug captured a meeting of FTA officials with John Williamson, CPUSA labor secretary. One of the resulting documents, which is typewritten, is not a transcription of what the bug recorded but rather a cogent summary of the discussion. The second one is a set of handwritten notes on the same meeting. These do not appear have been derived from the first document, so my guess is that they were taken directly from the bug.[114]

The key years in the connection between the Bureau and Carey were 1949 and 1950. In December 1948 the House Subcommittee on Education and Labor released the results of its three-month investigation of the UE. The subcommittee, according to the lead paragraph in the *New York Times*, "reported today that Russia controls the strategic US electrical industry through Communist domination" of the UE. This report established the boundaries within which both the UE and its numerous opponents would operate within the next four or five years. No matter that the issue was more complicated than this; it always came down to Russia and Communism.[115]

As the stakes grew higher in 1949 and 1950, Carey and the FBI grew closer. In March 1949 Carey and Hoover, in what may have been their only face-to-face contact, but which certainly was the most important meeting between Carey and the FBI, reached an understanding. There was, the labor leader told the Director, a UE meeting coming up in Ohio. He and "a number of his associates believed they were in a position to change the complexion of the Ohio group which in turn would have an effect upon the national organization." Undoubtedly thinking that evidence that key UE officers and staff were either CPUSA members or Party liners would convince the undecided to join the right-wing insurgency, Carey asked Hoover to provide him with FBI information on a "list of names he gave him." Hoover told Carey that Bureau files were "strictly confidential," but they might contain information "of a public source nature to which he could then be referred." Carey's words of caution which closed this meeting indicate that he not only wanted to keep secret his relationship with the FBI but also realized how damaging the knowledge of such a connection would be in the hands of his enemies: "Mr. Carey indicated that his contact with the Bureau should be treated as strictly confidential as it would be fatal to his efforts if it became known to certain elements in the CIO that he contacted the FBI."[116]

Les Finnegan handled much of the FBI information that flowed through the floodgates opened by this meeting. Carey's assistant, Finnegan was a former newspaper reporter and, according to the FBI, a member of the Socialist Party in 1940. Finnegan was "allowed to review at the Bureau blind memoranda" on a "large number of communists in the UE." While he apparently did this many times in 1949 and 1950, there is information about only two of those occasions. According to one, in January 1950 "blind memoranda were prepared on a list of seven persons under [UE] District #3 listed by Mr. Carey." The other indicates that Finnegan, probably as a result of Carey's visit with Ladd on January 12, "spent several days each week" from January 20 to February 10, 1950, "reviewing various blind memoranda from H. Fletcher to Mr. Ladd." Finnegan took notes but "was cautioned not to take down specific dates nor CP membership book numbers."[117]

The FBI had gone yet another step further in providing information to Carey. It was now providing him with access to memoranda that contained not just public source material but information that could have come to it only from another intelligence agency, an informant inside the Communist Party, or some sort of surveillance or break-in; this consisted specifically of dates—presumably of meetings and telephone conversations—and CPUSA membership numbers. Finnegan had to go to FBIHQ because of the sensitivity of the information to which he was being given access.

Both Carey and Finnegan eventually wound up on the Bureau's "Do Not Contact List" because they publicly criticized the FBI (perhaps because of a bad conscience). Well before this, however, they and others in the IUE had collected enough information to launch an effective attack on the UE.[118]

The stakes in the battle with the UE were extraordinarily high in the spring and summer of 1950. Carey and his group had focused all their attention on winning at the UE convention held in Cleveland in September 1949. They had more success than at any time in the past but still fell considerably short of overthrowing the Communists and their allies. The convention passed a set of six demands to be presented to Murray. If he did not accept them—and he clearly would not—the executive board of the union was authorized to withhold dues from the CIO.

The Carey group, some of whom had been fighting the UE leadership for almost ten years, decided that the battle within the UE was over. The day after the convention ended, its leadership met, called for secession from the UE, and established a steering committee to seek a union charter from the CIO. This union, free of Communists, would compete with the left-wing UE.

Murray, as expected, refused to accede to the demands. After the final meeting, held the night before the convention ended, the UE executive board implemented the convention's decision to withhold dues. In turn, the 1949 CIO convention expelled the UE and filed charges of Communist domination against ten other unions; nine were expelled in 1950. The Carey group received a charter for the IUE.

It was not just the entire prestige of the CIO that was at stake in this UE-IUE struggle; also at issue was Communism, the Cold War, and competing visions of the role trade unions should play in capitalist America. No less important to those involved were the hundreds of staff jobs, access to money and status, and future career opportunities that were at stake. For those who had somehow missed the significance of the battle and failed to notice which side had the most prestige, the speakers at the IUE's founding convention brought it sharply to their attention. Murray and Secretary of Labor Daniel Tobin gave speeches, as did Secretary of the Air Force Stuart Symington. President Harry S. Truman sent a letter praising the new union.

The IUE, as we have seen, had many weapons at its disposal, but one of the most potent—if not *the* most, given the context—was the issue of Communism. Very few of the many Communists in the UE ever admitted being Party members. A much greater number denied, at one time or another, that they were members. Almost all desperately tried to avoid facing the problem. Carey's relationship with Hoover was so important precisely because the FBI was providing information that the IUE could use in its battles. One of the places where it put this material to use was Pittsburgh.

The key dates for Local 601 were April 17 and June 1, 1950, when the membership voted on whether it would be represented by the UE or the IUE. In an amazingly high turnout of 90 percent, the IUE defeated the UE by 100 votes, 5,763 to 5,663. Since neither side won an absolute majority, the membership voted again, and this time the IUE won by 5,964 to 5,706. By year's end the IUE, which continued to win elections, represented about 80 percent of all Westinghouse workers.

Rice's public involvement in the UE battle diminished toward the end of 1949 and then virtually disappeared. This was due in part to Carey's concern about being called a "stooge of the hierarchy and the clergy," in part because of the ugly internal politics within the IUE—in which John M. Duffy had lost out—and in part because Rice's normal preference was to work out of sight, though the "Commies kept smoking [him] out." Some of it, though, also had to do with the fact that Rice, as he later remembered it, was convinced that the battle was over: the IUE had won long before the vote was held. This did not mean, however, that Rice was not active behind the scenes. He continued to advise Murray and Bill Hart, local Steelworkers' district director, ACTU president, and vehement anti-Communist, and called Carey several times to "tell him things he should know." Most important, as he admitted, "I've spoken to some judges on behalf of IUE, this almost no one knows."[119]

The "judges" probably were Blair Gunther and Michael Musmanno. Musmanno was the "public face" and the "most visible figure" of Americans Battling Communism (ABC), a militant Pittsburgh anti-Communist group established in 1947. Gunther was one of its founders, as were numerous other judges to whom Rice could have talked. The ABC, especially Gunther and another of its founders, Harry Alan Sherman, who had fought the UE during the war, was instrumental in the surfacing of

Matt Cvetic, a CPUSA member who had been reporting to the FBI since 1941.[120]

Cvetic first testified before HUAC on February 21, but his story broke in the papers the day before because Gunther had released the deposition he had taken. Cvetic then answered questions on two more days in February and four in March. His testimony received front-page coverage. He named names and organizations. The newspapers printed both and, in some cases, added addresses. From the UE the list included first Tom Fitzpatrick, then Tom Quinn, Steve Rosner, Leo Turner, Charlie Newell, and so on and so forth. Employers began firing those people it could, unions dismissed officers, and even the Pittsburgh Symphony cut loose a first violinist.

It has never been clear why Cvetic surfaced when he did. The best study of his career says that the FBI "certainly had nothing to do with" it. Is it possible that Rice did? That might be hanging too much on the "judges" reference. There were other actions instigated by judges, and Musmanno was responsible for several of them. What we do know, though, is that Cvetic's testimony was a critical component of the political context within which the Local 601 representation elections occurred.[121]

The IUE's campaign literature also contributed to that context. We turn now to several leaflets that probably used FBI information and several more that may have. It is virtually impossible to determine the precise source for any given IUE assertion, though it is worth the effort to try.

"Fitzpatrick the Patriot" is the first to be examined. Tom Fitzpatrick, a longtime leader in Local 601 and District 6, was a member of the CPUSA. This leaflet asserted his radicalism and provided evidence for it but did not produce any specific proof of Party activity. The FBI, it charged, had "cited" Fitzpatrick as the "leader of the Labor Group of the Communist Party in Western Penna." The handout then named four men on the UE payroll who, it asserted, "have been cited by the United States Government and the FBI as Communists or fellow travellers." The "fellow traveller" probably was added to account for Tom Quinn, who was not a member. The other three, Charles Newell, Steve Rosner, and Jack Sartisky, certainly were members. (A fifth person worked for the CPUSA and covered Local 601.)[122]

Fitzpatrick, Quinn, and Newell also were featured in "10 Long Years of Communist Rule!" The IUE national office probably produced the first part of this document, which demonstrated the ways in which the UE line paralleled the Communist Party's and how both differed from the CIO's. The next section laid out information on nine UE officers and/or staff members who had betrayed the "rank and file membership of the Union," who "remained as always loyal American citizens." The final section dealt specifically with District 6 and devoted the most space to Newell, Quinn, and Fitzpatrick, whose influence the IUE was working hard to neutralize. The fourth man, Stanley Loney, the current district president, may or may not have a Communist.[123]

The brochure included some information, especially for Fitzpatrick, that probably came from the FBI, whose file on him contained especially precise information on the connection between the CPUSA and Local 601. My hunch is that a good deal more that was attributed to other sources such as HUAC actually came from the Bureau. Citing the FBI or using information that could only have come from it was, I think, a last resort. The FBI probably was the IUE's final authority as to whether someone was or was not a Communist.[124]

The Bureau probably functioned in this way as a source for the IUE's list of two hundred Communists or former Communists who were working for the UE in late spring 1950 published in the May 22, 1950, issue of the *IUE News*. An accompanying note indicated that the list was the product of a "careful five-month study of UE employees" (in other words, from just about the time when Finnegan began regularly visiting FBIHQ until the date of publication). This list, which at least one IUE leader kept current as the years went on, was produced by a team of researchers consisting of "a group of IUE leaders, former UE officials, ex–Communist Party members, several research experts and two independent agencies."[125]

We can be sure about the origin of some of the names on this list. Someone in the IUE national office, probably Finnegan, put together a list of "UE international reps and field organizers who have solicited Communist Party memberships." There are no sources for most of these accusations, but several do note one. Harry Block, for example, provided six names for District 1, while James Click provided four for District 8. Sydney Mason, the longtime Party member and a staff member in District 1, is a less obvious but certain source.[126]

It is possible to offer educated surmises about some members of the "research team." J. B. Mathews, the former fellow-traveler turned anti-Communist researcher, and Benjamin Mandel, former Communist and HUAC's director of research, may have been involved, since HUAC had produced its own list of Communist Party members in the UE. If Mandel was cooperating—and given Finnegan's correspondence with him, it is probable—he surely would have given the IUE access to HUAC material. The research staff of the House Subcommittee on Education and Labor,

which as we have seen investigated the IUE in 1948, may have been implicated, and so may Counterattack, the anti-Communist organization put
together by former FBI agents and others.[127]

This said, we know that one of the "independent agencies" was certainly
the FBI. Through illegal and semilegal means, the Bureau had access not
only to Party membership lists and cards but also to secret UE-CPUSA
meetings. It is hard to imagine anyone having more certain information
about who working for the UE was a Communist and who was not. This
was then, I think, an extraordinarily accurate list.

The only other issue about this list is the timing of its publication. The
General Motors elections were held on February 28, but the UE had little
hope there. Those at Westinghouse were held on April 27. It is difficult to
understand—unless Finnegan's work was still unfinished—why the IUE
did not get the list out in time for those contests. It did appear in time for
the GE elections on May 25 and the run-off at Local 601 on June 1.

Even before the list appeared, however, Finnegan was providing information from what he later called his "Communist records." In February
1950 Al Hartnett, the IUE secretary-treasurer, wrote Finnegan, asking
him to send along "some background material" on Joe Kress, Fred Haug,
and Marie Reed, three organizers the UE had just sent into Erie. The
"material should be helpful," he thought, to the IUE representative working there. A week later he asked Finnegan to let him know—"as soon as
possible"—what he had on Herbert Nichols, a UE international representative. The next month he asked for "some propaganda on" Julian Emspak,
the secretary-treasurer of the UE.[128]

There must have been many demands for information from Finnegan's
stockpile, for in July 1950 he told Hartnett and two others to get the information from his secretary: "Eileen has the keys to my office safe which
contains Communist records of the UE people. Eileen is completely familiar with those records and can find the background of any particular
UE person you might be interested in much faster than you could. Therefore, will you please ask Eileen to hunt up whatever material you want."[129]

By late 1950 the IUE and other raiding unions had seriously hurt the
UE. It no longer existed at GM and was the minority union at GE, RCA,
and Westinghouse. It had lost more than 150,000 members. The battle was
not over—UE membership held stable for about the next two years—but
it would never be the same, as government attacks, raids, and CPUSA-
directed defections took their toll in the coming years.

Rice, then, was not the only Catholic who was working with the FBI and
other "outside" agencies in the battle against the Communists in CIO

unions, especially the UE. It is difficult to see where either he or the others drew a line at those with whom they would work. That they kept these relationships secret is indicative of their awareness that they were doing something that was, if not wrong, then certainly detrimental to their cause if ever discovered.

We cannot, however, leave it at this, since the story is considerably more complicated and interesting. No matter how ugly these alliances were, they are perfectly understandable in historical terms when we look briefly at what the Communist Party was and what it was doing. Because this was a trade union battle, we need to look first at the evidence for "Communist domination" of the UE and other CIO unions. Then we will move on to a brief discussion of other matters that framed the anti-Communist response.

The key to understanding how the Communist Party functioned in the UE is to comprehend that the distinction between membership and non-membership sometimes did not matter as often as has been argued. The issue was, I am convinced, whether or not non-Communists accepted the Party line. As James Matles argued at a meeting of UE Party members, "We will make a united front with anyone who will agree to three fundamental points: 1- Be against war with the USSR; 2- Defend the rights of Communists to hold office; 3- Agree to work with Communists." Where the CPUSA—or its line—controlled hiring and/or appointed positions in the UE, it was able to build an organization within the union and exert great influence.[130]

Making sure that the right people got hired was the simplest way to do this. From at least 1941 to 1947 Matles sent out a letter to all UE general vice presidents providing them with a one-paragraph description of those who applied for organizing jobs. In addition to basic biographical information—age, marital status, and so on—the applicant's organizing experience also was given. While this information often was indicative of the applicant's political tendencies, more important, I think, were the references Matles listed.

To take two examples: Seymour Siporin had work experience with the FTA and the Die Casters, but what would have solidified his pro-CPUSA politics, if not his membership, was his list of references: Edward Cheyfitz, a Party member; Grant Oakes, who at least worked closely with the Party; and Ernie DeMaio, a Communist. Charles Wright had no organizing experience but was a UE member in an Evansville, Indiana, plant. He "was acquainted" with Albert Fitzgerald, who defeated Carey for the presidency of the union and who worked with Communists, and Bill Sentner, an open Communist.[131]

There also was an internal Communist Party organization within the UE. Since it was secret, it is difficult to get at, but evidence sometimes floats to the surface. In late 1945 Sol Rosner, who had just taken a job in District 6 after working in District 8, asked what to do about his Party commitment: "What shall I do about political organization? Shall I talk to Tom or contact Roy instead?" "Tom" was of course Tom Fitzpatrick, then district president and member of the Party's district "buro." "Roy" was Roy Hudson, who, because he had been slow to condemn Earl Browder's World War II Communist line, had been demoted from head of trade union affairs to head of the Pittsburgh Communist Party. Here is Sentner's response: "With respect to the other matter you mentioned, I would suggest that you see the person in charge [Hudson] so as to secure first-hand information relative to the matter. I also would discuss the question with Tom so that any decisions you might arrive at will be mutually agreeable."[132]

The second bit of evidence I have found about the internal Party apparatus within the UE involves Elvis Swan. In 1943 Swan applied for a UE organizing job. Formerly a UE member and a shop chairman in one of its plants near Evansville, he currently was working for the Shipbuilders. "Acquainted" with Fitzgerald, Sentner, and Bob Logsdon, who worked with Communists, he went on staff as an organizer in Indiana. He ran into trouble doing his job in northern Indiana, wrote a letter to the UE national office criticizing district leadership, and was fired, apparently because he could not negotiate or "do political work." It was not fair, Swan argued, to let him go. He could do the job: "You can find out by contacting the chairman of the workers' political party in Evansville that I am capable of leading people politically and it is politically that they must be led through this crisis."[133]

The third bit of evidence I have found pertains to Joe Squires. Squires worked at a UE plant in St. Louis and was "acquainted" with Sentner and Otto Maschoff, a Communist. At some point Squires went on staff and worked out of St. Louis. In February 1946 the FBI learned, through a bug, that the UE wanted to move Squires temporarily to Fort Wayne, Indiana, but Ralph Shaw, head of the Communist Party in St. Louis, thought otherwise. Squires, the FBI reported, was "too busy in St. Louis with Party work." Someone was going to contact Sentner to see if Squires could stay. The same procedure was followed in June, when Squires had an "offer of a long term assignment" for the UE in Connecticut. Sentner, according to Squires, "had made arrangements to contact RALPH SHAW in order to obtain SHAW's approval for his transfer to New Haven."[134]

I have found one final case. In 1945 Sentner advised Frances Dodge whom to "see in the UE on a job." She was to talk to either Sidney Mason, at that time a Communist, or Charles Fay, almost certainly a Communist. "Tell them," he continued, "that I referred you to them and give them the straight stuff."[135]

This evidence hints at what further research will almost certainly demonstrate: there was at work in the UE a cadre premised on Marxist-Leninist principles and intimately—ideologically if not organizationally—tied to the USSR. It was far more than just the Party's infiltration of the UE and other unions, though, that mattered to the anti-Communists. As I have been arguing for a long time now, the Party and its politics were dangerously flawed. Hewing to an organizational model that partook more of "high modernism" and the capitalist-technocratic necessities of twentieth-century factory production than democracy or socialism, Party members concealed their affiliation and met secretly to make decisions that affected the organizations of which they were a part. What was important to them was the line at any given moment in time. That line came from the USSR. When it changed, so did the Communist. If not, he or she left the Party or was expelled.[136]

The Soviet Union was, as we now know in great detail and for which there was much evidence even at the time, a murderous regime that violated every basic human right and made a mockery of the fight for democracy that ordinary men and women had been waging for centuries. It did all this in the name of socialism. No wonder most American working-class men and women became anti-Communists of some sort or the other. Not only were their material lives considerably better in the United States than they would have been in the USSR, but also they lived in a country where they could worship as they pleased.

The Communist "city on the hill" was profoundly secularist and anti-religious. Even more than that, most CPUSA members and those who worked with them were contemptuous of religion and religious people. No matter how much the Party periodically tried to camouflage this, there was hardly an aware union member who came in contact with them who did not pick up on this basic orientation to the world. One of the significant fault lines in the UE Local 601 and 506 battles was the issue of religion and its role in the world.[137]

What the USSR did from 1945 through 1950 in Eastern Europe provided lesson after lesson in what Communism meant. It was not pretty. But the CPUSA and those who worked with it explicitly and implicitly defended it as part of a democratic-Communist upheaval. It may have been so to some degree and in some places, but the end result—very quick in coming—was the establishment of atheistic police states. Is it surprising that most of the Catholic working class, many of whom were not far removed from their Eastern European origins, became vehemently anti-Communist?

The spying that the USSR was doing in the United States, of course, was a related factor. There should by now be no doubt that the CPUSA was heavily involved in those efforts. It matters little at what level of the Party it occurred, how many members knew about it, and how many would have participated if asked. It matters little why it was being done. What counts is that the CPUSA, whose loyalty had demonstrably and repeatedly been shown to lie with the USSR, could be—and in fact was—tied to the transfer of information to an enemy of the United States.[138]

An anecdote in John Hoerr's book *Harry, Tom, and Father Rice* illustrates the multiple tragedies of all this. In February 1949 at a Local 601 meeting the anti-Communists introduced a resolution condemning the trial and conviction of Josef Cardinal Mindszenty in Hungary. Tom Fitzpatrick and others who spoke against the resolution were "booed off the floor." It, of course, passed. Tom Fitzpatrick was a good trade unionist and a good man; that is why he is one of three to whom my book *The CIO's Left-Led Unions* is dedicated. He was, though, a Communist, and that brought with it certain values and obligations. He would suffer mightily for his convictions, but they need to be recognized for what they were. Tragedy number one.[139]

Tom Quinn, also a good trade unionist and a good man, was not a Communist but worked closely with them. He, according to Hoerr, "regarded the [union's] stand on Mindszenty as 'ridiculous'" but chalked it up to right-wing maneuvering: "It seemed our leadership was kind of baited into that [position] by Father Rice and the ACTU. They would find issues to raise at membership meetings of that kind of controversial nature which would give the parish priests something to raise at Mass on Sundays before the meeting."[140]

Quinn did not get it. Rice and the ACTU may have been up to something, but that does not mean that the issue of Mindszenty did not matter. It went to the heart of what the Soviet Union was doing to Eastern Europe: What kind of society was being built there? It went to the heart of the CPUSA: Could it be independent of the USSR? When Quinn chose to work with the Communists, he chose to work within their framework, within the Communist Party line. He was not the only good man and good trade unionist to make this decision. It was understandable but also unfortunate. Tragedy number two.

Hoerr also does not get it. He is a fine writer and researcher whose excellent book on the steel industry I have taught many times.[141] He writes, "It is uncertain what the UE leaders hoped to accomplish by hewing to the Soviet line." A few sentences later he wonders "why Matles and his associates never came to understand" the ways in which their connection to the USSR "damaged their credibility in the eyes of many members and certainly of the public." The assumption behind these questions—that the commitment to Communism was like any other political choice and susceptible to reasoned analysis—permeates this otherwise splendid book. Hoerr, like so many other students of this period, fails to understand the significance of Matles's and other Communists' commitment to the USSR as a workers' utopia. His book therefore leads readers terribly astray at some key moments about the choices Quinn and others made. Tragedy number three.

Monsignor Rice has disappeared from these pages for quite a while. It is time to return to him. We now have a large context within which to think about him and the decisions he made to work closely with the FBI and other government agencies to combat Communists in the UE and other CIO unions.

From one perspective, Rice's work with the FBI and others was collaboration pure and simple. It meant going outside the trade union movement to use the resources of those who, while supposedly neutral, were opposed to virtually everything for which the CIO (and Rice) stood. It is for this reason, I think, that Rice repeatedly brought this cooperation to history's attention: he felt guilty about it; he had a "bad conscience." In a more general sense, but similarly, he sought forgiveness from those in the UE whom he had harmed. Rice was exceptional in his bad conscience.[142]

The monsignor, from another perspective, committed no wrong—no sin—when he worked with the FBI and other "outside" institutions. Communists and Communism were so dangerous, so evil, that getting rid of them and their influence was of paramount importance. That the evil and the danger were tied to another country made the task even more urgent. This is why, I think, Rice's confessions always were a bit pro forma. At some level he was still convinced that he did what he had to do and would do it again in the same way in the same situation. It was, he told me, a "just and beautiful fight."[143]

Means versus ends is one way of thinking about Rice's anti-Communist activities. In his mind the end justified the means; that is, Communism was so evil that for Rice, there were few illegitimate means of fighting it.

It is hard to see any other way of interpreting his final judgment in the car incident: "I am sorry that happened. I am sorry. It was not sinful. It was not sinful." His response to my question—"Did the ends justify the means?"—partook of the same reasoning: "I did not think I used impure means."[144]

Cheating in elections was not sinful either. After mentioning in a 1983 interview that anti-Communists in Schenectady had forged cards to order to win a representation election—presumably at Local 203—he proudly added, "I can't say that it bothered me in the slightest." And as he put it in a 1989 discussion of vote fraud in union elections, "For me actually, in my heart of hearts, so much depends on who steals the votes, how and for whose benefit."[145]

What happened after Communists and/or racketeers had been defeated always had been an important issue for Catholic labor activists. They knew that one of their fundamental tasks was to participate in the creation of a competent and responsible leadership to replace those who were thrown out of office. Without that, their work was essentially negative rather than positive.

Rice was never terribly concerned about this. Here, as in so many other ways, he differed from his fellow labor activists. When he withdrew from Local 601 it was, I think, with a sense of relief, because all that remained was the maneuvering over who would replace the Communists. To Rice this was a political question, not a moral one. As he wrote his bishop, "I've stayed away from the internal politics, because that is a dirty business, and cannot work out to the advantage of what is right."[146]

Those whom Rice had helped bring to power in Local 601, however, were from all evidence unprepared for running one of the largest union locals in the country. They quickly fell to fighting among themselves in the scramble for office and prestige. They, moreover, fought with their compatriots across the country for national office and prestige. Mike Fitzpatrick, "known as a schemer and a hard man to hold," was at the center of much of this contention. Here, as in so many other areas, he was much less the man than his brother Tom, the Communist.[147]

Rice's withdrawal from union affairs was formalized in 1952, when he was moved to a parish in Natrona, Pennsylvania. Six years later he was transferred to Washington, Pennsylvania, where he stayed until 1966, when he took up a parish in Homewood, a poor African American section of Pittsburgh. From 1954 until 1960 his column did not appear in the *Pittsburgh Catholic*.

His return to public life in the 1960s was marked by a set of commitments that matched the hard-and-fast moral absolutes that had guided his actions in the anti-Communist struggle: civil rights for African Americans and opposition to the Vietnam War. Both brought him into serious conflict with the white working class whose cause he had long championed. He in fact played no small role in the splintering of the Democratic coalition that he had implicitly helped build in the 1930s and 1940s.[148]

Might the tremendous disdain that he expressed for the white working class in the 1960s—which occurred at the same time that he was publicly criticizing himself for his activities several decades earlier—have had something to do with his understanding that he played at least a bit part in its creation?

Afterword

FATHER HUGH CALKINS, O.S.M., who wrote two weekly columns—
"Lights and Shadows" and "Two Worlds"—for the *Novena Notes* in the
1940s and 1950s, found little good in the world around him. A member, as
were two brothers and two nephews, of the Servites, or Friar Servants of
Mary, who oversaw the enormously popular Our Lady of Sorrows Friday
night ritual, Calkins railed constantly at secular evils. Sexual politics particularly concerned him. In one sense his writings, especially in the 1940s,
might be seen as an unending jeremiad against Americans' misuse of the
body. He firmly believed, moreover, in a patriarchy of the most traditional
kind. Calkins, finally, was a "black-hole" anti-Communist, who projected
onto "Reds" his deepest anxieties and desires. His metaphors more generally coded danger as female.[1]

J. Edgar Hoover would have entirely agreed with this Calkins. Not so,
however, with the one who consistently advocated social Catholicism. The
Servite regularly attacked racism and discrimination as un-Catholic behavior. In a story that he repeated periodically, Calkins told of Christ
"born a Negro" and lynched while saying Mass. He not only supported the
right of all workers to join unions but also backed specific strikes, for example, the telephone workers' strike of 1950, which few Catholic journalists even noticed. He reprinted the Detroit Association of Catholic Trade
Unionists' principles of "economic democracy" which laid out a Catholic
vision of a moral economy.[2]

Both social Catholicism and Catholic sexual politics were, for Calkins,
integral parts of the same "Catholic pattern." As he put it at one point,
Catholic thinking was "like a perfect necklace: Each part is linked

inseparably to the others. You can't pick some parts for acceptance and others for rejection." Part and parcel of this "Catholic Mind" was support for Franco's Spain, defense of the Inquisition, and a limited commitment to toleration for doing and thinking incorrectly.[3]

Until the mid-1980s or so this Catholic pattern ironically provided a big umbrella under which stood priests and bishops who, while believing in all of it, emphasized one piece over another. One looks in vain, though, for any discussion of the social issues that the U.S. Church used to stand for in the various position papers and joint declarations issued by Catholics and evangelicals since then. What has brought these two groups together is not just some sort of theological and doctrinal truce—if not agreement—but rather a common stance toward sexual politics, what Mark A. Noll and Carolyn Nystrom call "social-political cobelligerency" in the U.S. culture wars.[4]

The way contemporary Catholicism handles Calkins is suggestive of this narrowing of Catholic thinking. Calkins vehemently opposed not only artificial birth control but also the rhythm method for limiting conception. He was in fact, as Leslie Woodcock Tentler argues, a "near-apoplectic critic." It is impossible to find anything about Calkins's social Catholicism on the Internet these days, but there are numerous references to his critique of the rhythm method. His 1948 attack on it, "Rhythm: The Unhappy Compromise," is available on-line and regularly referred to by Catholics who are not content with opposing abortion. In it, as Tentler writes, Calkins seems to "regard" rhythm as "a mostly female plot."[5]

This book, in its focus on what brought the FBI and the Catholic Church together, might be seen as the prefiguring or prehistory of the Catholic-evangelical alliance that has become such an essential part of American political life. What united them both was a commitment to—and implementation of—a set of stances toward gender and sexual politics that originated in an essentialism and a conviction of male superiority, no matter the idiom in which it was couched, that prescribed women's subordination. The Church's refusal to apply to men the same litmus test in "culture of death" issues that it applies to women is indicative of the hierarchy's continuing interest—whether conscious or unconscious, intended or unintended—in the subjugation of women.[6]

It has often appeared in recent years that this is the only thing in which the hierarchy—and therefore the Church—is interested. Adopting a purely defensive and apologetic stance, it discourages, and if necessary suppresses, the kind of theological and intellectual work that might provide genuinely Catholic answers—here I am thinking of Radical Orthodoxy—to pressing modern issues faced by the laity. It stands aside while the Catholic majority on the Supreme Court goes about "repealing the 20th century." It, finally, ignores its own tradition of social Catholicism.[7]

ABBREVIATIONS

Manuscript Depositories

AAB: Archdiocesan Archives of Baltimore

AIS: Archives of Industrial Society, University of Pittsburgh

ALHUA: Archives of Labor History and Urban Affairs, Walter P. Reuther Library, Wayne State University

AND: Archives of the University of Notre Dame

AMPSJ: Archives of the Missouri Province of the Society of Jesus

ANYPSJ: Archives of the New York Province of the Society of Jesus

BAA: Baltimore Archdiocesan Archives

CAA: Chicago Archdiocesan Archives

CHS: Chicago Historical Society

CUAA: Catholic University of America Archives

DAA: Detroit Archdiocesan Archives

FDRL: Franklin Delano Roosevelt Library

GUA: Georgetown University Archives

HAA: Hartford Archdiocesan Archives

HCLA: Historical Collections and Labor Archives, Pattee-Paterno Library, Pennsylvania State University

HSTL: Harry S. Truman Library

LC: Library of Congress

MUDSC: Marquette University Department of Special Collections and University Archives

NA: National Archives

SAA: Seattle Archdiocesan Archives

SP: Special Collections, Robert W. Woodruff Library, Emory University

TDA: Toledo Diocesan Archives

UC: University of Chicago

UV: University of Virginia

WHMC: Western Historical Manuscript, University of Missouri–St. Louis

WrSU: Wright State University

MANUSCRIPT COLLECTIONS

AmP: *America* Papers, GUA
AP: Karl J. Alter Papers, TDA
ALASP: Association of Los Alamos Scientists Papers, UC
ASCP: Atomic Scientists of Chicago Papers, UC
CC: Chancery Collection, CAA
CCWLP: Catholic Council on Working Life Papers, CHS
CIOSTO: CIO Secretary-Treasurer Office, ALHUA
CORP: Charles Owen Rice Papers, AIS
CORP(m): Charles Owen Rice Papers (microfilm), HCLA
DCP: Daniel Cantwell Papers, CHS
DeACTU: Detroit Association of Catholic Trade Unionists Collection, ALHUA
EACP: Edward A. Conway Papers, Creighton University, Omaha
EA: The Albert Einstein Archives, The Jewish and National University Library, Jerusalem
FASAP: Federation of American Scientists Addendum Papers, UC
FASP: Federation of American Scientists Papers, UC
FBIHQ: Federal Bureau of Investigation, Headquarters Files, obtained through the Freedom of Information Act
FHP: Francis J. Haas Papers, CUAA
FMP: Francis P. Matthews Papers, HSTL
GHP: George Higgins Papers, CUAA
GJP: Gardner Jackson Papers, FDRL
HCP: Howard Curtiss Papers, HCLA
HD: William Higinbotham Diary, copy in author's possession
HRP: Harry Read Papers, CUAA
HRuP: Harold Ruttenberg Papers, HCLA
IUEA: International Electrical, Radio & Machine Workers of America Archives, Rutgers University
JaCP: James Click Papers, WHMC
JCP: John F. Cronin Papers (CCRO), UND
JDP: Joseph Donnelly Papers, HAA
JEHS: Scrapbooks, J. Edgar Hoover Memorabilia Collection, Record Group 65, NA
JNP: John Noll Papers (NOL), UND
LTP: Louis J. Twomey, S.J., Papers, Loyola University, New Orleans
MAP: Michael Amrine Papers, GUA
MBP: Meyer Bernstein Papers, HCLA
MFP: Melcher Family Papers, UV
NSG: Nathan Silvermaster Group, FBI Electronic Reading Room
NCAIP: National Committee on Atomic Information Papers, LC
OGS: National Catholic Welfare Conference/United States Catholic Conference Collection, Office of the General Secretary Papers, CUAA
OP: J. Robert Oppenheimer Papers, LC
RCP: Raymond Clancy Papers, ALHUA
RHP: Reynold Hillenbrand Papers, AND
RP: Joseph H. Rush Papers, UC
SAD: National Catholic Welfare Conference/United States Catholic Conference Collection, Social Action Department Papers, CUAA
SMP: Stephen Mitchell Papers, HSTL

TQP: Thomas Quinn Papers, AIS
UEA: United Electrical & Radio Archives, AIS
WPA: Works Progress Administration Papers, CSL
WJCP: William J. Campbell Papers, National Archives and Records Administration, Great Lakes Region
WSP: William Sentner Papers, Washington University, St. Louis

JOURNALS, NEWSPAPERS, AND PERIODICALS

A: *America*
AdR: *Advance Register* (Wichita)
AER: *American Eccesiastical Review*
AI: *Atomic Information*
AM: *American Magazine*
BAS: *Bulletin of the Atomic Scientists*
BT: *Brooklyn Tablet*
CA: *Catholic Action*
CCW: *Chicago Catholic Worker*
CHC: *Catholic Herald Citizen* (Milwaukee)
CM: *Catholic Mind*
CoR: *Congressional Record*
CoRA: *Congressional Record Appendix*
CPC: *Chicago Provincial Chronicle*
CR: *Catholic Review* (Baltimore)
CT: *Catholic Transcript* (Hartford)
CUB: *Catholic Universe Bulletin* (Cleveland)
DW: *Daily Worker*
HPR: *Homiletic and Pastoral Review*
JB(C): *Jesuit Bulletin* (Chicago Province)
JB(M): *Jesuit Bulletin* (Missouri Province)
LEB: *Law Enforcement Bulletin*
LH: *Labor History*
LL: *Labor Leader*
MC: *Michigan Catholic*
NCEAB: *National Catholic Education Association Bulletin*
NN: *Novena Notes*
NW: *New World*
NYT: *New York Times*
OSV: *Our Sunday Visitor*
PC: *Pittsburgh Catholic*
PPG: *Pittsburgh Post-Gazette*
PST: *Pittsburgh Sun-Telegraph*
R: *Rotarian*
RD: *Reader's Digest*
S: *The Sign*
SAN: *Social Action Notes for Priests*
SL: *Steel Labor*
SO: *Social Order*
U&E: *Union and Echo*
UEN: *UE News*

USCH: *U.S. Catholic Historian*
VS: *Vital Speeches of the Day*
W: *Work*
WE: *Wage-Earner*
WL: *Woodstock Letters*

NOTES

Introduction

1. "Edgar Hoover Calls Irreligion Nation's Menace," *CR*, November 11, 1942, 1; "Chief Crime Specialist Prescribes Old Fashioned Remedy," *NN*, April 16, 1948, 8; Tansey, "Chief of the FBI," *Our Catholic Messenger*, June 1952, JEHS; Gillese, America's No. 1 G-Man," *The Magnificat*, July 1954, 121.
2. Murray Polner and Jim O'Grady, *Disarmed and Dangerous: The Radical Times and Lives of Daniel and Philip Berrigan* (Boulder, Colo., 1998), 198, 229; Philip Berrigan, *Fighting the Lamb's War: Skirmishes with the American Empire* (Monroe, Maine, 1996), 96; Jack Nelson and Ronald J. Ostrow, *The FBI and the Berrigans: The Making of a Conspiracy* (New York, 1972).
3. I had planned to include a chapter on the FBI and the Knights of Columbus, the Holy Name Society, and the Catholic War Veterans—organizations of Catholic laymen—but as the book grew longer, the limitations of space prevented doing so.
4. Sanford J. Ungar, *FBI* (Boston, 1975), 12.
5. Wills, *Bare Ruined Choirs: Doubt, Prophecy, and Radical Religion* (New York, 1972), 233.
6. Kovel, *Red-Hunting in the Promised Land: Anticommunism and the Making of America* (New York, 1994).
7. Juster, *Disorderly Women: Sexual Politics and Evangelicalism in Revolutionary New England* (Ithaca, N.Y., 1994), 11.
8. "The Reminiscences of James B. Carey" (1960), 241, in the Oral History Collection of Columbia University.
9. I have pending requests for Rice's Pittsburgh Field Office and FBI Headquarters files.

1. The Creation of a Catholic Protestant and Protestant Catholics

1. 94-1-2597; 62-32073; 94-1-9758. These numbers identify FBI Headquarters files obtained by the author, unless otherwise noted, through the Freedom of Information Act. The most common FBI file contains three sets of numbers: the first is the classification number, the second the case number, and the final the serial or

document number. Many of the files that I have used, however, have as many as four sets because the classification encompassed so much. For example, 94-1-2597 is Research Matters, Subsection 1, case number 2597 (Georgetown University); 62-32073 is Miscellaneous, case number 32073 (Edmund Walsh S. J.). In 94-1-20353-6, used in the next note, 6 is document number 6 in case number 20353 (Holy Cross). Some documents, however, were not, in the Bureau's terminology, serialized. The best discussion of these matters is Ann Mari Buitrago aned Leon Andrew Immerman, *Are You Now or Have You Ever Been in the FBI Files? How to Secure and Interpret Your FBI Files* (New York, 1981).

2. L. B. Nichols Office Memorandum for Mr. Tolson, May 23, 1944, 94-1-20353-52; Hoover, "Standards of Law Enforcement," *Holy Cross Alumnus*, February–March 1941, 3–4; 94-1-14425; 66-6800-1-102; 94-41038; John T. Madigan to Director, October 10, 1942, 94-1-20353-6.

3. "Ordered desire," I think, is my phrase, but I could have picked it up from K. A. Cuordileone, *Manhood and American Political Culture in the Cold War* (New York, 2005). He regularly refers to "sexual disorder."

4. "Assistant Director J. J. McGuire Jr. Retires from the FBI," *LEB*, April 1961, 8; H. H. Clegg Memorandum to Tolson, October 20, 1950, 67-53404-NR [Not Recorded]; William A. Donaghy, S.J., to Hoover, December 13, 1956, 67-53404-NR ("old friend").

5. "A Graduate's Responsibility," June 29, 1944, 94-1-20353-36.

6. Ibid.

7. Ibid.

8. Broome to Hoover, July 18, 1944, 94-1-20353-52.

9. [Hynes] to Hoover, July 7, 1944, 94-1-20353-41. Hynes's name was not deleted in this letter when was it was released as a "see" reference.

10. Rubin, "The Traffic in Women: Notes on the 'Political Economy' of Sex," in Rayna R. Reiter, ed., *Toward an Anthropology of Women* (New York, 1975), 157–210.

11. Philip Gleason, *Contending with Modernity: Catholic Higher Education in the Twentieth Century* (New York, 1995), 81–85; Joseph R. Preville, "Fairfield University: The Emergence of a Modern Catholic Institution" (Ph.D. diss., Boston College, 1985), 3; Hoover, "Law Enforcement as a Career," January 20, 1947, 94-1-20353-74.

12. 94-1-658.

13. Löwy, *Redemption and Utopia: Jewish Libertarian Thought in Central Europe— A Study in Elective Affinity* (London, 1992), 6. Also see Lowy, *The War of Gods: Religion and Politics in Latin America* (London, 1996); James C. Scott, *Seeing Like a State: How Certain Schemes to Improve the Human Condition Have Failed* (New Haven, 1998), 5, 55, 219, 291.

14. [Deleted] to Director, May 23, 1960, 94-46287-72. I have not been able to find a copy of this speech. Also see "Seniors Hear Talk by FBI Inspector at Pathfinder Meeting," *The Hoya*, December 20, 1946. 1.

15. The most complete bibliographies of Hoover's articles and speeches are Frank Donner, *The Age of Surveillance: The Aims and Methods of America's Political Intelligence System* (New York, 1981), 468–77; Richard Gid Powers, *G-Men: Hoover's FBI in American Popular Culture* (Carbondale, Ill., 1983), 328–36. There are hundreds of additional items in JEHS.

16. Hoover, "Youth Adrift," S, June 1946, 36–38.

17. Hoover, "Kids Don't Want to Be Criminals," *Kiwanis Magazine*, September 1946, JEHS.

18. "The Christian Family," November 21, 1949, in *Our Bishops Speak* (Milwaukee, 1952), 155, 156.

19. Hoover, "Combatting Lawlessness," VS, February 15, 1938, 271 ("only way"); Hoover, "If I Had a Son," *University of Notre Dame Religious Bulletin*, September 21–22, 1938, enclosure in Father John F. O'Hara to Hoover, September 23, 1938, FBIHQ 94-1-6-658-119.

20. "Family Rosary Crusade Takes City by Storm," NW, October 5, 1951, 3; NW, January 17, 1947, 6; Jeffrey M. Burns, *American Catholics and the Family Crisis, 1930–1962: An Ideological and Organization Response* (New York, 1988), 188–93.

21. Kane, *Marriage and the Family: A Catholic Approach* (New York, 152), 64, 67; Thomas, "The Catholic Family in a Complex Society," SO, December 1954, 455.

22. *As I Remember Fordham: Selections from the Sesquicentennial Oral History Project* (New York, 1991), 139–40, 27, 32; Joseph E. Persico, *Casey: From the OSS to the CIA* (New York, 1990), 21; Michael O'Brien, *Vince: A Personal Biography of Vince Lombardi* (New York, 1987), 39, 188; Cox, *Liberty: Its Use and Abuse. Being the Principles of Ethics Basic and Applied*, 3rd rev. ed. (New York, 1946), 324, 326, 327.

23. Hoover, "Crime and Your Home," May 17, 1938, OF 10-B, FDRL.

24. Calkins, NN, January 30, 1948, 13; "Cardinal Lashes 'Printed Filth'; 1,700 Women Hear 'Call to Arms,'" NW, November 5, 1948, 1; "Cardinal Urges Madonna Ideal," NW, March 1, 1946, 1.

25. "When the Kidnapper Comes!" *The Delineator*, November 1933, 56.

26. LaFarge, *A Report on the American Jesuits* (New York, 1956), 24 ("the relationship"); LaFarge, *The Jesuits in Modern Times* (New York 1928), 48 ("should be"); Leonard A. Waters, "Sons and Their Mothers," JB(M), June 1954, 7 ("Sons of").

27. Robb, "I Remember J. Edgar Hoover," *Ladies Home Journal*, July 1972, 137; Powers, *Secrecy and Power: The Life of J. Edgar Hoover* (New York, 1987), 218; Joseph L. Schott, *No Left Turns* (New York, 1975), 5.

28. "J. Edgar Hoover Calls America Gullible," NYT, May 24, 1943, 10; Hoover, "A Nation's Call to Duty," June 11, 1942, VS, July 1, 1942, 555; Hoover, "Internal Defense of America," speech to Daughters of the American Revolution, April 17, 1944, CoR, April 19, 1944, A1885. The 1943 assertion was made while Hoover was discussing "international confidence men," but he clearly meant it much more generally.

29. Cox, *Liberty*, 171, vii; Ferdinand W. Schoberg, S.J., "Whither American Education," in Hunter Guthrie, S.J., and Gerald Walsh, eds., *A Philosophical Symposium on American Catholic Education: Proceedings of the Seventeenth Annual Convention of the Jesuit Philosophical Association of the Eastern States, Fordham University, September 4, 5, 6, 1940* (New York, 1941), 13n ("individual"); Robert I. Gannon, S.J., *After Black Coffee* (New York, 1947), 18; Hunter Guthrie, S.J., "The Sacred Fetish of Academic Freedom," [Georgetown University] *Alumni Magazine*, Summer 1950, 3; "Communism and Schools—J. Edgar Hoover's Views," *U.S. News and World Report*, November 26, 1954, 130–31.

30. Klaus Theweleit, *Male Fantasies*, vol. 1, *Women, Floods, Bodies, History* (Minneapolis, 1987), and vol. 2, *Male Bodies: Psychoanalyzing the White Terror* (Minneapolis, 1989); Elizabeth Grosz, *Volatile Bodies: Toward a Corporeal Feminism* (Bloomington, 1994); Calvin Thomas, *Male Matters: Masculinity, Anxiety, and the Male Body on the Line* (Urbana, 1996); Julia Kristeva, *The Powers of Horror: An Essay on Abjection* (New York, 1982); Luce Irigaray, "The 'Mechanics' of Fluids," in *This Sex Which Is Not One* (Ithaca, N.Y., 1985), 106–18. In what follows, while

I have kept the documentation to a bare minimum, the evidentiary basis for the generalizations consists of hundreds of examples drawn from reading Catholic newspapers and periodicals.

31. "Text of Cardinal Mundelein's Address at Jubilee Banquet," *NW*, October 31, 1930, 1; "Archbishop's Stirring Address Tells Maternity House Project; Cause and Cure of Bolshevism," *NW*, April 18, 1919, 5.

32. Hoover, "Law Enforcement Views Education for Leisure," *Education*, October 1950, 92–98.

33. "Modern Problems of Law Enforcement," *VS*, July 29, 1935, 682; "Sectional Rallies Launch Holy Name Campaign," *NW*, April 25, 1947, 9.

34. David Campbell, *Writing Security: United States Foreign Policy and the Politics of Identity* (Minneapolis, 1992), 96.

35. Hoover, "Law Enforcement and the Publisher," *LEB*, April 22, 1937, 4; Walsh, "Implementing Our Foreign Policy—the Spiritual Aspect," July 27, 1952, 62-32073-49; Cronin, "Asks Wisdom and Harmony for Labor," *CR*, September 6, 1940, 6.

36. Douglas, *Natural Symbols: Explorations in Cosmology* (New York, 1996), 74; *Achievement*, May 1948, JEHS; "Owen J. Shevlin Passes Away," *NW*, May 20, 1921, 12.

37. Eve Kosofsky Sedgwick, *Between Men: English Literature and Male Homosocial Desire* (New York, 1985).

38. Powers, *Secrecy and Power*, 9.

39. Jack Alexander, "The Director—II," *New Yorker*, October 2, 1937, 21.

40. Athan G. Theoharis and John Stuart Cox, *The Boss: J. Edgar Hoover and the Great American Inquisition* (Philadelphia, 1988), 40 ("Edgar would"); Powers, *Secrecy and Power*, 12 ("affectionate").

41. Powers, *Secrecy and Power*, 22–23.

42. Edward L. R. Elson, "J. Edgar Hoover—Churchman," *Presbyterian Life*, November 27, 1948, 4; Powers, *Secrecy and Power*, 13–15.

43. Robert W. Lynn and Elliot White, *The Big Little School: Two Hundred Years of the Sunday School*, 2nd ed. (Birmingham, Ala, 1980), 99 ("uniformity of"), 107 ("provided a"), 102 ("unity and"); Powers, *Secrecy and Power*, 19 ("organized like").

44. Hoover, "Sunday School Combats Crime," *Sunday School Builder*, June 1952, JEHS; "J. Edgar Hoover Speaks to Southern Baptists," *The Messenger*, October 4, 1951, JEHS; Lynn and White, *Big Little School*, 120 ("The fabric").

45. Theoharis and Cox, *The Boss*, 32 ("hit his stride"); Powers, *Secrecy and Power*, 32 ("reinforced"); Ralph de Toledano, *J. Edgar Hoover: The Man in His Time* (New York, 1973), 38–39.

46. Powers, *Secrecy and Power*, 28; Hester O'Neil, "Hoover's High School Days," *American Boy and Open Road*, July 1954, 35, O'Neil, "Hoover's School Days," *American Boy and Open Road*, September 1954, 22–23.

47. Powers, *Secrecy and Power*, 29.

48. Quoted in O'Neill, "Hoover's School Days," 24.

49. Gail Bederman, *Manliness and Civilization: A Cultural History of Gender and Race in the United States, 1880–1917* (Chicago, 1995); David I. Macleod, *Building Character in the American Boy: The Boy Scouts, YMCA, and Their Forerunners, 1870–1920* (Madison, 1983), 35 (quotes).

50. "Did You Happen to See," *Washington Times Herald*, April 24, 1950, JEHS; "Boss G-Man Schoolmate of Saginaw Y Secretary," unidentified Saginaw, Mich., newspaper, ca. May 19, 1936, JEHS; Macleod, *Building Character*, 89 (quotes).

51. O'Neill, "Hoover's School Days," 22 ("means work"); Powers, *Secrecy and Power,* 32.

52. Quoted in O'Neill, "Hoover's School Days," 24.

53. Alexander, "The Director—II," 21 ("practical struggles," "the book"); O'Neill, "Hoover's School Days," 8 ("A gentleman").

54. O'Neill, "Hoover's High School Days," 34; Curt Gentry, *J. Edgar Hoover: The Man and the Secrets* (New York, 1991), 66 ("He was").

55. Carol Smith-Rosenberg, "Female World of Love and Ritual: Relations between Women in Nineteenth-Century America," *Signs* 1 (1975): 1–30; E. Anthony Rotundo, *American Manhood: Transformations in Masculinity from the Revolution to the Modern Era* (New York, 1993), 46.

56. "G-Man Hoover Shrine Member," *Sundan's Red Fez,* March 1, 1937, JEHS; Gentry, *Hoover,* 148.

57. Gentry, *Hoover,* 67 ("unofficial"); de Toledano, *Hoover,* 42 ("took a"); Howard Locke, "Fingerprints on the Hands of Crime," *Kappa Alpha Journal,* March 1935, JEHS.

58. "D. N. Hoover," *Washington Times,* April 2, 1921, JEHS.

59. Ovid Demaris, *Director: An Oral Biography of J. Edgar Hoover* (New York, 1975), 6–7; Gentry, *Hoover,* 217.

60. Theoharis and Cox, *The Boss,* 73 ("anticipated"); Powers, *Secrecy and Power,* 92 ("exchanged").

61. Powers, *Secrecy and Power,* 170.

62. Ovid Demaris, "Private Life of Hoover," *Life,* September 1974, 74 ("it was"); Theoharis and Cox, *Boss,* 133 ("only personal").

63. Powers, *Secrecy and Power,* 260 ("only close"); Theoharis and Cox, *The Boss,* 109 ("attributes").

64. Theoharis and Cox, *The Boss,* 33 ("social interests"); Powers, *Secrecy and Power,* 171 ("relationship"). Compare the latter with Powers's more recent discussion of this issue, *Broken: The Troubled Past and Uncertain Future of the FBI* (New York, 2004), 241–42.

65. Summers, *Official and Confidential: The Secret Life of J. Edgar Hoover* (New York, 1994); Theoharis, *J. Edgar Hoover, Sex, and Crime: An Historical Antidote* (Chicago, 1995).

66. The discussion that follows is greatly indebted to Talal Asad, "On Discipline and Humility in Medieval Christian Ritual," in *Genealogies of Religion: Discipline and Reasons of Power in Christianity and Islam* (Baltimore, 1993), 125–67; and Sedgwick, *Between Men.*

67. For detailed discussions of the rule, see J. T. Dillon, *House of Formation: A Catholic Seminary in the 1950s* (Riverside, Calif., 2003); Raymond Hedin, *Married to the Church* (Bloomington, 1995).

68. Dubay, *The Seminary Rule: An Explanation of the Purposes Behind It and How Best to Carry It Out* (Westminister, Md., 1954), 19–20; Thomas H. McLaughlin, "Discipline in the Seminary," *NCEAB* 26 (1929): 699.

69. Mohan, "The Administration of Student Personnel at Quigley Preparatory Seminary" (M.A. thesis, DePaul University, 1944), 55.

70. Ibid., 55, 56.

71. Ibid., 56, 57.

72. Ibid., 64.

73. Ibid., 61, 66, 67.

74. Gibbons, *The Ambassador of Christ* (Baltimore, 1896), 69.

75. Ibid., 70, 71.

76. Ibid., 74–77.

77. Joseph M. White, *The Diocesan Seminary in the United States: A History from the 1780s to the Present* (Notre Dame, 1989). 263–64 ("We absolutely"); NCEAB 30 (1933): 613.

78. James Higgins, C.S.S.R., "Supervision of Reading and Movies in the Minor Seminary," *NCEAB* 46 (1949): 131, 132. At the LaSalle Institute, a card placed in front of the projector lens was used to censor movies; Dillon, *House of Formation*, 47.

79. Paul Schuster, S.D.S., "The Visiting-Day Problem in the Preparatory Seminary," *NCEAB* 30 (1933): 646–52; Dubay, *The Seminary Rule*, 92.

80. McHugh, "Experiences of a Prefect of Discipline," *NCEAB* 32 (1935): 301–2.

81. Brennan, "The Supervision of Leisure Time in the Boarding Minor Seminary," *NCEAB* 44 (1947): 177, 178.

82. Author's personal experience; Brennan, "Supervision of Leisure Time," 178, 179.

83. John E. Sexton and Arthur J. Riley, *History of St. John's Seminary, Brighton* (Brighton, Mass. 1945), 150 ("in certain"); Thomas J. Shelley, *Dunwoodie: The History of St. Joseph's Seminary, Yonkers, New York* (Westminister, Md., 1993), 188 ("repeatedly"); George E. O'Donnell, *St. Charles Seminary, Philadelphia: A History of the Theological Seminary of St. Charles Borromeo, Overbrook, Philadelphia, Pennsylvania, 1832–1964* (Philadelphia, 1964), 103.

84. Dubay, *The Seminary Rule*, 94–96.

85. Gibbons, *Ambassador of Christ*, 131, 133.

86. Ibid., 131, 136.

87. Ibid., 138.

88. Ibid., 141, 143–44.

89. McLaughlin, "Discipline in the Seminary," 699.

90. Gartland, ""Sex Education for Minor Seminarians," *NCEAB* 46 (1949): 136, 137.

91. Ibid., 137.

92. Ibid., 137, 138.

93. Ibid., 138.

94. Kirsch, "Presenting Chastity as a Positive Virtue," *NCEAB* 36 (1939): 564.

95. Murnion, *The Catholic Priest and the Changing Structure of Pastoral Ministry, New York, 1920–1970* (New York, 1978); Hedin, *Married to the Church*, 13; Marcuse, *Eros and Civilization: A Philosophical Inquiry into Freud* (Boston, 1974), 35. Also see Dillon, *House of Formation*, 95–99.

96. Joseph Donnelly, "Brotherhood of Priests," JDP, box 10, folder Priesthood (25th anniversary).

97. Theoharis and Cox, *The Boss*, 202–3; Powers, *Secrecy and Power*, 152; Sanford J. Ungar, *FBI* (Boston, 1975), 325–27; Gentry, *Hoover*, 347; B. W. Kunkel, "The Representation of Colleges in Graduate and Professional Schools of the United States," *Association of American Colleges Bulletin*, 1941, 454, 456, 460; Gannon to Hoover, May 8, 1945, 94-1-22668-4.

98. Powers, *G-Men*; Claire Bond Potter, *War on Crime: Bandits, G-Men, and the Politics of Mass Culture* (New Brunswick, N.J., 1998); William Beverly, "On the Lam: Fugitive Frontiers in the FBI Era" (Ph.D. diss., University of Florida, 1998), chap. 2. Daniel E. Ruth, *Inventing the Public Enemy: The Gangster in American Culture, 1918–1934* (Chicago, 1996); W. J. West, SAC, to Hoover, February 14, 1938, 94-1-5549-5.

99. Raymond J. H. Kennedy, S.J., to Hoover, February 29, 1940, 94-1-16103-1; Kennedy to Hoover, April 4, 1940, 94-1-16103-3; H. T. O'Connor to Hoover, September 27,

1940, 94-1-16103-6 (Canisius); 94-1-5549; [deleted] to Hoover, February 11, 1961, 94-1-5549-42.

100. G. B. Norris, SAC, St. Louis, to SAC, Springfield, Mo., March 3, 1940, 94-1-016403-1; A. C. Rutzen to Director, April 18, 1940, 94-1-016403-2 (St. Louis University); V. W. Peterson, SAC, to Director, March 1, 1940, 94-1-5549-12 (Boston College).

101. Hoover to Robert D. McCabe, November 20, 1951, 94-1-22668-19; [Paul Dietrich] to Hoover, n.d., 94-1-22668-21; M. A. Jones to Nichols, November 10, 1952, 94-1-22668-22; Hoover to [Dietrich], October 28, 1952, 94-1-22668-23; Hoover to [Dietrich], November 13, 1952, 94-1-22668-23; "Fordham Alumni Man FBI Posts," *The Ram*, December 17, 1952, 4; "Fordham's Athletes Strong in FBI Ranks," *The Ram*, January 6, 1953, 3 "FBI Looks to Fordham to Halt Aggressors," *The Ram*, February 6, 1953, 5.

102. Hoover, "Fordham Alumni in the FBI," *Fordham Life*, July 1957, 18; SAC, New York, to Director, April 16, 1957, and Director to New York SAC, May 26, 1957, 94-1-22668-36.

103. "Fordham Graduates Join FBI," enclosed in Hoover to Edward J. Klemonski, December 9, 1960, 94-1-22668-54.

104. Hoover to J. C. Foley, S.J., February 16, 1940, 94-1-2597-[?]; Nichols Office Memorandum for Tolson, May 23, 1944, 94-1-20353-52; "Memorandum Re: St. Louis University," attached to Nichols to Tolson, February 28, 1947, 94-1-16430-19x; "Special Agents of the FBI with Degrees from Canisius College," enclosed with Hoover to Daniel P. Moynihan Jr., May 11, 1961, 94-1-16103-23; J. B. Adams Office Memorandum to Mr. Callahan, February 25, 1966, 94-1-16103-30.

105. In 1937 Notre Dame had 7 alumni who were special agents; in 1941 about 20; in 1942 about 64; in 1950 96; and in 1954, 124. St. John's also contributed a good number of agents: in 1942 the number was 35 and in 1951, 91. In comparison, De-Paul had just 12 alumni special agents in 1951. See "Re: Notre Dame University," January 6, 1937, attached to L. B. Nichols Memorandum for Mr. Joseph, 94-1-658-13x; S. J. Drayton to Hoover, December 14, 1941, 94-1-658-149; Hoover to Father J. Hugh O'Donnell, C.S.C., February 4, 1942, 94-1-658-153; Hoover to Rudy Unger, October 12, 1950, 94-1-658-367; Hoover address at Notre Dame, February 22, 1954, enclosed in Hoover to H. G. Foster, February 15, 1954, 94-1-658-432; McGuire Memorandum for Nichols, April 4, 1942, 94-1-88-18; Hoover to Irene K. Murphy, August 21, 1951, 94-1-88-74; M. A. Jones Office Memorandum to Nichols, March 17, 1951, 94-1-1085-17.

106. "Militia of Christ," *JB(C)*, January 1947, 7 ("Militia"); "Ignatius of Loyola, Soldier and Saint," *JB(C)*, February 1953, 3 ("undertake"); "These Are Men," *JB(C)*, March 1943, 5; Schultenover, *A View from Home: On the Eve of the Modernist Crisis* (New York, 1993); *CPC*, March 1942, 47 ("We who"); H. B. Furay, "The Jesuits. Schock Troops," *Catholic Digest*, June 1947, 71; ("a good"); William J. O'Malley, S.J., *The Fifth Week* (Chicago, 1976), 128 ("guts); Gannon, *The Poor Old Liberal Arts* (New York, 1961), 29 ("to say"); "Training a Jesuit," *JB(C)*, June 1937, 4–8 ("drilling").

107. Morrow, *The Chief: A Memoir of Fathers and Sons* (New York, 1984), 116, 117; Buchanan, *Right from the Beginning* (Boston, 1988), 111–12. "The Pope's Marines" is the title of Buchanan's chapter on Gonzaga High.

108. "Conference of Professors of Philosophy," *WL* 54 (1925): 114 ("to defend"); "Philosophy and Life," *JB(C)*, March 1938, 6 ("the only").

109. Ong, *Fighting for Life: Context, Sexuality, and Consciousness* (Ithaca, N.Y., 1981),

123 ("resulted"); Ong, "Latin Language Study as a Renaissance Puberty Rite," *Studies in Philology* 56 (1959): 103–24.

110. Persico, *Casey*, 21.

111. Susan L. Poulson, "From Single-Sex to Coeducation: The Advent of Co-Education at Georgetown, 1965–1975," *USCH* 13, no. 4 (Fall 1995): 117, 117 n2; *As I Remember Fordham*, 4–5 ("many people").

112. *As I Remember Fordham*, 17; Douglas, *Purity and Danger: An Analysis of Concepts of Pollution and Danger* (Boston, 1979).

113. *The Catalogue of Holy Cross College, 1927–1928* (Worcester, Mass., 1928), 27 ("facts"); Jesuit Educational Association, *Teaching in Jesuit High Schools* (n.p., 1957), 1 ("formation"); *A Catalogue of Georgetown University* (1925), 59 ("Christian manhood"); William Patrick Leahy, "Jesuits, Catholics, and Higher Education in Twentieth-Century America" (Ph.D. diss., Stanford University, 1986), 59 ("manly piety").

114. *Holy Cross Catalog*, 23.

115. Ibid., 28 ("closer supervision"); *As I Remember Fordham*, 31–32, 109; O'Brien, *Vince*, 37; Califano, *Inside: A Public and Private Life* (New York, 2004), 38.

116. *Catalogue of Georgetown University*, 43 ("paternal"), 44; *Fordham University Bulletin of Information, 1929–1930* (New York, 1930), 27; *Holy Cross Catalogue*, 25; *JB(C)*, November 1942, 6; *Holy Cross Catalogue*, 25 ("unfair").

117. LaFarge, *Jesuits in Modern Times*, 53.

118. Carrabine, "Queen of the Society," *CPC*, December 1954, 45–48.

119. Gannon, *Poor Old Liberal Arts*, 10–13 ("emulation"); Jesuit Educational Association, *Teaching in Jesuit High Schools*, 175.

120. Patrick J. Clear, S.J., "Play Ball!" *JB(C)*, December 1952, 9–10; *CPC*, February 1945, 39, February 1943, 34, February 1940, 33, March 1946, 51, February 1952, 53–54; *JB(C)*, April 1943, 6l.

121. Ong, *Fighting for Life*, 123; *A Catalogue of Georgetown*, 43 ("friction"), 47 ("publicly").

122. *As I Remember Fordham*, 73 (quotes); David Maraniss, *When Pride Still Mattered: A Life of Vince Lombardi* (New York, 1999), 33.

123. *A Catalogue of Georgetown*, 43; Califano quoted in *A*, May 20, 1989, 471; *CPC*, November 1936, 17; *As I Remember Fordham*, 152; *Fordham University Bulletin*, 68–70; *Bulletin of the Undergraduate Sodalities* 2, no. 1 September 30, 1958. Also see the various sodality records at GUA.

124. *Fordham Universtiy Bulletin*, 68–70; *Holy Cross Catalog*, 148–54; Robert R. Moore, S.J., "Jesuit Students Honor Our Lady During May," *JB(C)*, May 1941, 4, 7; *As I Remember Fordham*, 28 ("outstanding event"), 91; Persico, *Casey*, 26 ("Mary. Mother").

125. Thomas Kselman and Steven Avella, "Marian Piety and the Cold War in the United States," *Catholic Historical Review* 72 (1986): 403–24; *CPC*, November 1949, 13, June 1949, 85, December 1950, 25; *JB(C)*, December 12, 1954, 9. Georgetown's student newspaper *The Hoya* is a good source for these devotions. For the senior class gift, see "1950 Class Gift to Georgetown," *Alumni Magazine*, Fall 1950, 11.

126. Johnson, "Mary and the Face of God," *Theological Studies* 50 (1989): 521; Gannon, *God in Education* (New York, 1943), 29.

127. Martin to Hoover, March 16, 1959, 94-1-9758-62.

128. Theoharis and Cox, *The Boss*, 109 ("athleticism"); "Successor to Burns May Not Look Like a Detective, But—," *Washington News*, December 27, 1924, JEHS; For-

lance M. Gillis, "The Idea of Character Formation in the Jesuit System of Education," in Guthrie and Walsh, *Philosophical Symposium*, 57 ("character").

129. "Manresans Hear Appeals to Guard United States," *CR*, January 27, 1939, enclosure in 94-1-9758-5. The Jesuits not only produced manpower for the FBI but also worked closely with it. Except for the case of Father Edwin Conway, S.J., who is the subject of chapter 5, and a brief discussion of Jesuit labor priests in chapter 6, however, I do not discuss the close relationship between Jesuits and the FBI. For the briefest outline of this cooperation, see Steve Rosswurm, "Manhood, Communism, and Americanism: The Federal Bureau of Investigation and American Jesuits, 1935–1960," Cushwa Center for the Study of American Catholicism, *Working Paper Series*, ser. 28, no. 2, Spring 1996.

130. "The Chalice from the FBI!" *The Manresan*, July 1951, JEHS (quotes).

131. Ibid.

132. *JB(C)*, January 1951, unpaginated back page.

2. *The Boss's Bishops*

1. Ed "Moose" Krause quoted in Murray Sperber, *Shake Down the Thunder: The Creation of Notre Dame Football* (New York, 1993), 368.

2. John J. Lechner, "J. Edgar Hoover," *Notre Dame Alumnus*, February 1937, 127 ("quiet mask-like); "J. Edgar Hoover, Here, Hits 'Mollycoddling' in Prisons," *South Bend Tribune*, January 11, 1937, JEHS.

3. *Religious Bulletin*, September 21–22, 1938, enclosure in O'Hara to Hoover, September 23, 1938, 94-1-658-119; O'Hara to Hoover, September 23, 1938; Hoover to O'Hara, October 19, 1938, 94-1-658-119.

4. O'Hara to Hoover, December 6, 1937, 94-1-658-108; Conroy to Hoover, April 1, 1943, 71-1642-1; *Catholic Standard and Times*, August 14, 1959, enclosure in Hoover to O'Hara, August 21, 1959, 94-50719-5.

5. Thomas T. McAvoy, *Father O'Hara of Notre Dame: The Cardinal-Archbishop of Philadelphia* (Notre Dame, 1967), 159.

6. O'Hara to Hoover, March 7, 1938, 94-1-658-113; Hoover, "Our Future," *CoRA*, May 11, 1942, A1715–A1717.

7. "Washington Banquet Complete Success," *The Manresan*, January 1939, 2, enclosure in 94-1-9758-8.

8. "Manresans Hear Appeals to Guard United States from Its External Foes," *CR*, January 27, 1939, 2. Hoover used much the same language to memorialize Curley when the bishop died in 1947. "Bishop McNamara Is Named Archdiocesan Administrator," *Washington Post*, May 18, 1947, JEHS.

9. "Washington Banquet Complete Success," 1. This item was one of the numerous issues of *The Manresan* that the FBI included, as public source material, in its release of 94-1-9758.

10. Hoover to Curley, January 24, 1939, 94-1-9758-7x.

11. James V. Catano, *Ragged Dicks: Masculinity, Steel, and the Rhetoric of the Self-Made Man* (Carbondale, Ill., 2001), 199–202 ("masculine authenticity"); Curley to Hoover, October 11, 1939, 94-1-152-4564; John Tracy Ellis, *Catholic Bishops: A Memoir* (Wilmington, Del., 1983), 47, 51.

12. Curley to Hoover, September 28, 1936, Curley Papers, H1280, AAB; R. C. Hendon Memorandum for Tolson, February 19, 1940, 62-32097-38.

13. Hoover to Vincent de Paul Fitzpatrick, December 4, 1942, 94-8-799-1 (editorial); "Launch a Protest," *CR*, December 24, 1943, 14 ("any self-induced").

14. "The Review Regrets," *CR*, August 20, 1943, 12.

15. Ibid.; "The Battle on the Home Front," *VS*, September 15, 1943, 736.

16. Kelley to Hoover, August 21, 1940, 65-28102-4.

17. Hoover to H. E. Andersen, August 30, 1940, 62-28102-9.

18. H. H. Clegg Memorandum for the Director, August 29, 1940, 65-28102-6.

19. Ibid.

20. Ibid.

21. Clegg Memorandum for Director, August 30, 1940, 65-28103-9.

22. Soucy Memorandum for the Director, September 9, 1940, 65-28102-9x.

23. Curley to Hoover, September 13, 1940, Curley Papers, H1294, AAB.

24. J. J. Kelly to Hoover, October 16, 1953, 62-98033-30. For the only extended discussion, as far as I know, of the connection between Hoover and a member of the Catholic hierarchy, see James F. Garneau, "The Director and His Eminence: The Working Relationship and Questions of Church and State as Reflected in Cardinal Cushing's FBI Files," *American Catholic Studies* 114, no. 2 (2003): 37–53. My conclusions are similar to Garneau's.

25. M. A. Jones Office Memorandum for Mr. Nichols, September 18, 1956, 94-46940-2.

26. SAC, Boston, Office Memorandum for Director, FBI, September 26, 1952, 62-98033-4; M. A. Jones Office Memorandum for Cartha DeLoach, February 3, 1959, 62-98033-101 ("noted for").

27. Nichols Memorandum for Tolson, September 25, 1952, 623-98033-1.

28. James M. O'Toole, *Militant and Triumphant: William Henry O'Connell and the Catholic Church in Boston, 1859–1944* (Notre Dame, 1992), 253 ("brilliant"); M. A. Jones Office Memorandum for Nichols, September 25, 1952, 62-98045-1; SAC, Boston Office, Memorandum for Director, September 27, 1952, 62-98033-7 ("future activities").

29. M. A. Jones Office Memorandum for Mr. Nichols, July 30, 1952, 62-98033-11.

30. "FBI Head Blames U.S. Ills on 'Spiritual Starvation,'" *Boston Daily Globe*, October 3, 1952, 94-37638-NR. The interview appeared in the *Pilot* on October 4, 1952.

31. Hoover to Minihan, September 30, 1952, 62-98033-8.

32. Minihan to Hoover, October 12, 1952, 62-98033-18.

33. Wally Crew, *Men of Spirit, Men of Sports* (Worcester, Mass., 1999), 64–65.

34. SAC, Boston, to Director, November 24, 1954, 94-46666-5; E. J. Powers to Hoover, January 3, 1955, 94-1-179-5-3.

35. Minihan to Hoover, February 6, 1953, 62-98033-[26]; Minihan to Hoover, May 12, 1956, 94-46666-14.

36. Joseph Dever, *Cushing of Boston: A Candid Portrait* (Boston, 1965), 41.

37. "Archbishop Hails FBI Director as Contemporary Paul Revere," *Pilot*, April 27, 1957, 94-37638-41.

38. Ibid.

39. J. J. Kelly to Hoover, October 16, 1953, 62-98033-30.

40. Laughlin to Hoover, December 18, 1958, 62-98033-86.

41. Sullivan Office Memorandum for A. H. Belmont, September 14, 1959, 62-98033-158.

42. Hoover to Cushing, July 29, 1958, 62-90833-72; Cushing to Hoover, July 31, 1958, 62-98033-73.

43. "J. Edgar Hoover Says Archbishop Inspired His Book," *Boston Globe*, February 24, 1958, enclosure in Laughlin to Hoover, February 24, 1958, 62-98033-61 ("To his"); Cushing to Director, February 21, 1958, 62-68033-58 ("leading clerical"). Cushing's letter enclosed the blurb.

44. "Archbishop Cushing Lauds FBI Head's Book," *GE News* (Medium Steam Turbine, Generator and Gear Department), March 7, 1958, enclosure in Dana C. Pierce to Hoover, March 7, 1958, 62-98033-62.

45. Cushing to Hoover, March 10, 1958, 62-98033-67.

46. "Address: Archbishop Cushing[,] Communion Breakfast[,] State Employees[,] November 16, 1958," enclosure in Laughlin to Hoover, November 14, 1958, 62-98033-90.

47. Laughlin to Hoover, November 14, 1958, 62-98033-90.

48. Laughlin to Hoover, December 8, 1958, 62-98033-86.

49. Cushing to Hoover, November 26, 1960, 62-98033-211; Hoover to Cushing, December 5, 1960, 62-98033-211.

50. "Bishop Noll Called Catholic Action Pioneer on Silver Episcopal Jubilee," *NW*, June 30, 1950, 1.

51. Richard Ginder, *With Ink and Crozier: A Biography of John Francis Noll, Fifth Bishop of Fort Wayne and Founder of Our Sunday Visitor* ([Huntington, Ind., [1952]), 254.

52. Ibid., 261.

53. Noll to Hoover, December 4, 1937, 71-1038-1.

54. Hoover to Noll, December 28, 1937, 71-10380-1.

55. Memorandum, January 1[o], 1938, 71-1038-[NR].

56. Edward A. Tamm Memorandum for the Director, March 12, 1938, 71-1038-7 ("quite some"); *Fort Wayne Journal Gazette*, February 19, 1938, enclosure in 71-1038-6; *OSV*, February 27, 1938, 94-8-328-2.

57. Tamm to Hoover, March 12, 1938.

58. Noll to Hoover, February 24, 1942, 71-1503-1 ("small lewd"); Newark Report, August 10, 1942, 71-1503-9 ("strip-tease").

59. SAC, Indianapolis, to Hoover, September 16, 194371-1583-10 ("disappointed"); Hoover to SAC, Indianapolis, February 17, 1943, 62-73947-2.

60. Noll to Hoover, April 22, 1953, 62-89703-41.

61. Ginder, *With Ink and Crozier*, 257 ("the more," "Frederick Collins"); Noll to American Medical Association, January 8, 1938, JNP, box 3, folder 4. Noll may well have written Ginder's biography; JNP, box 2, folder 30.

62. For the other two reports, see O'Hara to Hoover, December 6, 1937, 94-1-658-119; Conroy to Hoover, August 2, 1944, 62-26225-35-422. Hoover ordered his Chicago SAC to investigate the second report, which probably came from Bishop Bernard Sheil, but nothing seems to have come of it. William J. Campbell's reports on Communist agitation in Chicago to Sheil in 1932 and 1933 may also have been its source; see folder Catholic Church, Bishop and Cardinal, 1932–1940, box 1, folder Communism, 1931–1933, WJCP. Campbell's December 28, 1931, letter comes closest to making this assertion but does not include obscene literature in the "planned system of propaganda" he finds in the "public grade and high schools." .

63. Noll to Hoover, April 22, 1953; Hoover to SAC, Indianapolis, April 28, 1953, 62-89703-41.

64. Noll to Samuel Stritch, January 6, 1950, CC, box 3000; Noll to Hoover, September 10, 1953, 94-4-5831-2.

65. "A Felony Every Twenty Seconds," *OSV*, April 25, 1937, 94-8-328-2; Director to [deleted], February 10, 1958, 94-8-328-41; Ginder, "Right or Wrong" column, *OSV*, April 5, 1964, 94-8-328-109.

66. J. J. McGuire Memorandum for Nichols, May 27, 1942, 94-8-328-13.

67. "The Indispensable Supports," enclosure in Hoover to Monsignor Joseph R.

Crowley, January 8, 1963, 94-8-328; Hoover to [deleted], March 8, 1963, 94-8-328-105 ("I am"). The article appeared in the February 17, 1963, issue.

68. Nease Office Memorandum to Tolson, 94-8-328-47.

69. *OSV*, December 7, 1958, 11, enclosure in 94-8-328-48x.

70. Nease Office Memorandum to Tolson, January 14, 1959, 94-8-328-60.

71. Enclosure in 94-8-328-54 ("trends and"); *The Dome*, December 18, 1958, enclosure in 94-8-328-54 ("Americans can").

72. Nease Office Memorandum for Tolson, November 17, 1958, 94-8-328-47.

73. Ibid.

74. Ibid.

75. Nease Office Memorandum to Tolson, January 14, 1959, 94-8-328-60.

76. Conroy to McGuire, January 19, 1959, 94-8-328-61; M. A. Jones Office Memorandum to DeLoach, February 5, 1959, 94-8-328-55 ("brief public"); Conroy to McGuire, February 16, 1959, 94-8-328-58.

77. McGuire Office Memorandum to Tolson, May 26, 1959, 94-8-328-65 ("90%," "in view"); Conroy to Hoover, December 29, 1958, 94-8-328-51 ("must").

78. Conroy to McGuire, May 2, 1960, 94-8-328-74.

79. *OSV*, September 16, 1940, enclosure in 94-8-328-9; *OSV*, December 13, 1942, enclosure in 94-8-328-17.

80. Thomas C. Reeves puts Sheen's FBI file to good use in his biography *America's Bishop: The Life and Times of Fulton J. Sheen* (San Francisco, 2001). My emphasis is very different, though.

81. Kathleen Fields, "Bishop Fulton J. Sheen: An American Catholic Response to the Twentieth Century" (Ph.D. diss., University of Notre Dame, 1988), 222, 224 n22, 232, 233, 246, 251, 265.

82. Ibid., 331.

83. [Deleted] to Hoover, January 12, 1943, 94-4-6389-1 ("strongly indicted"); [deleted] to League of Catholic Laymen, January 3, 1944, 94-4-6389-5 ("pro-fascist").

84. Sheen to Hoover, April 21, 1944, 94-4-6389-7.

85. Edward Scheidt to Hoover, May 14, 1947, 94-4-6389-11.

86. Sheen to Hoover, February 19, 1958, 94-4-6389-50.

87. Hoover to Sheen, September 14, 1950, 94-4-6389-15; Hoover to Sheen, September 30, 1957, 94-4-6389-48.

88. Ladd Memorandum for Tamm, February 8, 1944, 94-4-6389-6.

89. Conroy Teletype to Hoover, October 10, 1945, 100-63-121. Robert P. Newman kindly provided me with a copy of Budenz's file.

90. Ladd Office Memorandum to Director, October 12, 1945, 100-63-125.

91. Coyne Office Memorandum to Ladd, October 19, 1945, 100-63-126.

92. Ibid.

93. Ibid.

94. Ibid.

95. W. C. Strickland Office Memorandum for Ladd, November 26, 1945, 100-63-136.

96. Tamm Office Memorandum for the Director, November 30, 1945, 100-63-149.

97. See Ladd Memorandum for Director, October 29, 1948, 94-4-6389-14, for the suggestion that the FBI was routinely checking on potential converts. For Sheen's assertions and the Bureau's response, see "Congressional Aide Held as Red Agent, Sheen Says," *PM Daily*, March 25, 1946, 3, and "Red Spy Seized by Congress, Sheen Charges," *Washington Times-Herald*, March 25, 1946, 1, enclosures in Ladd Office Memorandum to Hoover, March 25, 1946, 94-4-6389-9; "Says Russians Tried Spy Scheme on Him," unidentified newspaper clipping, [November [1?], 1946], 94-4-6389-A; M. A. Jones Office Memorandum to Nichols, May

4, 1953, 94-4-6389-21; *Treasure in Clay: The Autobiography of Fulton J. Sheen* (New York, 1980), 85-87. Also see Mary Jude Yablonsky, "A Rhetorical Analysis of Selected Television Speeches of Archbishop Fulton J. Sheen on Communism, 1952–1956" (Ph.D. diss., Ohio State University, 1974), 37; Reeves, *America's Bishop,* 207.

98. Galvin to Hoover, March 10, 1942, 94-1-20733-18.

99. Hoover to Spellman, March 23, 1942, 94-1-20733-20; John Cooney, *The American Pope: The Life and Times of Francis Cardinal Spellman* (New York, 1986), 16 ("powerhouse"). Cooney uses FBI material, but only sporadically and seldom productively.

100. Spencer J. Drayton to Hoover, June 16, 1942, 94-4-5826-3. The names of those present at the luncheon were deleted in the version of this serial that was released in the Spellman file. When, however, the same serial was released as a "see" reference for Bishop Bryan McEntegart, the names were present.

101. Spellman, *The Road to Victory* (New York, 1942), 4, 5, 16.

102. Ibid., 28, 52, 53.

103. Hoover to Spellman, November 18, 1942, 94-4-5826-[6]; Spellman to Hoover, November 25, 1942, 94-4-5826-5.

104. Spellman to Hoover, November 30, 1942, 94-4-5826-8; "Notable Service," *BT,* November 28, 1942, enclosure in 94-4-5826-8; Hoover to Spellman, December 10, 1942, 94-4-5826-8.

105. Spellman to Hoover, May 10, 1944, 94-4-5286-NR; Hoover to Spellman, January 10, 1946, 94-4-5826-13; Spellman to Hoover, June 3, 1963, 94-4-5826-58.

106. Spellman to Hoover, November 20, 1953, 94-4-5826-[32]; Hoover to Spellman, November 29, 1953, 94-4-5826-33.

107. "Communism and Schools—J. Edgar Hoover's Views," *U.S. News & World Report,* November 26, 1954, 131, 130; Spellman to Hoover, November 22, 1954, and Hoover to Spellman, November 29, 1954, 94-4-5826-33.

108. [Deleted] to Hoover, October 9, 1946, 94-4-5826-25; Boardman to Hoover, September 26, 1952, 94-4-5826-31; Kelly to Hoover, March 1, 1954, 94-4-5826-NR.

109. SAC, New York, Office Memorandum for Director, FBI December 20, 1954, 94-4-5826-34.

110. [Deleted] to Director, June 2, 1944, 94-4-5826-9. O'Hara's name is deleted in serials 9, 10, and 11 of 94-4-3701 but was not excised in E. E. Conroy to Hoover, September 25, 1944, 94-4-3701-12. These serials were entirely withheld in the FBI's release of 94-4-3701 (O'Hara). I received them, however, as "see" references in the Spellman release.

111. Hoover to SAC, New York, July 3, 1944, 94-4-3701-10.

112. [Deleted] Office Memorandum to [deleted], April 20, 1955, 94-4-5826-NR.

113. Ibid.

114. E. E. Conroy to Director, July 12, 1944, 62-26225-35-394.

115. Hoover to Spellman, July 21, 1944, 62-26225-35-414; Hoover to Conroy, July 20, 1944, 62-26225-35-394.

116. Ladd Office Memorandum for Director, March 26, 1946, 94-3-4-20-787x; Thomas Blantz interview with Cronin, March 17, 1978, 34.

117. Nichols Office Memorandum for Tolson, February 23, 1956, 62-92038-10.

118. Ibid. ("I don't," "We can"); Nichols Office Memorandum to Tolson, February 28, 1956, 62-92038-11 ("is unpredictable").

119. Kelly to Hoover, December 28, 1954, 94-4-5826-35.

120. Director to SAC, New York, January 6, 1955, 94-4-5826-38. (I am working here from a version of this document processed under my FOI appeal 87-1489.)

121. Ibid. The Dies Committee, forerunner of HUAC, was so called for its chairman, Congressman Martin Dies Jr. of Texas.
122. "Address of His Eminence, Francis Cardinal Spellman," June 28, 1946, *CoR*, A3806.
123. Harry Read Memorandum for James B. Carey, November 3, 1951, CIOSTO, box 1, folder Miscellaneous Persons S.
124. "Archbishop O'Boyle Calls Home Bulwark against Communism," *Washington Star*, March 16, 1953, A-8, 94-38790-A.
125. O'Boyle's speech, 94-38790-11x1.
126. Ibid.

3. *Assistant to the Director Edward Tamm and His Chicago Connections*

1. "Teachers Held Last Hope of Saving World," *Buffalo Courier-Express*, September 24, 1947, 6.
2. "Speech to Be Given Before Public Service Employees," 94-38399-3. Brief quotations from the speech appeared the next day in the *Buffalo Courier-Express*, September 24, 1947, 6.
3. Ibid.
4. Ibid.
5. Claire Bond Potter uses Tamm's early career in the Bureau as an example of Hoover's creation of a "masculinized, professional model" for "police experts," but does not note that Tamm was Catholic; see Potter, *War on Crime: Bandits, G-Men, and the Politics of Mass Culture* (New Brunswick, N.J., 1998), 48–49.
6. Tamm Testimony, "Stenographic Transcript of Hearings before the Subcommittee of the Committee on the Judiciary, United States Senate," February 18, 1948, I, 77-37864-7 ("economically"); Tamm to Director, August 19, 1930, 67-15585-1 ("I have); Keith to the Director, August 19, 1930, 67-15585-2 ("gentlemanly demeanor"); Nathan Memorandum for the Director, August 27, 1930, 67-15585-3.
7. "Successor to Burns May Not Look Like a Detective, But—," *Washington News*, December 27, 1924, JEHS ("old gum-shoe"); *FBI Manual of Instruction* (Washington, D.C., 1927), 144, Athan Theoharis, ed., *FBI Manuals of Instruction* microfilm (1983), reel 1 ("Applicants for").
8. Washington, D.C., Report, September 10, 1930, 67-15585-6.
9. Butte Report, September 11, 1930, 67-15585-8; D. O. Smith Memorandum for the Director, September 20, 1930, 67-15585-13.
10. Keith to Director, December 11, 1930, 67-15585-21.
11. Gus T. Jones to Director, January 15, 1931, 67-15585-24; J. R. Burdge to Director, February 19, 1931, 67-15585-27 ("thorough and").
12. Burdge to Director, February 19, 1930, 67-15585-28.
13. Baughman Memorandum for the Director, April 3, 1931, 67-15585-31.
14. Connelly to Director, November 3, 1931, 67-15585-43.
15. Connelly to Director, December 14, 1933, 67-15585-80; Tamm to Director, December 20, 1933, 67-15585-81.
16. Tamm to Hoover, January [21], 1934, 67-15585-89.
17. *Newark Evening News*, June 17, 1933, 67-15585-[NR]; *New York Times*, June 18, 1933, sec. 2, 5; Philip Gleason, *Contending with Modernity: Catholic Higher Education in the Twentieth Century* (New York, 1995), 90 ("Catholic Vassar"); *NYT*, January 31, 1934, 14.
18. Director to Tamm, May 25, 1934, 67-15585-95; "Bandits Have Code Like Old Pirate Maps," *NYT*, April 15, 1934, 29.

19. Hoover Memorandum for Tamm, July 25, 1934, 67-15585-101.
20. Hoover Memoradum for Tolson, Quinn, Tamm, Lester, September 5, 1934, 67-15585-104; Hoover Memorandum for Tamm, September 7, 1934, 67-15585-105; Hoover Memorandum for Tolson and Tamm, September 7, 1934, 67-15585-106; Hoover Memorandum for Tolson and Tamm, September 15, 1934, 67-15585-108; Hoover Memorandum for Tamm, September 15, 1934, 67-15585-109; Hoover Memorandum for Tamm, September 15, 1934, 67-15585-110.
21. Hoover to Tamm, October 3, 1934, 67-15585-113.
22. Quoted in Bryan Burrough, *Public Enemies: America's Greatest Crime Wave and the Birth of the FBI, 1933–1934* (New York, 2004), 450, 500.
23. Tamm Memorandum for the Director, November 2, 1934, 67-15585-121.
24. Hoover Memorandum for Tamm, November 3, 1934, 67-15585-120.
25. Andrew Tully, *The FBI's Most Famous Cases* (New York, 1965), 243; J. R. Calhoun to Tamm, July 13, 1938, 67-15585-253 ("We have").
26. Tamm to Hoover, July 13, 1934, 67-15585-98; Tamm to Calhoun, July 18, 1938, 67-15585-253.
27. Hoover Testimony, "Stenographic Transcript of Hearings," February 18, 1948, I, 77-37864-7.
28. Gold Dust Twins Telegram to Hoover, September 19, 1936, 67-15585-[205].
29. Theoharis, *Chasing Spies: How the FBI Failed in Counterintelligence but Promoted the Politics of McCarthyism in the Cold War Years* (Chicago, 2002), 244.
30. Hoover to Tamm, June 5, 1939, 67-15585-266.
31. Hoover to Tamm, March 23, 1945, 67-155850-[NR] ("grand job"); Hoover to Tamm, July 6, 1945, 67-15585-327 ("planning and").
32. Tamm's medical examination, May 18, 1945, 67-155850-325.
33. Ibid. For Tamm's detailed accounting of several days of work, one in 1939 and the other in 1940, well before the U.S. entry into the war, see Tamm Memorandum for the Director, May 9, 1939, 67-15585-265; Tamm Memorandum for the Director, September 26, 1940, 67-15585-282.
34. Medical examination, May 18, 1945.
35. Hoover to Tamm, May 25, 1945, 67-15585-324.
36. Theoharis, *Chasing Spies*, 111.
37. Ibid., 94.
38. On Soviet espionage, see Katherine A. S. Sibley, *Red Spies in America: Stolen Secrets and the Dawn of the Cold War* (Lawrence, Kans., 2004); Allen Weinstein and Alexander Vassiliev, *The Haunted Wood: Soviet Espionage in America—The Stalin Era* (New York, 1999); John Earl Haynes and Harvey Klehr, *Venona: Decoding Soviet Esponage in America* (New Haven, 1999); Steven T. Usdin, *Engineering Communism: How Two Americans Spied for Stalin and Founded the Soviet Silicon Valley* (New Haven, 2005). On the CPUSA and Soviet espionage, see Harvey Klehr et al., *The Secret World of American Communism* (New Haven, 1995); Klehr et al., *The Soviet World of American Communism* (New Haven, 1998); R. Bruce Craig, *Treasonable Doubt: The Harry Dexter White Spy Case* (Lawrence, Kans., 2004); Allen Weinstein, *Perjury: The Hiss-Chambers Case* (New York, 1979); Ronald Radosh and Joyce Milton, *The Rosenberg File: A Search for Truth* (New York, 1983). On the CPUSA and CIO, 100-7602 (Roy Hudson) and 100-11687 (John Williamson); Victor Rabinowitz, *Unrepentant Leftist: A Lawyer's Memoir* (Urbana, 1996); John J. Abt, *Advocate and Activist: Memoirs of an American Communist Lawyer* (Urbana, 1993); Steve Rosswurm, "The Wondrous Tale of an FBI Bug: What It Tells Us about Communism, Anti-Communism, and the CIO Leadership," *American Communist History* 2, no. 1 (June 2003): 3–20.

39. This information comes from "symbol number sensitive source index" cards obtained from the FBI through the Freedom of Information and Privacy Act.

40. J. Edgar Hoover Memo to Lawrence M. C. Smith, August 15, 1942, 100-7602-[NR] (preceding document is 100-87602-116), symbol number sensitive source index card.

41. Tamm Memorandum to the Director, November 5, 1945, reproduced in Athan Theoharis, ed., *From the Secret Files of J. Edgar Hoover* (Chicago, 1991), 89.

42. Tamm Memorandum for the Director, May 31, 1946, 61-63-[169x1].

43. Ladd Memorandum to Hoover, February 27, 1946, in *Final Report of the Select Committee to Study Governmental Operations with Respect to Intelligence Activities* (Washington, D.C., 1976), bk. 3, 430.

44. Ibid.

45. For this bug there is not only a symbol number sensitive source card but also a serialized record of its installation; Philadelphia teletype, January 1, 1947, 100-11687-[147]. Two reports, one typed and the other handwritten, which resulted from this surveillance are in CIOSTO, box 109, folder Hearings, FTA, Correspondence 1946–1949.

46. Steven M. Avella, in *This Confident Church: Catholic Leadership and Life in Chicago, 1940–1965* (Notre Dame, 1992), provides essential background for this section of the chapter. He has, moreover, considerable information on the Tamm connection.

47. See serials 17–37 in 94-4-1411; Avella, *This Confident Church*, 5–12.

48. Avella, *This Confident Church*, 18–20, 104. Burke also knew Tamm—and undoubtedly everyone else discussed in this section—on a first-name basis but probably was too busy running the archdiocese to play the kind of role that Fitzgerald did. Burke addressed a letter to Tamm "Dear Ed" on May 7, 1946, CC, box 2975.

49. Fitzgerald to Hoover, May 1, 1958, 94-48305-4; SAC, Chicago, Office Memorandum to Director, February 18, 1955, 94-48305-1.

50. "John Fitzgerald Memoir," copy in author's possession. Steven Avella kindly gave me a copy of this unpaginated document.

51. Tamm to Stritch, October 28, 1947 (attached to Stritch to Tamm, November 23, 1947); Tamm to Stritch, April 9, 1946 (attached to Tamm to Stritch, November 16, 1946); Tamm to Stritch, November 6, 1948, CC, boxes 2982, 2973, 2989.

52. Stritch to Cicognani, February 27, 1947, and its attachment "Memorandum: The President's Personal Representative at the Vatican," CC, box 2976. For a fairly good indication that Tamm was giving information to Stritch, see Stritch to Cicognani, May 9, 1947, CC, box 29876. Less certain as evidence is Stritch to Cicognani, May 21, 1947, attached to Cicognani to Stritch, December 12, 1947, CC, box 2980.

53. "Moscow Subsidies for the Italian Communists"; "Memo: Aid to Italy From the United States" ("espionage services"); and "Confidential—Additional to Memo," attached to Stritch to Cicognani, May 16, 1947, CC, box 2976, folder Apostolic Delegate.

54. Stritch to Tamm, November 23, 1947, CC, box 2982. My hunch is that this bit of business concerned Italy—which is why I have included it here—and involved Senator J. Howard McGrath, the Rhode Island Democrat and future attorney general.

55. Fitzgerald to Tamm, April 1, 1949, CC, box 2996. Handwritten in pencil on this letter is the notation "re Eritrea & Libiya." "Libya," March 29, 1949, is in box 2993, and "Eritrea," March 29, 1949, in box 2992.

56. Tamm to Stritch, June 26, 1946, attached to Tamm to Stritch, October 16, 1946, CC, box 2973 ("tremendously impressed"; "I am"); Stritch to Tamm, July 22, 1946, attached to Tamm to Stritch, November 16, 1946, CC, box 2973 ("I have").

57. Tamm to Stritch, January 4, 1946 (quotes), attached to Tamm to Stritch, November 16, 1946, CC, box 2973; Stritch to Tamm, January 8, 1946, attached to Tamm to Stritch, October 16, 1946, CC, box 2973.

58. Tamm to Bishop Duane G. Hunt, January 4, 1946, enclosed with Tamm to Stritch, January 4, 1946 ("confidentially"); and Tamm to Hunt, March 12, 1946, attached to Tamm to Stritch, October 16, 1946, CC, box 2973.

59. Burke to Archbishop Joseph T. McGucken, December 17, 1942; Peter O'Brien, O.P., to Burke, December 18, 1942; and De Salto to Burke, January 8, 1943, CC, box 2946.

60. Stritch to Cicognani, August 25, 1942, CC, box 2946.

61. Stritch to Cicognani, November 10, 1946, CC, box 2969.

62. Memo, July 15, 1949, attached to Casey memo, n.d., CC, box 2991.

63. Tamm to Fitzgerald, November 19, 1945 (quotations); and Stritch to Father Tanner, November 27, 1945, CC, boxes 2965, 2968.

64. [Fitzgerald] Memo to His Eminence, August 2, 1948, CC, box 2983.

65. Fitzgerald to Thomas O'Neil, October 8, 1948, CC, box 2986.

66. Ibid.

67. Campbell to Sheil, February 1, 1932, Catholic Church, Bishop and Cardinal, 1932–1940, box 1, folder Communism, 1931–1933, WJCP; "Note" with Hoover to Campbell, July 9, 1959, 62-89058-2. There apparently was another problem in 1939, but the lines describing it are deleted.

68. SAC Auerbach to Director, June 19, 1959, 62-89058-2; "Note" with Hoover to Campbell, July 9, 1959, 62-89058-2.

69. Correspondence/Project, box 21, folder FBI 1967–1968, WJCP.

70. Porter McKeever, *Adlai Stevenson: His Life and Legacy* (New York, 1989), 205.

71. Mitchell to Fitzgerald, February 10, 1949, SMP, box 1, folder 1949 (3) ("good lunch"); Mitchell to William Ayers, August 11, 1949, SMP, box 1, folder 1949 (2); Mitchell to Krock, May 19, 1948, SMP, box 1, folder 1948 (2) (delighted at").

72. Stritch to Howard J. Carroll, March 4, 1950, CC, box 3000, folder NCWC Monsignor Carroll. Stritch's "OFF THE RECORD" appointment with Truman, which Tamm arranged, may also have had to do with this loan; www.trumanlibrary.org/calendar/main.php?currYear+1950&currMonth=7&currDay=31 (accessed June 10, 2009).

73. Mitchell to Tamm, May 6, 1948, SMP, box 1, folder 1948 (2) ("Fitz could"); Mitchell to Tamm, February 18, 1948, SMP, box 1, folder 1948 (2) ("Your ears"); Mitchell to Tamm, February 8, 1951, SMP, box 2, folder 1952–1953 ("I passed").

74. Mitchell to Durand Smith, March 28, 1949, SMP, box 1, folder 1949 (2).

75. "From the Desk," *NW*, January 31, 1947, 1 ("men in"); "Cardinal, FBI Official Tell Holy Name Men to Wake Up Christian Peoples," *NW*, October 31, 1947, 3; "Edward Tamm Named to U.S. District Court," *NW*, February 6, 1948, 3; "Named Again," *NW*, July 2, 1948, 14.

76. *NW*, July 21, 1950, 4.

77. John Crewdson, "Seeing Red," *Chicago Sunday Tribune*, March 26, 1986, 16; Make Mills, Industrial Detail, to Commissioner of Police, June 14, 1937, United States Congress, Senate, Committee on Education and Labor, "Violations of Free Speech and Rights of Labor," Exhibit 1627-C, 5161.

78. This discussion is based on the correspondence in WJCP, Catholic Church, Bishop and Cardinal 1932–1940, box 1, folder Communism 1931–1933.

79. Stritch to Brogan, December 27, 1944, Stritch Personal Papers, box 2826, AAC ("I think"); Brogan to Stritch, February 21, 1945, CC, box 2967.

80. Meehan to Father Cletus O'Donnell, August 3, 1949, attached to Father Frank Coyle to Burke, August 29, 1949, CC, box 2990 ("all Catholics"). The information on the individuals comes from letters attached to Coyle's letter.

81. Folder "[1949]—Meehan, Thomas, Rev," CC, box 2993.

82. Heimoski to Meehan, January 28, 1949, ibid. For Dunne's discussion of the play's origins as well as an account of the Chicago production, see *King's Pawn: The Memoirs of George H. Dunne, S.J.* (Chicago, 1990), 132–36, 177–79, 211.

83. Tamm to Stritch, December 20, 1947, CC, box 2981. I have found no evidence to support Curtis Gentry's discussion of Hoover's response to Tamm's departure in *J. Edgar Hoover: The Man and the Secrets* (New York, 1991), 336.

84. "Truman Names Tamm to Bench," *Washington Times Herald*, JEHS ("as a"); Tamm to Stritch, February 3, 1948, attached to Tamm to Stritch, April 9, 1948, CC, box 2988 ("Were it").

85. Stritch to Tamm, March 11, 1948, attached to Stritch to Tamm, September 29, 1948, CC, box 2989 ("Junior"); Mitchell to Tamm, May 6, 1948, SMP, box 1, folder 1948 (2) ("St. Louis").

86. Tamm Memorandum for the Director, February 7, 1948, 67-15585-361; Nichols Memorandum for Tolson, February 10, 1948, 67-15585-362.

87. J. P. Mohr Memorandum for Tolson, February 16, 1948 ("I told"); and Nichols Memorandum for Tolson, February 17, 1948, in Athan Theoharis, ed., *Louis B. Nichols Official and Confidential File* (microfilm, 1983), reel 15, frames 211, 234.

88. "Missouri Vote Fraud Inquiry Enters Tamm Judgeship Quiz," *Washington Times-Herald*, February 19, 1948, JEHS.

89. "Tamm Assumes Vote Quiz Blame," *Washington Times-Herald*, February 20, 1948, JEHS.

90. This memorandum, which apparently is unserialized, can be found in section 2 of Tamm's 67-15585 file.

91. "Another Hearing on Tamm Set for Next Week," *Washington Evening Star*, March 3, 1948, 67-15585-NR.

92. "Senate Group to Give Formal Report on Friday on Tamm as Justice," *Washington Star*, May 4, 1948, JEHS; Mitchell to Dilliard, May 6, 1948, SMP, box 1, folder 1948(2); Tamm to Stritch, June 21, 1948, CC, Box 2988.

93. "Truman Names 11 Rebuffed by GOP," *NYT*, June 23, 1948, 17.

94. Tamm to Hoover, June 23, 1948, 67-15585-366; Hoover to Tamm, June 29, 1948, 67-15585-[NR].

95. "'Interim' Judge Tamm Problem for District Court," *Washington Daily News*, June 29, 1948, JEHS.

96. "3 Recess Appointees Held Entitled to Pay," *NYT*, August 27, 1948, 7 ("could continue"); "Tamm Will Get Permanent Post on D.C. Bench," *Washington Times-Herald*, November 5, 1948, JEHS.

97. *Washington Star*, October 20, 1958, B1, 67-15585-NR.

98. "N.L.R.B. Is Enjoined," *NYT*, July 21, 1954, 30.

99. Quoted in "U.S. Appeals Court Judge Edward A. Tamm, 79, Dies," *Washington Post*, September 23, 1985, 6, 67-15585-NR.

100. Ibid.

101. Tamm to Hoover, June 23, 1948, 67-15585-366.

102. Tamm to Hoover, September 2, 1958, 67-15585. This item appears to be unserialized; it is section 4.

103. Tamm to Hoover, May 3, 1960, 94-44876-46 ("tremendously impressed"); Tamm

to Hoover, November 11, 1960, 94-44876-53 ("Your views"); Tamm to Hoover, October 24, 1966, 67-15585-421 ("constitutes a").

104. Tamm to Kelley, June 20, 1974, 94-44876-125; Tamm to Kelley, October 10, 1973, 67-15585-439.

105. Norman W. Philcox to Hoover, April 10, 1961, 67-15585-?; Boston Teletype to Director, July 31, 1954, 94-44876-12; New York SAC to Director, June 15, 1956, 94-44876-15; San Francisco SAC Airtel to Director, July 11, 1958, 94-44876-28.

106. Hoover Memorandum for Tolson, Belmont, Sullivan, and DeLoach, January 14, 1965, in Theoharis, *Nichols Official and Confidential File*, microfilm reel 1, frame 8.

107. Hoover to Tamm, October 7, 1958, 94-44876-31. The information on the contents of the memoranda on Edwards comes from Alexander Charns, *Cloak and Gavel: FBI Wiretaps, Bugs, Informers, and the Supreme Court* (Urbana, 1992), xiv n24. The memoranda were not included in the FBI's release to me of this file.

108. Hoover Memorandum for Tolson, Mohr, Callahan, and Bishop, January 11, 1971, 94-44876-NR.

109. 94-38399-3.

110. Gentry, *J. Edgar Hoover*, 46, 180.

111. Ibid., 227; Tolson Memorandum for the Director, March 21, 1941, in Athan Theoharis, ed., *The "Do Not File" File* (microfilm, 1989), reel 1, frame 27 ("maintenance of").

112. William M. Halsey, *The Survival of American Innocence: Catholicism in an Era of Disillusionment, 1920–1940* (Notre Dame, 1980); Gentry, *Hoover*, 133 ("We were").

4. *Father John F. Cronin and the Bishops' Report on Communism*

1. Karl Alter to Cronin, October 19, 1946, AP, box 4, folder 33. Peter H. Irons seems to have been the first to discover Cronin's authorship of these pamphlets; see Irons, "America's Cold War Crusade: Domestic Politics and Foreign Policy, 1942–1948" (Ph.D. diss., Boston University, 1972), 87–98; Irons, "American Business and the Origins of McCarthyism: The Cold War Crusade of the United States Chamber of Commerce," in Robert Griffith and Athan Theoharis, eds., *The Specter: Original Essays on the Cold War and the Origins of McCarthyism* (New York, 1974), 72–89.

2. Steve Rosswurm, "The FBI and the CIO from 1940 to 1955," paper presented at the Organization of American Historians' Meeting, Philadelphia, April 1987.

3. Garry Wills, *Nixon Agonistes: The Crisis of the Self-Made Man* (Boston, 1970), 25–30. Cronin later affirmed to Thomas C. Reeves that Wills had "described" his role in the Hiss affair "accurately"; Cronin to Reeves, June 8, 1977, JCP, box 2, folder 15.

4. Cronin to Alter and Alter to Cronin, November 5, 1945, AP, box 7, folder 6. For discussion of Cronin's report, see Irons, "America's Cold War Crusade," 77–182; Earl Boyea, "The National Catholic Welfare Conference: An Experience in Episcopal Leadership" (Ph.D. diss., Catholic University, 1987), 412–24; Athan Theoharis, *Chasing Spies: How the FBI Failed in Counterintelligence but Promoted the Politics of McCarthyism in the Cold War Years* (Chicago, 2002), 144–48; John T. Donovan, *Crusader in the Cold War: A Biography of Fr. John F. Cronin, S.S. (1908–1994)* (New York, 2005), chap. 2.

5. Much of this information is drawn from an interview with Father James Cronin, Father John Cronin's brother, on June 26, 1995, at St. Joan of Arc, Aberdeen, Maryland. Also see Donovan, *Crusader in the Cold War*, chap. 1.

6. Cronin, *Cardinal Newman: His Theory of Knowledge* (Washington, D.C., 1935).

7. Cronin, "Economics of the Spirit," *S*, April 1940, 535 ("unified and"); Cronin, "A Living Wage Today," *S*, June 1938, 647 ("set up"); Cronin, "Decline of American Capitalism," *The Christian Front*, July–August 1938, 108 ("passive and"). (This is not the publication put out by Father Charles Coughlin.)

8. Cronin, "Decline," 108.

9. Cronin, "Asks Wisdom and Harmony for Labor," *CR*, September 6, 1940, 6 ("At all"); Cronin, "Lessons Written in Blood," *S*, December, 1940, 272 (remaining quotations).

10. Cronin, "Hope Long Deferred," *S*, February 1941, 400–402.

11. Cronin, "Says Labor Must Select Good Leaders," *CR*, September 5, 1941, 10 ("The fighter"); Cronin, "The Destiny of Labor," *S*, December 1941, 279 (remaining quotations).

12. Cronin, "Men Who Lead Labor," *S*, July 1941, 718–21.

13. Cronin, "Asks Wisdom and Harmony for Labor," *CR*, September 6, 1940, 6.

14. Ibid., 6 ("Here we"); Cronin, "Says Labor and Business Need Reform," *CR*, September 13, 1940, 12 ("broad festering"); "Father Cronin Urges Unity of Good Will," *CR*, September 20, 1940, 12 ("organic unity"); Cronin, "Freedom Defended," *HPR*, June 1941, 923 ("evil germs"); Cronin, "Says Decision Must Be Made by the Nation," *CR*, August 22, 1941, 3 ("cancer which").

15. Cronin, "Saviours of Society," *AER*, June 1941, 514.

16. See Joshua B. Freeman and Steve Rosswurm, "The Education of an Anti-Communist: Father John F. Cronin and the Baltimore Labor Movement," *LH* 33, no. 2 (Spring 1992): 217–47. Also see Vernon L. Pedersen, *The Communist Party in Maryland, 1919–1957* (Urbana, 2001), chaps. 6, 7, 8; Albert Vetere Lannon, *Second String Red: The Life of Al Lannon, American Communist* (Lanham, Md., 1999), chap. 10; Donovan, *Crusader in the Cold War*, 16–25.

17. Cronin to Father John Hayes, March 21, 1944, SAD, box 8, folder 15.

18. "Communist Activities," November 5, 1942, attached to Cronin to Ready, November 5, 1942, OGS, box 32, folder 1939–1942.

19. Cronin, "Further Thoughts on Parish Social Action," *The Priest*, February 1945, 18.

20. Captain [deleted] F.A., "Memorandum for the Officer in Charge," June 23, 1943, 100-242224-2, John Cronin FBI Files, box 1, folder 6, MUDSC.

21. Noll to Alter, March 27, 1941, AP, box 3, folder 21.

22. The "dog" quote is from "Max" to "Maloney," a "house note" from the *Milwaukee Tribune* editor to Arch Ward at the *Tribune*. The other quotations are from McGowan to Monsignor Michael Ready, May 26, 1944. Both items, along with other pertinent correspondence, are in AP, box 4, folder 6.

23. R. A. McGowan, "Clergy Hail Schools of Catholic Action," *CA*, August 1937, 16.

24. McGowan to Hayes, August 16, 1939, SAD, box 2, folder 16.

25. Ibid., box 41, folder Social Action Surveys.

26. Cronin to Hayes, November 17, 1942, SAD, box 8, folder 14.

27. Hayes to Father Vincent Breen, November 22, 1943, SAD, box 8, folder 1.

28. Cronin to Mooney, October 27, 1942, OGS, box 23, folder 1939–1942.

29. Cronin, "Communist Activities," November 11, 1942, attached to Cronin to Ready, November 11, 1942, ibid.; "General Intelligence Memorandum," September 4, 1942, Maryland Manuscripts 4008, Maryland Room, McKeldin Library, University of Maryland; Pedersen, *The Communist Party in Maryland*.

30. Cronin, "Communist Activities."

31. Ibid.

32. Ibid.

33. Cronin to Stritch, May 15, 1943, attached to Stritch to Cronin, May 22, 1943; Stritch to Cronin, May 22, 1943, CC, box 2953.

34. Ready to Mooney, April 17, 1944, OGS, box 23, folder 1944.

35. Administrative Board Minutes, November 12, 1944, OGS, box 64.

36. Alter to Ready, July 31, 1944, OGS, box 4, folder Personnel 1944–1945.

37. Cronin to Alter, November 18, 1944, SAD, box 2, folder 15.

38. Cronin to McGowan, November 18, 1944, ibid.

39. "Report on the Investigation of Communism," November 13–December 31, 1944, OGS, box 24, folder Communism . . . Report.

40. J. K. Mumford Memorandum for D. M. Ladd, November 17, 1944, 100-337494-1.

41. [Deleted] Memorandum for Ladd, November 30, 1944, 100-337494-2.

42. Cronin to Read, December 20, 1944, HRP, box 3, folder 3.

43. Stritch to Brogan, December 27, 1944, Stritch Personal Papers, box 2826, AAC.

44. Alter to Cronin, December 26, 1944, OGS, box 24, folder Communism . . . Report; Cronin to Alter, December 30, 1944, AP, box 7, folder 4.

45. Alter to Cronin, January 2, 1945, AP, box 7, folder 5.

46. Cronin to Carroll, December 30, 1944; Cronin to Higgins, January 19, 1945, SAD, box 8, folder 16 ("piled-up work"); "Report on Communist Investigation, February 1, 1945," OGS, box 24, folder Communism . . . Report ("very sharp").

47. "Report on Communist Investigation, February 1, 1945."

48. August Raymond Ogden, *The Dies Committee: A Study of the Special House Committee for the Investigation of Un-American Activities, 1938–1944*, 2nd rev. ed. (Washington, D.C., 1945), 63 ("weirdest collections"); "Report on Communist Investigation, February 1, 1945" (remaining quotations).

49. Read to Higgins, January 26, 1945, HRP, box 10, folder Professional Correspondence and Other Papers Miscellaneous; "Report on Communist Investigation, February 1, 1945."

50. Cronin to Alter, February 1, 1945, AP, box 7, folder 5. This naval intelligence connection may have come through Howard Carroll of the NCWC (see his handwritten pencil comments on Cronin to Carroll, December 30, 1944) or O'Hara (see Cronin to Alter, "Report on Communist Investigation, February, 1945," both OGS, box 24, folder Communism . . . Report).

51. "Report on Communist Investigation . . . February, 1945" ("some exceptions"); Brogan to Stritch, February 21, 1945, CC, box 2967 ("most cooperative"). See Drayton to Director, January 16, 1945, 100-337494-2x1; Ladd Memorandum for Tamm, January 16, 1945, 100-337494-2x2; Hoover to Drayton, February 7, 1945, 100-337494-2x2. Brogan mentions Campbell in a second letter to Stritch dated February 21. The first set of answers is in CC, box 2966.

52. Cronin to Alter, March 2, 1945, AP, box 7, folder 5. For Smith's connections to intelligence agencies, see Steve Rosswurm, "Manhood, Communism, and Americanism: The Federal Bureau of Investigation and American Jesuits, 1935–1960," Cushwa Center for the Study of American Catholicism, *Working Papers Series*, ser. 28, no. 2, Spring 1996, 7–9.

53. E. E. Conroy Evaluation of Bierly, March 31, 1944, 67-176012-NR.

54. Cronin to Higgins, March 17, 1945, SAD, box 8, folder 16.

55. Cronin to Alter, March 25, 1945, AP, box 7, folder 5.

56. Alter to Cronin, March 27, 1945, ibid. ("wonderful job"); Cronin to Alter, March 25, 1945 ("other sources").

57. Ladd Memorandum to Tamm, April 5, 1945, 100-337494-4.

58. Ladd Memorandum to Tamm, April 12, 1945, 100-337494-5.

59. Cronin to Carroll, April 8, 1945, OGS, box 24, folder Communism . . . Report.

60. Administrative Board Minutes, April 10, 1945, OGS, box 64.

61. Alter to Cronin, March 27, 1945, AP, box 7, folder 5.

62. Cronin to Alter, April 2, 1945, ibid.

63. Ibid.

64. Cronin to Alter, May 1, 1945, AP, box 7, folder 5.

65. OGS, box 24, folder Communism . . . Report.

66. Ibid. I have located the following responses: "Confidential Questionnaire on Communism," CC, box 2966; Haas, "Answer to Questionnaire on Communism," FHP, box 2; "Questionnaire on Local Activities of Communists," AP, box 7, folder 5; Folder "NCWC-Communism—1945," DeACTU, box 29; see also Steven M. Avella and Elizabeth McKeown, eds., *Public Voices: Catholics in the American Context* (Maryknoll, N.Y., 1999), 237–42; David J. O'Brien, *Faith and Friendship: Catholicism in the Diocese of Syracuse, 1886–1986* (Syracuse, N.Y., 1986), 287.

67. OGS, box 24, folder Communism . . . Report.

68. "Report on Communist Investigation, April, 1945" ("filling in"); "Report on Communist Investigation, May, 1945" ("thus reduce"), OGS, box 24, folder Communism . . . Report."

69. "Report on Communist Investigation, May, 1945."

70. My guess, supported by Athan Theoharis to Rosswurm, September 27, 2005, is that Tamm wrote this uninitialed comment on an unserialized routing slip in 100-337494. (Hoover certainly did not.) The paper trail for the final approval is incomplete and indirect. In neither Cronin's FBIHQ file, 94-35404, nor the one captioned "Social Action Department (National Catholic Welfare Conference)," 100-337494, is anything said explicitly about the FBI decision to provide hundreds of pages of information to Cronin in the summer and fall of 1945. What there is, however, is Hoover's notation, in a letter to Chicago SAC Drayton, June 28, 1945, 100-337494-7, that FBIHQ was in the "process of preparing answers"; Hoover's transmittal of information to Cronin through Father Robert Lloyd, S.J., in Hoover to [Lloyd], October 24, 1945, 100-3-1177, and September 13, 1945, 94-4-3263-62. Also see Tamm's Memorandum for the Director, January 2, 1946, 94-35404-46X.

71. Cronin to Alter, May 1, 1945 ("certain delicate"), and Cronin to Alter, May 12, 1945 ("My own"), AP, box 7, folder 5.

72. Cronin to Alter, June 5, 1945 ("high official"), and Cronin to Alter, June 16, 1945, ("grapevine"), ibid.

73. "Report on the Communist Investigation," June, 1945, OGS, box 24, Communism . . . Report. By the time Cronin wrote this report, which he sent on June 30, he probably had received the first FBI memorandum. Dated June 13, 1945, it was captioned "Financial Resources of the Communist Political Association." The "set of memoranda" given to Cronin is in L. L. Tyler Office Memorandum for Tamm, June 28, 1947, 94-35404-55.

74. "Report on the Communist Investigation," June 1945 ("necessary to," "the leader"); Cronin to Dempsey, June 5, 1945, AP, box 7, folder 5 ("economic law").

75. Cronin to Higgins, July 17, 1945, SAD, box 8, folder 16.

76. Ibid.

77. Ibid.

78. Ibid.

79. Ibid.

80. Brogan to Stritch, July 13, 1945, attached to Stritch to Brogan, July 16, 1945, CC, box 2964.

81. Stritch to Alter, July 16, 1945, AP, box 13, folder 28 ("spent a"); Cronin to Stritch, July 26, 1945, CC, box 2967.

82. "Report on the Communist Investigation for August, 1945," OGS, box 24, folder Communism . . . Report.

83. Katherine A. S. Sibley, *Red Spies in America: Stolen Secrets and the Dawn of the Cold War* (Lawrence, Kans., 2004), 165–66; Gregg Herken, *Brotherhood of the Bomb: The Tangled Lives and Loyalties of Robert Oppenheimer, Ernest Lawrence, and Edward Teller* (New York, 2002), 218.

84. Cronin to Alter, September 6, 1945, AP, box 7, folder 5; Cronin to Carroll, October 7, 1945, OGS, Box 24, folder Communism . . . Report; Robert Chadwell Williams, *Klaus Fuchs, Atomic Spy* (Cambridge, Mass., 1987), 78.

85. "Report on the Communist Investigation for August, 1945."

86. If this scenario seems farfetched, consider this: Monsignor Charles Owen Rice picked up the story of atomic secrets and Soviet espionage from Pittsburgh Field Office agents. Their account, as he remembered it years later, contained much that is now known to be true; Rosswurm interview with Rice, June 12, 1986, St. Anne's Rectory, Castle Shannon, Pittsburgh.

87. Victor Rabinowitz, *Unrepentant Leftist: A Lawyer's Memoir* (Urbana, 1996), 39.

88. Cronin to Alter, September 6, 1945.

89. Binder attached to L. L. Tyler Memorandum for Tamm, June 28, 1947, 94-35404-55; Hoover to Lloyd, September 13, 1945; Hoover to [Lloyd], October 24, 1945.

90. "Report of Communism Investigation, September, 1945," OGS, box 24, folder Communism . . . Report. It is possible, in my discussion of Murphy here and in the remainder of the chapter, that I have underestimated the importance of Mandel and Isaac Don Levine; see, for example, Cronin to Harland H. Vinnedge, May 30, 1974, JCP, box 2, folder 25.

91. Ted Morgan, *A Covert Life: Jay Lovestone, Communist, Anti-Communist, and Spymaster* (New York, 1999), 146–51, 149 ("saw himself); D. M. Ladd to the Director, October 18, 1947, 62-85541-1 ("old line").

92. Cronin to Carroll, September 25, 1945 ("discuss the"), and September 29, 1945 ("is as"), OGS, box 24 folder Communism . . . Report; Cronin to Alter, September 29, 1945, AP, box 7, folder 5 ("has quite").

93. "Report of Communist Investigation," September 1945, folder Communism . . . Report."

94. Cronin to Carroll, October 21, 1945, OGS, box 24, folder Communism . . . Report; Allen Weinstein, *Perjury: The Hiss-Chambers Case* (New York, 1979), 347; Sullivan, *The Bureau: My Thirty Years in Hoover's FBI* (New York, 1979), 36, 39. Weinstein draws from his interview with Cronin. I requested access to it, but Weinstein did not respond; Rosswurm to Weinstein, July 28, 1989, carbon copy in possession of author.

95. Cronin to Carroll, October 7, 1945, OGS, box 24, folder Communism . . . Report."

96. Cronin to Carroll, October 21, 1945 (quotations), and Carroll to Cronin, October 29, 1945, ibid.

97. Cronin to Stritch, November 4, 1945 ("contacts"), and Stritch to Cronin, November 9, 1945 ("confidentially"), CC, box 2964; Cronin to Alter, November 5, 1945, AP, box 7, folder 6 ("Each of").

98. Minutes of the Meeting of the Administrative Board, NCWC, November 12, 1945, CC, box 2968.

99. [Alter] to Carroll, November 28, 1945, and Alter to Your Excellency, December 4, 1945, OGS, box 24, folder "Communism . . . Report."

100. Cronin, "The Problem of American Communism in 1945: Facts and Recommendations," 2–4, FMP.

101. Ibid., 5–6.

102. Ibid., 11, 15.

103. Ibid., 15.

104. Ibid., 23, 30.

105. Cronin to Alter, November 5, 1945.

106. Steve Rosswurm, "Communism and the CIO: Catholics and the 1944 Presidential Campaign," *USCH*, 19, no. 4 (Fall 2001): 73–86.

107. Cronin, "Problem of Communism," 44a.

108. Ibid.

109. Ibid., 48.

110. Ibid., 49.

111. Ibid.

112. Ibid., 50. Josephine Adams, Harold Young, Nathan Witt, Harold White (i.e., Harry Dexter White), and Edwin S. Smith were the other five. The four were Frank Coe, Harold Glasser, Michael Greenberg, and Allen Rosenberg. See Lauren Kessler, *Clever Girl: Elizabeth Bentley, The Spy Who Ushered in the McCarthy Era* (New York, 2003), 325, 132n.

113. Cronin, "Problem of Communism," 50.

114. Ibid., 55, 60.

115. Ibid., 61.

116. Ibid., 66.

117. Ibid., 67, 69, 70.

118. Ibid., 71.

119. Ibid., 80.

120. Alter to Carroll, November 1, 1945, OGS, box 88, folder, 1945.

121. Cronin to Alter, November 13, 1945, AP, box 7, folder 6.

122. Ibid.

123. Cronin to Alter, December 8, 1945, AP, box 7, folder 6.

124. Alter to Cronin, December 12, 1945 ("a clear"), and Alter to Cronin, December 22, 1945 ("outlining your"), ibid.

125. Donovan, *Crusader in the Cold War*, 165–67; Weinstein, *Perjury*; Ronald Radosh and Joyce Milton, *The Rosenberg File: A Search for the Truth* (New York, 1983); John Earl Haynes and Harvey Klehr, *Venona: Decoding Soviet Espionage in America* (New Haven, 1999); R. Bruce Craig, *Treasonable Doubt: The Harry Dexter White Spy Case* (Lawrence, Kans., 2004); Katherine A. S. Silbey, *Red Spies in America: Stolen Secrets and the Dawn of the Cold War* (Lawrence, Kans., 2004); Steven T. Usdin, *Engineering Communism: How Two Americans Spied for Stalin and Founded the Soviet Silicon Valley* (New Haven, 2005); 100-7602 (Roy Hudson); 100-11687 (John Williamson); Victor Rabinowitz, *Unrepentant Leftist: A Lawyer's Memoir* (Urbana, 1996); John J. Abt, *Advocate and Activist: Memoirs of an American Communist Lawyer* (Urbana, 1993); Steve Rosswurm, "The Wondrous Tale of an FBI Bug: What It Tells Us about Communism, Anti-Communism, and the CIO Leadership," *American Communist History* 2, no. 1 (June 2003): 3–20; Tamm Memorandum for Hoover, November 20, 1945, 100-337494-9.

126. Jerry W. Sanders, *Peddlers of Crisis: The Committee on the Present Danger and the Politics of Containment* (Boston, 1983).

127. Melvyn P. Leffler, *The Specter of Communism: The United States and the Origins of the Cold War, 1917–1953* (New York, 1994), 36, 52. For the stunning research that provides the particulars for this generalization, see Leffler, *A Preponderance of Power: National Security, the Truman Administration, and the Cold War* (Stanford, 1992).

128. Cronin, "The Problem of American Communism," 62.

129. Noll to Cronin, April 17, 1945, JNP, box 2, folder 30; Noll to Sheil, May 24, 1945, WJCP, Correspondence, box 6, folder 1945–1946.

130. Monaghan to Higgins, n.d., SAD, box 9, folder 12.

131. HAR to Father Daniel Cantwell, December 18, 1945, DCP, box 1, folder 5.

132. Cronin to Carroll, July 18, 1946, OGS, box 23, folder 1946. An almost identical letter went to Alter on July 18, 1946, AP, box 4, folder 30.

133. Cronin to Alter, February 9, 1946, AP, box 7, folder 7.

134. *Washington Post*, March 11, 1946, 1; handwritten comment on D. M. Ladd Memorandum for The Director, March 11, 1946, 94-35404-3.

135. D. M. Ladd Memorandum to Director, March 11, 1946, 100-17828-[26?] ("well acquainted"); J. C. Strickland Memorandum to Ladd, March 26, 1946, 100-17828-[24?] ("derogatory information"); Strickland to Ladd, March 29, 1946, 100-17828-25; *FBI File on J. Robert Oppenheimer* (microfilm, 1979), reel 1. I learned of this incident from Sibley, *Red Spies in America*, 201. Cronin's name is deleted in the memoranda, but there is no doubt the reference is to him.

136. Walter to Robert E. Stripling, March 31, 1948, Cronin FBI Files, box 1, folder 5, MUDSC.

137. Cronin, "Dean Acheson," OGS, box 23, folder 1949.

138. Cronin to Alter, December 8, 1945.

5. A Jesuit Informant

1. Conway to Rev. Father Provincial, April 24, 1954, EACP. I researched Conway's papers at Creighton University, where he was teaching when he died. They had been, from all appearances, untouched since then. The papers, closed to researchers, are now at the Midwest Jesuit Archives in St. Louis. I have photocopies of the most important documents. I came across Joseph S. Rossi's extensive discussion of Conway's activities at the UN's founding conference long after I had drafted this chapter, but it confirms much of what I assert about Conway's modus operandi, personality, and character traits; see, for example, Rossi, *American Catholics and the Formation of the United Nations* (Lanham, Md., 1993), 20, 47–49, 52, 117–18, 185–87, 284. Rossi did not research in the EACP.

2. Jessica Wang discusses Conway's role in Melcher's firing in *American Science in an Age of Anxiety: Scientists, Anticommunism, and the Cold War* (Chapel Hill, 1999), 67–74, but she did not look at nearly as wide a range of sources as I have taken into account. Her analysis, moreover, is considerably different. Alice Kimball Smith, who may have known a good bit more than she revealed about the Melcher firing, repeats the official version in *A Peril and a Hope: The Scientists Movement in America, 1945–1947* (Chicago, 1965), 324–28. Rossi, for no apparent reason, quotes from one of Conway's reports on his meeting with the FBI in *American Catholics*, 269 n65. Donald A. Strickland devotes very little attention to the NCAI and none to the Melcher incident, but his book helps establish the context of the NCAI; see Strickland, *Scientists in Politics: The Atomic Scientists Movement, 1945–1946* (West Lafayette, Ind., 1968).

3. These generalizations are based on a wide-ranging set of sources, but especially EACP. For the "Pattern for Peace," see "Religious Leaders Issue Peace Plan," *NYT*, October 7, 1943, 15; for the UN recommendations, see "Three Faiths Map Ideas for Charter," *NYT*, April 5, 1945, 14.

4. On the funding of Conway's activities, see Conway to Father Zacheus Maher, August 17, 1943, EACP; and McGowan to Alter, February 16, 1945, AP, box 4, folder 14.

5. Maher to Conway, April 11, 1945, EACP.

6. Paul Boyer, *By the Bomb's Early Light: American Thought and Culture at the Dawn of the Atomic Age* (New York, 1985), 22.

7. "Monopoly of Atom Seen as Visionary," *NYT*, November 9, 1945, 3.

8. Conway, "Participation in the Development of Our National Policy on Atomic Development," December 12, 1945, EACP; Conway to Joseph A. Rock, S.J., December 5, 1945, EACP ("informal advisor"). The only thing approaching official approval that I have found for Conway's participation in the NCAI is a reference to a memo from Carroll to him on January 2, 1946. The NCWC's secretary general had sent Conway's December 12 memo to Stritch, who wrote: "'I am returning the report of Father Conway. It is very interesting. I hope that he carries on in this work"; Conway, "Memorandum to H.E. Cardinal Stritch," April 29, 1946, CC, box 2973.

9. Conway, "Participation in the Development."

10. "Report on Further Activities in Connection with Public Policy on Atomic Energy," December 20, 1945, EACP. (There also is a copy in OGS, box 93, folder U.S. Gov't.: Atomic Energy, 1945.) Victor Rabinowitz notes that Popper was "close" to the Party, "if not [a] member"; Rabinowitz, *Unrepentant Leftist: A Lawyer's Memoir* (Urbana, 1996), 122.

11. Conway to Alter, January 14, 1946, OGS, box 93, folder U.S. Gov't.: Atomic Energy, 1946, 1948. (There also is a copy in AP, box 4, folder 25, and EACP.) For the Dublin group, see "World Government Is Urged to Bar Ruin in Atomic War," *NYT*, October 17, 1945, 1.

12. Conway, "Memorandum to H.E. Cardinal Stritch," April 29, 1946; Guy Hottel, SAC, Washington, D.C., Field Office (FO), to Hoover, January 17, 1947, Washington FO File, 65-4736-63 ("close personal"); Hottel, Washington FO SAC, to Hoover, March 12, 1946, 100-344452-5X; Conway, "Memorandum to Stritch"; Hottel, Washington FO SAC, to Hoover, March 12, 1946; Cronin to Alter, March 9, 1946, AP, box 7, folder 7. I have assumed that Conway's memo and the letter to Alter of January 14 refer to the same initial visit. As for the first Hottel item, I do not think that the deleted reference could be to anyone other than Conway. Jessica Wang shared with me the Washington FO files (65-4736) on FAS. All further references to these files will be from her copies received under the FOIA.

13. D. M. Ladd Memorandum to Director, March 11, 1946, 100-344452-[5].

14. Hottel to Hoover, January 17, 1947.

15. Harvey Klehr, John Earl Haynes, and Kyrill M. Anderson, The *Soviet World of American Communism* (New Haven, 1998), 139 n24 ("Soviet security"); John Earl Haynes and Harvey Klehr, *Early Cold War Spies: The Espionage Trials That Shaped American Politics* (New York, 2006); Athan Theoharis, *Chasing Spies: How the FBI Failed in Counterintelligence but Promoted the Politics of McCarthyism in the Cold War Years* (Chicago, 2002).

16. Haynes and Klehr, *Early Cold War Spies*; Theoharis, *Chasing Spies*.

17. Conway, "Memorandum to Stritch" (quotations); [deleted] to Hottel, April 5, 1946, WFO 65-4736-11; [deleted] to Hottel, May 14, 1946, Washington FO, 65-

4736-13; [deleted] to Hottel, June 4, 1946, Washington FO, 65-4736-18; [deleted] to Hottel, June 14, 1946, Washington FO, 65-4736-19. The quotations throughout this discussion are from Conway's memo unless otherwise noted.

18. "Attention Ickes and Roosevelt!" *New Leader*, April 27, 1946, 5.

19. For Calkins, see Richard G. Hewlett and Oscar E. Anderson Jr., *The New World: A History of the United States Atomic Energy Commission*, vol. 1, *1939–1946* (Berkeley, 1990), 487. There are no references in NSG to Calkins. John Abt, Hillman's adviser and the general counsel of his union, was a secret CPUSA member, but there is no indication that Conway had his influence in mind.

20. Smith, *A Peril and a Hope*, 240, 397–98, 400–401 (Bell); NSG, no. 4, 113–14 (Falk). I checked the master index to the HUAC hearings as well as the indexes in Lauren Kessler, *Clever Girl: Elizabeth Bentley, the Spy Who Ushered in the McCarthy Era* (New York, 2003); John Earl Haynes and Harvey Klehr, *Venona: Decoding Soviet Espionage in America* (New Haven, 1999); R. Bruce Craig, *Treasonable Doubt: The Harvey Dexter White Spy Case* (Lawrence, Kans., 2003); Michael J. Ybarra, *Washington Gone Crazy: Senator Pat McCarran and the Great American Communist Hunt* (Hanover, N.H., 2004); Allen Weinstein and Alexander Vassiliev, *The Haunted Wood: Soviet Espionage in America—the Stalin Era* (New York, 1999).

21. Ellen Schrecker, *Many Are the Crimes: McCarthyism in America* (Boston, 1998), 43; HUAC, *Hearings on H.R. 1884 and H.R. 2122, March 24–28, 1947* (Washington, D.C., 1947), 138, 139, 141; 100-44542.

22. Concerning Lamb and Margolin, the Bureau may have confused two Margolins: one named Olga, the other Olya. During the GREGORY investigation the Bureau picked up on a Margolin, who was close to a key subject. At one point the report spelled her name Olga, at another Olya. This Margolin was working for the State Department. See NSG, no. 2, 263; no. 5, 243, 250; Haynes and Klehr, *Venona*, 113–14. For Lamb, see "4 CIO 'Left-Wing' Aide Quits," *NYT*, July 23, 1947, 12; Irving Richter, *Labor's Struggles, 1945–1950: A Participant's View* (New York, 1994), 25 ("close to"). For Helen Lamb, see NSG, no. 5, 249. Richter has a somewhat different characterization of Lamb several sentences later. There is an innocuous mention in NSG, no. 4, 156.

23. Haynes and Klehr, *Venona*, 152–57 (Straight). The NCAI material in Jackson's papers at the FDRL, box 57, is primarily for NCAI's later history.

24. Melcher to Frances Day, November 13, 1946, MFP, box 24.

25. MFP; *Melcher on Melcher—From Boyhood to Bowker and Beyond: The Catalogue of an Exhibition in Commemoration of the Second Anniversary of the Gift to the University of Virginia Library of the Papers of Daniel Melcher* (Charlottesville, 1995); John Tebbel, *A History of Book Publishing in the United States*, vol. 4 (New York, 1981).

26. Ted R. Gamble to Ralph McDonald, January 25, 1946, FASP, box 19, folder 2 ("turned in"); Melcher to Ralph E. Shikes, October 26, 1943, and Melcher to "Dear Family," January 24, 1943, MFP, box 24. The surviving Schools at War material, Record Group 56, NA, consists almost entirely of anonymously produced brochures and flyers.

27. Melcher to Ed and Lou, December 5, 1945; Melcher to Ellie, December 9, 1945; Melcher to Mom and Dad, September 11, 1945; Melcher to Joseph Gaer, June 8, 1944; Melcher to Fred, [1944?]; Melcher to Ted Wilson, June 22, 1945; and Melcher to Lewis Merrill, December 15, 1946, all MFP, box 24; Julia L. Mickenberg, *Learning from the Left: Children's Literature, the Cold War, and Radical Politics in the United States* (New York, 2006), 14 n42.

28. Segure to Melcher, October 6, 1946, February 10, 1947, and September 16, 1948;

Melcher to Bacon, January 22, 1945; Bacon to Melcher, January 25, 1945, and [June 1945], all MFP. On Bacon, see Mickenberg, *Learning from the Left*.

29. For the Keeneys, see Haynes and Klehr, *Venona*, 178–80; "Testimony of Philip O. Keeney and Mary Jane Keeney and Statement Regarding Their Background," *Hearings before the Committee on Un-American Activities*, House of Representatives, Eighty-first Congress, 1st sess., May 24, 25, and June 9, 1949 (Washington, D.C., 1949), 254; "Hello from Peggy and Dan Melcher," August 1946, NCAIP, box 68, folder Daniel Melcher—Memos. The reference is to "Angus Keeny," but I have no doubt that this is the same person as Philip Keeney. Melcher notes that he currently was in Japan, as was Philip Keeney. For Wasserman, see NSG, no. 4, 36 ("a strongly"), 262, 279–81.

30. NSG, no. 4, 281 ("been in"); no. 4, 155; no. 5, 233; Haynes and Klehr, *Venona*, 100–104; NSG, no. 4, 155, 262, 275.

31. NSG, no. 4, 172, 281; no. 5, 35–36, 37, 41; Haynes and Klehr, *Venona*, 111, 113–14; Melcher to Harry S. Wender, September 12, 1946, MFP, box 24.

32. Marzani, *The Education of a Reluctant Radical: From Pentagon to Penitentiary*, bk. 4 (New York, 1995), 97; Alan Strachan to Dick [Leonard], February 23, 1947, WPRP, box 88, folder 5; "4 CIO 'Left-Wing' Aide Quits," 12. For Marzani, also see Washington, D.C., Report, July 31, 1942, 77-23443-9.

33. See Mickenberg, *Learning from the Left*, esp. 11–12, 12 n35, 142, 225, 230, 274.

34. Marzani, *Education*, 156.

35. "The Reminiscences of William A. Higinbotham," 1998, 2, in the Oral History Collection of Columbia University; "Interview with Robert F. Bacher," Caltech Archives, 1983, 68, oralhistories.library.caltech.edu/93/01/OH_Bacher_R.pfd (accessed August 13, 2007).

36. Higinbotham to Rev. A. Powell Davies, July 21, 1947; Higinbotham to Oppenheimer, November 27, 1946, OP, box 120, folder General Correspondence July–December 1946. For Gold's *Daily Worker* article, see my discussion at the end of this chapter.

37. "Reminiscences of Higinbotham," 39–40.

38. Ibid., 40; Chicago Report, October 10, 1946, 100-344452-22; SAC, Chicago, to Director, FBI, December 17, 1946, 100-344452-3[2]; Wang, *American Science*, 74, 74 n93; Strickland, *Scientists in Politics*, 89.

39. Amrine to Maude Lennox, December 25, 1949, MAP, box 2, folder 35; 140-26111; 116-68437; www.aip.org/history/ead/aip_goudsmit/20000092_content.html (accessed March 19, 2006).

40. Armrine to Lennox, December 25, 1949; George A. Albee, "Exploring a Controversy," *American Psychologist*, March 2002, 162 ("in-house").

41. Higinbotham to Melba Phillips, January 16, 194[6], FASAP, box 1, folder 11002.

42. "Notes on Employment of Michael Amrine by FAS," FASAP, box 1, folder 11004.

43. "Statement of Michael Amrine[,] July 22, 1946," OGS, box 93, folder U.S. Gov't.: Atomic Energy, 1946–1948 (unless otherwise noted, the discussion that follows is drawn from this document); "Conway, "Memorandum re Activities of National Committee on Atomic Information" ("lengthy deposition," "instigation"); Robert Franklin Maddox, *The Senatorial Career of Harley Martin Kilgore* (New York, 1981), 52–53, ("became"); NSG, no. 2, 171, 173, 180; no. 4, 119, 125, 128; no. 5, 146, 182, 183, 189, 249, 269. Conway did not date the second item; the suggested archival date is July 1946. On the basis of internal evidence, however, it can be narrowed down much further: from July 23 to July 26, 1946.

44. Smith, *A Peril and a Hope*, 151.

45. Higinbotham [Memo?], January 3, 1946, ASCP, box 14, folder 5.

46. Unless otherwise noted, the discussion that follows comes from "Hello from Peggy and Dan Melcher," August 1946; Melcher to NCAI Executive Committee, June 3, 1946, NCAIP, box 62, folder Executive Committee (misc.); Melcher's report contained in Council Meeting of the Federation of American Scientists, June 22–23, 1946, ASCP, box 14, folder 2. The pamphlet *Education for Survival* was one of NCAI's most popular pieces of literature.

47. Nancy Larrick, "Eight Weeks in the National Committee on Atomic Information or *Pattern of Political Action*," MFP, box 24. Larrick included appendixes in the document, but they have not survived.

48. Hewlett and Anderson, *The New World*, chaps. 13, 14.

49. Higinbotham to Maurice Shapiro, March 1, 1946, FASAP, box 1, folder 11003 ("completely changed"); Higinbotham to All Sites, March 1, 1946, ASCP, box 14, folder 7 ("like the," "It is").

50. Higinbotham to Richard Sill, March 19, 1946 ("discredit scientists," "state that"); Higinbotham to Leo Brewer, March 19, 1946 ("difficult," "smeared"); Higinbotham to Sill, March 19, 1946, ("We could"), FASAP, box 1, folder 11003; "New Attack by McCarthy," *NYT*, October 24, 1950, 7.

51. Higinbotham to Sill, March 19, 1946; Conway to Mrs. Raymond Mahon, March 20, 1946, EACP.

52. "59 Groups Support Civil Atom Rule," *NYT*, March 22, 1946, 2; Hewlett and Anderson, *New World*, 510 ("there were").

53. Melvyn Leffler, *A Preponderance of Power: National Security, the Truman Administration, and the Cold War* (Stanford, 1993), 109.

54. NCAIP, box 96; Phillips to Lamb, April 25, 1946, FASAP, box 1, folder 11003; "Summary of Published Facts Concerning Canadian Spy Case," FASAP, box 7, folder 21057; Higinbotham, Phillips, and Rush to Dear Sir, May 8, 1946, FASAP, box 7, folder 21056F ("unfortunate effect").

55. M to Simpson, June 5, 1946, FASAP, box 1, folder 11005.

56. Higinbotham to the Administrative Committee, July 18, 1946, OP, box 120, folder FAS General Correspondence, July–December 1946 ("for editorializing"); Larrick, "Eight Weeks" ("There had"). Larrick dates this meeting as June 19, but there is no doubt that this is the one that occurred on June 9.

57. "Statement of Michael Amrine[,] July 22, 1946."

58. Ibid.

59. Ibid., Higinbotham to the Administrative Committee, July 18, 1946. Amrine's dating of the interview and the resulting discussions with Melcher do not fit with Higinbotham's account, but the gist of their stories appears to be accurate.

60. "Statement of Michael Amrine[,] July 22, 1946"; "Vetoing the Veto," *DW*, June 17, 1946, 7.

61. Handwritten notes on "Memorandum to Council Delegates," June 4, 1946, ASCP, box 16, folder 7.

62. "[?] Atomic Information," June 20, 1946, MAP, box 18, folder 16 ("political beliefs"); "Digest of a letter of June 21, from Amrine to Jackson transmitting Red-baiting charges which were dismissed, but which were followed by 5 Executive Committee Sessions closed to the Director," attached to Melcher to NCAI Executive Committee, August 6, 1946, ASCP, box 17, folder 14 (Amrine and Higinbotham absent); HD, June 18, 1946. William B. Higinbotham, Willy's son, shared his father's diary with me.

63. "Digest of a letter of June 21."

64. Melcher to Higinbotham, June 21, 1946, NCAIP, box 64, folder W. A. Higinbotham—Memos.

65. Larrick, "Eight Weeks"; "Report on the Meeting of the Executive Committee of the NCAI," June 23, 1946, ASCP, box 17, folder 14, UC.
66. Larrick, "Eight Weeks."
67. "[?] Atomic Information"; *AI*, April 22, 1946, 2, and June 3, 1946, 3.
68. *AI*, June 3, 1946, 3, and June 17, 1946, 9.
69. *AI*, April 22, 1946, 6 ("atomic bomb"), "[?] Atomic Information."
70. Larrick, "Eight Weeks"; Higinbotham to the Administrative Committee, July 18, 1946; "Report on the Meeting of the Executive Committee of the NCAI," June 23, 1946.
71. Conway to Alter, June 29, 1946, AP, box 4, folder 29. Amrine's comment ("Digest of a Letter of June 21") that he had seen Conway and knew that he had Higinbotham's proxy for the June 23 meeting suggests that the priest was secretly meeting with both.
72. Conway Memo to Carroll, May 31, 1946, EACP ("FBI contact"); Conway to Alter, June 13, 1946, AP, box 4, folder 29 ("continuing his"); Conway, "Report on E. A. Conway's Activities with National Committee on Atomic Information," [July 9, 1946], EACP ("phoned the," "had word," "she had").
73. Washington D.C. Report, September 17, 1946, 100-344452-77.
74. "Statement of Michael Amrine," July 22, 1946 ("and now"); "Report," July 9, 1946 ("red-baiting," "convinced that").
75. "Report," July 9, 1946 ("I have"); HD, July 1, 1946 ("Mike aroused").
76. Melcher to Bacon, March 27, 1943, MFP, box 24; "Statement of Michael Amrine," July 22, 1946.
77. HD, July 3, 1946 ("all upset"); Marzani, *Education*, 202; John J. Abt, *Advocate and Activist: Memoirs of an American Communist Lawyer* (Urbana, 1993), 117.
78. "Statement of Michael Amrine," July 22, 1946.
79. HD, July 4, 1946.
80. Strickland, *Scientists in Politics*, 52 ("private science"); Simpson to McDonald, July 5, 1946, reproduced, apparently in toto, in "Minutes of the Policy Committee Meeting of NCAI," July 27, 1946, FASP, box 19, folder 3; HD, July 5, 1946.
81. Larrick, "Eight Weeks ("on advice," "No interest");" Melcher, "Six Months of NCAI Activity, July 7, 1946, ASCP, box 14, folder 5; Higinbotham to Administrative Committee, July 18, 1946.
82. "Minutes," NCAI Executive Committee, July 7, 1946, ASCP, box 17, folder 14.
83. Ibid. ("extended discussion," "expressed much," "aspects," "desirable procedures," "correcting staff"); Higinbotham to Administrative Committee, July 18, 1946 (remaining quotations).
84. Conway to Alter, July 8, 1946, AP, box 4, folder 30 ("done on other"); Conway, "Memorandum re Activities," [July 23—July 26, 1946] ("the arguments"); Conway to Alter, July 8, 1946; Higinbotham to Administrative Committee, July 18, 1946 ("Any redbaiting").
85. HD, July 7, 1946.
86. Higinbotham to Administrative Committee, July 18, 1946 ("fairest," "the man"); HD, July 11, 1946 (remaining quotations).
87. Larrick, "Eight Weeks."
88. HD, July 11, 1946 ("told him," "this is"); Melcher Memo to McDonald, July 8, 1946, attached to Melcher to Oppenheimer, July 12, 1946, and Melcher to Oppenheimer, August 6, 1946, OP, box 138, folder NCAI (remaining quotations).
89. Melcher Memo to McDonald, July 8, 1946. All quotations in the discussion that follows are from this source. Two things about this memo are unclear. First, did

Melcher ever send it to McDonald? (I think he did). Second, did Melcher write it before or after he and the NCAI chair met on July 8? (I think before). My guess is that Melcher's giving the letter to McDonald triggered the meeting.

90. For his father's pressure, see Melcher to Melcher, April 13, 1946, July 10, 1946, MFP, box 24.

91. "Preliminary Report," June 26, 1946, *Congressional Record*, July 17, 1946, 92, pt. 7: 9257-9258; C. P. Trussell, "Peril to Security Seen in Oak Ridge," *NYT*, July 12, 1946, 5.

92. "Scientist Ridicules Charges," *NYT*, July 12, 1946, 5 ("naïve"); Rush to Atomic Scientists of Chicago, July 12, 1946, ASCP, box 15, folder 3 ("except in"); HD, July 13, 1946 (remaining quotations).

93. Maher to Conway, April 11, 1945, EACP.

94. Hottel to Director, July 10, 1946, 100-344452-13; Hottel to Director, July 23, 1946, 1009-344452-10; Washington FO Report, September 17, 1946, 100-344452-17; [deleted] to Hottel, July 23, 1946, Washington FO 65-4736-28; [deleted] to Hottel, July 31, 1946, Washington FO 65-4736-30; Conway, "Memorandum re Activities," [July 23–July 26, 1946] (all quotations). Most likely the FBI got a copy of the letter through a break-in at Melcher's house, since I strongly doubt that he would have left it lying around the office. McDonald may also have been the source, if Melcher had given it to him. Conway did not name the FBI as the source of the "proof" about Marzani, but it could not have been anyone else.

95. Conway, "Memorandum re Activities," [July 23–July 26, 1946].

96. Conway, "Memorandum re Activities," [July 23–July 26, 1946]; HD, July 14, 1946 ("He has"). I have assumed that Conway's reference to "an assistant to the Attorney General" means an assistant attorney general.

97. Kai Bird and Martin J. Sherwin, *American Prometheus: The Triumph and Tragedy of J. Robert Oppenheimer* (New York, 2005), 89; 100-346735; William A. Higinbotham et al. to McDonald, July 17, 1946, EA, 40-495 (quotations).

98. Francis T. Bonner, "Melba Newell Philllips (1907–[2004])," in Louise S. Grinstein et al., eds., *Women in Chemistry and Physics: A Bibliographic Sourcebook* (Westport, Conn., 1993), 488–94; Melcher to Einstein, July 18, 1946, EA, 40-494; Phillips to McDonald, July 17, 1946, FASA, box 1, folder 11006 (quotations).

99. HD, July 16, 1946.

100. Conway, "Memorandum re Activities," [July 23–July 26, 1946].

101. Higinbotham to Administrative Committee, July 18, 1946.

102. Ibid.

103. Ibid.

104. Melcher to Kenneth Leslie, February 11, 1947, MFP, box 24; Larrick, "Eight Weeks."

105. HD, July 19, 1946 ("This is"), and July 20, 1946 ("Decided about"); Amrine to Simpson, July 25, 1946, AP, box 18, folder 16 ("Present plans"); Conway, "Memorandum re Activities," [July 23–July 26, 1946].

106. McDonald to Administrative Committee of Federation of American Scientists, July 20, 1946, OGS, box 93, folder U.S. Gov't.: Atomic Energy: 1946–1948.

107. Melcher to Ruth Kistin, July 23, 1946, NCAIP, box 66, folder Ruth Kisten—Memos; Melcher to Edward L. Bernays, July 26, 1946, NCAIP, box 18, folder June 1946; HD, July 21, 22, 26, 1946; Conway, "Activities of the National Committee on Atomic Information," August 6, 1946, OGS, box 93, folder U.S. Gov't.: Atomic Energy, 1946–1948.

108. HD, July 21, 1946 ("Republicans feel," "stop or," "not so"); Higinbotham, "Memorandum to All Associations," July 25, 1945, ASCP, box 14, folder 7.

109. HD, July 24, 1946; Amrine to Simpson, July 25, 1946; HD, July 26, 1946.
110. Higinbotham and Rush to McDonald, July 26, 1946, OP, box 120, folder FAS General Correspondence, July–December, 1946.
111. Waldo Cohn to Executive Committee, NCAI, July 26, 1946, ASCP, box 17, folder 14; HD, July 27, 1946 (all quotations).
112. Melcher to Einstein, July 18, 1946; Higinbotham et al. to McDonald, July 17, 1946.
113. HD, July 27, 1946. There is no letter from Mrs. Condon around this date in EA.
114. Ibid.
115. HD, July 28, 1946.
116. Larrick, "Eight Weeks"; HD, July 29, 1946.
117. HD, July 30, 1946 ("more picking," "about a"), and July 31, 1946 (remaining quotations).
118. Rose W. Alpher et al. to Executive Committee, July 29, 1946, FASP, box 19, folder 2 (all quotations). The separate resignation letters of the two staff members have not survived, but Alpher's letter indicates that they were turned in. Only a stenographer and one of the "shipping boys" stayed; see "Hello from Peggy and Dan Melcher," August 1946.
119. Larrick to McDonald, July 29, 1946, FASP, box 19, folder 7; Britten to McDonald, July 31, 1946, attached to Melcher to Oppenheimer, July 8, 1946. Britten also signed Alpher's letter.
120. Higinbotham to Council Members, July 31, 1946, ASCP, box 14, folder 7; Schiff to McDonald, August 2, 1946, and Walter C. Michels to Higinbotham, August 8, 1946, NCAIP, box 46, folder Association of Philadelphia Scientists; Maury Shapiro to Phillips, August 6, 1946, ALASP, box 4, folder 8; Higinbotham to Robert S. Rochlin, August 7, 1946; Rush to Victor Lewinson, August 8, 1946; Rush to Shapiro, August 10, 1946; Higinbotham to Joseph Willets, August 13, 1946; Rush to Waldo Cohn, August 13, 1946, all FASAP, box 1, folder 11007.
121. HD, August 5, 1946 ("Melcher &"); Melcher to Einstein, July 31, 1946, EA, 40-499-1; McDonald to Einstein, August 5, 1946, and Einstein to McDonald, August 7, 1946, NCAIP, box 33, folder Einstein; HD, August 3, 1946 ("political issues"); EOD office memo to McDonald, August 14, 1946; Muste to McDonald, August 14, 1946; and McDonald to Muste and Swomley, August 26, 1946, NCAIP, box 33, folder Ralph McDonald. For Melcher's communication with Einstein, see EA 40-498, 40-500.
122. Conway, "Activities," August 6, 1946; "Communists Ousted from Atomic Unit," *Minneapolis Sunday Tribune*, August 4, 1946, 1, 10; Smith, *A Peril and a Hope*, 327–28; HD, August 7, 1946. Finney's article, despite Alice Kimball Smith's assertions in *A Peril and a Hope*, was fairly accurate in its main contours.
123. Higinbotham to Clark, August 4, 1946. Higinbotham kept a copy of this letter in his diary.
124. Conway, "Activities," August 6, 1946.
125. Stritch to Alter, July 22, 1946, and Alter to Conway, July 23, 1946, AP, box 4, folder 30; Conway, "Activities in Connection with National Committee on Atomic Information," August 20, [1946], OGS, box 93, folder U.S. Gov't.: Atomic Energy, 1946–1948 ("get a man"); McDonald Memorandum, August 30, 1946 ("writer on"); Smith, *A Peril and a Hope*, 328; Conway to Alter, September 19, 1946, AP, box 4, folder 32 ("forging along").
126. HD, October 31, 1946 ("an awful"), November 4, 1946; Higinbotham to Joseph Schaffner, November 8, 1946, and Higinbotham to Simpson, November 8, 1946, FASA, box 1, folder 11010; Simpson to Higinbotham, November 13, 1946, ASCP, box 13, folder 16; HD, November 6, 1946.

127. Casgrain to Conway, January 22, February 12, March 14 ("Such things"), March 24, April 1, 1947, NCAIP, box 32, folder Conway; Smith, *A Peril and a Hope*, 329; Glashen to Conway, n.d., NCAIP, box 32, folder Conway.

128. McDonald to Robert E. Marshak, January 7, 1949, FASP, box 49, folder 6.

129. The evidence indicates that Conway's interaction with the FBI waned as he left Washington for a position at St. Louis University and then Creighton. It waxed, however, for Amrine and Higinbotham as the former took a job at Brookhaven for a year and the latter for the rest of his life. Both men, but especially Higinbotham, had been and were situated where they could—and presumably thought they should—provide information to the FBI. For Conway, see Conway, "Behind the Baruch-Wallace Controversy on Control of Atomic Energy," October 10, 1946, AP, box 4, folder 34; Director to SAC, Washington, D.C., February 6, 1947, Washington FO 65-47326-79; Hottel, SAC, Washington FO, to Hoover, January 17, 1947, Washington FO 65-4736-63; Conway to Alter, January 15, 1947, AP, box 6, folder 21; Conway to Carroll, February 12, 1947, OGS, box 93, folder U.S. Gov't.: Atomic Energy 1946–1948. For Higinbotham, see HD; "Notes for Chapter Nine," note 4, www.brotherhoodofthebomb.com (accessed May 29, 2008); 100-346735. For Amrine, see 116-68437; Amrine to Stickle, March 25, 194[7], MAP, box 18, folder 16. (The letter is dated 1946, but that cannot be correct.)

130. Conway, "Behind the Baruch-Wallace Controversy on Control of Atomic Energy," October 10, 1946, AP, box 4, folder 34; Haynes and Klehr, *Venona*, 118, 119, 121, 128.

131. "Reminiscences of Higinbotham," 247.

132. Rush to John H. Gibbud, [after September 12, 1946], RP, box 2, folder 7.

133. Gold, "Can Atombomb Be Compared to Hitler Program of Murder?," *DW*, November 21, 1946, enclosed in Higinbotham to Oppenheimer, November 27, 1946, OP, box 120, folder General Correspondence, July–December 1946.

134. Bird and Sherwin, *American Prometheus*, 138, 172; Amrine to Morrison, July 22, FASAP, box 1, folder 11006; Amrine to Morrison, n.d. ("unnecessary"), and Morrison to Amrine, July 28, 1946 ("what we"), MAP, box 18, folder 16.

135. Kovel, *Red Hunting in the Promised Land: Anticommunism and the Making of America* (New York, 1994); Powers, *Not Without Honor: The History of American Anticommunism* (New York, 1995).

136. Melcher to F. R. von Windigger, March 1, 1946, NCAIP, box 18, folder March 1946 ("the proverbial"); Melcher to Day, October 12, 1946; Melcher to Harold Young, October 12, 1946; Melcher to Segure, September 10, 1948; and Melcher to Abe Seitz, November 1, 1948, MFP, box 24; Newark Report, June 18, 1962, 140-26111-14 ("general reputation").

137. "Some notes on A.I. copy policy," DM to EM, April 15, 1946, NCAIP, box 68, folder Marzani.

138. Melcher to Leslie, October 20, 1946.

139. There is a suggestion as to the FBI's conclusion about Melcher in *Melcher on Melcher*, 29. It is rather mysterious, but the document could not be located in Melcher's papers, nor did I find it in Melcher's FBI material.

6. Anti-communism in the CIO

1. Rice, "Response," in Steve Rosswurm, ed., "Symposium on *Fighter with a Heart: Writings of Monsignor Charles Owen Rice*," *LH* 40 (1999): 67. See Rice's 1990 newspaper column "Ghosts, Demons In: Flying Saucers Out," in Charles J. Mc-Collester, ed., *Fighter with a Heart: Writings of Charles Owen Rice, Pittsburgh Labor Priest* (Pittsburgh, 1996), 225–26.

2. Schatz, *The Electrical Workers: A History of Labor at General Electric and Westing-house, 1923–1960* (Urbana, 1983); McGeever, *Rev. Charles Owen Rice: Apostle of Contradiction* (Pittsburgh, 1989); Rice to Monsignor George C. Higgins, May 22, 1989, GHP, Correspondence, Hierarchy and Clergy.

3. Rice's concern about researchers working on his life can be seen in his correspondence with Monsignor George M. Higgins, GHP, Correspondence, Hierarchy and Clergy.

4. Gilpin, "Left by Themselves: A History of the United Farm Equipment and Metal Workers of America, 1938–1955" (senior thesis, Lake Forest College, 1981); Ross-wurm and Gilpin, "The FBI and the Farm Equipment Workers: FBI Surveillance Records as a Source for CIO Labor History," *LH* 27 (1986): 485–505.

5. Christopher Bailey, "Fr. Kazincy," *PC*, October 9, 1994, reprinted in *Pennsylvania Labor History Notes*, December 1994; William Z. Foster, *The Great Steel Strike and Its Lessons* (New York, 1920), 1187–118, 121–22; *SL*, August 20, 1936, 6.

6. Kenneth J. Heineman, *A Catholic New Deal: Religion and Reform in Depression Pittsburgh* (University Park, Pa., 1999), 123; "2,500 Attend Park Works Lodge Picnic," *SL*, August 26, 1937, 2; Rice to Clinton Golden, February 18, 1938, CORP, box 8, folder CIO 1937–1940; "Priest Defends Labor's Political Activities," *NW*, July 22, 1938; John L. Mayo to Rice, January 12, February 3, 1939, and George Medrick to Rice, June 21, 1939, CORP, box 8, folder CIO 1937–1940; "Priest Lauds Lewis, Other CIO Officers," *SL*, July 28, 1939, 3; Ernest Webb and M. Smiley to Rice, July 12, 1939, CORP, box 8, folder 1937–1940 ("went over"); Joseph F. Gallagher to Rice, n.d., and John F. Murray and Sam Nicastra to Rice, August 8, 1939, CORP, box 8, folder CIO 1937–1940 ("very anxious"); W. L. McGarry to Rice, December 12, 1939, CORP, box 25, folder 1939; "SWOC District Convention Here," *Allentown Morning Call*, January 14, 1940, 5, HCP, box 1, folder 14; T. Louis Majors to Rice, [Ap]ril 29, 1940, CORP, box 8, folder CIO 1937–1940; "Steelworkers' Picnic Sunday in Lincoln Park," *Bethlehem Globe Times*, July 12, 1940, HCP, box 1, folder 14; "'Hubbard Strikers Seek Only Orderly Conduct'— Father Rice," *PST*, September 30, 1940," Helping Those Arrested in Hubbard Fight," *PST*, September 30, 1940, HRuP, box 3, folder 13. Rice was invited to speak in Rankin, Pennsylvania, in February 1938, but it is unclear whether or not he did so; Anthony Santella to Rice, February 19, 1938, CORP, 8, folder 1937–1940. Rice also participated in radio programs for the Bethlehem organizing drive; Frank Fernbach Oral History, vol. 2, 24, HCLA; MBP, box 5, folder 6. See chap. 4 in Heineman, *A Catholic New Deal*, for a superb discussion of Catholics and SWOC in 1937. The Rice Papers at the University of Pittsburgh have been reorganized since I intensively researched them, so some of my citations are not relevant to the way they are now organized. I have chosen to leave them as they are rather than attempt to alter them from one form to the other.

7. McCollester, *Fighter with a Heart*, 230.

8. Heineman, *A Catholic New Deal*, 130–31 and passim; McGeever, *Rice*, 46–48.

9. Gilligan to Hayes, April 21, 1942, SAD, box 41, folder Social Action Survey; Kern to Hayes, April 7, 1943, SAD, box 41, folder Priest Study Group.

10. Rice to Boyle, n.d., CORP, folder 57.

11. Boyle to Rice, November 26, 1940, and March 28, 1941; Rice to Boyle, October 9, 1941 ("insults"), ibid.

12. Bishop William Foery telegram to Rice, June 26, 1938; Julius Rothman to Rice, November 22, 1938; and David J. McDonald to Rice, November 29, 1938, CORP, box 25, folder 1938; Kempton A. Williams to Rice, July 21, 1939, CORP, box 8,

folder CIO 1937–1940; *Ledger* [monthly newspaper of Local 16 of the United Office and Professional Workers Union], October 1937, 8, CORP(m), reel A; Rice to Bishop Edward F. Gibbons, May 7, 1938, CORP, box 25, folder 1938.

13. *193. CIO Convention Proceedings (Washington, D.C., 1938)*, 8.

14. "Not Many Reds in C.I.O. Except in New York," *CHC*, October 16, 1937, 2 ("'communistic," "ill-advised"); "Catholic Priest Lauds the CIO," *Textile Worker of New England*, August 1937, CORP(m), reel A (remaining quotations).

15. Rice to P. A. Bray, February 25, 1938, CORP, box 25, folder 1938 ("honey-combed," "surprisingly small," "many CIO," "extremely difficult"); Rice to Father Paul James Francis, April 4, 1939, CORP, box 22, folder UAW, April 4, 1939 (remaining quotations).

16. Quoted in Heineman, *A Catholic New Deal*, 156, 168.

17. Rice to Bishop Edmund F. Gibbons, May 7, 1938, CORP, box 25, folder 1938.

18. Gerald Zahavi, "'Communism Is No Bug-A-Boo': Communism and Left-Wing Unionism in Fulton County, New York, 1933-1950," *LH* 33 (1992): 169–77; "Leather Workers Reject CIO Affiliation at Mass Meeting," *Gloversville Morning Herald*, April 20, 1938, 3 (quotations).

19. Rice to Gibbons, May 7, 1938. .

20. "Leather Workers Reject CIO Affiliation at Mass Meeting."

21. Schatz, *Electrical Workers*, pt. 4; McGeever, *Rice*, chaps. 2, 3, 4; Philip Jenkins, *The Cold War at Home: The Red Scare in Pennsylvania, 1945–1960* (Chapel Hill, 1999), chap. 5; John P. Hoerr, *Harry, Tom, and Father Rice: Accusation and Betrayal in America's Cold War* (Pittsburgh, 2005).

22. Rice to Kersten, August 26, 1948, CORP, box 25, folder 1948. This letter, with the date given as August 26, 1946, not 1948, also is in *LH* 31 (1990): 405.

23. Rosswurm interview with Monsignor Charles Owen Rice, June 12, 1986, St. Anne's Rectory, Castle Shannon, Pittsburgh.

24. "The FBI and the CIO from 1940 to 1955," presented at the Organization of American Historians' Meeting, Philadelphia, April 1987.

25. *LH* 30 (1989): 449–62.

26. Diamond, "To the Editor," *LH* 31 (Summer 1990): 398, 402.

27. Diamond, "Labor History vs. Labor Historiography: The FBI, James B. Carey, and the Association of Catholic Trade Unionists," in *Religion, Ideology, and Nationalism in Europe and America: Essays Presented in Honor of Yehoshua Arieli* (Jerusalem, 1986), 299–328; Diamond, *Compromised Campus: The Collaboration of Universities with the Intelligence Community, 1945–1955* (New York, 1992).

28. Rice, "To the Editor," *LH* 31 (Summer 1990): 403. Rice first mentioned this interpretation of the incident in a letter to me of April 13, 1988, in which he commented on the scholarly paper that contained my assertion about the car.

29. Rosswurm, "The Catholic Church and the Left-Unions: Labor Priests, Labor Schools, and the ACTU," in Rosswurm, ed., *The CIO's Left-Led Unions* (New Brunswick, N.J., 1992), 132, 132 n39. I referred here to both the *Labor History* piece as well as Rice's letter.

30. McGeever interview with Rice, May 21, 1983, in author's possession; Rosswurm interview with Rice. These interviews are the source for the information about Duffy unless otherwise noted.

31. McGeever, *Rice*, 78.

32. *Progress*, January 1949, 10, CORP(m), reel B; McGeever, *Rice*, 119; McGeever interview with Rice, May 21, 1983. Rice's discussion of Duffy's expulsion was

quite disingenuous; *PC*, June 3, 1948, and September 30, 1948, TQP. He does not mention this expulsion in "A Good Man"; *PC*, November 30, 1961, 4.

33. ["Progressive Group"], [Fall 1949], CORP, box 8, folder Communism in Labor Movement, 1947–1950.

34. Rice, "A Good Man," 4.

35. Rice to Father Andrew Dzmura, July 3, 1948, CORP, box 22, folder United Electrical Workers, 1947–1949.

36. Rosswurm interview with Rice.

37. "Demand Action to Stem Layoffs," *Voice of the UE*, June 17, 1949, 1; "3,000 Vote in Election at UE-601," *PPG*, August 15, 1949, 1; "Probe Tied to UE Election," *PPG*, August 7, 1949, 3.

38. Ingrid Jewel, "Reds Bore in U.E. at Westinghouse," *PPG*, July 31, 1949, sec. 2, 1.

39. "'Quislings' Inspired UE Probe, Leftists Says," *PPG*, August 4, 1949, 1 ("an ambitious); "UE Leftists to Defy U.S. Probe," *PPG*, August 5, 1949, 1 ("With oratory"). Rice adopted the same strategy when he talked to the city's other paper, the *Sun-Telegraph*; "UE Chief Hits Father Rice on Red Probe," *PST*, August 4, 1949, 1, 2.

40. Rice to Dear Friend, August 1949, CORP, box 22, folder UE Correspondence A–C, 1949–1950; "UE Chief Hits Father Rice on Red Probe," *PST*, August 4, 1949, 2; "UE Leftists to Defy U.S. Probe," and "Un-Americans Call Hearing to Affect UE Elections," *Daily Worker*, August 8, 1949, 8, CORP, box 22, folder UE Corrrespondence A–C ("I won't").

41. "UE Leftists Refuse to Tell of Red Ties," *PPG*, August 11, 1949, 2.

42. "3,000 Vote in Election at UE-601," *PPG*, August 15, 1949, 1; "Left-Wingers Defeated in UE Vote," *PPG*, August 16, 1949, 1.

43. Michael Harrington, "Catholics in the Labor Movement: A Case History," *LH* 1 (1960): 257, 240 n30; Thomas E. Crehan, "Fr. Charles Owen Rice: Communism and Labor, 1938–1950" (M.A. thesis, Duquesne University, 1964), 75 ("the wrong"); McGeever, *Rice*, 125 ("suckered"); Rosswurm interview with Rice ("used," "set up"); McCollester, *Fighter with a Heart*, xvii (remaining quotations).

44. "Statement of William H. Peeler, Sr.," August 28, 1952, UEA, D6-308.

45. Ibid.

46. Ibid.

47. Ibid.; "The Boys in the Back Room," *UEN*, August 22, 1949, 4.

48. Goldstein, "UnAmerican Hearing Exposed as Plot by Outsiders to Keep Grip on UE Local," *UEN*, August 22, 1949, 4, 5.

49. "Here We Go Again,"*UEN*, August 22, 1949, 2.

50. Read Appointment Book, November 14, 1949, April 4, 1950, box 18, HRP; Frank Tavenner to Finnegan, September 2, 1949, IUEA, A2.05, folder "Communist Party: Marcel Scherer, 1949"; Finnegan to Benjamin Mandel, August 16, 1949, IUEA, A2.05, folder "Correspondence . . . Convention May–August, 1949," IUEA; Finnegan to Carey and Al Hartnett, [March 15–April 18, 1951], IUEA, B1.19, folder "Staff: Memos—Interoffice "Les Finnegan, 1949–1951"; Joseph T. Hawkins to Murray, October 1950, CIOSTO, box 64, folder UE May–December 1950. Archivists have reorganized the IUEA since I researched in them.

51. Finnegan to Smith, [July or August 1949], IUEA, A2.05, folder "Correspondence . . . Convention May–August, 1949"; "Daily Reminder," February 6, June 1, 2, 30, September 6, November 11, 1950, CIOSTO, box 256; "Daily Reminder," January 26, December 20, 1951, CIOSTO, box 256.

52. "Daily Reminder," April 24, May 8, June 22, 1950.

53. "Daily Reminder," June 1, December 19, December 21, 1950; "Sure, Philco Loves

Carey," *UEN*, November 28, 1949, 10; "Westinghouse Pays Salaries while Carey's CIO-IUE Organizers Travel," *The Dispatcher*, April 28, 1950, 9.

54. Damon Stetson, "To Speed UE Court Cases," *Newark Evening News*, December 3, 1949, 2; "Mr. Carey," n.d., CIOSTO, box 51, folder IUE 1950; CIOSTO, box 175, folder IUE 1949–1950.

55. "Forty-niners," IUEA, box 124, folder "Memo—Les Finnegan—1960"; IUE Local 755 Collection, IUE Local 804 Collection, IUE District Council 7 Collection (MS-49), IUE District Council 7 Collection (MS-116), and IUE Local 801 Collection, all WrSU; Steven Gietscher interview with Oakie Wornstaff, July 16, 1976, 15–16 (transcript), WrSU; Wornstaff interview, July 16, 1976, 10, and Gietscher interview with Wesley Steinhilber, December 6, 1976, pt. 1, 26–28 (transcript), WrSU; Gietscher interview with Robert Elsner, August 27, 1976, 24, 29, 32 (transcript), WrSU. See the numerous memos on individual UE officers and organizers in MS-49, box 2, folder 2, and box 11, folder 11. For the Dayton UE, see Joseph L. Mason, "Radicalism in Industrial Unions: The United Electrical Workers in Dayton, 1937–1955" (M.A. thesis, Wright State University, 1998).

56. Harrington, "Catholics in the Labor Movement," 257; Ronald L. Filippelli, "A Second Oral History Interview with Monsignor Charles Owen Rice," April 5, 1968, HCLA; Rice, "The Tragic Purge of 1948," *Blueprint for the Christian Reshaping of Society* (February 1977): 4. The paragraph in which Rice discusses the FBI in this last article was excised from the version published in McCollester, *Fighter with a Heart*, 96–98. Rice's discussion of the FBI in "Confessions of an Anti-Communist" also has been deleted in this collection.

57. The number of pages that Rice received comes from letters from the FBI to him dated November 30, 1977, and April 17, 1978. They were with the FBI material at his office. I am thankful to Suzanne Rinni, whose correspondence and sharing of FBI documents was of critical importance in the earliest days of this project. Patrick McGeever quite generously shared the FBI material that he received as a result of his FOI/PA request.

58. Rosswurm interview with Rice. Rice's story about repeating FBI information is verified in Carey's file, Pittsburgh Report, January 12, 1942, 62-62426-25.

59. Rosswurm interview with Rice.

60. Director, FBI, to SAC, Pittsburgh, May 26, 1947, 62-83517-1. McGeever also received a copy of this serial.

61. "To the Loyal American Workers of UE Local 601, UERWA !!!" December 1941, CORP(m), reel B; Rosswurm, "Manhood, Communism, and Americanism: The Federal Bureau of Investigation and American Jesuits, 1935–1960," Cushwa Center for the Study of American Catholicism, *Working Paper Series*, ser. 28, no. 2, Spring 1996, 7–9.

62. "Correlation Summary," December 14, 1970, 62-83517-6, 7, 8. This is a lengthy document, so I have provided page numbers. I am working here from McGeever's copy rather than from my handwritten notes taken from Rice's copy.

63. Ibid., 9.

64. Ibid., 9, 19, 20.

65. Ibid., 10.

66. Rosswurm, "The Wondrous Tale of an FBI Bug: What It Tells Us about Communism, Anti-Communism, and the CIO Leadership," *American Communist History* 2 (June 2003): 3–20.

67. May 21, 1983, interview with McGeever. The claim in the first sentence of this paragraph sounds like typical Rice self-promotion, but it could have been true.

68. Rosswurm, "Wondrous Tale of an FBI Bug," 19; Rice to Benjamin Masse, S.J., October 30, 1946, AmP, Box 49, folder 18, GUA. The talk with Murray, Rice wrote in this letter, occurred "some months ago."

69. Rosswurm, "Wondrous Tale of an FBI Bug," 15.

70. "Association of Catholic Trade Unionists," April 7, 1947, enclosure to SAC, Pittsburgh to Director, FBI, May 5, 1947, 100-80258-12; "Catholic Trade Unionists," April 15, 1947, enclosure to SAC, Pittsburgh to Director, FBI, 100-80258-11; "Association of Catholic Trade Unionists," May 20, 1947, "Association of Catholic Trade Unionists," May 20, 1947, 100-80258-1[4]. The first memo inexplicably reports that business said to have been done on April 15 in serial eleven of this file already had been accomplished.

71. "Association of Catholic Trade Unionists," September 26, 1947, 100-80258-15.

72. Rice, letter to the editor, *LH* 31 (1990): 403; Diamond, "Labor History vs. Labor Historiography," 325; Pittsburgh Reports, June 16, 1944, and August 7, 1946, 100-326165-1, 100-326165-7.

73. Filippeli, "Second Oral History Interview," 14.

74. Read to Marguerite Gahagan, December 18, 1948, HRP, box 3, folder ACTU; Rice to Joe [Sullivan], December 20, 1949, DeACTU, box 33, folder Riesel; Matles to General Executive Board etc., February 2, 1948, UEA, PM-129; *Progress*, May 1949, 12, CORP(m), reel B; Nichols, "Memorandum for Mr. Tolson," April 17, 1948, 62-83517-2 (quotations). This last source is another document that McGeever provided. In a letter of May 24, 2005, the FBI told me that it has no main file on Riesel. I do not see how this could be possible.

75. McGeever, *Rice*, 112.

76. [Deleted] Memo for SAC, March 22, 1950, Pittsburgh 100-655-14. I am again working from a McGeever document.

77. Rice to Bishop John F. Dearden, CORP, box 23, folder 515.

78. For Carey's testimony, see Joseph A. Loftus, "Electrical Union a Russian Front Says Carey of CIO," *NYT*, September 3, 1948, 1, 4. For the UE's refutation, see Ronald L. Filippelli, "UE: An Uncertain Legacy," *Political Power and Social Theory* 4 (1984): 237; "Basmajianon Leave," *NYT*, September 4, 1948, 26; *UE 1948 Convention Proceedings* (New York, 1948), 93–114. For the IUE's continuing assertions, see "Summary Report to the GE Conference Board," August 16, 1950, attached to "Organizational Report . . . August 25, 1950," IUEA, A.1.04, folder "Organizational Reports; Re: GE-UE Collusion;" GJP, box 37, folder IUE.

79. Memo for SAC, March 22, 1950.

80. Louis J. Twomey, S.J., "Go the Workingmen . . . Go to the Poor," *CM*, December 1938, 323 ("evils," "subversive elements"); Rosswurm, "Communism and the CIO: Catholics and the 1944 Presidential Election," *USCH* 19, no. 4 (Fall 2001): 78, 80, 82–86; Rosswurm, "Manhood, Communism, and Americanism," 7–9; Rosswurm, "The Catholic Church and the Left-Led Unions," 136.

81. Deborah Bernhardt interview with Father Philip Carey (transcript), February 19, 1981, Tamiment Library, 6; Carey to Editor, *Wage Earner*, [1944], DeACTU, box 11, folder Philip Carey ("sucked in"); Carey to Twomey, [November, 1951?], LTP ("I can").

82. Carey to Hoover, November 19, 1953, 14-4053-5809; Bernhardt interview with Carey, 43. Carey never uses the term "industrial squad," but it is clear from the context that this is what he is referring to.

83. "Minister Replies to Editorial in Tribune," *Tampa Morning Tribune*, March 10, 1944, 14. McAtee's stand was widely covered in the Catholic labor press: "Florida Priest Defends His Right to Protest against Anti-Labor Bills," *W*, April 1944, 7;

"Priest Answers Challenge," *LL*, April, 1944, 7; "Priest Answers Challenge," *LL*, April 20, 1944, 1.

84. McNally to Rice, April 7, 1947, CORP, box 22, folder Transport Workers, 1937–1940.

85. Ibid.

86. McNally to Rice, August 11, 1947, CORP, box 25, folder 1947.

87. Comey to Hoover, May 31, 1945, 94-1-9758-14x4.

88. SAC, Philadelphia, to Director, May 26, 1955, 94-46287-43; Comey to Carey, February 9, 1953; Director to Comey, June 1, 1955, 94-46287-43. Josh Freeman kindly provided me with a photocopy of Comey's letter to Carey which he made from the original in the Xavier Labor School papers at the ANYPSJ. It was not there when I went through the material in 1988.

89. Seattle Report, June 17, 1942, 100-80258-2.

90. Monsignor John F. Gallagher to Victor LoPinto, November 15, 1940, Organizations, ACTU, 1938–1958, SAA; Father Charles Keenen, S.J., to Hayes, August 24, 1941, SAD, box 41, folder Social Action Survey; Father Joseph Dougherty to Leo Hagen, September 5, 1941, Chancery Memo to *Progress*, September 16, 1941, and Shaughnessy, "Memorandum," August 31, 1942, Organizations, ACTU, 1938–1958, SAA.

91. Seattle Report, June 17, 1942.

92. Shaughnessy, "Memorandum" ("anti-clericalism"); Reinhold to Father Daniel Cantwell, November 4, 1942, DCP, box 1, folder 3; 100-90147 ("where he"); Seattle Report, June 17, 1942 (remaining quotations). For Reinhold, see Jay P. Corrin, *Catholic Intellectuals and the Challenge of Democracy* (Notre Dame, 2002). chap. 10.

93. This portrait draws upon many disparate sources, but a good starting place is Ste. Marie's vertical file at Wayne State University in Detroit.

94. Bugas to Hoover, March 31, 1942, 100-26844-11.

95. SAC, Chicago, to Director, February 26, 1942, 100-44933-2. Read provides an outline of his CIO career in "Even Errors of Past 10 Years Help Swell Accomplishment," *WE*, September 1949, 4.

96. Hoover to SAC, New York, May 25, 1943, 100-80258-5.

97. Diamond, "Labor History vs. Labor Historiography," 323 ("interview Paul," "maintain contact"); Cronin to Bishop Karl Alter, June 5, 1945, AP, box 7, folder 5 ("now working"). The context provides the identity of "my friends." I could not find the source for the "interview Paul" quote in the ACTU file that was released to me; according to 322, n17, that is where it should be found. The second document also was not released in the ACTU file I received.

98. Director to New York Field Office, May 25, 1943, as discussed in S. J. Drayton to Director, July 7, 1943, 100-44933-3; Read to Monsignor [Reynold Hillenbrand], May 9, 1943, CCWLP, box 1, folder 1941–1943.

99. "Harry C. Read," August 8, 1946, enclosure in Ladd to Tamm, August 8, 1946, 100-44933-4.

100. Ibid.

101. Harry Read Appointment Books, February 24, 1948, January 10, 1949, January 19 and 30, 1950, HRP, box 18.

102. Ibid., February 4, 1948; Rice to Dearden, May 13, 1950; "Parole Hearing Sought by Kersten for Joe Fay," *Milwaukee Journal*, October 16, 1953, 1, 2.

103. G. A. Nease, Memorandum for the Director, August 31, 1948, 62-62426-58.

104. "August 24, 1948," 62-62426-56.

105. On Carey as a CP member, see J. S. Adams Memorandum for A. Rosen, March

29, 1941, 62-62426-5; Washington Report, April 2, 1941, 62-62426; New York Report, April 3, 1941, 62-62426-7. On the investigations, see Hoover Memorandum for Matthew F. McGuire, April 5, 1941, 62-62426-7; Hoover Memorandum for Wayne Coy, July 15, 1942, 62-62426-36.

106. "Statement of James Barron Carey made in the presence of Special Agents [deleted] and [deleted] and Stenographer [deleted] of the Federal Bureau of Investigation. Questions by Agent [deleted]," May 9, 1942, Washington Field Office Report, May 27, 1942, 62-62426-36.

107. New York City Report, April 3, 1941, 62-62426-7; Ronald L. Filippelli and Mark D. McColloch, *Cold War in the Working Class: The Rise and Decline of the United Electrical Workers* (Albany, N.Y., 1995), 36, 58-64; "The Reminiscences of Jacob Samuel Potofsky," 1963–64, 663, in the Oral History Collection of Columbia University.

108. "Correlation Summary," 24, December 9, 1960, 62-62426-96.

109. D. M. Ladd Memorandum to Tamm, March 13, 1944, 62-62426-42.

110. Tamm Office Memorandum for Director, March 14, 1944, 62-62426-43.

111. Ibid.

112. Ladd Memorandum for Tamm, March 23, 1944, 62-62426-41.

113. Tamm Office Memorandum for Hoover, March 14, 1944.

114. The source for the installation of the bug comes from a "symbol number sensitive source index" card obtained through the FOI/PA. (There also is a serialized record of the bug's installation; Philadelphia teletype, January 1, 1947, 100-11687-[147]). For the memorandum and notes, see CIOSTO, box 109, folder Hearings, FTA, Correspondence 1946–1949.

115. "Electrical Union Is Accused as Red," *NYT*, December 20, 1948, 7.

116. Hoover Memorandum for Tolson and Ladd, April 13, 1949, 62-62426-NR.

117. L. B. Nichols Office Memorandum for Tolson, February 9, 1945; Baumgardner Memorandum to Belmont, April 21, 1959, 62-62426-NR ("allowed to"); "Correlation Summary," 80, December 9, 1960, 62-62426-96 ("blind memoranda"); "Daily Reminder," January 12, 1950, CIOSTO, box 256; "Correlation Summary," 67, July 14, 1954, 100-326165-42; "Correlation Summary," 84, December 9, 1960, 62-62426-96 (remaining quotations). The FBI released the Finnegan documents in a letter of August 24, 2001. Most of the file numbers are impossible to read. This entry does not specifically name Finnegan as the person taking the notes, but on the basis of the document previously discussed, I have assumed that he is the person who went to FBIHQ.

118. For Carey, see Hoover Memorandum for Ladd et al., January 18, 1954, 62-62426-80; for Finnegan, see M. A. Jones Memorandum to DeLoach, December 6, 1965, Finnegan release.

119. Rice to Dearden, May 13, 1950; McGeever interview with Rice, May 21, 1983.

120. Jenkins, *The Cold War at Home*, 78, 79; Daniel J. Leab, *I Was a Communist for the FBI: The Unhappy Life and Times of Matt Cvetic* (University Park, Pa., 2000), 51–52.

121. Leab, *I Was a Communist*, 50 ("certainly had"); Jenkins, *Cold War at Home*, 81.

122. "Fitzpatrick the Patriot," 601 Records, Box 5, folder F, AIS (quotations); Hoerr, *Harry, Tom, and Father Rice*, 130.

123. 601 Records, box 4, folder DD—Communism Red Baiting, AIS.

124. 100-326165.

125. "200 UE Communists Named!" *IUE News*, May 22, 1950, GJP, box 37, folder IUE-CIO (quotations); Oversize, JaCP.

126. IUEA, A2.05, folder "UE Organizers and International Reps in Communist Party"; folder "Communist Party: Sidney Mason, 1949 Affidavits and Explanation."

127. "Hearings Regarding Communist Infiltration . . . Part I," in *Hearings before the Committee on Un-American Activities, House of Representatives*, 81 Cong., 1st sess., August 9 and 10, 1949, 653–81.

128. Hartnett to Finnegan, February 16, 1950, IUEA, B1.19, folder "Finnegan" ("some background");. Hartnett to Finnegan, February 23, 1950, IUEA, B1.19, folder "Finnegan" ("as soon"); Hartnett to Finnegan, March 23, 1950, IUEA, B1.19, folder "Finnegan" ("some propaganda"). All five names are on the IUE list of two hundred.

129. Finnegan to Hartnett et al., July 14, 1950, IUEA, B1.19, folder "Finnegan."

130. Sidney Mason, "The Communist Party and Fitzgerald," IUEA, A2.05 folder "Sidney Mason, 1949 Affidavits and Explanation." This meeting took place in 1946, but it is clear that Matles was arguing that this was the policy that had governed the Communist Party's UE work since 1940. It probably was true from 1935 on.

131. Matles to All General Vice Presidents, April 25, 1941 (Siporin), Matles to All Members of the General Executive Board, April 11, 1944 (Wright), WSP, ser. 5, box 10, folder National Office Correspondence.

132. Rosner to Sentner, November 8, 1945, WSP, ser. 1, box 5, folder District Election Campaign (1945); Pittsburgh Report, August 7, 1946, 100-326165-7 ("buro"); Sentner to Rosner, November 20, 1945, ser. 1, box 5, folder District Election Campaign (1945). My hunch is that this is the "Steve Rosner" named by Cvetic and targeted in "Fitzpatrick the Patriot."

133. Matles to All Members of the General Executive Board, June 1, 1943, WSP, ser. 5, box 10, folder National Office Correspondence ("Acquainted"); Swan to Matles, August 1, 1947, UEA, O-1445 (remaining quotations).

134. Matles to All Members of the General Executive Board, August 20, 1943, WSP, ser. 5, box 10, folder National Office Correspondence ("acquainted"); St. Louis Report, August 26, 1946, 100-18332-51, WSP. (remaining quotations).

135. Sentner to Dodge, February 14, 1945, WSP, ser. 6, box 1, folder correspondence.

136. Rosswurm, "Introduction: An Overview and Preliminary Assessment of the CIO's Expelled Unions," in Rosswurm, *CIO's Left-Led Unions*, 1–17; Rosswurm, "Coming to Terms with Monsignor Charles Owen Rice: Religious Belief, Political Commitment, and Historical Practice," Pennsylvania Labor History Society Meeting, Pittsburgh, September 1998; Rosswurm, "Some Thoughts on the CIO's Cold War Purge," Wisconsin Labor History Society Meeting, Milwaukee, May 2001; Rosswurm, "Religion and Chicago's Working People," Labor and Working-Class History Association Panel, Newberry Library, January 2003; Rosswurm, ["Bryan Palmer's Optics of Power,"] *LH* 49 (2008): 369–71; James C. Scott, *Seeing Like a State: How Certain Schemes to Improve the Human Condition Have Failed* (New Haven, 1998), chap. 5. How this played itself out in one CPUSA life can be seen in James R. Barrett, *William Z. Foster and the Tragedy of American Radicalism* (Urbana, 1999).

137. Schatz, *Electrical Workers*.

138. Allen Weinstein, *Perjury: The Hiss-Chambers Case* (New York, 1978); Ronald Radosh and Joyce Milton, *The Rosenberg File: A Search for the Truth* (New York, 1983); Joseph Albright and Marcia Kunstel, *Bombshell: The Secret Story of America's Unknown Atomic Spy Conspiracy* (New York, 1997); Weinstein and Alexander Vassiliev, *The Haunted Wood: Soviet Espionage in America—the Stalin Era* (New York, 1999); John Earl Haynes and Harvey Klehr, *Venona: Decoding Soviet*

Espionage in America (New Haven, 1999); R. Bruce Craig, *Treasonable Doubt: The Harvey Dexter White Spy Case* (Lawrence, Kans., 2003); Katherine A. S. Sibley, *Red Spies in America: Stolen Secrets and the Dawn of the Cold War* (Lawrence, Kans., 2004); Steven T. Usdin, *Engineering Communism: How Two Americans Spied for Stalin and Founded the Soviet Silicon Valley* (New Haven, 2005).

139. Hoerr, *Harry, Tom, and Father Rice*, 111.

140. Ibid.

141. Hoerr, *And the Wolf Finally Came: The Decline of the American Steel Industry* (Pittsburgh, 1988).

142. McGeever, *Rice*, 227–28. Also see Hoerr, *Harry, Tom, and Father Rice*, 253.

143. Rosswurm interview with Rice. Also see McCollester, *Fighter with a Heart*, 230.

144. Rosswurm interview with Rice.

145. McGeever interview with Rice, May 21, 1983 ("I can't); Rice, "Confessions," 456. McCollester excised the paragraph (and the following one) in which this quotation appeared in *Fighter with a Heart*, 102. After the sentence quoted in the text Rice continues, "Sadly it must be related that my wild and most enjoyable college extracurricular career was assisted by the 'stealing' of a vote, one vote."

146. Rice to Dearden, May 13, 1950.

147. Ibid. For Mike Fitzpatrick, see Peeler, "Statement"; IUEA, B1.1., folder Field Representaive: "Fitzpatrick, Michael: 1950–1952"; *Cub*, March 21, 1952, 4.

148. Kenneth J. Henineman, "Reformation: Monsignor Charles Owen Rice and the Fragmentation of the New Deal Electoral Coalition in Pittsburgh, 1960–1972," *Pennsylvania History* 71 (2004): 53–85; Kenneth J. Heineman, "Iron City Trinity: The Triumph and the Trials of Catholic Social Activism in Pittsburgh, 1932–1972," *USCH* 22, no. 2 (Spring 2004): 121–45.

Afterword

1. These generalizations are based on an extensive and intensive reading of *NN*. For a stunning example of Calkins's projection and anti-Communism, see "St. George and Our Lady," *NN*, April 23, 1948, 8–9.

2. Calkins, "Christ the Negro," *NN*, January 21, 1944, 7.

3. Calkins, "Two Worlds," *NN*, September 8, 1944.

4. Noll and Nystrom, *Is the Reformation Over? An Evangelical Assessment of Contemporary Roman Catholicism* (Grand Rapids, 2005), 192. The authors might disagree with my emphasis here, but I think it follows from their discussion.

5. Tentler, *Catholics and Contraception: An American History* (Ithaca, N.Y., 2004), 176, 180. www.sspx.org/against_the_sound_bites/rhythm_unhappy_compromise. htm (accessed July 5, 2008).

6. Christine E. Gudorf, "To Make a Seamless Garment, Use a Single Piece of Cloth," in Patricia Beattie Jung, ed., *Abortion and Catholicism: The American Debate* (New York, 1988), 279–96. Rosemary Radford Ruether alerted me to Gudorf's essay "'Consistent Life Ethic' Is Inconsistent," *National Catholic Reporter*, November 17, 2006, 13–14.

7. Simon Lazarus, "Repealing the 20 Century," prospect.org/cs/articles?article =repealing_the_20th_century (accessed July 31, 2008); Lazarus and Harper Jean Tobin, "Justice Scalia's Two-Front War," www.prospect.org/cs/articles?article =justice_scalias_two_front_war (accessed March 7, 2008). For an introduction to Radical Orthodoxy's thinking on the contemporary, see John Milbank, "The Gospel of Affinity," in *Being Reconciled: Ontology and Pardon* (New York, 2003), 187–211.

Index

Acheson-Lilienthal report, 202

Alter, Karl, and Social Action Department, 149–50, 174–75

Americans Battling Communism, 263

anti-Communism: and Curley, 57–58; and Cushing, 65. *See also* Communism; *entries for individuals*

antimodernism, 2, 4, 65, 71, 81, 86

Amrine, Michael, 195–96; analysis of *Atomic Information*, 203–6; and Conway, 181, 206–7, 213–16; and FBI, 197, 222, 325n29; FBI deposition of, 197–98, 202–3; and Larrick, 203; and Melcher, 196–98, 202–3, 204; political views of, 196–98, 223–24; and Urey, 196

Aquinas, Thomas, 45, 81

Association of Catholic Trade Unionists, 136, 144–47, 151, 160, 173; Chicago chapter, 254–55; Detroit chapter, 254–55; and FBI, 245, 248, 253–57; Seattle chapter, 253–54

Bacon, Betty, 192

Baruch Report, 202–3

Baughman, Thomas, 28–29, 101

Bell, Rachel, 187–90, 201

Bentley, Elizabeth, 85, 172, 185–86; and Sheen, 83

Bierly, Kenneth, 154

birth control, 58, 276

Bishops' Report: and Alter/Cronin, 152, 154, 156; and Chicago FBI, 162, 166–67; and Chicago Red Squad, 151; and Communists in CIO, 170–71, 179; and Communists in government, 171–72; and Curley, 150; and FBI, 150–51, 156, 159–60; and Huffman, 152–53, 156–57; and Murphy, 159, 175; and National Catholic Welfare Conference Administrative Board, 146–49, 167; and O'Hara, 152, 155, 157; and positive program, 150, 154–55, 158, 160, 162, 173; and questionnaires, 150–51, 158, 303n5, 304n66. *See also* Cronin, John F; Tamm, Edward A.

Blessed Virgin Mary. *See* Mary, Saint

Bobich, George, 248

borders, 17, 19, 21, 41, 46

Boston College, 42

boundaries, 19–22, 34, 41

Budenz, Louis, 167; and Sheen, 83–86; and Tamm, 111

bulwarks. *See under* metaphors

Calkins, Hugh, 16–17, 275–76

Campbell, William: and Bishops' Report, 122, 153; and Chicago, 118–20, 121; and Chicago Red Squad, 119, 122; and Communism, 119, 293n62; and FBI, 119–20; and Tamm, 120, 123

Canisius College, 42; number of FBI agents as alumni, 44

Carey, James B., 7; anti-Communist activities of, 243–44; and FBI, 112, 245, 257–62; UE on, 242–43

Carey, Phillip: and FBI, 250–51; and New York City Red Squad, 251

Casey, William, 45, 49

Catholic Church: and alliance with FBI, 12, 22; UE on, 242–43. *See also entries for individuals*

Catholic University of America, 67, 80, 90

Catholic Youth Organization, 89, 94, 119

Chicago Red Squad, 119, 122–23

Christophers, 97–98

CINRAD, 185–86

Clark, Tom, 216–17, 220

College of the, Holy Cross. *See* Holy Cross, College of the

Comey, Dennis, 250; and FBI, 252–53

Commoner, Barry, 197–98

communion breakfasts, 13, 42, 69, 77, 82–83, 252

Communism: Catholic ways of fighting, 145, 147–48, 231–33; and Cushing, 65; and Hoover, 63, 66–67; and Noll, 71; and obscene literature, 54–55, 74; and Sheen, 80; and Social Action Department, 231–32. *See also* anti-Communism

Condon, Edward, 178

Condon, Mrs. Edward, 218

Conroy, E. E., 84

contest, 12, 40; and Hoover, 25, 27–28; and Jesuits, 12, 45, 47–49. *See also* homosociality; masculinity

Conway, Edward A., 6; accused of anti-Semitism, 219, 225; and Communism, 212, 222–23; and Cronin, 185; disposition of papers of, 307n1; and FBI, 180–81, 183, 185–86, 206–7, 213, 221, 315n129; and Melcher, 191, 206, 213–14; pre-NCAI career, 181–83; and reports on NCAI, 183–91; and Social Action Department, 184–85; and Stritch, 180, 182, 189. *See also* Amrine, Michael; Higinbotham, William; Melcher, Daniel

Copeland, Charles, 241

Counterattack, 77, 134, 154, 266

Cox, Ignatius, 16, 18, 45

Coyne, J. P., 84–86

Creighton University, 47, 120, 307n1, 315n129

crime, 4, 22, 66; and Catholics, 58, 75–76, 80, 89, 121, 139; and Hoover, 10, 14–15, 54, 63, 66, 72, 76, 80

crisis, 4, 26, 48, 56; women and, 17, 41, 58; and World War II, 10–11, 58, 75, 80, 88, 255

Cronin, John, 5, 21, 93, 135, 255; and Alter, 149–50, 174–75; and Baltimore FBI, 136, 150–51, 154, 162; and Baltimore shipyards, 136–37, 140–42, 145, 147–48; and Chamber of Commerce pamphlets, 133; and Chicago FBI, 166; and Chicago Red Squad, 122; and Communism, 138–39, 167–74, 176; and Dies Committee, 154, 158, 161; and FBI, 142, 150–51, 156, 159–60, 162, 165–66; and Hiss, 134, 165–66, 171–72, 175–76; and Murphy, 164–66, 175, 178; and New York City Red Squad, 153–54; and New York FBI, 153, 162; and Office of Naval Intelligence, 153; others' opinion of, 142, 177–78; and Smith, 154, 179; and Social Action Department, 174–75, 177; and social Catholicism, 137—140, 155, 161–62; and somatic metaphors, 21, 138–39; and Soviet espionage, 163–64, 176, 178; and Stritch, 148; and Tamm, 156, 159–60. *See also* Bishops' Report

Curley, Michael J., 4, 56–61, 136

Cushing, Richard, 61–70, 167

Cvetic, Matt, 263–64

DeLacy, Hugh, 208

DePaul University, number of FBI agents as alumni, 289n105

desire, 19, 22, 66; and gender, 3, 45; ordered, 10, 22; reeducation of, 37, 39–41

Diamond, Sigmund, 236–37

Doherty, Tom: and FBI, 255

Donnelly, Joseph, 145, 148, 230
Donohue, Hugh: and FBI, 153
Douglas, Helen Gahagan, 189
Douglas, Mary, 21, 46
Duffy, John, 237–38, 241, 263
Dunne, George, 123

ecumenical activity: 140–41, 182
Einstein, Albert, 203, 211, 218
elective affinity, 13
Engerman, George, 207–8
essentialism, 3, 12, 16, 276

Falk, Joy, 187–88, 190, 210; and Conway, 190, 210
family: Catholic view of, 15; Hoover view of, 14–15
Federal Bureau of Investigation (FBI): *See* Hoover, J. Edgar; *entries for individuals*
Federation of American Scientists, 183, 188
Finnegan, Les: and AEC, 243; and FBI, 261–62, 265–66; and HUAC, 243
Finney, Nat, 216, 220
Fitzgerald, John, 112–13; and FBI files, 118; and Tamm, 113, 120–21, 123
Fitzpatrick, Tom, 240, 242, 248, 264–65, 268, 270
Fordham Law School, 10
Fordham University, 86; and FBI, 42–44; number of FBI agents as alumni, 43; and masculinity, 46–49
Founding Fathers, 2, 11, 66
freedom: Catholic view of, 18, 55, 121; Hoover view of, 18; Jesuit view of, 18
Fuller, Helen, 187, 189–90

Gannon, Robert, 42, 50, 97
gender: and Catholic/FBI alliance, 2–3, 12–13, 16–17, 22. *See also* homosociality; masculinity
Georgetown University, 64, 99; and Hoover, 9–10, 107; number of FBI agents as alumni, 44; and masculinity, 48–49
Gillmor, Dan, 207
Ginder, Richard, 75

Goldstein, Betty, 242
Gordon, William, 257
GREGORY, 185–86, 191, 191–94, 197, 225
Groves, Leslie, 195, 200

Haas, Francis, 145, 155
Haldeman-Julius Company, 94
Halpern, Freda, 187–90
Hawkins, Joe, 243
Hayes, John, 144–46, 149, 160
Higgins, George, 95, 149, 153–55, 161–62, 174–75, 179
Higinbotham, William, 188, 194–95; and Conway, 181, 213–16; and FBI, 222, 315n129; and firing of "Susie," 195, 215; and McCarthy charges, 200; and Melcher, 194, 198, 204; political views of, 195, 223
Hillman, Sydney, 187, 189
Hiss, Alger, 5, 113. *See also* Cronin, John F.
Holy Cross, College of the, 10, 12, 47, 181; number of FBI agents as alumni, 44
Holy Name Society, 54, 57, 106, 121
home: and Hoover, 11, 75, 89; and Noll, 79
homosexuality: and Hoover, 26–30, 106
homosociality, 12, 22; and Catholics, 41, 50; and Hoover, 26–28, 30; and Jesuits, 12, 44–46, 50. *See also* gender; masculinity
Hoover, J. Edgar: and body, 3; and cadets, 25–26; and Carey, 259–60; and Communism, 63, 66–67; and contest, 25, 27–28; and crime, 10, 14–15, 54, 63, 66, 72, 76, 80; in debate club, 25; and family, 14–15; and freedom, 18; and home, 11, 75, 89; and homosexuality, 26–30, 106; and homosociality, 26–28, 30; juvenile delinquency, 55, 66, 75, 89 and masculinity, 3, 81; and metaphors, 14, 20–22; and Notre Dame, 13, 15, 54–55; and mother, 23, 29; and obscene literature, 54–55 and Sunday School, 24
House Un-American Activities Committee, and NCAI/FAS, 201, 212–13, 217. *See also* Rice, Charles Owen

Jackson, Gardner: anti-Communism of, 190–91; and Melcher, 187, 191, 202–4, 210

Jesuits, 9, 12; and contest, 12, 47–49; and FBI, 291n129; and homosociality, 12, 50; and masculinity, 45–46, 50; and patriarchy, 16–17

Johnson, Clyde, 248

Joliot-Curie, Frederick, 205

juvenile delinquency, 4, 22, 55; and Catholics, 55; and Hoover, 55, 66, 75, 89; and Spellman, 89, 92–93

Keith, J. M., 99

Keller, James, 97–98, 173

Kelley, Francis J., 59–61

Knights of Columbus, 62, 66, 69, 87, 134

Kovel, Joel, 6, 224, 275

labor priests, 135, 145, 229–30

Ladd, D. M., 84, 110–11, 126, 256

LaFarge, John, 17, 47

Lamb, Helen, 190

Lamb, Robert, 187, 190

Larrick, Nancy, 194, 218–19; memo of, 202, 211, 215

Laughlin, Leo L., 67, 69, 84

Lloyd, Robert S., 10, 50–52, 160, 164

Loney, Stanley, 265

Loyola University (Chicago), 49, 119

Manresa Retreat House, 10, 50–51

Margolin, Olya, 187, 190

Mary, Saint, 40, 49–50

Marzani, Carl, 208; characterization of Melcher, 194

Marzani, Edith, 188, 193, 208, 213–14, 229

masculinity: and Catholicism, 227–28, 238; and Cushing, 65; and Minihan, 64; and order, 23, 30, 32–33, 38; and plain-spokenness, 56–57, 65. *See also* contest; gender; homosociality

Mason, Sydney, 265, 267

Masters, Dexter, 208, 216

Masters of Deceit: and Cushing, 67–68; and *Our Sunday Visitor*, 78; and Sheen, 82

Mathews, Francis, 116, 133–34

Matles, James, 243, 267–68, 271

May, Alan Nunn, 186, 200–201, 205

McAtee, John: and FBI, 250–52

McCarran, Patrick, 115, 116

McDonald, Ralph: and Melcher, 205, 215–16

McGowan, Raymond, 95, 143–44, 174–75

McGuire, John J., 10, 78–79

McIntyre, James, 157, 175

McMahon, Brien, 183, 188, 190, 200, 213

Meehan, Thomas, 16, 122–23

Melcher, Daniel, 7; career before NCAI, 191–92, 198; and GREGORY targets, 193–94; and McDonald, 210–12; NCAI accomplishments, 199–200; and opponents, 190, 211–12, 218; politics of, 192–94, 198, 206, 224; and staff, 187–88, 192–94

Merrill, Lewis, 192

metaphors: 3, 6, 18–22, 47–48, 81, 90, 96; and the body, 19–20, 139; bulwarks, 20, 22; and Catholics, 20–22; and gender, 3, 19–20; and Hoover, 14, 20–22; medical, 20–21, 38, 139

Mindszenty, Josef, 51, 270

Minihan, Jeremiah, 62–65

Monaghan, John, 177

Mooney, Edward, 146, 148

Nathan, Harold, 99

National Committee for Atomic Information: firing of Melcher, 202–6; founding of, 183; history post-Melcher firing, 221; staff resigns, 218–20. *See also entries for individuals*

National Council of Catholic Men, 62

National Council of Catholic Women, 61–62, 112

National Organization for Decent Literature, 72

Nelson, John, 248

Newell, Charles, 264–65

New York City Red Squad, 153–54, 251

Nichols, Louis B, 61, 125

Nixon, Richard, 5, 134

Noll, John F, 4, 70–80, 161, 177

Notre Dame, University of, 65, 87; and Budenz, 85–86; and Hoover, 13, 15,

54–55; number of FBI agents as alumni, 289n105; and O'Hara, 53–55
Novena Notes, 1, 275

O'Boyle, Patrick, 95–96
obscene literature, 4, 22; and Hoover, 54–55; and Noll, 71–75
O'Donnell, Hugh, 85–86
O'Hara, John, 53–56, 88, 91–92
Ong, Walter, 45, 48
Oppenheimer, Robert, 178, 180, 189, 195, 211, 223
order: and society, 11, 26, 47, 95; and seminary, 41. *See also* gender; homosociality; masculinity
Our Sunday Visitor, 70–80

Panzino, Frank, 241–42
patriarchal authority, 47, 50
patriarchal family, 3, 12; Catholic view of, 15–16, 95; Hoover's view of, 15, 54
patriarchy, 2–3, 55; and Jesuits, 44
Peeler, William, 241–42
Phillips, Melba, 189, 214, 217–19
Plain Talk, 134
Powers, Richard Gid, 18, 26

Quinn, Tom, 241–42, 264–65, 270–71

Read, Harry: and anti-Communist activities, 243, 254–57; and assessment of O'Boyle, 95; and Bishops' Report, 151, 153, 158, 170; and FBI, 254–56
Ready, Michael, 148–51
Red Squad: Chicago, 119, 122–23, 151, 153; New York City, 153–54, 251
Regis College, 181–82
Reid, Helen, 209–10, 212, 218
Reinhold, H. R., 177, 253–54
Rice, Charles Owen, 7–8; and Boyle, 229–30; character of, 229, 238; and Chevrolet, 234–37; and FBI, 244–50, 271–73, 305n86; and historians, 226–27, 236–37, 241; and House Un-American Activities Committee, 239–43; and Murray, 237–38, 247; and support for CIO, 228, 230–33; and

UE #506, 239, 248; and UE #601, 234, 239–43, 263–65; and UE #610, 248–49
Richter, Irving, 190
Rosner, Steve, 264, 268, 323n132
Rush, Joseph, 213, 216–17, 222–23
Ryan, John A., 143–44, 154

Sartisky, Jack, 264
Schimmel, Herbert, 188, 190, 197
secularism, 65, 70
seminary: and Hoover, 32; and obedience, 31–34; and rule, 31, 35–37; and West Point, 33
Sentner, William, 258, 267–69
sex/gender system, 12, 276
Sheen, Fulton J., 4, 80–86, 97
Sheil, Bernard J., 119, 122, 177, 234
Simpson, John, 208–9, 216–17
smear campaigns, 59, 67–70, 75–79
Smith, William J., 179; and FBI, 246, 250, 303n52
Social Action Department, 142–45, 155, 174–75, 231–32
Soviet espionage: and Canada, 185–86, 189, 199, 201; and USA, 185–86
Soucy, E. A., 60–61, 167
Spellman, Francis, 4–5, 77, 86–95, 97; and Bishops' Report, 149, 151–54, 156, 162, 166
St. John University, number of FBI agents as alumni, 289n105
St. Louis University, 42, 181; number of FBI agents as alumni, 44
Ste. Marie, Paul, 254
Straight, Michael, 187, 191
Stritch, Samuel: and Chicago Red Squad, 122–23, 151, 153; and Hoover, 112; and Tamm, 113–18, 123–25
Sugure, Rose, 192
Sullivan, Gael, 114–15, 118
Sullivan, William C., 67, 166
Szilard, Leo, 189, 209

Tamm, Edward, 5, 73, 87, 256; and Budenz, 85–86; and Carey, 259–60; and Cronin leaks, 109, 112; and Eucharistic Congress speech, 97–98, 131–32; and FBI communist matters,

109–11; and FBI sensitive matters, 106–7; and Hoover, 98, 100, 102–3, 105, 128–32; and international Catholic Church; and judicial position, 123–27; as judge, 128–31; and Mitchell, 120–21, 124; and UN San Francisco conference, 108, 113, 159–60l and USA Catholic Church, 115–18
Tamm, Quinn, 60–61
Tentative Confidential Report on Communism, 156–59
Theoharis, Athan, 30, 107
Tolson, Clyde, 29–30, 93–94, 99, 101
Turner, Leo, 264

UE (United Electrical, Radio and Machine Workers of America): and CPUSA, 267–69; in Dayton, 244; Local #601, 234, 239–40, 263–66

University of Notre Dame. *See* Notre Dame, University of,
Urey, Harold, 189, 196, 204, 217

Vida, Ernest, 242

Wallace, Henry, 187, 222
Walsh, Edmund, 10, 21
Walter, Francis, 178–79, 239–43
Wasserman, Ursula, 193, 207
Weber, Paul, 150, 159, 170; and FBI, 255
Whisner, Robert, 240, 242
White, Henry Dexter, 89
Winterrowd, E. E., 85–86
Winthrop, John, 97, 114, 132
Wright, John J., 13, 62

Young, Harold, 187